# A Portal to Paradise

# A Portal to Paradise

## 11,537 years,

MORE OR LESS,

*on the northeast slope of the Chiricahua Mountains,*

BEING A FAIRLY ACCURATE AND OCCASIONALLY
ANECDOTAL HISTORY OF THAT PART OF

## Cochise County, Arizona,

*and the country immediately adjacent,*

REPLETE WITH TALES OF

## glory AND greed,

## heroism AND depravity,

## and plain hard work

## Alden Hayes

FAILED FARMER, BANKRUPT CATTLEMAN,
SOMETIME SMOKE-CHASER, ONE-TIME PARK RANGER,
AND OVER-THE-HILL ARCHAEOLOGIST

*The University of Arizona Press*

TUCSON

The University of Arizona Press
© 1999 The Arizona Board of Regents
First printing
All rights reserved
This book is printed on acid-free, archival-quality paper.
Manufactured in the United States of America
04   03   02   01   00   99     6   5   4   3   2   1

Library of Congress Cataloging-in-Publication Data
Hayes, Alden C.
A portal to paradise : 11,537 years, more or less, on the
northeast slope of the Chiricahua Mountains : being a fairly
accurate and occasionally anecdotal history of that part of Cochise
County, Arizona, and the country immediately adjacent, replete with
tales of glory and greed, heroism and depravity, and plain hard
work / Alden Hayes.
p. cm.   Includes bibliographical references (p. ).
ISBN 0-8165-1785-1 (acid-free, archival-quality paper)
1. Cochise County (Ariz.)—History. I. Title.
F817.C5 H39 1999
979.1'53—ddc21
98-40077
CIP

British Library Cataloguing-in-Publication Data
A catalogue record for this book is available from the British Library.

*Frontispiece*: Cathedral Rock at the mouth of Cave Creek Canyon

Many men and a few women who have known this part of the country and who were important to its story have been memorialized in the names of creeks, mountains, springs, or trails. This book is dedicated to some who knew the Chiricahuas and were important to its story, but who never had a place named for them:

Domingo Jironza, Old Plume, Lt. Juan C. Tápia, Mary Chenowth, Jim Hancock, Joe Wheeler, Emmett Powers, Jack Maloney, Ralph Morrow, Birt Roberds, Nacho Flores, Jane Greenamyer

# Contents

# Illustrations

Cathedral Rock *frontispiece*

*following page 48*
Looking down Turkey Creek Canyon
Barfoot Park
The San Simon Cienega
A Chiricahua Apache family's camp of the 1880s
Merejildo Grijalva
J. L. Coryell and his son George
Jim Hughes with either Milt Hicks or Jack Mackenzie
Loco, a Chihenne chief
Gus and Mary Chenowth's place on the San Simon Cienega
Gus Chenowth at his cienega ranch
Sgt. Neil Erickson of the Fourth Cavalry
Emma Peterson
Officers and scouts at the Mud Springs vedette
Frank Hands at his place in Pinery Canyon
The Hall family at their Z Bar T ranch
Katie and Maggie Noland at the ranch on Oak Creek

*following page 169*
Riding one and leading one up Market Street in Paradise
Waiting for the stage at the Hayes Hotel in Paradise

# Maps

# Preface

My first visit to southeastern Arizona was brief. It was the middle of a cold December night in 1936 when, with two other fellows from Albuquerque, I drove south on Highway 80 up the San Simon Valley, heading for Bahia Kino. Somewhere between Apache and the Bernardino siding, we pulled off the road and climbed into the back of my 1928 Model A Ford delivery wagon to get a little sleep. We were on our way again before daylight, and I never saw a thing but the car's light on the road in front of me.

The next time was more memorable. In April 1941 my bride and I drove tandem into Granite Gap, she in an open roadster and I in a pickup truck with all our belongings—they didn't fill it. She was in the lead and stopped just west of the top of the divide. She had been here before and wanted to show me the view. The valley that spread out below us was a golden sheet of Mexican poppies, and beyond loomed the dark wall of the Chiricahua Mountains. Gretchen pointed out the gash made by Cave Creek Canyon, our destination and future home. Her father had just bought an apple orchard in the canyon's mouth and had asked us to help him farm it. The prospect of spending my life in such a setting was exciting. More than fifty years later the grandeur hasn't diminished, though seldom have the flowers again been so rambunctious.

At the entrance to the canyon, Portal was strung out under sycamores and live oaks on the floodplain of the creek's left bank. It boasted two emporiums: white-painted Newman's Store next to the bridge and, facing it a hundred yards away, Cave Creek Grocery in a small stuccoed adobe. A little farther up the creek was a two-room school, each room in a separate building, with twin two-holer privies back-to-back in the rear. There were thirteen residences. Most were wood-frame structures, but two were adobe, two were built of creek-bottom boulders, and one was a tent over a lumber frame.

There were four households just below Portal, six more on up the canyon, and a couple of bachelors lived on Silver Creek three miles west. Farther up that road in Paradise, there were six occupied houses and about as many between there and Whitetail Canyon. The people in that country of the Cave Creek and Turkey Creek drainages, along with Whitetail, made up a community that kept the one-teacher-eight-grades school going, voted on election day as a single precinct, buried its dead in Graveyard Canyon, and held frequent potluck picnics at Sunny Flat. Much of it gathered at about five in the afternoon to pick up the mail in Portal.

Both stores had gas pumps, carried groceries, horseshoes, and work gloves, and each had a kerosene barrel for lamp oil. Newman's had a beer license and an attached dance hall, while Cave Creek Grocery had the post office. It was a standoff. They were in direct and unfriendly competition, but most of the populace felt it wasn't good policy to take sides. Playing no favorites, most of us split our trade.

Both stores had benches flanking their doors where, around mail time, observations were made about the weather, news was shared, and old-timers told stories. I wish now that I'd made more time for those stories. I always cocked an ear, and I often scribbled a note when I got back to the house, because here the *real* West was being revealed. Though most of the genuine trailblazers were gone, several of the local old folks were born in, or had moved early to, Arizona Territory. Most of them had come west from Texas and other points east to locate around here between 1900 and 1910—too late to worry about Indians but early enough to become well acquainted with many who had.

Dignified, white-mustached, and eighty-one, Emmett Powers in white shirt, open vest, and flat-brimmed cattleman's Stetson looked like he'd stepped off the set of a Tom Mix movie—the sheriff or the grandfather of the girl who had ridden into the sunset with the hero. "Daddy" Powers introduced me to George Franklin when I sat down next to them in front of Newman's Store. Mr. Franklin, looking like the namesake of Rustler's Park, with his hat plumb and level on his head and his shirt collar buttoned up to his Adam's apple, sat with his left leg over his knee and his foot pulled tight against the right calf. His back was straight, and his pale blue eyes flickered briefly in my direction and then stared ahead over the top of Stuart Mountain at something I couldn't see. He didn't say anything, but I was sure he was thinking, "This country has gone to hell, filling up with dude kids like this."

I was a dude all right, but not a city dude. I'd spent some time in the hardwoods of the Kishwaukee River bottoms in Illinois and in the hemlocks and maples of Michigan when I was growing up. I had considerable skill with a canoe, could hit with an ax the spot I was looking at, and could hold up one end of a crosscut saw. Two of those skills were fairly useful in the Chiricahuas. Canoeing wasn't one of them. I had spent two or three months on a gentle horse, but I wasn't a horseman. I had put in a couple of summers picking fruit on a Michigan farm, but I couldn't hitch a team.

When we settled onto Sierra Linda Ranch, we had to hire Pete Domínguez to milk for us. He was a good teacher. I learned to milk and he lost his job. We got a little bunch of Rhode Island Red hens for fresh eggs, and I was amazed to learn that hens didn't need a rooster in attendance but could lay eggs without having been bred.

Blackie Stidham and Sam Moseley were patient with me and taught me to shoe my own horses. Sam denied being a farrier.

"A farrier shapes a shoe to fit. I just sort of whittle at the hoof till it fits whatever shoe I can find," he told me.

About horsemanship he was equally casual. "You just straddle him and let your legs hang down."

"Uncle" Ed Epley, another old post office benchwarmer, had come from Texas as a boomer in 1903 to make his fortune in the mining game. Though weighing no more than 125 pounds soaking wet, he was all gristle and had drilled countless yards into the hard limestone with a single jack. I had never been in mining country and didn't even know the vocabulary: adit, gangue, stope, winze. One evening when all were socializing after graduation exercises at the schoolhouse, I asked Ed to educate me about mines.

"A mine is a hole in the ground, and a miner is the darn fool at the bottom of it," he told me. "There isn't much more to know."

He didn't really feel that way about it. Well into his eighties he was still driving steel, blasting, and mucking, ever optimistic that he was on the brink of bonanza.

Though I never learned much more about mining, I worked hard at learning how to make water run uphill; to prune fruit trees; to mix sulfur, arsenic, and lime for spraying coddling moths; to prune grape vines; to keep a tractor running; to stretch wire; to grease the windmill and change the leathers; and to ease cattle from one place to another without scattering them from hell to breakfast. I wasn't a *good* hand, but I could plug up a hole until a better one came along. I also learned something about modifying the behavior of a forest fire, about packing a mule, and about finding my way from Rattlesnake Peak to Barfoot Park in the dark.

Emma Maloney was a hard-bitten lady raised on a mountain ranch working horseback with fractious cows, making her own soap, rendering skunks for harness oil, canning venison, and making fruit leather. She set high standards for her own behavior and that of her neighbors, and was never shy about speaking her mind. I ran into her in the store one April evening when I had been trying to put a spray on the apple blossoms but had been forced to quit because of high wind, and we compared notes on the prospect of the creek staying up long enough for another irrigation.

She started to leave but turned back to say, "You know, Alden, when you first come here ever'body gave you about six months, but by God, I think you're going to make it."

I couldn't have been prouder.

Well, I *did* make it for sixteen years, but then after a combination of bad luck, poor judgment, and five years of drought, we left, taking with us a wealth of experience, a treasure of memories, two sons, and thirty thousand dollars of debt. We also took with us a sense of identity with jagged rhyolite cliffs and Apache pines, with clear creeks purling under sycamores and mustang grapes, with mesquite and snakeweed, buckskin grass and desert marigolds.

When we were able, nineteen years later, we returned to the Chiricahuas—not to grow apples or grapes or to run cattle. I hoped to write a history of this part of the world. At first I planned to include the entire Chiricahua range. I wasn't long learning that was too ambitious, so I confined myself to the area I knew best and had personally made footprints and horse tracks in—the east side of the mountains between Apache Pass and Tex Canyon, the adjacent San Simon Valley, and the west fringes of the Peloncillo Mountains on the valley's east side. Occasionally I had to wander farther afield when events in a broader area had a direct bearing on local concerns.

Within that area there is a human community, the limits of which are vague and have varied over the decades. Post offices have opened and closed in a dozen locations, and the ill-defined center of the population has shifted, but it has remained one community. Portal can't really be separated from Paradise, six miles away.

I used my meager notes and my recollections of what I'd heard, and though I was too late to sit down with those old-timers—they'd all slipped away—I talked with many of their children and grandchildren. Census records, the county register, the files of the Arizona Historical Society, and old newspapers have helped a lot, but the thing has gone slowly. Almost one thousand feet above the canyon bottom, just a little northeast of the base of Cathedral Rock, is a lichen-splotched slab of yellow-rose rhyolite hanging over the creek. It is cracked through, and a piece of it about the size of the Cochise County courthouse rests on a forty-five-degree angle. Nothing holds it there but the friction of the two surfaces. Someday it will slip off and crash through oak and piñon with a hell of a roar. I spend a lot of time keeping an eye on it. I'd hate to miss it.

I haven't organized my story into categories such as "Law and Order," "The Cattle Industry," "Mining," or "The Life of James Covington Hancock." When I was very small, I would sometimes worry about what I would do if it rained or if I became mute when the teacher asked me to multiply nine by eight. My mother told me, "Alden, just take one step at a time." Following her advice has made me a pretty good walker but also kind of pedestrian. So, taking one step at a time, my story is chronological. I discuss the salient events of 1854 before I get into 1876, but this is a story, not a treatise. There is no hypothesis, no theory, and no conclusion. Don't look for the meaning of it all. I'm not sure there is any.

If there is a theme, it is that one aspect of life can't be sealed off from another. To get a feeling for a time, it is necessary to realize that while miners were drilling into Crystal Ridge, cowboys were moving steers to market and farmers were cutting hay. And the three occupations weren't always neatly separated. In a week's time one man might work at all of them.

This isn't meant to be a piece of scholarship, but it isn't fiction either. I didn't make it up, and it is as accurate as I could make it. There are no footnotes or citations to back up my interpretation of events, but I consulted more than 200 published sources and got something useful out of 180 of them. Naturally, some were worth more than others. Without Charles Polzer and Tom Naylor, I wouldn't have known of the 1695 military expedition to Turkey Creek. The works of Eve Ball, Angie Debo, Bill Griffen, Ed Sweeney, and Dan Thrapp were invaluable in sorting out the Apache wars, and though I used my own words, Jeff Burton provided most of the facts regarding the activities of the various Blackjacks.

People I have interviewed formally or who have contributed something through a windy told at a barbecue or by a throwaway offhand remark include Harry Burrall, Dorothy Chamberlain, Amos and La-Dorna Chenowth, Jim and Sally Coryell, Grace Sanford Cox, Jim Frank Cox, Cliff Darnell, Ruey Darrow, Charles C. DiPeso, Leo Domínguez, Ed and "Bee" Epley, Ben Erickson, Emma Erickson, Ignacio Flores, Elmer and Mamie Pattison Franklin, Rosalie Kennedy Gilliland, Bill Gurnett, Larry R. Gurnett, Emil Haury, Glennis Byers Hayes, Cindy Hayostek, Virginia S. Hershey, Maurine Reed Hicks, Addie Washburn Hill, George W. Hilliard, Natalie Hoxie,

Pamela Hulme, Dorothy Chenowth Jessee, Jeff Jordan, Irene Hancock Kennedy, Lulu Pearl Hale Larman, Vince Lee, Anita Lester, Charles McGlone, Jack and Emma Sanders Maloney, Isabel May, Audrey Morrow Miller, Bill and Guy Miller, Carson and Ralph Morrow, Wayne Morrow, Mora Moseley, Sam Moseley, George Newman, Gordon Newman, Jr., A. F. Noland, A. F. Noland, Jr., Tom Noland, Van Noland, Oscar and LaVerne Pague Olney, Ben and Alma Pague, Robert Pague, D. D. Parramore, Joyce Merchant Peters, Herbert Reay, Walter Reed, Cristóbal Rendón, Finley and Sally Darnell Richards, Ed and Lillian Erickson Riggs, Claudine Saenz, Bill Sanders, Frank Sanford, Bessie Epley Siler, James Chenowth Simmons, Charlie Smith, A. B. "Blackie" Stidham, Maryan Stidham, Pat Stoltz, Elsie and Myriam Toles, Jay Van Orden, Lula Reed Walker, Reed and Elmore Walker, Brooks White, John P. Wilson, and Arthur Zachau, Jr.

Through correspondence or by furnishing documents or photos, Jan Baker, Mildred Reed Clapp, Ed Francis, Roland L. Frazier (whose mother was a Barfoot), Phyllis de la Garza, Annabel Hall, Edna Hastings, Cindy Hayostek, Eleanor Hoppe (a Parramore descendant), Georgia Walker Lee, Jim McDonald, Lynn Mitchell, Richard Y. Murray, Pete Rawdon, Minette Harris Smith, and Ted Troller have been generous, as have the libraries of the Arizona Historical Society, the Bisbee Mining and Historical Museum, the Cochise County Historical Society, the Coronado National Forest, the Mendocino County Historical Society, and the Western Heritage Center.

Jeanne Williams has been helpful with motherly advice, and Bob Morse has been patient with my computer illiteracy and generous with his time in getting me out of electronic snares. David Laird read the original manuscript and made helpful suggestions for its improvement. Karen Hayes has copied photos, made prints, provided me with photos of her own, told me when my sentences were getting unwieldy, and with loving brutality edited the original draft. Most important, she has been patient with my testiness—gritting her teeth because patience doesn't come much more easily to her than it does to me.

# The Setting

But the most marked sight is the Sierra Chiricahui. It is a formidable chain, and terribly rugged, abrupt ledges, cut up and twisted, pinnacles, crags, and precipices.

**Adolph Bandelier**

Along the Mexican border, between El Paso on the Rio Grande and Tubac on the Santa Cruz, is a stretch of country made up of narrow, northwest-southeast-trending chains of mountains separating wider valleys. That piece of country, almost three hundred miles wide and a hundred or so from north to south, sprawls across parts of four states: Chihuahua and Sonora, Arizona and New Mexico. But it is pretty much like itself from one end to the other. Within it no plain or valley is so wide that a person can't see mountains both east and west. From every mountain crest one can look across valleys on both sides and see more mountains beyond them.

With some differences the area has a common history—geologic as well as contemporary—and, again with minor variations, the same flora and fauna. And it has the same feel to it, so it ought to have a name to distinguish it, as the Staked Plains do, or the Northwest Coast or the Northern Rockies.

Geography is always transitional. You can't pinpoint the exact line where you step out of this nameless country, but without question the Chiricahua Mountains are in its middle. Elevations range from

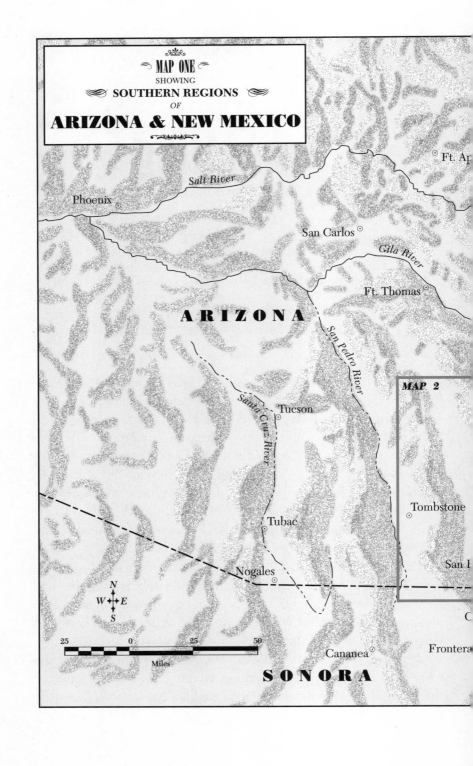

MAP ONE
SHOWING
SOUTHERN REGIONS
OF
ARIZONA & NEW MEXICO

Salt River

Phoenix ⊙

San Carlos ⊙

Gila River

Ft. Ap

Ft. Thomas ⊙

A R I Z O N A

San Pedro River

Santa Cruz River

Tucson ⊙

MAP 2

Tubac ⊙

Tombstone ⊙

San

Nogales ⊙

N
W ✦ E
S

25        0        25        50

Miles

Cananea ⊙

Frontera

S O N O R A

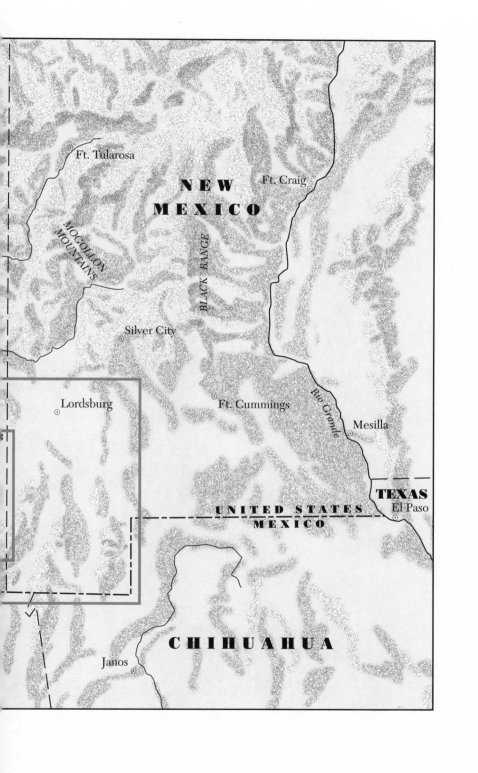

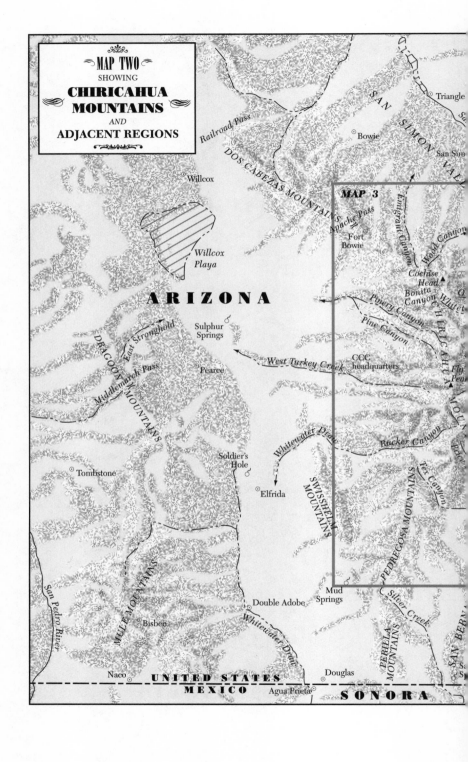

SHOWING

**CHIRICAHUA MOUNTAINS**

AND

**ADJACENT REGIONS**

Triangle

San Simon Valley

Bowie

San Sim

Railroad Pass

DOS CABEZAS MOUNTAINS

Willcox

**MAP 3**

Apache Pass

Emigrant Canyon

Wood Canyon

Fort Bowie

Willcox Playa

Cochise Head

Bonita Canyon

White

**A R I Z O N A**

Pinery Canyon

Pine Canyon

CHIRICAHUA MOUN

Sulphur Springs

East Stronghold

Fly Pea

West Turkey Creek

CCC headquarters

DRAGOON MOUNTAINS

Pearce

Middlemarch Pass

Whitewater Draw

Rucker Canyon

Pine

Tombstone

Soldier's Hole

Tex Canyon

SWISSHELM MOUNTAINS

Elfrida

PEDREGOSA MOUNTAINS

San Pedro River

MULE MOUNTAINS

Mud Springs

Silver Creek

Double Adobe

SAN BERN

Bisbee

Whitewater Draw

PERILLA MOUNTAINS

Douglas

S S

Naco

**U N I T E D   S T A T E S**

**M E X I C O**

Agua Prieta

**S O N O R A**

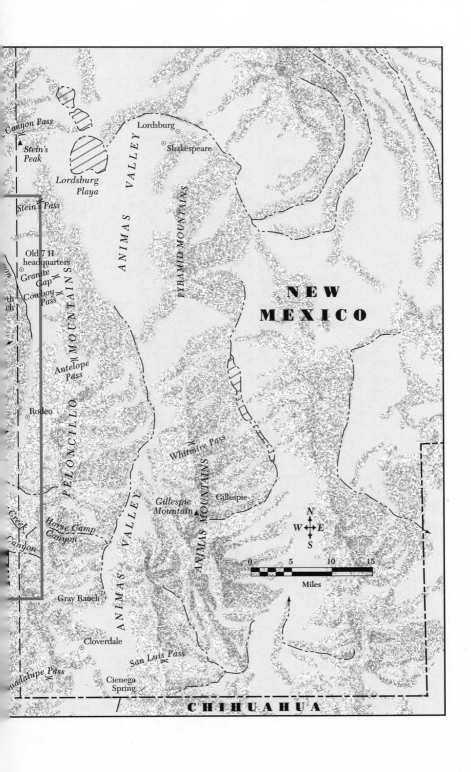

Canyon Pass

Stein's
Peak

Stein's Pass

Lordsburg

Shakespeare

Lordsburg
Playa

ANIMAS VALLEY

PYRAMID MOUNTAINS

NEW
MEXICO

Old 7 H
headquarters

Granite
Gap

Cowboy
Pass

ch

PELONCILLO MOUNTAINS

Antelope
Pass

Rodeo

Whitmire Pass

Gillespie
Mountain

Gillespie

ANIMAS MOUNTAINS

N

W    E

S

Creek

Canyon

Horse Camp
Canyon

ANIMAS VALLEY

0          5         10        15

Miles

Gray Ranch

Cloverdale

San Luis Pass

nadalupe Pass

Cienega
Spring

CHIHUAHUA

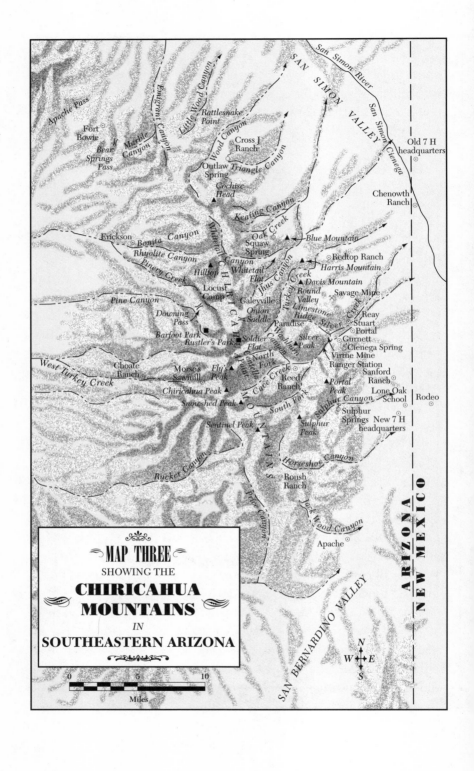

MAP THREE

SHOWING THE

**CHIRICAHUA MOUNTAINS**

IN

**SOUTHEASTERN ARIZONA**

0    5    10

Miles

4,000 to 10,000 feet above sea level. The highest points are confined to small areas, and most of the country averages between 4,500 and 5,500 feet. It is that elevation that keeps the country from being brutally hot despite its latitude only eleven degrees north of the Tropic of Cancer.

The mountains were created when sedimentary limestone and sandstone deposited under Paleozoic seas were rumpled by the horizontal compression exerted by tectonic plates floating on deep seas of magma. The folds and wrinkles of the limestone resulted in parallel ridges. Some were so tight they cracked open and "faulted" when one side of the fold dropped and the other pushed up over it.

The core's molten rock escaped through the weakened surface crust as oozing lava or more explosively as clouds of incandescent pulverized rock, which were deposited above or along the sides of the folded limestone. The period of fire lasted about seventy million years, ending in a final burp less than a million years ago when little volcanoes on the divide of the San Bernardino and San Simon Valleys east of the Chiricahuas deposited their cinder cones.

None of the valleys in the border country now have permanent live streams. The Santa Cruz, the San Pedro, and the San Simon all drain north into the Gila River but are often dry for months at a time. The Mimbres River, the Animas Valley, and the Sulphur Springs Valley are interior drainage basins having no outlets, but their waters collect in playas that in wet seasons are shallow lakes—inches deep and miles across—and when dry are glaring expanses of alkali. The San Simon and Sulphur Springs Valleys each have almost imperceptible divides at their southern ends near the border, which separate them from the Río San Bernardino and Whitewater Draw, respectively, which drain into the Río Yaqui and the Sea of Cortez.

This isn't a desert like the Sahara or Death Valley. There is vegetation everywhere—even bare rock is often lichen covered. But the plants are species that can survive long periods without water. Precipitation ranges from as high as thirty-five or forty inches a year— much of it as snowfall—in the narrow islands above 9,000 feet, down to about eight inches in the valley bottoms. By one definition a desert is an area where the rate of evaporation exceeds precipitation. All but the northern exposures of the highest ridges would qualify under those terms. If every morning you bet it won't be cloudy, you'll win most of your bets.

Rainfall is more or less evenly divided between what falls in violent summer thunderstorms and what comes as soft winter drizzles. Spring and fall are usually sunny and dry. A factor that adds to the spring drought is the wind that sucks winter moisture out of the ground, often evaporating snow before it can melt into the soil. By June most living things have no memory of rain or expectation of seeing it again.

The summer solstice begins to turn things around. It is time to start watching the clouds for "dry lightning" and for virga, "Arizona rain," which falls through the cumulus clouds but evaporates before touching the parched ground. On the south side of the border, one can hope for real rain by the twenty-fourth of June, the feast day of San Juan Bautista. On the American side of the fence, one has to wait for the Fourth of July.

Moisture in the mountains keeps the creeks and springs flowing and maintains the water table. Precipitation in the high country is twice that of the skirts of the mountain. In contrast, at the bottom of the valley at San Simon, ten miles from the foothills, the annual average is barely half as much.

Precipitation varies widely from year to year, so averages don't mean much. The average rainfall at Portal is 17.04 inches, but the range is from 27.94 in 1919 down to 4.21 inches in 1956. Several years in a row will be wetter than usual—or drier.

The rapid climb of a mile of elevation from the valley floor to the tops of the high peaks makes for a striking change in vegetation, from the heat- and drought-resistant plants of the Chihuahuan Desert— black grama and fluff grass, creosote bush, mariola, and tarbush—to the spruce, fir, and aspen forests of the mountains.

On the mountains' ridges there are further differences between the north sides, where sunlit hours are short, and the south sides, which are exposed to the full force of the sun. On a high ridge one can stand in a dense forest of Douglas fir and aspen in an environment not unlike that of British Columbia. A stroll of a few hundred yards over the crest will put one in an open woodland of yellow pine and manzanita, with scattered mescal and even claret cup cactus. It's not unlike Mexico's Sierra Madre. The lower slopes and foothills are clothed in juniper and live oak on the cooler exposures, and sotol, mescal, and mountain mahogany on the sunnier sides.

In canyon bottoms, where there is live water much of the year, there are narrow bands of rich woodland dominated by sycamore, but with velvet ash, silver-leaf oak, madrone, chokecherry, and coyote willow in abundance. The drier arroyos are lined with desert willow and hackberry.

Another environment here has its own distinctive vegetation. Marshes, or cienegas, exist at flat, alluvium-filled spots with seeps that keep the soil moist. They are distinguished by expanses of sacaton, a tall bunch grass, and tules (cattails and rushes) in areas where permanent water stands. Groves of cottonwood and black willow are typical. A seeming anomaly in the desert, a large cienega will shelter mallards and teal, herons and ibis.

Historically, antelope grazed the open valleys, mule deer the foothills and bajadas, desert bighorn the rocky slopes and peaks, turkey and whitetail deer the higher country. Several Mexican mammals not found farther north occur along the border. Javelinas graze apparently painlessly on prickly pear cactus, and coatis, or *chulos*, travel in bands through the wooded creek bottoms. Three tropical cats are occasional visitors: margay, ocelot, and jaguar. The Mexican gray wolf, or lobo, has been exterminated—several times—but occasionally one is reported to have drifted back north out of the Sierra Madre.

Several Mexican owls and hawks, as well as seven species of hummingbirds, make their only United States appearance in this narrow strip of border country. The white-winged dove, the harlequin or "fool" quail, and the elegant trogon nest in the Chiricahuas. Thick-billed parrots once also occurred in large flocks in the pines of these mountains but were hunted out years ago.

Topographically, the Chiricahuas are a bow-shaped range, with the belly to the east, running for 150 miles to end in low hills at the Mexican border. The range is separated from the Pinaleño range to the north by Railroad Pass, five miles wide, which itself connects the Sulphur Springs Valley and the San Simon. The latter valley at this point is at it widest, about twenty-five miles across. This long, single range is called by several names. At the north end of the chain the Dos Cabezas Mountains end at Apache Pass. At the central part of the range, the Chiricahuas are higher and broader, about eighteen miles from valley to valley. South of a high saddle dividing the head of Tex Canyon on the east side and Rucker Canyon dropping to the west, for no reasons of geomorphology, the range is called the Pedregosas. Ten miles farther south there is a more obvious break at Silver Creek. From there to the border, a string of lower, timberless hills are the Perillas. Nestled close to the west side and paralleling the Pedregosas is a narrow ridge of limestone, the Swisshelms. Often all five of the names are subsumed under the name of the Chiricahua Mountains.

# A Portal to Paradise

## Chapter 1

# The Indian Pioneers

In the spring of 1952, Emil Haury pulled into a gas station in Benson. The attendant, eyeing the load of duffel bags, tarps, and tools, said, "Looks like you're going hunting. There's no open season now, is there?"

"Yes, it's elephant season," Emil told him.

**Emil Haury**

The first spear-armed men who came out of the north into southeastern Arizona, followed by women carrying babies or skin bags of jerky, were the only true pathfinders. When they walked into the Sulphur Springs and San Simon Valleys about twelve thousand years ago, they had no one to point the way.

The terrain was almost the same as it is today, but ancient freshwater Lake Cochise filled much of the Sulphur Springs Valley and drained south into the Río Yaqui; the alkaline flat west of Lordsburg and the Playas Valley had outlets to the sea. The climate was cooler and wetter. Total precipitation wasn't much greater, but more of it came as snow and less of it evaporated. The San Simon River was a live stream flanked by marsh. Timber reached down the slopes to the valley's edge, pine trees covered the foothills, and deciduous oaks and hickory trees lined the tributary watercourses. Valleys were open meadows where small horses, llamalike camels, tapirs, four-horned antelope, and huge long-horned bison grazed—and elephants.

Emil Haury of the University of Arizona was hunting one of those elephants on Greenbush Draw near Naco on the border, where a few months earlier two spear points and several heavy bones had been found in the arroyo's bank. Haury excavated the site, finding evidence that a mammoth was killed there by at least eight spears and that the hunters took what meat they could handle, leaving the rest of the carcass. Their finely flaked spear points with longitudinal grooves at the base on each face were a distinctive type known as Clovis Fluted, named for the first find of the kind associated with mammoth bones near Clovis, New Mexico.

While Haury's crew was uncovering the kill, rancher Edward Lehner found old bones exposed in an arroyo bank near his house on the San Pedro River, a mile below the mouth of Greenbush Draw. The Arizona State Museum identified them as bits of mammoth teeth, and when Haury explored the deposit later, he uncovered parts of eight mammoths and a bison. Scattered throughout were thirteen Clovis spear points and several stone knives and choppers. Charred oak, ash, and pine in hearths nearby had radiocarbon dates showing that on several occasions between eleven and twelve thousand years ago, young mammoths had been ambushed at a water hole and butchered there. The hunters cooked some meat on the spot but left spear heads embedded in meat they couldn't carry.

No similar find has been made in the San Simon Valley, but the early hunters were surely there. The game was. In the 1970s Finley Richards spotted from horseback a piece of tusk on the surface of an old terrace of San Simon Creek. A paleontologist at the University of New Mexico verified that it was an elephant's. More recently bison bones were found in the eroded creek bank north of San Simon. Eventually someone will find in the sloughing banks of the creek evidence of another postglacial slaughter where a twelve-foot hairy elephant, trunk lifted in a squeal of rage, was stabbed to death by a party of daring hunters.

Elephants were already on the way out, and by 8000 B.C. none were left. Their extinction about four thousand years after man's entry into North America may have been hastened by overkill, but that time was also the beginning of a climate change from cool and moist to warm and dry. The deciduous groves in the valleys died of thirst, pines retreated up the slopes, and mesquite began to appear along the watercourses—in a time that also saw the end of horses, camels, giant bison, ground sloths, tapirs, and several species of antelope and carnivores.

The big game hunters of ten millennia ago adapted to new ways of living, relying more on collecting fruits, roots, and seeds. People still killed deer, set snares for squirrels, and drove rabbits and quail into nets, but now they got more food from wild onions, the tubers of wild potatoes, piñon nuts, acorns, and meal ground from grass seed. The many deep, cylindrical mortar holes found in bedrock in the foothills probably date from this long period of hunting and gathering.

People also milled grass seeds on metates with shallow stone basins and oval grinding surfaces, using manos, or grinding stones, that were about the size and shape of hamburger buns. In hunting they launched spears with an atlatl, or spear thrower, an eighteen- to twenty-inch stick that, in effect, lengthened the hunter's arm. Instead of Clovis points, they used cruder triangular points with deep corner notches.

A site in Cave Creek has contributed much to our knowledge of the period. By 1923 John Hands, a rancher and mining man, had made enough of a stake to retire. For the thirty-seven years he had tramped the country, he had ignored the broken bits of pottery, the traces of old walls, and the metates and other stone tools left by Indians. Then, in 1924, Byron Cummings of the University of Arizona hired him, as an experienced powder man, to accompany him to Mexico to help excavate a site covered by a recent lava flow. Hands blasted away the rock overburden and was himself fired with an enthusiasm for antiquity that burned for the rest of his life.

For ten years Hands worked at other digs in the Southwest. In 1936 he helped Gila Pueblo, a private research institution in Globe, Arizona, excavate a large midden on his ranch just outside the entrance to Cave Creek Canyon. The site, extending for a hundred yards along the north side of Cave Creek Cienega, became a defining source of knowledge for this stage of culture.

The long era of little change in customs lasted from about 5000 to 2000 B.C. Meat was probably 25 percent of the diet, but the major emphasis was on gathering fruits, roots, and seeds. By 1000 B.C. some people were growing corn introduced from Mexico, though they first may have nurtured native species such as careless weed (amaranth).

Archaeologists looked into several sites both older and younger than the Hands midden before they found evidence of the succeeding stage. Then on two sites, one on Whitewater Draw near McNeal and another on the San Pedro River, they found the earliest "architecture," dating from between 2000 and 1500 B.C. to a century or so before the Christian era. The dwellings were shallow, oval basins with hardened clay floors measuring about six by ten feet. Fire-reddened soil suggested that fires had been built on the floors. Probably switches or poles surrounded the depressions to make a frame for a thatched or hide-covered wickiup.

Other artifacts were similar to those of the preceding period, with only minor change. There was no pottery. The number of items seems meager, but we know from perishable material found in dry caves occupied at the same time that the people had wooden tools, clothing of hides, sandals made of yucca fiber, and skillfully woven baskets.

Before those house sites were found, however, a site representative of the succeeding stage—that with the first pottery—was excavated on an outwash fan of Cave Creek about two miles below Portal. Though Hands had discovered the site, he died two years before the dig.

Cave Creek Village, as the site was named, was a cluster of seven houses similar to the earlier ones, but they were a bit larger and showed evidence of an attempt to plaster floors and walls. Each house had a fire pit, although some cooking had been done outside. Stone artifacts were unchanged from the earlier phase, but bracelets and beads made of shell imported from the Gulf of California were found.

The chief new artifact was a plain gray to red-brown pottery. Like corn, this came from southern Mexico, where pottery had been made for a thousand years. Both squash and beans had been added to the crops by this time—roughly A.D. 100. The bow and arrow appeared, although atlatls were still used for another three to four hundred years.

With the development of substantial housing, the introduction of pottery, and the adoption of horticulture, the homogeneous, region-wide hunting and gathering culture that had lasted several millennia came to an end. As sedentary farmers, the people in one part of the Southwest began developing different ways of doing things from those in other sections.

South of the Colorado Plateau in southwestern New Mexico and southeastern Arizona and well down into northwestern Chihuahua, people developed the Mogollon culture, distinct from the Hohokam in the desert to the west and from the Anasazi in the north. Within the larger Mogollon area, in the vicinity of the Chiricahua Mountains, a branch of the Mogollon followed a similar but recognizably differ-ent pattern. Some of those distinctions were spelled out at San Simon Village on Gold Gulch, ten miles west of Bowie.

The fifty-four houses excavated there spanned a period of several centuries from about A.D. 1. By about A.D. 300 the houses were ten-by twelve-foot rectangles in pits one-and-a-half to three feet deep. Near the middle of one long side was a narrow ramped entryway with a fire pit just inside. An arrangement of posts supported the walls and roof. In addition to the earlier plain pottery were a polished red plain ware and a polished brown pottery painted with simple broad-line red decoration.

By the ninth century pottery had begun to be more elaborately decorated. Some three hundred years earlier the knowledge of mak-ing pottery had spread from south to north, and it is possible that the first pottery made in what is now the United States was shaped within sight of the Chiricahuas. But by the 800s innovation moved from north to south.

There is no proof that *people* moved down from the Colorado Pla-teau, but the flood of ideas from that direction increased. By A.D. 1000 pottery design followed the black-on-white Anasazi tradition.

A more striking change occurred in housing. The communities of scattered pit houses became rows of above-ground rooms joined together, small pueblos made of stone and hand-shaped loaves of adobe, or jacales of posts and adobe.

In the 1200s the San Simon Valley was marginal to the Hohokam culture of the western desert, to the Casas Grandes culture of Chihuahua, and to the Mimbres branch of the Mogollon, whose center was in southwestern New Mexico. On the surface of unexcavated sites in the canyon mouths of Jhus, Sulphur, Cave Creek, and Horseshoe, one can find pottery pertaining to all those cultures. It is not clear which ware was acquired in trade and which was made here. Since the excavation of San Simon Village, little archaeology has been done in eastern Cochise County, and many questions remain unanswered. We do know that about A.D. 1300, over most of Cochise County, on the upper Gila, around the Animas range to the east, and a little way into Mexico, large pueblos were built of stone and adobe—some with well over one hundred rooms and often with more than one story. The occupants of these houses cremated their dead and made a distinctive red pottery painted with black-and-white designs.

This combination of traits, which first appeared in the 1200s on the upper tributaries of the Salt River, was undoubtedly a blending of local custom with traits introduced by an immigration of people from the Four Corners country, which by 1300 was totally abandoned. The ideas, if not the people, spread rapidly to the Hohokam in the desert valleys of the Salt and middle Gila, as well as to the south.

These sites exist on both sides of the Chiricahuas and in the Animas Valley, but there has been little systematic study of them. Pueblo Viejo, at the junction of the San Simon River and the Gila, which was probably the largest prehistoric settlement in southeastern Arizona, was described by early explorers as a series of large compounds extending for three or four miles along the Gila's south bank. Sadly, the entire site was plowed, planted, or paved before it could be properly investigated. A small undamaged piece of Pueblo Viejo was excavated in the 1970s by careful amateurs, Vera and Jack Mills of Elfrida, who got geomagnetic samples from two fireplaces that dated to about A.D. 1360 and 1405.

The Millses also excavated about a third of a community on West

Turkey Creek occupied in late 1300s, where several compounds of large one-story adobe rooms surrounded open plazas. In addition to remains of corn, beans, and squash, they found seeds indicating that cotton was grown. The couple also dug part of a similar site on the Anderson ranch in Price Canyon, on the east side of the Chiricahuas.

There are remains of sites occupied between the 1200s and the 1400s at the mouth of every major canyon emerging from the Chiricahuas, the Peloncillos, and the Animas Mountains and at every seep in the valleys, but there is scant evidence of a sedentary people in this part of the Southwest after 1400. There are hints that some of the population of southeastern Arizona wound up in Cíbola, the province surrounding present-day Zuni Pueblo, where the *conquistadores* found the inhabitants burning their dead in an un-Anasazi fashion. Archaeologists have found the pottery of those people reminiscent of the polychromes of the Gila River drainage. As populous as the Zuni country had become at the time of European contact, it seems unlikely that it accommodated all the people of southwestern New Mexico and southeastern Arizona. Nor does the possible migration of some of the people explain the depopulation of the latter large area.

It probably wasn't totally vacated. From a small pueblo on Deer Creek in the Animas Mountains have come carbon-14 dates of 1565 to 1620. The site was probably occupied by the Janos or Jocomes people the Spaniards encountered in those years. But the story of the time between 1400 and the mid-1500s is on a blank page, and for the next one hundred years the ink is blurred.

When Coronado, with pennons flapping, brought his army and the flocks to feed it north to the expected riches of the fabled Seven Cities, he passed through a stretch of unpopulated land extending from the *rancherías* of the Piman-speaking peoples in Sonora to the villages of the Zunis. In spite of much diligent scholarship, we don't know his precise route.

If he went down the San Pedro, as conventional wisdom has it, he would have passed a Sobáipuri village near present-day Fairbank and couldn't have missed it. A much easier route, one certainly known to his Indian guides, would have been down the San Simon to Pueblo

Viejo—perhaps the abandoned Chichilticale recorded by the expedition. That more easterly route might have *appeared* unoccupied. The Jocomes the Spaniards found in the Chiricahuas a hundred years later may have been a backsliding remnant of the earlier civilization, who quietly withdrew into the canyons to avoid contact with the imposing army column.

Archaeology is only about seventy-five years old in Cochise County. There are still floating pieces of data and holes to fill with pieces that are yet to be found.

The mountains had the name first, and the people, the Chiricahua Apaches, were named for the range at the center of their territory.

Apaches were newcomers to the Southwest, having arrived on the plains of southeastern Colorado and northeastern New Mexico shortly before the Spaniards. They reached the border country probably no sooner than the early 1600s. Their ancestors were among the last to come from Asia. All Apaches speak Athapaskan, and their speech is so similar to the tongues spoken on the Mackenzie and Yukon Rivers that linguists believe that the northern and southern Athapaskans have been separated for no more than a thousand years.

The Spanish applied the name Apache to all the southern Athapaskans as early as the late 1500s. The origin of the word is usually ascribed to the Zuni word *apachu*, "enemy." The Apaches called themselves *ende*—"the people"—or *nde, dinde*, or *diné*, depending on the dialect.

There are seven distinct tribes of southern Athapaskans, though they weren't always separate. The Kiowa-Apaches were pulling away about the time the first Apaches probed the high plains. By the 1700s the Jicarillas in northeastern New Mexico and the Lipans in west Texas were developing their own dialects. The speech of the others is still closely enough related that Chiricahuas, Mescaleros, Western Apaches, and Navajos can, with difficulty, understand each other. The Western Apaches, or Coyoteros, of east-central Arizona and the Mescaleros of southeastern New Mexico each recognize the Chiricahuas of southeastern Arizona and southwestern New Mexico as a people closely related to themselves but of a different tribe.

The label Chiricahua Apaches was originally applied to a band that ranged from the Huachuca and Whetstone Mountains east to the Animas Mountains, and from south of the Gila Valley to a short way below the present international border. The Chiricahua Mountains were central to the area, which included the Mules, the Dragoons, the Dos Cabezas, and the Peloncillos. The Apache term for these people was Chokonende or Chokonen (pronounced Ch'kahnen). Prominent Chokonen leaders were Cochise, Chihuahua, and Naiche.

A more numerous group now included under the umbrella term Chiricahua was the Chihenne, or Red Paint People, who ranged east of the Chokonen to the Rio Grande and north to the San Agustin Plains. They were known by many names to Mexicans and Americans, depending on where they were encountered. A favorite camp was near hot springs in the northwest quarter of their territory in Cañada Alamosa, about sixty miles southwest of Socorro, New Mexico. While they were there, they were known as Apaches de Ojo Caliente, or Warm Springs Apaches, to white men, and that name is often applied to all the Chihenne. Well-known leaders were Mangas Coloradas, Victorio, Nana, and Loco.

A third band was the Ndenda (Enemy People), so named for their ferocity in battle. Their country was the boot heel of New Mexico and the adjacent part of the state of Chihuahua, south into the Sierra Madre as far as the Río Aros. The Ndenda weren't always recognized by their Mexican and American enemies as other than extensions of the Warm Springs or Chokonen, and it is likely that the name is recent, dating from the hostilities of the mid-1800s. Juh was an outstanding Ndenda leader.

Tribal identity as a political entity was of so little importance to the Apaches that they had no name for it. Primary allegiance was to the extended family—a couple with their unmarried children, their married daughters with *their* families, and possibly a widowed parent of the older woman—a unit that might number from a dozen to twenty or thirty. Within this large family there was much interdependence.

When a man married, he lived near his wife's parents. Though he had his own household, the game he killed was theirs, to be cooked with his wife's help in his mother-in-law's camp. The head of the family was the oldest man, but for many of his decisions he had the advice of his wife—or wives, for it was permitted to have more than one, though it wasn't common. When a man took another wife, she was likely to be his sister-in-law because it was his duty to care for his wife's widowed sister.

Sometimes several extended families camped together and were called by a name referring to a commonly used campsite or to their leader. These were likely to be short-term or seasonal arrangements, however, because large concentrations of people could quickly use up available food sources.

At least two such groups were recognized within the Ndenda: the Tsebekinende (Stone House People) and the Dzilthdaklizhende (Blue Mountain People) to the south of them. One group of families of the Chokonen was known as the Tsegatahende (Rock Pocket People), a name descriptive of Cave Creek Canyon and other steep-walled canyons of the Chiricahua Mountains. The group led by Cochise was called Chishende, Cochise's People.

The Chihenne included, in addition to the Warm Springs group, the Mimbreños on the Mimbres River (also called the Coppermine or Santa Rita Apaches) and the Mogollon Apaches (or Gileños) on the upper tributaries of the Gila River. The latter, Geronimo's people, were usually lumped with the Chihenne but were sometimes thought of as a distinct band called the Bedonkohe.

All of these bands—the Chokonen, the Chihenne, and the Ndenda —were Chiricahuas. They intermarried, visited back and forth, and frequently joined forces in war. They weren't confined to their favored ranges, for the earth and its resources belonged to all.

A *nantan*, or leader, of a band was called *capitán* by the Mexicans and chief by the Americans, but he didn't inherit his position, nor was he always elected. He earned his position through force of character, oratory, hunting or raiding skill, or by the reputation of being right more often than other men. The title was informal, and the man's authority was no greater than his ability to make it stick. Those who had confidence in him followed him. If too many of his decisions were bad, dissatisfied family heads would take their people off to join another group. He led by persuasion, not by command. Thus, the groups were not static. A strong leader might attract families to swell his group, but drought, shortage of game, squabbles, or a poor crop of mesquite beans could cause followers to leave. Often the son of a chief succeeded him, having acquired the qualities of leadership from his father through training or genes.

Unlike other Apache bands, the Chokonen claim they never planted corn but made their living solely by hunting and gathering. Men usually hunted in small groups that shared the kill. Deer was the most important game, but pronghorn and mountain sheep were also taken. Boys practiced archery on quail, rabbits, and squirrels. Bears were taboo because of a power they had to make a person sick. Snakes weren't eaten, nor were fish because they looked a bit like snakes.

Hunting required more than skill and stamina. Aware of being part of nature, the Apaches believed that all the elements and creatures had the power to harm the irreverent and to reward those who showed proper respect. Through ritual the hunter asked the deer to give itself up, and when he killed one he offered thanks with a pinch of pollen, and out of respect he avoided stepping over the body while it was being skinned and butchered.

Often wild plants provided the greater part of subsistence, and gathering them was the woman's task. Customarily, several women went out together, their burden baskets carried on tumplines. They also observed rituals of thanks, and when they dug up roots of the wild potato, they put the top back to return to the earth part of what it had supplied. Gathering required knowledge of the country, of where a specific plant could be found and the season it could be harvested. Camps were moved frequently to be at the right place at the right time. Nearly 6,000 feet of elevation change from the valley floor to the top of Chiricahua Peak furnished a great variety of vegetation with something ready to eat at every season.

In the valley the first sunny days of February brought out the wide leaves of cañaigre, or sorrel (*Rumex sp.*), which were cut when young to be boiled as greens. In early spring tender cattail shoots were pulled at the San Simon Cienega, and the heads of the yucca cut off and baked. In late May yucca flower buds were picked to be eaten raw or boiled.

By June south-facing slopes of the foothills provided sotol and mescal, whose flower stalks, emerging like giant asparagus, were cut, roasted, and peeled. In shaded gulches and on north-facing slopes, the pink flowers of the New Mexico locust were picked and used like yucca flowers. After a few rains in July, purslane, careless weed, and lamb's quarters were gathered for greens, and in August seeds of the latter two species and those of sunflowers, buckskin grass *(Panicum obtusum)*, and sand dropseed *(Sporobilis dendsiflora)* were ground into meal. September was a good time for hackberry, acorns, walnuts, juniper, and madrone berries and piñon nuts. Berries on the squaw-bush *(Rhus trilobata* and *R. microphylla)* and buckthorn lasted into November.

In winter months there was little to collect except the inner bark of box elder, aspen, or ponderosa pine, and times would have been hard if not for mesquite beans and mescal. Between them, these two big staples, gathered in the late spring and summer and dried for storage, provided a large part of Chokonen diet.

All of the several species of mescal, or century plant, were used for food. The most plentiful and most desirable was *Agave palmeri*, which was also the largest, with leaves up to three feet long. It grows scattered on open, grassy foothills and up into oak woodlands to 6,500 feet. A smaller mescal, *A. parryi*, with wide, foot-long leaves, grows in clusters in the oaks and chaparral at 5,000 feet and up into the pines at 8,000 feet on southern exposures. Mescal could be collected at any season but was juiciest just before blooming in May.

Gathering mescal was a major effort in which men also took part. They cut off the plant at ground level with a sharpened stick, then chopped off the leaves with a broad-bladed stone knife and carried the large white crowns to a pit eight to ten feet across and three feet deep, which they had lined with stones. Then they filled the pit with firewood, burned it down to coals, and covered the hot stones with green grass. The largest mescal head was blessed with pollen before it was put into the pit. Once filled, the pit was covered with the cut-off leaves and the earth from the pit. Baking lasted through two nights, and the mescal was taken out early the second morning. The charred outsides were trimmed off, and the hearts, now brown with natural sugar, provided an immediate feast of sweet pulp. The remaining mescal was sliced and pounded into cakes and spread out to dry for storage.

The second staple was mesquite beans, gathered from a shrub or small tree that grows from the valleys up into the foothills to about 5,500 feet. Though seldom more than ten feet high, mesquites growing in sheltered places and along streambeds are sometimes double that height. By June the sweet eight-inch-long bean pods are edible and will continue to be after they mature and turn yellow. They are best gathered in the summer as they mature, however, before worms, high winds, and pack rats reduce the size of the crop. The beans were chewed for the sweet pulp and juice, then the quid of fiber was spit out. Beans were also dried and ground, and the flour was winnowed from the fiber and mixed with water to drink as *pinole* or was baked into cakes.

It was probably from the O'odham and the Tarahumaras that the Apaches learned to make tulapai—from *tulthpai*, "gray water"—a fermented drink made of sprouted corn or cactus fruit.

An economy based on scattered and seasonally available resources required frequent moves, so shelter needed to be simple, quickly erected, and easily abandoned. The traditional Chiricahua wickiup was made by stabbing the butts of long flexible poles into the ground, tying their tips together in a domelike frame, and thatching it with sacaton or beargrass or covering it with hides. For short stops this shelter could be quite small, but for a stay of several weeks it might be twelve feet across at the floor and high enough to stand in.

In early times the Apaches often helped themselves to the corn of the sedentary Opatas and Pimas, though it wasn't a significant contribution to the food supply. But by the time the Spaniards were established on the Santa Cruz, the upper San Pedro, and in Chihuahua, the Apaches were raiding for livestock as an extension of their hunting pattern and an important part of their economy. Some danger was involved, but raiding wasn't war. A Chokonen on a raid was simply hunting big game in the form of domestic stock. The Mexican rancher was, at first, looked upon as a reluctant servant, and as in more conventional hunting, care was taken to leave a little for seed.

Defensive warfare, or wars of retaliation and revenge, occurred but were considered activities separate from gathering cattle. Unlike the Indians of the Plains, the Apaches didn't glorify and make a game of war.

Before the establishment of Spanish ranches in the early 1700s, Apaches penetrated infrequently into what is now Mexico. Once the ranches provided inviting targets, however, beef and horse meat gradually became staples and permitted the Apache population to grow larger than the wild foods of the semiarid country could support. By the mid-1800s they had become dependent on raiding for their livelihood. To halt the raiding, the Spaniards from time to time concentrated Apaches around the presidios and issued rations. When a pinch for funds or a change in policy brought an end to rationing, the Apaches reverted to raiding.

During the late 1800s Caucasian intrusions reduced Apache foraging territory, making raiding more necessary for survival. As Mexican and American settlers grew in numbers, they were increasingly able to protect their property and to retaliate, and the distinction between warfare and raiding became blurred.

Chiricahua Apache life wasn't solely taken up with making a living. Their system of beliefs was and is a rich one. Its cardinal difference from Western religions is in its sense of man being at one with nature, a part of it rather than its God-appointed master. Man, born of earth and sky, is a fellow inhabitant with the fox, the raven, and the cottonwood tree, all of whom have spiritual selves like his.

Though they occupied these mountains for 350 years, the Chokonen left little trace of their presence. A rare pictograph, a storage basket cached in a crack in a cliff face, a pottery jar hidden in a cave, and the mescal-baking pits of fire-cracked rock make up the scant tangible evidence. But through a history that is legend around the edges and a tradition that will outlast those few material things, this remains "Apache country."

# Chapter 2

# Spanish Exploration

We could see large, splendid, and fertile valleys covered and enriched with very beautiful meadows, prairies, springs, rivers, and streams. . . . This fertile and attractive land is adorned and endowed with fine mountain ranges . . . large madrone trees, many very tall nut-bearing walnut trees, Castile prune trees, and wild grapes.

**Baltazar de Obregón**

In 1527 the bungled Spanish expedition to conquer Florida came to an end with a shipwreck in the Gulf of Mexico. Four survivors led by Alvar Núñez Cabeza de Vaca spent ten years working their way up the Rio Grande to the vicinity of El Paso and then across northwestern Mexico to Sinaloa, where they stumbled, footsore and nearly naked, into a party of Spanish slavers. One of the weary travelers was Estevan, a black Moor from the coast of Morocco.

Indians on the Rio Grande told the foursome about people on the upper reaches of the river who lived in towns of stone houses several stories high. With repetition, the survivors' tales were exaggerated until the Spaniards easily convinced themselves that another bonanza lay in Cíbola, which they related to seven mythical golden cities west of Atlantis. The name Cíbola is a Hispanicized version of the Zunis' word for their country.

In late 1538 Mexico's viceroy sent Fray Marcos, a French priest from Nice, north to reconnoiter. Accompanied by Pima Indians and by Estevan for his linguistic skill and knowledge of the country, Marcos was escorted to Culiacán by the new governor of Nueva Galicia, Francisco Vásquez de Coronado. The friar then went up the coast, where he divided his party, sending the Moor ahead with Pima guides. Thus the first "Spaniard" to see Arizona was African, and the second was French.

On his journey across the continent two years earlier, the African had picked up not only languages and knowledge of the terrain, but also a shaman's bag of tricks. After leaving Marcos, he proceeded grandly north with his escort. Arrayed in feathers and accompanied by rattles, whistles, and drums, he so impressed the people along the way that they showered him with gifts, which he accepted as his due. When he reached Cíbola, he was so demanding that the Zunis killed him and, according to tradition, ground his bones.

Word of the killing reached the slower-moving Marcos at Chichilticale, pueblo ruins a week's journey south of Cíbola, and though the friar claimed to have seen from a hill the village where the Moor died and could verify its splendor, there is doubt that he went any farther after hearing from his Pima retainers about Zuni inhospitality.

A century of research has gone into plotting the course followed by Estevan, Fray Marcos, and later Coronado from Mexico to the Zuni villages, but few scholars have known the country as well as Charles Di Peso of the Amerind Foundation at Dragoon, Arizona. Di Peso believed the route went up the Bavispe River to San Bernardino Springs, thence down the San Simon Valley, over Antelope Pass into the Animas Valley, and north to the upper Gila Valley. Prior scholars favored a route down the San Pedro to cross the Gila, thence northeast to Zuni—a conclusion that, given the nature of the terrain between the confluence of those streams and Zuni, is hard to accept.

We know from contemporary sources that the Indians of Sonora knew the Zuni people through trade. The Spaniards followed established paths, guided by men who had walked them. It makes sense that those guides would take the easy low road. That trail would be the one that skirted the east flank of the White Mountains and Escudilla Peak, leading to Zuni Salt Lake and on to Cíbola.

A modification of the route suggested by Di Peso might go down the San Simon Valley to the Gila, thence north by way of the San Francisco River. That would have been a better-watered trail than one past Lordsburg Playa, and it would have brought them to Pueblo Viejo or to a contemporary ruin on the upper Gila near Cliff—either one a good bet to be Marcos's Chichilticale.

It is possible that Jocomes from the Chiricahua Mountains' east side saw Estevan as he passed and watched Fray Marcos trudge along after him and return again the way he had come.

When the viceroy got the friar's glowing report, he sent a frontier veteran, Melchior Díaz, to verify his account. In November Díaz departed with fifteen *caballeros* and a few Indians. His were the first horses in Arizona—Marcos and Estevan had been afoot. It was midwinter, and the high country was snowed in when he reached Chichilticale and the beginning of the lonely, unoccupied stretch, so Díaz wintered on the Gila, learning about Cíbola from local people who knew it well. These people, probably Jocomes, were hunters with no fixed residence. They painted a less colorful picture of the mud and stone villages than Fray Marcos had, and warned Díaz that the Zunis had told them of the Moor's death and that the Spaniards would not be welcome.

Meanwhile, a major expedition was organized in Mexico to leave in the spring of 1540, led by Coronado. The force, nearly as large as the one that had wrested the Aztec empire from Moctezuma twenty years before, was made up of three hundred fighting men, mostly young adventurers who supplied their own equipment and mounts. They were accompanied by several hundred Indians whose numbers swelled and ebbed as the army moved along—Tarascans and Aztecs from the Mexican plateau, Pimas and Opatas from the frontier.

From Culiacán, Coronado went on ahead with about a hundred horsemen; the friars, including Marcos de Niza; and some of the Indian auxiliaries, leading them north in advance of the main body. The support trains and the herds of livestock, larder-on-the-hoof, necessarily moved slower.

This party, much larger than those of the Moor, Marcos, or Díaz, raised a bigger dust as it passed east of the Chiricahuas—if, indeed, that was their route. Coronado's encounter with the Zunis; his discovery of the Grand Canyon, the Hopi towns, and the pueblos on the Rio Grande; and his terminus in south-central Kansas are not part of this story, but before the expedition returned to Mexico, there were to be nine more passages of the road from Mexico to Cíbola via Chichilticale.

In the spring of 1542, discouraged by the failure to find plunder and weakened by hunger, with many of their horses lost and their commander injured, the army retraced its steps. Two days below Chichilticale, they met a relief pack train of food, possibly in the vicinity of the San Simon Cienega. After a welcome feast the army marched on south to Sinaloa.

In a little less than three years, fifteen parties of Spaniards had passed north or south. Not for three hundred years would there be so much non-native traffic in the vicinity.

Subsequent explorations bypassed this part of the frontier. The expedition of Oñate to establish Spanish settlement in northern New Mexico in 1598 followed a more direct route north through Chihuahua. In August 1680 the Pueblo Indians of the upper Rio Grande revolted, killed many colonists, and drove the surviving two thousand or so south to El Paso. The first Spanish settlers in northwestern Chihuahua were New Mexican refugees, many of whom settled around Casas Grandes.

Indian unrest continued, and in 1685 Governor Don Diego Jironza, to quell outbreaks of the Janos and Jocomes to the west, set up a *presidio*, or garrison, at the village of Janos to control them. But trouble continued, and within a year the Jocomes and Janos were for the first time joined by Apaches in the attacks, thus beginning a harassment of settlers that continued for two hundred years.

Jesuit missions had been established in northern Sonora in the mid-1600s, but permanent Spanish settlement had not followed as quickly as in Chihuahua. Their appetite whetted by success, the raiding tribes expanded their interests to the Opata villages in Sonora. The Spanish, having made Christians of the Opatas, were obliged by law to defend them. To do this, in 1690 they put a presidio at an Opata community thirty miles south of Agua Prieta on the present border and aptly named it Fronteras. The presence of a few soldiers on a lonely river, however, did little to discourage the Jocomes from stealing cattle and gathering Opata corn, and the raids continued. The base from which these raids were launched was principally the Chiricahua Mountains.

A year after founding the Fronteras presidio, Jironza was relieved of his governorship of New Mexico and made general of the military forces in Sonora, assigned to protect the missions, the growing number of Spanish ranches, and the peaceful Indian population. He was replaced as governor by Don Diego de Vargas, who was soon to win fame for leading the reconquest of northern New Mexico. In the meantime, like his predecessor, he had to protect his flanks.

In October 1691 Vargas took his soldiers from El Paso to Janos to join Gen. Juan Fernández de la Fuente and his troops. The combined force then went northwest in search of hostile Indians by way of the San Bernardino Valley and the San Simon. North of the present border they joined troops from Fronteras commanded by Francisco Ramírez de Salazar, a New Mexico colonist driven out by the Pueblo rebellion. On the Gila River they attacked an Apache rancheria. They may have been the first white men since Coronado to see the jagged profile of Cochise Head in the Chiricahuas.

Expeditions like that of Vargas were ineffective in discouraging raids by the unsettled tribes. In November 1694, after a fierce fight, General Jironza from Fronteras beat back an attack on a peaceful Opata village at Batepito, thirty miles south of San Bernardino Springs. Occasional dispatches to Mexico City from the northern frontier mentioned Apaches, but Jocomes and Janos were spoken of as the leading threat to peace.

In May 1695 the governor of Nueva Viscaya, which included most of northwestern Mexico, sent word to General Fernández at Janos to join forces with Gen. Domingo Terán de los Ríos to quell the hostile Indians once and for all. It was the first of many "final solutions" to be promulgated in the succeeding 190 years.

The army of 126 men, almost half of them Indian allies, left Janos the following month. General Fernández's journal makes it possible to plot their movements, precisely in some instances and with educated conjecture in others. Their first contact with the enemy was at Cuchuvérachic, a small rancheria on the Río San Bernardino twenty miles southeast of Agua Prieta. After a three-day skirmish, Fernández sent several captives out to the scattered bands of Jocomes and Apaches to ask them to meet with him in the Chiricahua Mountains to discuss peace.

The generals then moved up to the spring at San Bernardino to await a response. They had barely made camp when messages from Jironza, who was fifty miles south marching to join them, told of a rebellion of the Pimas of Sonora. The killing of a priest had been avenged by an overzealous Spanish officer when he enticed the Pimas to a conference and then opened fire, killing dozens of them, most of whom were innocent. The betrayal had aroused the heretofore loyal Pimas who had not been involved in the padre's death. In their rage they burned two missions and several ranches. Governor Jironza requested Fernández and Terán to return to help him put down the immediate danger of a Pima uprising.

Fernández, believing he was close to accomplishing something, was reluctant to turn back. He made a day's march of sixteen leagues north to the springs of Las Lágrimas de San Pedro—"St. Peter's Tears." Sixteen of the Spanish 2.63-mile leagues is about forty-two miles, which on a direct route passing just west of Parramore Crater could have landed them at an unnamed seep on Sulphur Draw, due east of Darnell Peak and west of the present town of Rodeo. The next morning, "after traveling about one league," they reached a spring where they found the warm ashes of more than forty fires. This may have been Anderson Seep, near the roping arena on the Three Triangle Ranch east of Portal Peak. They went on for "about three leagues" on a "fresh trail that went up a heavily wooded canyon into the Chiricahua Mountains." At Anderson Seep they were about three leagues from the narrows of Cave Creek Canyon above Portal.

There they met a corporal returning from a scout he had been sent on, who reported that he had found recently abandoned camps in the mouth of another canyon two leagues away. He took the army to them, probably in East Turkey Creek.

The scouts' approach had alarmed the Indians, evidently Jocomes, who had gone up to a defensive position in two rocky peaks on the column's left, from which they yelled down at the troops. They seem to have been in the bare, whitish rocks on Silver Peak's north shoulder. A Spanish-speaking Indian worked his way down to a safe talking distance, and through palaver both parties avowed peaceful intent. The Indians agreed to send runners to outlying rancherias to bring people in to a council. To show their sincerity, the soldiers put up four crosses in their camp "a quarter of a league away." This may have been at Soldier Flat, two-thirds of a mile northeast of the white rocks. The Spaniards named the canyon La Cañada de las Paces de San Pedro—"The Peace, or Treaties, of St. Peter," whose feast day it was.

After several days of vainly waiting in the Lágrimas camp for the Indians to show up, the generals reluctantly returned to San Bernardino Springs, where another urgent message from Jironza reached them, asking that they join him at Cocóspera. They did so and spent July and August "pacifying" the Pimas.

Fernández was anxious to get back north to deal with the Indians he had talked with in June. He persuaded Terán and Jironza to join him, and also Capt. Nicolás de Higuera, who had come north with a company from Sinaloa. On September 9, 1695, the combined forces of Spanish soldiers and large contingents of Opata, Concho, and Pima allies left Cocóspera and marched down the San Pedro River to the Sobáipuri village of Quíburi, the ruins of which can still be traced below Fairbank, west of Tombstone.

The Sobáipuri, an eastern branch of Pimas, occupied the San Pedro Valley in permanent settlements under Chief Coro. Three years before, the Jesuit missionary Eusebio Kino had made a nominal Christian and an ally of Coro, who warned the soldiers that the Apaches planned to ambush them in the Chiricahuas. Such a large force was in no danger from scattered unorganized bands, however, and Coro joined them with ten of his men.

Leaving Quíburi, the army crossed the Dragoons, made a dry camp
in the Sulphur Springs Valley, and sent a party out to find water. The
muddy water found the next day was needed. It was the first since
leaving the San Pedro, and many of the men, Terán among them, were
ill with chills and fever. At this point they were probably on Whitewater Draw, south of the Squaretop Hills, a dozen miles west of the central part of the Chiricahuas. Coro's scouts had located Jocomes in a
canyon on the west slope of the range. Directions and distances traveled later in the campaign make it likely they were in Rucker Canyon.

In the afternoon Lt. Antonio de Solís, Jironza's second-in-
command, took a mounted party ahead and found a rancheria near
the mouth of the canyon, but the Indians had fled. The next morning they found livestock whose brands identified them as having been
taken from the pueblo of Cuquiárachic, an Opata settlement near
Fronteras, so they torched the wickiups.

When the main army joined them at the smoking camp, scouts
went out to find where the Indians had gone. Two prisoners were
taken and interrogated with the help of an Opata who could speak
the Jocome language. They learned that most of the Indians were on
the Gila River but that there were many Jocomes and a few Apaches
closer in the Pinaleños and the Dos Cabezas Mountains.

During that night one hundred Pimas recruited at Cocóspera
quietly slipped out to return home.

The following morning Fernández's first need was a better source
of water. Again he sent Antonio de Solís out to find it. Solís by then
was about the only able-bodied officer in the command. General
Terán was helpless with fever, Jironza not much better, and Fernández himself was unwell. Solís and his patrol returned at midday, having found a pond three leagues north. This spot may have been in the
sacaton and live oaks at the mouth of West Turkey Creek. Carrying
the sick on litters, the army didn't reach the new camp until almost
midnight.

Fernández was determined to find the enemy, and again the duty
fell to Solís. By late afternoon the following day, he left with most
of the men still able to march and fight—sixty-four soldiers and one

hundred Indians. A few hours out, he took two prisoners and sent one back to Fernández. He intended to use the other as a guide, but when the man balked, he had him shot. Early on the second day, Solís surprised a rancheria, and "the Indians tried to escape up the arroyos of a small sierra which fell toward the land of the Sobáipuris, about eight leagues west of the Santa Rosa Mountains [the Pinaleños]." This action happened on a foray that "took him well north into the valley of Quíburi."

The "valley of the Quíburi" is the San Pedro Valley, the "land of the Sobáipuris." The small sierra may have been the outlying hills at the south end of the Winchesters, where arroyos drain west by way of Tres Alamos Wash into the San Pedro. In any event, the fire-eating lieutenant charged into those Indians, killed thirteen, including their head man, and captured the rest. Arrogantly, he sent two of the captives to the Apaches on the Gila, with orders that they come to the San Simon Cienega to surrender. Two old men, too feeble to march, he shot.

By midafternoon the next day, Solís was back with the main body of the army. In two-and-a-half days he had ridden fifty miles out, then back with forty-five prisoners.

The men had been in the field for five months. More than half were sick, probably with malaria, and those who were not were close to exhaustion. Fernández's objective was to reach the Indians on the Gila, though he must have begun to lose heart. The "victory" of an army of more than three hundred over a band of perhaps fifty or sixty, including women and children, was galling to him. In frustration, he had five of the Jocome prisoners shot and their bodies hung. With Christian "charity" he first had the two men and three women instructed in the faith and baptized.

Again Solís, showing no more mercy on his own body than on another's, led a party of soldiers to find a pass through the north end of the mountains—and water—three hundred men and one hundred horses had drained the water hole. The rest of the troops, their allies, and their prisoners followed slowly and painfully, many carried on litters. Through a day of agony and thirst, they struggled north through a pass they called San Felipe, out into the San Simon Valley—a march of nine leagues. San Felipe may have been Apache Pass, but since they missed Apache Springs, a mile off the trail, they may have gone through Bear Springs Pass, reaching the valley after a hike of about twenty-five miles.

On the morning of September 25, Fernández led the van himself to make one last effort to get to the Gila and the Apaches. This valley was more familiar to him. He had passed through it with Vargas five years before. Desperate to find water for his weakening command, he rode on ahead along the northeast side of the Dos Cabezas Mountains to water holes he knew to the north.

The pools he sought had dried up, and he was ranging about for other water when a messenger from the army crawling along behind him brought word that Jironza and Terán could go no farther. Fernández saw that further campaigning was futile. He returned and sent runners to all the water-searching parties to assemble at the *"rincón* of the Las Animas mountains" (the Dos Cabezas) ten miles north of San Felipe Pass. Some of the strongest went back into the mountains to carry water from tanks in the rocks down to the sick. Terán wrote his will.

The Spanish word *rincón,* "inside corner," when used as a topographical term, refers to a box canyon, or an open place with higher country on three sides. Buckeye Canyon, on the north side of the Dos Cabezas, fits the distance given in the Fernández journal. Near the midpoint of the range, north of the two-headed peak that gives its name to the range, the rincon is flanked by Rough Mountain on the east and Maverick Mountain on the west.

On September 26, with hardly enough able-bodied men to wrangle the horses, the general took his bedraggled troops to water at the San Simon Cienega. They retraced the previous day's route, then skirted the north end of the Chiricahuas on a grueling hike, a straggling column miles long dragging itself across the shadeless plain. By noon they had made six leagues, a little over fifteen miles, and they found water holes, possibly at the mouth of Emigrant Canyon, where the men got a drink. It was six leagues farther to the cienega. The strong didn't get there until sundown, and the litters not until hours after dark. Some of the Indians deserted the column and didn't get there at all.

Fernández describes their camp as "facing the canyon where the enemy made peace with us last June," and indeed, from the downstream end of the cienega, one can see the white rocks on the side of Silver Peak.

After a conference the following morning, the officers decided to stay for a few days to rest both men and horses. While the sick lay back in exhaustion and gaunt horses grazed the sacaton meadows, two patrols went out to look for Indians. A sergeant led a patrol "about seven leagues north" to the Peñol de Alonso Pérez. The *peñol*, a rocky eminence or cliff, may have been Stein's Peak at about six leagues, or sixteen miles, north of the cienega. A corporal took eighteen men back to the site of the "treaty" in Turkey Creek, where he found the crosses still in place but the Indians' camp abandoned.

Late on the third day at the cienega, the officers gathered at Jironza's tent for a council. Terán, too sick to stand, was represented by his ensign, who reported that two-thirds of his men were sick and the rest near total exhaustion. He voted to call it quits. A third of Higuera's Sinaloans were down, and even the indomitable Solís admitted that most of the Sonoran force was incapacitated and that the Indian allies wanted to go home—170 had already done so. Each officer had his say, and it was the reluctant unanimous opinion that the campaign should be brought to an end. Spanish authority dealt harshly with failure, and each man's declaration was carefully recorded in justification before the generals concurred and gave orders to depart in the morning.

The news of the decision spread quickly, and by morning on September 30 those Opatas, Pimas, and Sobáipuris who had not already decamped or died of the fever were gone.

It was too late for Terán. At midnight Fernández got word that the general was dead. Not wanting to bury his comrade in unconsecrated

ground, he had the body lashed to the back of a pack mule and detailed a squad of the strongest men to ride hard for a burial at Janos,
fifty leagues southeast.

Before the commands separated, two prisoners were selected to
present to the governor. The officers divided the rest. Although Spanish law forbade slavery, forcing heathens to work while they were
given instruction in the Christian faith was tolerated. In the midafternoon they moved out, Jironza and Higuera going south by way of San
Bernardino. Fernández, with his own and Terán's troops, reached
Janos on October 6, 1695, in just over three days.

In a four-month campaign the army had seen some new country
and added a bit to the knowledge of the terrain, but it could claim no
progress toward containment of the hostile tribes.

Spanish penetration into this area didn't end with that 1695 expedition, but subsequent expeditions were equally ineffective. Indian
raids became more frequent as settlement increased on the upper Río
Sonora and tributaries of the Río Yaqui. The new settlers' herds were
an irresistible target to the Apaches, whose strength and increasing
numbers were made possible, in part, by those herds. In 1704 Janos,
Jocomes, and Chiricahua Apaches together raided Bacanuchi, south
of modern Cananea; Terrenate, on the upper Río Santa Cruz; and
Teuricachi, near Fronteras.

In 1717 most of the Janos and Jocomes were settled around the
Janos presidio and eventually lost their ethnic identity through ab-
sorption into the Mexican population. Probably the now-dominant
Apaches took in some of both of those groups. After 1730 only the
name Apache is heard in regard to pillage and plunder, and passage
through their territory by any other than a large armed party was only
by Apache sufferance.

In 1700 the Jesuits extended the missions to the Pimas in the Santa
Cruz Valley by putting a priest at San Xavier del Bac and one at
Guevavi the next year, but it wasn't until soldiers were garrisoned at
Tubac in 1753 that Spanish ranchers felt secure enough to settle in

what is now Arizona. Soon there were several hundred settlers between Sonoita and Tubac, a population that fluctuated as the crown's military policy and the intensity of Apache raiding sought a balance. This thin line of European settlement along the Santa Cruz never reached north of Tucson, and except for scattered, chancy, and short-lived mines or cattle stations, Spaniards seldom tried to live east of that valley.

Punitive expeditions were made against the Apaches on their home ground annually. In 1747 an ambitious winter expedition marched from the Rio Grande to the Río Mimbres but didn't reach the Chiricahuas. They nearly froze and they saw no Apaches.

A campaign in 1756 was a two-pronged attack in which a party from Janos marched north past the Animas Mountains to the Gila to meet a force from Fronteras under Gabriel Antonio de Vildósola. The combined army of soldiers and Opata and Tarahumara Indians killed a few Apaches on the Gila near the ruins of Pueblo Viejo and at the north end of the Peloncillos. As they headed south, they ignored more Indian sign "because of the impossibility of operating in the Sierra Chiguicagui, an extremely rugged range . . . a great lofty spine some fifteen leagues long."

In 1766 Lt. Juan Bautista de Anza of the Fronteras garrison stormed an Apache stronghold in the Chiricahuas and captured a chief. Promoted to the command of Tubac presidio, he campaigned in the Pinaleños and the Peloncillos, and in 1771 he returned to the Pinaleños to surprise an Apache camp, where he killed nine and took some prisoners. Anza was a fine soldier who later established the colony at San Francisco in Alta California and as governor of New Mexico explored far north onto the high plains, but here he had a big job and little to work with.

In the spring of 1774, a new presidio at San Bernardino, a half-day ride from the Chiricahuas, was manned intermittently until about 1789 by troops from the Fronteras garrison.

Between 1777 and 1788, Anza's successor, Pedro de Allande de Saavedra, another energetic soldier, made numerous campaigns from

Tucson to the Peloncillos. On a big sweep in 1784 across the Santa Teresa Mountains and south to the Dos Cabezas, his tally of the enemy was sixteen, including three women and four children.

Meanwhile, military activity against the Apaches continued from the south. In 1780 Capt. José Antonio Vildósola swept down the San Simon Valley and east to Pinos Altos, fruitlessly scouring the country. The next year the Chokonen returned the compliment with more success. A renegade Spaniard, José María González, who at fifteen had been captured by Apaches at Cucurpe, led a raid on his old home from a rancheria at the north end of the Chiricahuas. His attack killed fifteen, including his own father.

Another futile Spanish expedition commanded by Alférez Domingo Vergara left Fronteras in the spring of 1785 and reconnoitered the Chiricahua Mountains, finding that the Indians had burned off the country, denying them forage for their horses.

It's not surprising that Spanish campaigns were ineffective. Troops were thinly spread across a wide frontier and were poorly equipped. Each soldier was supposed to have a musket or carbine, two pistols, a lance, a bull-hide shield, and an arrow-proof heavy leather jacket. The remuda was to have six horses and a pack mule for each trooper. A 1787 inspection of the Tucson presidio revealed that Allande's seventy-three men were short eighty-two horses and twenty-two mules, and the stock on hand was in poor shape. They had only sixty-four muskets, and half the pistols were unusable. Only a third of the men had leather jackets.

Spanish policy for dealing with the Apaches was as inconsistent as American policy would be a hundred years later. In twenty years it went from one of containment, to one of extermination, to a plan of "divide and conquer." In the mid-1780s the Apaches were invited to settle at the presidios, where they would be supplied provisions in the hope that, weakened by coddling with rations of tobacco, sugar, wheat, and beef, they could be contained. Moral destruction might work where extermination wasn't possible.

A contingent of over four hundred Chokonen from the Chiricahua Mountains, led by Chicanstegé, were induced to settle at Bacoachi in 1787. When the chief saw troop movements in the vicinity, he became nervous and left, taking most of the Indians with him. By June only about a hundred remained. Some of them were recruited to help attack those who had refused to come in to enjoy the benefits of Christian civilization.

On a sortie to the Gila with Chokonen auxiliaries in the fall of 1788, Capt. Manuel de Echeagaray sent a note by an Apache runner from the Santa Teresa Mountains to his home base. In thirty-six hours the messenger ran to Arispe, traveling 196 miles. Small wonder that it took two hundred years to whip the Nde.

Peace wasn't constant, but for almost forty years conditions were quiet enough for tentative Spanish settlement in what had been totally hostile country. During this tenuous peace, miners from Chihuahua built a triangular earthen fort in the middle of Chihenne country and began to dig for copper at Santa Rita del Cobre, at the south end of the Pinos Altos Mountains.

There is evidence that in the 1790s there were short-lived *estancias* at San Bernardino and Agua Prieta. Then, after Mexico's independence from Spain in 1821, Ignacio Pérez was granted four *sitios*, about twenty-seven square miles, around San Bernardino Springs, and he moved in four hundred head of cattle. He didn't confine his range to the seventeen thousand acres of the four sitios, and it is possible that a large adobe corral at the upper end of San Simon Cienega, traces of which remained in the 1940s, dated from that period.

The Mexican government was unable to continue rationing the tame Apaches at the presidios, and they began to drift back to their old range and old ways. By the 1830s their increased harassment caused Pérez to give up, leaving behind an estimated hundred thousand head of ungathered cattle. Vaqueros had ridden the valley only about ten years when it and the Chiricahua Mountains again knew only Apaches and a rare Mexican war party.

## Chapter 3

# The First Gringos

It is a general impression amongst the lower classes in Mexico that the Americans are half savages, and perfectly uncivilized. The specimens they see in Northern Mexico are certainly not remarkably polished in manners or appearance, being generally rough backwoodsmen.

**George Ruxton**

Whether any of the wide-ranging mountain men of the fur trade of the early 1800s saw the Chiricahua Mountains we have no record. None were diarists and few were literate, but we do know that in the winter of 1825–26 and again the following year, several Americans trapped the Gila River and its tributaries. There probably was little prospect of beaver up the San Simon from the Gila, but it is likely that curiosity led some of the adventurers to see what lay to the south of the cottonwood-sheltered valley.

One of those who probably knew the Chiricahuas was Jim Kirker, an Irishman who had fought the British as a privateer and sold liquor in New York and groceries in St. Louis before joining a trapping expedition up the Missouri in 1822. In two years on the plains and in the Rocky Mountains, he was introduced to Indian fighting by the Arikara and the Blackfoot. He joined a goods train to Santa Fe, and the trip was so profitable he made another in 1825 and applied for Mexican citizenship to ease the way into various entrepreneurial activities, some of them legal.

In 1826 he trapped the upper Gila, then settled in, making Santa Rita del Cobre his headquarters for several years of trapping in the winter, when fur was prime, and mining in the summer, when it wasn't.

Kirker became friendly with an educated Apache subchief, Juan José Compá, who became his entry into the fringes of Apache society and helped him learn the language, trade for beaver, and swap firearms for rustled livestock. It's possible that he, not one to dwell on the niceties, took part in raids himself.

Ore from Santa Rita went to a smelter at Corralitos by pack train on a trail that skirted the Burro Mountains and went between the Animas and Alamo Hueco ranges to Janos and Corralitos. The trail had been used for almost two hundred years by Apache raiding parties, but Kirker's friendship with Compá helped protect the trail from Apache attack. In 1831 he moved to a more strategic location at Janos, where he married Rita García and, as Don Santiago Kirker, or "Quirque," sired a large family.

Alliances last only as long as they are convenient for both parties. In the spring of 1837, while Don Santiago was away, Compá and his Chiricahuas attacked the Janos–Santa Rita mule train and started harassing settlers in Chihuahua and Sonora. Unable to protect the citizens, the governor of Sonora gave permission to another expatriate, Missourian John J. Johnson, to pursue the Apaches for the reward of half the recovered livestock.

Johnson recruited sixteen American frontiersman, borrowed a small cannon, and went into the field. From Fronteras they followed the broad trail of the raiders and their stolen stock and in a week came upon an Apache camp at the Animas Mountains.

Johnson's small force was greatly outnumbered. He was no fool and realized that the situation called more for guile than gallantry. Pretending to be a peaceful trader, he enticed the Apaches into his camp to barter. As soon as he had a suitably bunched target, he let go a charge of chain shot from a cannon concealed under a pile of pack saddles and blankets while he and his companions opened fire with their individual weapons. The volley killed twenty Indians and wounded an equal number. As the "traders" retreated toward Janos, the Indians counterattacked, losing seven more men doing so. Johnson claimed he didn't get enough horses to make the slaughter worthwhile.

Deception and murder were not repaid with trust and peace. The Apaches stepped up their raiding, killed a band of trappers on the Gila, wiped out a wagon train, forced the shutdown of the Santa Rita mines, and continued to run off livestock from Mexican ranches. Kirker's eye was cocked at the main chance. He could no longer run with the Apaches, but he *could* use his past friendships and his knowledge of Indian ways to fight them. He recruited a gang of hard-riding cutthroats, largely Shawnee and Delaware Indians displaced from the Ohio River, and contracted with the governor of Chihuahua for Apache scalps at a hundred pesos each. There were complaints that not all the black hair he presented for payment came from Apache heads, but many Apaches were killed for pay. Jim later boasted that he got 487.

Kirker's scalp-hunting career peaked on a July night in 1846 at Galeana, south of Casas Grandes. Though not loath to do battle when it was necessary, Kirker, like Johnson, would take an easier course when it offered itself. The townsmen feasted a large band of Chiricahuas, supplying them well with *sotol*. While they lay in mass stupor, Kirker and his men, aided by local citizens, beat in the heads of 130. When a new governor, Francisco García Conde, took office in 1840, he canceled the agreement as disgraceful, but a few years later his successor renewed the contract.

The Mexican War and the rush to California gold that followed brought the first *known* non-Indian Norteamericanos within sight of the Chiricahua Mountains, but they all hurried on by the north end and the south without penetrating the canyons. The war with Mexico was waged primarily to acquire Texas, but once under way, it was natural to go for a bigger piece of the pie.

Gen. Stephen Watts Kearny and his Army of the West took Santa Fe easily. Then, leaving his main force behind, in October 1846 he took a hundred men and two howitzers and headed for California with Kit Carson as his guide. His trail from the Rio Grande to Santa Rita del Cobre and down the Gila would become familiar to many, owing to the presence in Kearny's flying column of William H. Emory, a lieutenant in the Topographical Engineers. So that the United States could know what the western country, once taken, was like, Emory was assigned to map the route and describe in detail the land and its plants and wildlife. His report, published by Congress two years later, was an immediately popular guidebook for emigrants and gold seekers. But Emory didn't see the Chiricahuas. His beautiful map shows an emptiness south of the Pinaleños, noting that it was "believed by Mr. [Antoine] Leroux to be an open prairie"—probably a reference to what later became Railroad Pass, the route of the Southern Pacific tracks and Interstate 10. Leroux's information also indicates that if he hadn't been there, he knew someone who had.

A second California-bound column was a battalion of Mormons recruited from a gathering preparing to cross the plains to a promised land. President James Polk cut a deal with their leader, Brigham Young: in return for a year's enlistment, five hundred able-bodied of the faithful would be paid for their trip to the West and be allowed to keep their issue of clothing and their weapons.

Under the command of Lt. Col. Philip St. George Cooke of the First Dragoons, a tall, red-bearded Virginian, the Mormon Battalion followed Kearny's men down the Rio Grande a few weeks behind them. At Albuquerque, Cooke took on several mountain men, including a half-blood Cherokee named Powell Weaver (known to the Mexicans as Paulino), Antoine Leroux, and Jean Baptiste Charbonneau of St. Louis, the son of Sacagawea.

The column followed Kearny's route to Santa Rita, but from there, burdened with a train of thirty wagons, they required an easier road. The guides took them down the old Janos trail and then struck southwest across the dry plains, yellow with cured grama grass. They skirted the treeless Coyote Hills, crossed the salt flat of Playas "Lake," and went through the Animas Mountains at Whitmire Pass.

Colonel Cooke had much on his mind: the care of five hundred men in uncharted country, short rations, worn-down mules, and the expectation of battle when he arrived in California. But he wasn't too preoccupied to appreciate his surroundings. On the twenty-fifth of November he wrote in his journal:

> There is much that is strange on this vast table-land, studded with peaks and mountains of every shape; but this afternoon all must have been struck with the quiet beauty of the scene before us. The mountain passed, before us was a smooth plain, inclined always to the right but unbounded in front. Waving with the south wind, the tall grama and buffalo grass received from the slant sunshine a golden sheen; and the whole had a rich blue and purple setting of long mountain ranges on either side. The light, the shadow, and the varying distances gave variety and beauty of hue: the near heights dotted with cedar, the silvered granite peaks, and the distant lofty summits of the Gila mountains [the Chiricahuas]. The sun with its pencil of rays, touched all with the bright effect of the skillful painter, whilst the tree tops of the Las Animas gave the promise, which the bracing air welcomed, of the well-warmed bivouac.

They had one more pass to negotiate, one that required the Mormon boys to earn their twenty-three cents a day.

Hoping to replace some of his played-out horses and mules, Cooke sent out his scouts to locate Apaches to induce them to come in to trade while he attempted to find a way across the mountains to Rancho San Bernardino. He proceeded south up the Animas Valley, with the tree-darkened slopes of the Animas sierra on his left and the lower Peloncillos on his right.

South of the mouth of Cloverdale Creek, Cooke swung west to penetrate the mountains. It was a wrong turn. Paulino Weaver might have led him a mile or two farther to Guadalupe Pass, but Weaver was out looking for Indians. The ascent to the top of the divide wasn't difficult. The floor of the Animas Valley is five hundred feet higher than the valleys west of the range, and the slope up from the valley is relatively gentle. It is a steeper plunge off the west side, with eroded pinnacles, cliffs, and canyons.

Cooke was dismayed at the view from the crest and sent men to search for an easier crossing. They didn't find one. When the scouts came back in the evening, Leroux assured the commander there was no better way down. They had found an Indian, however, a Chokonen leader called Manuelito, who probably wouldn't have come with them if he hadn't been drunk. As the effects of drink wore off, he became uncomfortable with his situation.

The Apache had reason to be nervous. It had been only four months since Jim Kirker's slaughter of Chiricahuas at Galeana. Colonel Cooke assured him that he had nothing to fear, and the Indian left saying he would meet the soldiers at San Bernardino but that they had few mules, having lost many mounts when they were pursued after a recent raid in Mexico. The raid he referred to had been undertaken to avenge the Apaches killed at Galeana.

Convinced he had to jump off into Guadalupe Canyon, Cooke set his men to building a trail with axes and crowbars down the west side. By lowering the wagons over the steeper places with ropes, in three days they reached the bottom, where they joined the west end of Guadalupe Pass on the old Spanish trail from Janos to Tucson. The road they had been seeking was only a mile south of the rocky gulch they had fought their way down.

After they emerged from the pass onto the caliche desert spattered with greasewood and whitethorn, it was an easy day's hike to the deep sacaton grass in the bottoms surrounding San Bernardino Springs, where Manuelito rode out to greet them. With Manuelito was a "superior chief," who may have been Narbona, and several other men, one of whom may have been Cochise, one of Narbona's rising young warriors. The trading was disappointing, and the Americans got only three mules. Cooke wasn't impressed with the Apaches, whom he found to be "poor, dirty Indians . . . ugly and squalid." There were other points of view. The journal of one of his soldiers remarked that the women were "very good looking, plump pieces of baggage."

The battalion rested for a day near the abandoned adobes, feasting on the meat of wild cattle, before going on west for eighteen miles to camp at the little cienega of Agua Prieta on their way to Tucson and California.

Two years after Cooke's crossing of the Guadalupes, another march was made that way when Maj. Lawrence P. Graham blundered through with elements of the First Dragoons, en route from Nuevo León to California. At Galeana they had heard of Kirker's big killing in 1846, and they picked up one of his men, "Guno" (perhaps Gounod), for a guide. They rode on to Janos and took the old Tucson trail, reaching Guadalupe Pass on September 30, 1848.

Though their route took them to the pass Cooke had been looking for, they had almost as much difficulty. Their problem was their commander. Though brave and experienced, Major Graham was also a roaring drunk, called "Old Whiskey Barrel" by his men. One wagon hauled his whiskey; another carried the whore he had picked up in Chihuahua. It isn't unusual for soldiers to be critical of their officers, but two journals kept on the march agree that this fellow was hard to work for. He wouldn't permit scouts ahead of the column, and though he was often too drunk to sit his horse, he insisted on picking the route and each campsite. When he was passed out in his woman's wagon, things went more smoothly.

On the second day in the pass, they lost three wagons in flash floods. The third day they rested and combed the creekbed for lost gear. The fourth day they reached the valley, having taken four days to make fourteen miles. They rode on past Bernardino and to Agua Prieta, but they made a dry camp there. Swaying in the saddle, Major Graham picked a campsite in a mesquite thicket and refused permission to scout the area for water. In the morning they found they had picketed the horses two hundred yards from clear pools.

In February 1848 the treaty of Guadalupe Hidalgo ended the Mexican War and ceded to the United States all of Mexico north of the Rio Grande and the Gila. Eight days before the signing, gold was discovered in California, and soon thousands of veterans and other adventurers were headed west.

There were several routes, but argonauts from below the Mason-Dixon Line tended to take the southern route down the Gila River. It was estimated that in 1849, between six and eight thousand used one of the trails converging on the lower Gila at the Pima villages. Another count that year reckoned that four hundred California-bound wagons had gone through El Paso by midsummer.

A typical party was one of fifty-three men who left east Texas in March 1849 under the leadership of Isaac Duval. They traveled horseback, each man with a pack mule. From El Paso they were guided across northwestern Chihuahua by a merchant named Johnston, probably the semiretired scalp hunter. At Corralitos they found the smelters busy, thanks to an armed guard of fifty men. The gold seekers went on the next day to Janos, where they were wakened in the middle of the night by the arrival of Gen. Félix Zuloaga and a company of soldiers with a handful of Apache prisoners in tow.

The general was there for a scheduled meeting with the Apaches to exchange prisoners. He announced his intention of ambushing them in the plaza from concealed spots and invited the Americans to join in. Half the party volunteered, but in their inexperience and eagerness they gave away the show, and the Indians were frightened off.

From Janos the Forty-niners rode north to camp near the south end of the Animas Mountains. The next day an advance party of eighteen rode ahead through San Luis Pass in open country with scattered junipers and oaks.

On the west side they came on a large party of Apaches who advanced aggressively. The white men fired a few warning shots at them and then surrounded their pack animals to work their way out of the pass and down into the Animas Valley. The Indians kept their distance and, launching an occasional arrow at them, followed menacingly. Bunched up, the Americans slowly made their way to a lone willow at Cienega Spring about three miles from the west end of the pass, intending to make a stand.

Three hours behind, the rest of the Duval party topped the divide without knowing the dangerous situation the advance was in. One man climbed a hill to look for those who had gone ahead and spied Indians out in the valley, spread out and riding toward them. Fearing an attack, they, too, formed a hollow square around the pack stock. The Apaches withdrew to let them pass but followed at a safe distance until the Americans were rejoined at the spring.

A chief wearing a skull cap with a cluster of hawk feathers rode up slowly with two warriors and called out in Spanish that he wanted to talk. A Texan named Davis laid down his rifle and advanced, indicating the chief should do the same. The Indian refused to leave his weapons but continued to come on with his bodyguard. Seeing this, the white man picked up his rifle, and several of his partners joined him. The Indians retreated. After a few measures of this cotillion of mistrust, the two unarmed spokesmen exchanged some words. The chief said the Mexicans called him Mangas Coloradas and that he was a friend of the Americans. Davis told him that they weren't looking for trouble but would just as soon fight as not. He agreed that the Apaches could come into camp at four o'clock—indicating the time with a wave of his arm at the sun.

At the appointed hour the Apaches came back, armed with bows, lances, and a few smoothbore muskets. The groups arranged themselves in such a way that neither could have an advantage. Mangas Coloradas said he liked Americans and wanted them to join him in killing Mexicans. If the Americans hadn't interfered the other day, he would have wiped out Janos. Mexicans, "the damned Christians," had forced the Apaches into the mountains, where the only way they could live was by preying on those who'd taken the better land. But Indians and Americans, being heathens, were alike. The Forty-niners wanted to trade their worn-out mules for fresh animals, but the Indians couldn't spare any.

The next morning the travelers crossed the valley to and through Guadalupe Pass to camp in the ruins of Rancho San Bernardino. They killed a wild bull for meat and rested there two days before riding west past herds of wild cattle. They saw spiraling pillars of smoke from the Pedregosa Mountains on their right, which they supposed signaled their progress.

Shortly after the Duval party passed through, John Joel Glanton, carrying on the work of Kirker and Johnson, got a scalp-hunting contract with the state of Chihuahua. He left Janos in October with fifty Mexican and American adventurers. From a camp in Skeleton Canyon, he combed the Chiricahuas for two weeks but returned without seeing an Apache.

One of the southern roads to California eventually became the route of the Overland Mail, then with minor deviations was followed by the Southern Pacific Railroad and Interstate 10. This route was pioneered by Jack Hays, a veteran of the Texas Rangers.

In June 1849 Hays left San Antonio with a herd of two hundred cattle on a route across west Texas that he himself had plotted the year before. He was joined along the way by several independent companies of travelers, who elected him their leader for the way through Apache country.

By September the train of about one hundred men and the herd had reached Cooke's Road. They followed it to a point about twenty-five miles south of the Santa Rita mines. Hays hoped to take the cut-off hinted at by the note on Emory's map that said the land south of the Pinaleños was "open prairie." He was not sure of the route or whether he could find water, but he struck out to the southwest. Near the south end of the Burro Mountains, he met Mexican soldiers campaigning against the Apaches, who confirmed Hays's hunch about the shortcut and described the country and watering places for him. The party then went across the ground that would one day be Lordsburg and passed south of the playa, went through the Peloncillos at Stein's Pass, and, after reaching San Simon Creek, went up the arroyo to camp on the east side of the cienega, where they found "the grass good & wood plenty."

The next morning, angling northwest toward the Chiricahuas, they had a hard pull through greasewood and mesquite, made more unpleasant by blowing dust, to a dry camp, probably on Wood Canyon Wash, just east of Rattlesnake Point. The next morning they got a late start because of strayed stock and made only five miles, crossing the many arroyos draining Wood Mountain. They found some water in Little Wood Canyon and laid over a day while scouts went ahead to find the pass. On October 24:

> "The road was tolerable good till we reached the pass which was indeed a romantic one. We followed the bed of a dry arroya [*sic*] where there was scarcely room for the waggon wheels. . . . We, however, came safely through & camped . . . at a little stream, or a spring, gently flowing from the rocks."

They may have been the first Americans to see Apache Pass and to drink the cool water of Apache Spring in the shade of the chittamwood and hackberry trees.

Several herds of Texas cattle were driven to the West Coast in 1849, either by Cooke's Road or the one in Chihuahua. The profit on a steer more than made up for some death loss from thirst crossing the desert. That same year a herd of five hundred sheep was driven from Santa Fe to Tucson and on to San Francisco, where they were sold at an 800 percent profit. This began a thriving trade that continued for ten years, with about one hundred thousand New Mexico wethers taken to California markets.

After Francis Aubrey trailed five thousand head of sheep, ten freight wagons, and a hundred mules from northern New Mexico to the coast by the trail pioneered by Jack Hays, the route through Apache Pass became the principal southern road to California.

A large party of over two hundred that took that trail later in 1849 included Leonard Reed and his twenty-year-old son, Stephen. The Reeds, from Jackson County, Missouri, had gone to Texas the year before, intending to settle, but the news from California excited them and they didn't stay long. The sight from Granite Gap of the rugged profile of Cochise Head and the dark entrance to Cave Creek Canyon stayed in Stephen's memory, as did a night they camped at Apache Spring. Twenty-six years later he returned to spend the rest of his life.

All of the southern roads went through Mexican territory or a region that was in dispute. The treaty that ended the Mexican War was vague about the new boundary line from the Rio Grande to the headwaters of the Gila River. The two nations created a joint boundary commission to reconcile differences, and John Russell Bartlett, a scholarly book salesman from Rhode Island, was appointed to represent the United States. As cofounder of the American Ethnological Society, he had an academic interest in Indians but didn't know one. Though his managerial experience was scant, he had good political connections.

The commission was organized during the administration of lame-duck President Polk, who appointed Andrew Gray to be chief surveyor. Newly sworn President Zachary Taylor, appointed Bartlett to be commissioner, answerable to the secretary of state. The War Department assigned Lt. Col. Louis Craig and his Third Infantry to escort duty, and Lt. Col. John D. Graham, the sober brother of "Old Whiskey Barrel," to be head of the "Topographical Scientific Corps," with 2d Lt. Amiel Whipple as his assistant. By the time the work began, Taylor had died in office and was succeeded by Millard Fillmore. A clear line of responsibility and authority was never established.

Bartlett wasn't solely to blame for the expedition's confusion, but he compounded it. He hired a crew of friends: his brother, George, to be supply officer and Dr. Thomas Webb, cofounder of the American Ethnological Society, to be his personal physician and secretary. Webb, in turn, enlisted John Cremony of the *Boston Herald*, a Mexican War veteran whose duties were undefined. By late fall 1850 Bartlett met in El Paso with his Mexican counterpart, Gen. Pedro García Conde. The American commissioner supplied himself well at government expense and enjoyed himself hugely, dispensing and receiving hospitality. Between luncheons and soirees on both sides of the river, he and the Mexican agreed on an initial point for the survey, forty miles north of El Paso.

Bartlett was at a disadvantage. He didn't know the country and had little experience in the world of affairs. On the other hand, García Conde (the younger brother of the Governor Conde who had stopped Kirker's scalp hunting) was a distinguished soldier, had been director of the military college in Mexico City, and as a native of Arispe,

Sonora, was familiar with the entire frontier. And he possibly had a better head for wine. Bartlett didn't wait for his surveyor and astronomer to report for duty. In their absence he appointed Lieutenant Whipple to be acting surveyor and directed him to sign the agreement.

With the datum point established in April 1851, the commissioner, in his custom-made carriage, led his retinue to the copper mines at Santa Rita. While awaiting the arrival of the engineers, he made the acquaintance of Mangas Coloradas, who was camped nearby. Indulging his interest in ethnology, Bartlett embraced the chief, proposed eternal brotherhood, and started listing an Apache vocabulary. His motives were decent, but there was a note of condescension in his journal. He believed Indians should be treated with a combination of benevolence and firmness.

The benevolence lay in having a suit of clothes made for Mangas Coloradas and distributing cloth and knives to all his men. Though such things were readily to be had for the taking in Mexico, the Apaches accepted them as tokens of friendship.

Bartlett's firmness had another result. During an argument a teamster in his party shot an Indian, who died a few days later. Mangas Coloradas and his son, Ponce, came to Bartlett asking that he hang the killer or give him to the Apaches so they could do it. Bartlett was sympathetic but explained that American justice was more deliberate. He would send the culprit to Santa Fe for trial. The Apaches had no faith that a Mexican in home territory would be punished for killing an Indian, and insisted that Bartlett live up to his affirmation of fairness. Bartlett stood by his refusal, and the Apaches protested.

The discussion had gone on long enough. The Apaches were forgetting that they were savages. The commissioner reminded them that the United States was all-powerful and that, if they didn't behave, they would be wiped from the face of the earth. Bartlett lost more than his patience. Shortly after this last face-off, the Apaches left for Mexico, driving before them most of the survey's livestock. Whipple, who had salvaged a horse, made a futile pursuit. As he rode up on Ponce, who was serving as rear guard, the warrior bared his bottom and slapped his rump in derision before disappearing in the dust of the Janos road.

Waiting for his topographers, Bartlett made a side trip to Fronteras. In the Playas Valley, as he approached Whitmire Pass in the Animas Mountains, near the spot where Colonel Cooke had been so moved to rapture, he made this comment in his journal:

> "The vegetable world presents scarcely more interest than the animal world [he had just made unflattering notes on horned lizards]. The flowers are almost entirely of that most unbecoming of all hues, yellow—varying from sulphur color to orange—and glaring in the bright sunlight. One becomes sickened and disgusted with the ever-recurring sameness of plain, mountain, plant, and every living thing."

It was May and the prairie was carpeted with poppies. Beauty *is* in the eye of the beholder.

When Andrew Gray arrived to apply himself to the technical aspects of the survey, he immediately objected to the selection of the initial point so far up the Rio Grande. It gave to Mexico the only ground suitable for a railroad. He also protested that Bartlett hadn't had the authority to appoint Whipple to act for him; hence the initial point accepted by Bartlett was void. He was willing to accept the latter's leadership in logistical matters, but in surveying he believed Bartlett should defer to him. Colonel Graham further muddied the waters. Though he agreed with Gray about the datum point, he felt that both the civilians should be subordinate to him, the senior military officer. Lieutenant Whipple, subordinate to everyone, kept his mouth shut.

Bartlett and Gray fired off dispatches to Washington, detailing their arguments. Pending decision from that quarter, the survey got under way in August. Though the location of the boundary between the Rio Grande and the Gila depended on that vital starting point, there was no question about the Gila River below the San Pedro, so they departed for the west, mapping the country as they went.

Unlike Kearny and Cooke, Bartlett hadn't hired one of the crude mountain men, which may explain why he crossed the Burro Moun-

tains instead of taking an easier route around their south end, but
from those heights he guided on the cone-shaped peak of "El Pilon-
cillo, or Sugarloaf," now known as Stein's Peak. The party crossed the
wide valley, hugged the north side of the peak, and entered Doubtful
Canyon. Coming out of the pass to overlook the San Simon Valley, he
wrote in his journal on September 2: "A broad open plain appeared
before us about twenty-five miles across, bounded by a lofty and continuous range known as the Sierra Chiricahui . . . with an irregular
and jagged summit, often exhibiting picturesque and fantastic forms."

They dropped down to San Simon's arroyo close to where today's
highway crosses. They went up that "dry ravine" for eight miles and
camped on the cienega, where an artist sketched a view of the Chiricahuas to the southwest, and then faced east to make another of
Cienega Peak on the north side of Granite Gap. Heavy rain that evening made for slow, muddy travel the next day. They struck out northwest to get around the mountains, where they "followed a trail up a
ravine, and there discovered a spring and fine pool of crystal water."
They had arrived at Apache Springs. Working on west, they reached
the San Pedro in the vicinity of St. David, where they found the water
difficult to reach because of the sheer eight-foot banks.

There Gray got word that the secretary of the interior had relieved
him. He returned to San Antonio, leaving Whipple to map the boundary westward. Colonel Graham's office was abolished, and William
Emory, now a major, was appointed to take over both jobs. He agreed
with Gray about the initial point, but he mapped the Rio Grande
from El Paso to the gulf with dispatch.

Three years of confusion and bickering ended when the survey was
disbanded in 1853, with the boundary not established. It didn't matter
anymore. The United States was anxious to get an all-weather route
for a San Antonio to San Diego railroad, and after months of talk in
Mexico City, President Fillmore's envoy, James Gadsden, worked out
a trade. For ten million dollars Mexico would cede all territory south
of the Gila to the present border. Not everyone was happy. Gadsden
had asked for a line farther south to give the United States a port on
the Sea of Cortez, but Mexico was leery of American shipping hug-

ging their shores. And some Missourians, not wanting a railroad that would compete with their chosen route from St. Louis, didn't want a purchase at all.

By April 1854 the treaty was ratified. Major Emory surveyed the new boundary in eleven months without any fuss and for much less than the five hundred thousand dollars spent by the earlier survey.

When John Augustus Chenowth came through Apache Pass on his way to northern California that same year, he made the entire trip from Tennessee on United States soil. Gus, at a rough-and-ready twenty years, came from sturdy stock. A first cousin, Thomas J. Jackson, who was then a professor of military tactics at Virginia Military Institute, was to earn the nickname "Stonewall." Like the Reeds, many years after first seeing southern Arizona, Chenowth returned to the Chiricahuas and the San Simon Valley.

The funds spent so freely by Bartlett were not a total waste. In 1854 Bartlett published at his own expense his *Personal Narrative of Explorations*. He wasn't a good manager of men, mules, and money, but he was a scholar and had taken scholars with him whose names are still familiar to botanists and zoologists today. Quartermaster George Thurber was a botanist who spent his spare time collecting, at one time narrowly escaping death when an Apache loosed an arrow at him as he put a specimen in his plant press. John H. Clark, a zoologist, became the namesake of the Clark's spiny lizard that lives on the north wall of my house.

The name of Charles Wright, another botanist in the party, is applied to several xeric species. His acquaintance with the Southwest antedated that of his fellows. The diarist who recorded the progress of the train led by Jack Hays in 1849 notes that east of the Pecos River they ran into "a man named Wright," who had come from New York to Galveston by ship but was broke and had been trying to attach himself to a westering train. He was blundering along by himself, getting by with occasional handouts. "He is a botanist & quite a short man; he cut a curious figure carrying a huge portfolia [*sic*] with good-sized plants and flowers which he was preserving."

The three surgeons also made collections. Bartlett's friend Dr.

Webb was mainly interested in minerals, but he also picked up insects and other things zoological. Dr. C. C. Parry's name is attached to species of yucca and agave, and Dr. John M. Bigelow was also a botanist. Arthur Schott, Emory's assistant surveyor, collected everything he could pick up and press or pickle, adding more than one hundred new vertebrates to the scientific record.

James Russell Bartlett went back to Providence to serve seventeen years as Rhode Island's secretary of state. For mapping the Gila River, Amiel Whipple was rewarded with a survey of his own when the army sent him to plot the course for a railroad across the Colorado Plateau above the Mogollon Rim. Not disdaining expert guidance, he took Antoine Leroux along. Whipple was a brevet brigadier general when he died of wounds received at Chancellorsville. Emory survived the Civil War to retire as a major general the year before Custer's early retirement at Little Bighorn.

Looking down Turkey Creek Canyon from near its head. Limestone Mountain is at left in the distance, and Silver Peak is at the right. The white rocks near the center inspired the early name for the mountain and the canyon.

Barfoot Park and the site of the Riggs, and later the Sweeney, sawmill (lower left). Ida's Peak is near the center, and the Sulphur Springs Valley is in the distance. At the extreme right, behind Barfoot Peak, is the top of Rough Mesa in Chiricahua National Monument, with Dos Cabezas Peak beyond.

The San Simon Cienega looking toward Portal Peak (once Bear Mountain).

A Chiricahua Apache family's camp of the 1880s, with typical brush-covered bush wickiups.

Merejildo Grijalva, captive of Cochise, interpreter for the Apache agents, and guide and scout for the army.

J. L. Coryell and his son George in the early 1880s, about eight years after they met Billy the Kid on the Mimbres River.

Jim Hughes (left) with either Milt Hicks or Jack Mackenzie a few days after they participated in the bloody robbery of Mexican smugglers in Skeleton Canyon.

Loco, the Chihenne chief who led his people past Galeyville to Mexico in 1882.

Gus and Mary
Chenowth's place on
the San Simon Cienega
about 1914.

Gus Chenowth at his cienega ranch circa 1910 with the coach he bought for family use from the California District Stage Line when it closed down.

Sgt. Neil Erickson of the Fourth Cavalry at Fort Huachuca in about 1885.

Emma Peterson at Fort Bowie before her marriage to Neil Erickson.

Officers and scouts at the Mud Springs vedette during the final Geronimo campaign of 1886.

Frank Hands at his place in Pinery Canyon in 1895, preparing to leave with the troops pursuing the Apaches who had killed his brother, Alfred

The Hall family at their Z Bar T ranch on Whitetail Creek in 1906. Standing, left to right are George T. "Dad" Colvin, George Hall, Charles, Fred, and Nancy. In the front row are John, Robert D. Hall, Henry Theador, Henrietta Rogers Hall, and William Edward.

Not all cow work was done by men. Katie and Maggie Noland have one stretched out at the ranch on Oak Creek.

## Chapter 4

# Arizona Territory

The view of this *cañon* in the morning with the sun-light reflected from its deep recesses, and upright walls rising majestically on all sides to a height of several thousand feet, tapering like spires amid the clouds, presented a scene of grandeur and beauty rarely excelled.

**Andrew Belcher Gray**

Congress didn't foresee that one day Tucson would be a winter resort and that there were millions in copper and silver locked in the rock south of the Gila River. The $10 million spent for that desert, about fifty-seven cents an acre, was only to acquire the easiest route to California from the southern states. The ink was hardly dry on the document of the 1853 Gadsden Treaty before the Texas Western Railroad fielded a party to survey a route from San Antonio to San Diego. The railroad was so eager that their expedition got underway six months before the treaty was ratified.

To head the survey, the company picked an experienced frontiersman, Andrew Belcher Gray, the principal surveyor with Bartlett's Boundary Commission. Born in Virginia, Gray left home before he'd learned to shave to be an apprentice on a survey of the Mississippi delta. At eighteen he joined the new Texas navy and surveyed the boundary with the United States. Then the U.S. War Department hired him to survey Michigan's Keweenaw Peninsula. Gray spent the Mexican War with the Texas Rangers fighting Comanches, and by

December 1853 he was in San Antonio assembling an outfit for the
railroad survey.

Gray chose an old companion to be executive officer, wagon boss,
and logician. Peter Brady was an Annapolis graduate who, after two
years in the U.S. Navy, resigned his commission to join the Texas
Rangers. Brady did most of the hiring—all frontiersmen and mostly
veterans of the recent war. Walter W. deLacey, an old schoolmate,
became assistant surveyor, and Charles Schuchard, a Hessian and
graduate of the Freiburg School of Mines, was the expedition's artist.
Schuchard was no tenderfoot either, having been to California with
the Forty-niners.

In mid-February 1854 Gray's party reached El Paso del Norte, the
old settlement on the south side of the Rio Grande, and from there
headed northwest, mapping as they went. Somewhere north of where
Deming is today, they cut Cooke's Wagon Road, followed it for about
forty-five miles, then turned west, heading for an opening in the low,
bare Peloncillo Mountains. They crossed an old lava flow and went up
a gentle slope over a grassy prairie for five miles to La Puerta, now
Antelope Pass.

Here they turned northwest to descend and camp next to water
in the sacaton meadow of the San Simon Cienega, nine miles away,
where Gray had camped three years before with Bartlett. While the
morning coffee boiled and the horses were wrangled, sunlight hit the
tops of the rugged peaks of the Chiricahuas, beckoning the adventuresome Andrew Gray to the place he called the Grand Canyon of
the Chiricahuas.

"The camp was moved across the valley to the mouth of a bold
and rugged *cañon*, ten miles from the Sauz springs [an old name for
the San Simon], and facing La Puerta," Gray wrote. They had put
their new camp on Cave Creek Cienega, where an "abundance of
pure water was found . . . a couple of men . . . returned with information that a mile above was a mountain stream, fringed with large
pines, and the ground carpeted, as it was all around us, with luxuriant grama."

Today there are no pines a mile above the cienega, but it is likely that any such timber, pine or cypress, that may have existed was used up in building cabins before 1900. The "luxuriant grama" is now all but totally replaced by mesquite, catclaw, and horehound.

The surveyors moved south along the foothills, poking into the entrances of the canyons, then swung northwest toward Castle Dome and Mud Springs on an Indian trail with fresh moccasin tracks. It would be forty-seven years before the El Paso and Southwestern Railroad laid steel into the place Gray called Dome Mountain Pass.

At the same time Lt. John G. Parke of the Corps of Topographical Engineers left the Pima villages on the Gila River on a similar mission—to find a feasible railroad route to the east. Parke was mapping a road through Apache Pass while Gray was working south of him in the same range. The following year Parke returned and found Railroad Pass between the Dos Cabezas and the Pinaleños. Gray himself later endorsed that as the best way to go, and it was there the Southern Pacific laid track in 1880.

His survey done, Gray settled in Tucson, from where he surveyed mining property and mapped the Pima and Papago reservations. When Texas seceded in 1861, he returned east to join the Confederate army and didn't survive the war. His La Puerta became Antelope Pass, and his Grand Cañon is now Cave Creek Canyon, but Gray Mountain, flanking the south side of his Puerta, is a reminder of his passing through.

The railroad to California would be delayed, but the swelling American presence on the West Coast demanded better communication than provided by the five-month voyage around the tip of South America. For business and government, mail was the first concern.

After much haggling, Congress passed a bill to provide mail service to the coast on three roads: one through South Pass in Wyoming, another on the Santa Fe Trail and west from Albuquerque, and the third from El Paso to San Diego via Yuma.

James Birch, a stage-line operator in California, got the contract to provide semimonthly deliveries between San Antonio and San Diego, with service to start on the first of July 1857. He had less than four months to get service into operation and was in the East at the time.

By the time he could get word to his San Francisco agent, there were only eleven days before the mail was scheduled to leave San Diego, but it left on time by pack mule. The first westbound mail left San Antonio on July 9. Only a few days before the mail came into Apache Pass, Indians attacked a wagon train there, killing two men, but the mail went through without incident, arriving in San Diego on August 31.

Though there were small bands of miners in the Santa Rita and Patagonia Mountains who needed protection, it was primarily for the safety of the road to California that Fort Buchanan was established near Sonoita in the fall of 1857 by a detachment of the First Dragoons under command of Maj. Enoch Steen (for whom "Stein's" Pass was later named).

The San Antonio and San Diego Mail didn't wait for the new government road but used the trails blazed by Colonel Cooke and Jack Hays and well beaten out by the passage of thousands of emigrants. At first the eastbound San Diego–to–Tucson leg was carried entirely by pack mules, the "Jackass Mail." A wagon carried the first westbound mail, accompanied by an armed guard and a remuda of mules. The first coach made the trip in September 1857. By November twenty-five coaches were rolling, carrying passengers at two hundred dollars a head, and the company had four hundred mules to pull the stages in hitches of four or six, depending on the character of the road. For the first few months fresh mules were driven alongside the coach, but soon way stations were set up in charge of a stationmaster who kept a change of mules.

Meanwhile, the Pacific Wagon Road Office, with a $200,000 appropriation for a road from El Paso to San Diego, had hired James B. Leach to build the first leg of it to Yuma. In October he started with eighty men and worked along the track already used by the stage line, crossing the river in the vicinity of today's Las Cruces. They cleared trees, brush, and rocks from a road eighteen feet wide on the straightaway and twenty-five feet on the curves. They dug a few wells, constructed dirt tanks for catching runoff water, and had removed an estimated fifty thousand cubic feet from cuts by the time they reached Yuma a year later.

The rigors of a stage trip from Texas to Tucson was described by a young man who paid $150 for a ticket from San Antonio. At Fort Fillmore, a day's run from El Paso, the party got a night's rest, but in the next three days they stopped only briefly to water and feed the mules, fry sow belly, and boil coffee. Sleep was grabbed by nods between lurches of the wagon. They splashed through a trickle of water in the Mimbres River, but the San Simon was dry. At Apache Springs, four days out of El Paso, the passengers were able to wash the caked dust from their faces, sit at a table, take off their shoes, and stretch out for a few hours' rest before the four-day run to Tucson. Travelers could get from San Antonio to the Pacific in remarkably short time but would arrive red-eyed from lack of sleep, bruised, constipated, and smelling ripe from three weeks in the same clothes.

The life of the San Antonio and San Diego Mail was short. The postmaster general awarded a contract to the Overland Mail Company, better known as the Butterfield Mail for its founder, to carry mail from St. Louis to San Francisco. The Butterfield didn't get underway until September 1858, but once its coaches were rolling, the government canceled the contract of the SA&SD. For a year both companies carried passengers from El Paso to San Diego, but without the mail contract the earlier company had to abandon its route west of El Paso.

The Overland Mail used the low-slung "Celerity Wagon," better suited to rough terrain than the Concord coach, but as Raphael Pumpelly complained, it was still not luxurious. In 1860, as a passenger bound for the mines of the Tubac district, he complained:

> As the occupants of the front and middle seats faced each other, it was necessary for these six to interlock their knees; and there being room inside for only ten of the twelve legs, each side of the coach was graced by a foot, now dangling near the wheel, now trying in vain to find a place of support. . . . My immediate neighbors were a tall Missourian with his wife and daughters . . . the woman . . . ever following the dis-

gusting habit of dipping, filling the air, and covering her clothes with snuff; the girls for days overcome with seasickness, and in this having no regard for the clothes of their neighbors. ("Pumpelly's Arizona")

Early way stations were little more than tents or brush ramadas, but by the spring of 1858 a construction crew was working its way west erecting more substantial facilities. Though earlier travelers usually crossed the Peloncillos by Stein's Pass or Granite Gap to take advantage of grass and water on the cienega, the mail lines used a shorter route through Doubtful Canyon, where a station was placed near a spring at the east entrance. Another station was built on the east bank of San Simon Creek just north of the present-day railroad tracks, and a more elaborate one in Apache Pass, below the spring.

When the crew arrived to put up the new station in Apache Pass, they were met by soldiers from Fort Buchanan looking for stolen stock. With them was a young civilian, James Tevis, who joined the work gang and left a description of the completed station: "A stone corral was built with portholes in every stall. Inside, on the southwest corner were built, in 'L' shape, the kitchen and sleeping rooms. At the west end, on the inside of the corral, space about ten feet wide was apportioned for a grain room, and here were kept the arms and ammunition."

While the work on the station was underway, officials of the Santa Rita Mining Company, bound for Tubac, came through the pass with a train of machinery-laden wagons and a large herd of mules and camped at the west entrance to the pass. During the night the Chokonen chief, Cochise, slipped in from his rancheria in Goodwin Canyon a couple of miles away and made off with all the mules.

The mining men footed it back to the station, where the agent, Anthony Elder, provided them with mounts and helped them follow the trail of the stolen stock through the Sulphur Springs Valley to the border, where customs officials forbade them to follow the Apaches into Mexico. The frustrated pursuers looped back by way of San Bernardino Springs and down the San Simon Valley to return to the

Apache Pass Station, possibly the first gringos to pass that way since A. B. Gray four years earlier.

Elder, after ten futile days in the saddle, got back to his post tired, in a poor frame of mind, and mad at Apaches. He dismounted at the station, where a crowd of Indians were gathered, and displayed his pique by laying about him with a quirt. The guilty Indians were still in Mexico, and those who felt the sting of Elder's wrath were members of Esquinaline's outfit. Before serious damage was done, Esquinaline, older and less volatile than Cochise, calmed everyone down, the agent as well as the Apaches he had stirred up. The gift of ten sacks of corn from the company stores helped soothe injured dignity.

Michael McNeese, the division chief for the Overland, to further calm the waters, put Elder in charge of the company's supply trains and promoted Tevis from the construction gang to be agent of the Apache Pass Station. He was there to officiate when the first coaches of John Butterfield's Overland Mail come through in the early fall of 1858.

James Henry Tevis had been a soldier of fortune in Nicaragua. After returning home, he crossed the plains to Arizona, where he trapped for a time on the Aravaipa and the Gila with Moses Carson, Kit's brother. During his two years at Apache Pass, Tevis had little affection for Cochise, whom he thought to be contentious and dangerous. However, he became friendly with Esquinaline, whose normal range was the southern end of the Chiricahua and Peloncillo Mountains but who, at the time, was spending much time with Cochise's band around the pass.

With only two stages a week, the agent didn't have demanding duties, and he spent a lot of time in Esquinaline's company, learning his language and exploring the mountains. On one occasion the two camped on the San Simon Cienega. Instead of returning to Apache Pass by rounding the north end of the mountains, Esquinaline led him back by a shortcut up Whitetail Canyon to Indian Creek and over into Wood Canyon to Bear Springs Pass, making Tevis probably the first white man to travel the Josephine Trail.

During the first years after the Gadsden Purchase, the Chokonen bushwhacked an occasional careless traveler but mostly confined
their raiding to the settlements in Sonora. As long as they weren't
bothered, the Americans in the territory looked upon the activity
below the border more or less benignly. Whenever Esquinaline was
on an expedition down south, Jim Tevis saw to it that the family of his
friend was safe and comfortable.

Relations with the Indians in New Mexico (Arizona was still part
of New Mexico until the Civil War) were the responsibility of the
territorial governor in Santa Fe, who also served as superintendent
of Indian Affairs. In 1855 Gov. David Meriwether had the help of
Dr. Michael Steck in dealing with the Apaches. Steck was one of the
few officials in the Southwest who treated Indians fairly and compe-
tently. He set up an agency at Fort Thorn on the Rio Grande, near
present-day Hatch, and by 1858 he had successfully encouraged the
Chihenne of Warm Springs and the Río Mimbres to settle down to
grow corn and refrain from pillage. In 1859 he tried to extend his influence to the Apaches of Cochise's band.

In December Steck arrived at Apache Pass with three wagon loads
of gifts for an estimated six hundred Chokonen: bolts of cloth, blankets, and kettles. Though not impressed with the handout, Cochise
agreed to keep the peace, communicating through his interpreter, a
young Mexican prisoner the Apaches called El Chivero. Steck was attracted to the lad, whose true name was Merejildo Grijalva. When
Cochise was away, James Tevis helped El Chivero escape by putting
him on the eastbound stage for Mesilla, where Steck picked him up
for employment at the agency.

For a time Cochise was true to his word and didn't molest travelers
along the Butterfield trail. The parole didn't apply to Mexico, however, and shortly after meeting with Steck, Chokonen raided Fronteras and the Río Moctezuma. Unlike the Chihenne, they had never
farmed and had no intention of starting.

Early in 1860 Tevis himself left Apache Pass. His reasons are not
clear, but his memoirs, written a quarter of a century later, allude
to his increasing unpopularity with Cochise and an accusation by his

supervisor that his accounts were sloppy. At any rate, he threw in with his predecessor, Anthony Elder, in a little ranch at Canutillo, upriver from El Paso. However, his temperament wasn't suited to breaking clods, and when gold was discovered at Pinos Altos in the hills north of today's Silver City, Tevis was one of the first to arrive at the new diggings. The rush of American prospectors into a favorite Chihenne range brought on inevitable friction. The accommodation of red man and white that Michael Steck had built up began to break down in December when Apaches killed and ate a miner's mule.

Knowing that Tevis had experience with Indians, his fellows called upon him to help teach the savages a lesson. Tevis didn't think that the loss of a mule was sufficient cause for war. He was used to sacrificing an animal now and then to his neighbors, but flattered by the prospectors' request for his leadership, he acceded. The end result was that the miners jumped a small rancheria about twelve miles south of the camp, killed the head man, Elías, and took all the livestock.

Even though Mangas Coloradas took this as an unfriendly act, he continued to try to get along. The Americans knew he would be affronted by their raid and were leery of him. When he came into Pinos Altos on a peaceful visit, they grabbed him, tied him to a tree, and flogged him with harness leather. This taught Mangas Coloradas a lesson, but not the one intended. The fragile peace with the Chihennes crumbled, and the rupture of the more tentative accord with the Chokonen was about to follow.

In late January 1861, only a few weeks after the killing of Elías, a party of Apaches, probably Coyoteros, raided John Ward's ranch on Sonoita Creek, getting away with a bunch of cattle and Ward's twelve-year-old stepson, Felix. Word quickly reached nearby Fort Buchanan, and 2d Lt. George N. Bascom was sent in pursuit with 1st Sgt. Reuben F. Bernard and a detachment of the First Dragoons. The cattle the Indians were driving from Ward's ranch should have left an obvious trail, but the detail returned to the post apparently having lost it.

The Chiricahuas were the closest Indians and were blamed for the act. Bascom was sent to Apache Pass to do what was necessary to find the boy and recover the cattle. He led fifty-four men from C Company of the Seventh Infantry. John Ward went with them. On foot, the men took six days to reach the pass on February 3. At the western approach they met Sgt. Daniel Robinson with thirteen men from the Seventh returning to Buchanan from wagon-train escort duty. Robinson turned back, adding his men to Bascom's strength.

The stage-line employees knew nothing of the raid on the Ward ranch, but Bascom sent word to Cochise at his Goodwin Canyon camp that he wanted.to talk with him, then made camp a short distance from the station. Expecting only coffee and a visit, Cochise showed up the next evening with his wife, some of their children, a brother, and two or three younger male relatives. With all seated in the tent, the lieutenant stated his purpose. Cochise explained that his people weren't involved, that probably the Coyoteros had the boy and that he would try to recover him.

Here started a chain of blunders, bad decisions, and inept actions that soured gringo-Apache relations for a decade. Bascom had courage but little experience. Although he had been an officer almost three years, that time had been mostly in garrison.

Bascom told Cochise he didn't believe him and would hold him and the rest of the people in the tent as hostages against the return of the boy. Cochise, in a rage, sprang to his feet drawing a knife, slashed open the tent, and ran up the slope as the soldiers fired at him. His brother also tried to flee but was wounded and retaken. The others were all held. Realizing that more had been torn than the tent, Bascom moved his command to the corral at the stage station to hole up.

In the morning hundreds of Apache men appeared on the hill south of the station with a white flag, and a parley was arranged with four men to a side. Cochise advanced to meet Bascom, who was accompanied by John Ward and two sergeants. Again Bascom demanded the boy; again Cochise denied having him. As they were talking, three mail-company employees who were acquainted with the Indians and evidently had little faith in the soldier's ability to make any headway with the palaver came out to speak with some of the Apaches off to one side. Several warriors tried to seize them, and things rapidly came to pieces.

James Wallace, a relief stage driver, was grabbed and held. Stationmaster Charles Culver broke away and ran for the corral, along with roustabout William Welch. Seeing this, Cochise and the three who sided him turned to run back to the hill under the cover of Apache fire. The Bascom party, too, wheeled and ran for the station while the soldiers at the corral returned the Indian fire. Before he reached the stone wall of the corral, Culver took a ball in the back but was pulled to safety, but Welch was killed, probably by a wild shot from the corral.

Throughout the day there was an ineffectual popping of shots between the corral and the arroyo of Siphon Canyon. The soldiers were on the alert all night. Toward noon the next day Cochise showed up on the slope of the ridge east of the station with Jim Wallace in tow by a rope around his neck, his arms bound, offering to trade him and twenty army mules for his relatives. It was no trade, as Bascom insisted on the return of the Wade boy.

That afternoon José Antonio Montoya's five-wagon freight train unwittingly came into the pass from the west. At the top of the divide, it was surrounded and quickly overcome by Apaches, who unhitched and herded away the mules. The teamsters were tortured and lanced to death, and Cochise made hostages of three Americans with the train. He had Wallace write a note to Bascom to tell him that Cochise now had four prisoners to exchange for his family. He left it on a tree near the burning wagons.

The westbound stage, much earlier than expected, made it safely up Siphon Canyon to the station, where the occupants learned how lucky they were to have done so.

The eastbound stage entered the pass before daylight on the seventh. The Indians knew the schedule and had pulled rocks into the road. When the driver got down to clear the way, fire from the slopes wounded him and killed a mule. The passengers spilled out to get the driver into the coach and cut the dead mule out of the harness. One of them climbed up to take the lines, lashed the mules into a dead run, and pulled up to the station with no further loss. Among the passengers was Lt. John Rogers Cooke, whose father, Col. Philip St.

George Cooke, had pioneered the wagon road around the south end of the Chiricahuas.

With daylight Bascom made a cautious move. The mules hadn't been watered in two days, so he detailed Sergeant Robinson with a squad of men to provide protection for soldiers leading the mules, a few at a time, to water and back to the corral.

One can imagine the conditions at the Apache Spring Station by dark on February 7. A corral about fifty by thirty-five feet held fifty to sixty mules. The small stone house and storage shed couldn't have housed many of the eighty or so people, who included Bascom and his sixty-seven soldiers and John Ward, three surviving Overland employees, the Indian hostages, the four men on the eastbound stage, and the driver of the westbound stage. Most of the men probably bedded down outside the corral next to the walls, where they could jump for cover if they had to.

Although the besieged hadn't seen an Apache in a day and a half, it was reasonable to assume that there were still more angry Indians out there than armed men at the station. Two badly wounded men needed help. The lieutenant detailed Corporal Fraber and five men to slip out after dark and make their way back to Fort Buchanan.

No Indians were seen because Cochise had taken the band's women and children into the mountains for their safety, leaving only a few scouts to keep track of the Americans. It was the scouts who had fired on the stage, their numbers too few to press the attack. In the meantime, word had spread and Cochise had been joined by his father-in-law, Mangas Coloradas, still smarting from his manhandling, and by a coming leader from the upper Gila Valley whom the Mexicans called Geronimo.

The morning of the eighth the soldiers awoke with snow on their blankets and melted some to make coffee. With no sign of Indians, Bascom ordered another mule watering, but this time the mules were taken in a bunch. No sooner was the stock shouldered together around the spring than Apaches swept in to cut them off from the corral. Robinson's guard on the ridge scattered them with rifle fire, but more came in from the east and ran off the mules. One soldier was killed and two were wounded.

It had been two days since Cochise had left Wallace's note. He didn't know that Bascom hadn't seen it and, having no reply, assumed he wouldn't get one. He took the hostages to the pass near the burned wagons, where they were mutilated and lanced to death, then he left for Mexico. That evening Corporal Fraber reached Fort Buchanan.

For the next two days Bascom did nothing. He had thought there was little danger and then had lost his mules. He wouldn't make that mistake again.

Dr. Bernard Irwin, the post surgeon at Fort Buchanan, left on the morning of February 9 with eleven mounted infantrymen for Apache Pass, and word had been sent to Fort Breckenridge, which dispatched a force of seventy dragoons. While approaching the pass, Irwin's party ran into a small band of Apaches in the Dos Cabezas foothills, probably Coyoteros returning to the Gila with Mexican livestock. The soldiers captured several horses and took three prisoners. Bascom was glad to see them when they arrived at the beleaguered corral the evening of the tenth.

The reinforcements from Fort Buchanan weren't enough to be of much use, however, and for another four days Bascom, not realizing the Indians had left, hunkered down at the station, venturing out only as far as the spring to fill canteens.

The dragoons arrived on the fourteenth and for three days scoured the area of the pass, finding only abandoned wickiups where the ashes were cold. One of the patrols found the bodies of Wallace and the three Americans who were with Montoya's wagons.

The stages began running again, and on February 18, leaving a small guard detachment behind, the soldiers left the pass. Near the burned wagons at the top of the divide, Bascom had six Apaches hanged from four oak trees. They were Cochise's younger brother, Coyuntura, two young warriors who had accompanied him to the tent on the sixth, and the three Coyoteros taken by Dr. Irwin. He let the woman go with two children, one of whom was probably Cochise's young son, Naiche.

As is often the case, revenge was taken on the innocent. Bascom had made Cochise suffer for the kidnapping of the Ward boy, who had been taken by the Coyoteros. Cochise got his revenge for the death of his brother by killing four white men who had nothing to do with it. Bascom again got back at Cochise for that killing by hanging Apaches who weren't guilty of it.

The affair was over. It had cost the lives of fifteen Mexicans and Americans and at least ten Apaches. At least eighty-six mules were lost. John Ward's cattle were never recovered, and his stepson, Felix, grew up among the Pinal Apaches. The damage did not end there. Hundreds more would die, red and white, before there was quiet between the Gila and the Sierra Madre.

On the day that Lieutenant Bascom lost his mules to Cochise at Apache Springs, Jefferson Davis was selected to be president of the Confederate States in Montgomery, Alabama, an event that aggravated the growing interracial conflict in the Southwest.

In March the post office canceled the Overland Mail's contract in order to move the route out of Confederate territory. The San Antonio–San Diego company hoped to get the line operating again and to make some kind of arrangement with John Butterfield, who still had men, mules, and equipment in the field. Men from both companies left Mesilla together in late April, traveling west to inventory and transfer property. James Giddings acted for the San Antonio company. The Overland was represented by division agent Michael McNeese, Anthony Elder, a driver named Briggs, who drove the stage, and a fourth employee, Sam Neely.

On April 27 the stage reached Barney's Station (three miles east of the center of Lordsburg, at the bend of I-10), where they learned that two parties had left for San Simon three and four days before. They had been expected to return but hadn't been seen. The stage traveled through the night to Stein's Peak Station, at the entrance to Doubtful Canyon in the Peloncillos.

At dawn Cochise and his warriors ambushed the stage as it approached the station. The driver and Elder, riding beside him, were killed in the first attack. With no hands on the reins, the frightened mules stampeded and weren't stopped until the vehicle capsized a mile and a half up the trail, at the entry to the pass.

The other three men freed themselves from the wreckage and,

from the cover of the rocks, put up a fight in which Neely fell early. Michael McNeese knew Cochise, and perhaps toward evening he tried to talk his way out of the predicament. If so, it was a ploy that didn't work. He and Giddings were taken alive and hung by the ankles from two trees, with their heads a foot and a half above the ground. Their arms were spread and their hands tied to stakes in the ground, and small fires were built below their heads. Their bodies were so mutilated they were unrecognizable and were identified only by default: they weren't Neely, Elder, or Briggs.

That afternoon two of the mules, bruised and bleeding, came into Barney's Station. Word was sent to Fort McLane, three hours' hard ride to the northeast. A few miles east of Stein's Peak, soldiers sent to investigate met an eastbound wagon train belonging to William Grant, an army contractor who had lost his mules to Cochise when attacked at the abandoned station on San Simon Creek. Grant's men and their military escort pursued them and succeeded in recovering enough of the mules for the freighter to proceed with his wagons into the pass, where he found the trail strewn with papers and other mail and scraps of harness. He then came on the suspended bodies of McNeese and Giddings.

Grant had now survived two scrapes. He had been a passenger in the stage that was attacked in Apache Pass back in February.

Cochise was engaged in a war of revenge for the killing of his relatives. If he captured a few mules or took some weapons while making war, well and good, but his purpose was to cause pain and suffering. Ignorant of American politics, he attributed the abandonment of the stage line to his own hostile actions.

In May, operating out of the Chiricahuas, Cochise made raids on Sonoita Creek, the stage station at the San Pedro crossing, and at the Canoa ranch, south of Tucson. In June he attacked Fort Buchanan, killed three soldiers, and ran off all the livestock. At the same time Mangas Coloradas was busy farther east attacking travelers and miners.

When Fort Sumter surrendered to the South Carolinians two weeks before the Doubtful Canyon attack, there were fewer than thirteen thousand men in the entire U.S. Army, and there was more urgency to the threat of a Confederate occupation of Washington than to Apache raids on western mines and ranches.

On July 10 troops at Fort Breckenridge set fire to the post and marched up the San Pedro River for Fort Buchanan, which was then burned and abandoned. By August most of the borderland, except for Tucson and a small enclave around Tubac, was deserted. The Apaches believed they had run the Americans off.

In August 1861 Col. John Baylor and his Texas troops, having arrived in Mesilla, proclaimed himself governor of the Confederate state of Arizona, a piece of country roughly corresponding to the southern third of New Mexico, from Texas to the Colorado River, with Mesilla to be its capital. In December Baylor was joined by Brig. Gen. Henry H. Sibley, with three regiments of Confederate cavalry and some cannon, who assumed command of the "Army of New Mexico."

After sending Capt. Sherod Hunter with a troop of "Arizona Rangers" to occupy Tucson and to secure a route to California's gold, Sibley began his advance northward. Col. Edward Canby and four thousand Union regulars from the abandoned western forts, along with the recently recruited First Regiment of New Mexico Volunteers, awaited him at Fort Craig.

The outnumbered rebels suckered Canby out into the open at a flat called Valverde. By the time the opposing regiments were in position, Sibley was too drunk to play an active part, but his subordinate officers, lacking orders, charged and won the day. One of the Union men to fall, a year and two days after his departure from Apache Pass, was Capt. George Nicholas Bascom.

Sibley's advance to Colorado was soon whipped by Colorado Volunteers and logistics, and by July 1862 the Confederates were back in El Paso. Before Hunter got to Yuma, that crossing was in the hands of Col. James H. Carleton, who had left California with a column of California Volunteers. Before Carleton reached Tucson, Captain Hunter's overwhelmingly outnumbered Texans, like the Union troops that had been called east the previous year, were ordered to abandon Arizona.

The political fate of the West was to be decided on the Atlantic Coast, but it was the Apaches who owned Arizona. They attacked the El Paso–bound Texans at Dragoon Springs, killed two men, and got many of the horses and mules and all the wagons.

Carleton, now a brigadier general, occupied Tucson on May 20. Because of the large force of twenty-five hundred men, with hundreds of saddle, pack, and draft animals, he broke his command into smaller parties to avoid taxing the limited water sources. In June the advance party reached Apache Pass and had a guarded meeting with Cochise. In the evening three soldiers strayed away from their camp and were lanced to death, but the reconnaissance patrol continued on to the Rio Grande the next day.

In July a larger party under Capt. Thomas Roberts left Tucson with a wagon train and two cannons. At Dragoon Springs Roberts divided his command, leaving Capt. John Cremony with the wagons and men to guard them while he went ahead to check the water supply at Apache Springs. As he entered the pass on the fifteenth, he was fired on from the hills but made his way to the abandoned station. The Indians held the spring and wouldn't let the soldiers get to water until Roberts unlimbered his cannon and blasted the high ground above the spring to scatter them.

After getting water, Roberts started back to escort Cremony, sending five cavalrymen ahead to warn him to exercise caution. The latter were attacked as they left the pass, but after a running fight during which they shot Mangas Coloradas in the chest, severely wounding him, they made it through to reach the wagon train at Ewell's Station, fifteen miles west. Roberts's foot soldiers arrived there at 2 A.M. but got little rest. The command moved out at 5 A.M. to march back to the pass.

In the night the Apaches had reoccupied their breastworks at the water, and Captain Roberts repeated his action of the day before, advancing on foot after softening the resistance with cannon fire. It wasn't a major battle. Two soldiers were killed and two wounded, and Roberts estimated ten dead Indians, but in the past day and a half he had marched seventy miles and put in several hours of fire fight.

Reporting to Carleton, he advised him that if a permanent guard wasn't stationed at Apache Springs, every passing force would have to fight for water.

Captain Cremony, who had seen the pass under more peaceful conditions with the Bartlett Survey, took an advance guard of cavalry and left the pass for the San Simon Cienega. In the arroyo of Bear Gulch, they came upon the scattered bodies of thirteen miners, riddled by bullets and bristling with arrows. Cremony believed they had been ambushed by Chihenne under Mangas Coloradas, about half of the party falling in the first volley and the rest run down and lanced as they fled.

When General Carleton arrived at the pass ten days later with the main body of Californians, he established Camp Bowie, named for Col. George Washington Bowie, commander of the Fifth California Infantry. Before marching for the Rio Grande, he detailed one hundred men of the Fifth to make up the first garrison.

With the territory saved for the Union, General Carleton turned his attention to the protection of its citizens from the depredations of the Indians. Palaver and diplomacy weren't in James Henry Carleton's bag of tricks. An old career officer, he had been fighting Indians from the Missouri to the Rio Grande for twenty years. He was convinced that only by dealing out death and destruction could the Apaches be contained.

Within a year of his arrival in Arizona, in addition to reactivating old Fort Breckenridge and establishing Camp Bowie, Carleton had staffed other new posts: Fort West at Pinos Altos, Fort Cummings under Cooke's Peak, Fort Lowell at Tucson, Fort Goodwin on the Gila River, and Camp Wallen on Babocomari Creek. He was determined to make the territory safe.

## Chapter 5

# Cochise

He was a remarkably fine looking man fully six feet tall, as straight as an arrow, and well proportioned, the typical Indian face, rather long, high cheek bones, clear keen eye, and a Roman nose. His cheeks were slightly painted with vermilion. He carried himself at all times with great dignity, and was always treated with the utmost respect.

**Lt. Joseph A. Sladen, 1896**

Confederate Arizona, the southern third of the original New Mexico Territory, hadn't lasted long. After the rebels retreated to Texas, Congress created an Arizona for the Union by dividing New Mexico north to south, putting the boundary where it is today. President Lincoln signed the bill in February 1863.

The new territory was only a paper concept at first, but in May prospectors led by old mountain men Pauline Weaver and Joe Walker discovered gold in the Bradshaw Mountains. To protect the sudden population of the vicinity from the Yavapais and from each other, Whipple Barracks was garrisoned with California troops. The new post, named for Lt. Amiel Whipple, who had surveyed that country after working for Bartlett, was declared the capital.

Soon after the appointed officers of the territory arrived, the seat of the government was moved a short distance to the mining camp of Prescott. There the territorial legislature divided Arizona into four counties named for Indian tribes: Yavapai, Pima, Mojave, and Yuma.

Pima County, with Tucson the county seat, ran east to the New Mexico line.

The boom in central Arizona didn't affect the Chiricahua Mountains. The first census, in 1864, shows a total population in what is now Cochise County to have been fifty-one soldiers and seven civilians, all in Apache Pass. There were no women. Of course, it wasn't practicable to make a head count of Apaches, who weren't citizens anyway.

Counted or not, Apaches still owned the southeastern corner of the territory, and one of their principal occupations was still raiding. An incident in January 1863 contributed to mutual distrust. Joe Walker's party, on their way from Pinos Altos to their discovery of gold farther west, had had a few brushes with Apaches and wanted to ensure their safety with a valuable hostage. They sought a parley with Mangas Coloradas. The chief had gone to Janos to be treated for the wound he had received at Apache Pass. Recovered, he was back in his Pinos Altos stamping ground. He saw the futility of fighting off the increasing numbers of Americans, and at seventy he was ready for peace and agreed to meet. But Walker's men, joined by an army detachment, took him prisoner.

On their way to nearby Fort McLane with their captive, they camped with soldiers whose commander put Mangas Coloradas under the guard of two of his men. During the night the guards amused themselves by tormenting their prisoner, and when he protested they shot and killed him "while attempting to escape." It's not likely they had direct orders to kill him, but it is probable that his death was intended. The guards were warned not to let him get away and probably understood that it was hoped that he would try to. At the shots the officer of the guard came to look but walked away. One man robbed the corpse of trinkets, and another took his scalp. In the morning the body was buried, but the surgeon had it exhumed and cut off the head for phrenological examination "in the interests of science."

To carry out Carleton's order to kill all male Apaches he could run to ground, General West relentlessly attacked the now-leaderless

Chihenne. In six months after the murder of Mangas Coloradas, soldiers claimed to have killed eighty-five of them.

Cochise had gone to Mexico after the fight at Apache Pass, but in July of that year, 1863, he came to the aid of his father-in-law's people. A large party of Apaches severely damaged a wagon train in Cooke's Canyon and two weeks later ambushed a detachment of California Volunteers in the same place. Over near the Rio Grande they killed a Lieutenant Bargie and cut off his head. Going the murderers of Mangas Coloradas one better, they cut open his chest and tore out his heart. In August Cochise was back in the Chiricahuas running off the Camp Bowie horse herd.

Events followed that pattern for the rest of the year and throughout 1864. Energetic patrols from Bowie, Fort Goodwin, and Fort McLane destroyed Apache camps in the Chiricahuas and the Pinaleños when they could find them, but they seldom reached them before the Indians had fled, and not many were killed.

One of the scouting expeditions initiated by Carleton penetrated deep into the Chiricahuas. It left Camp Bowie in July 1864, led by Captain Thomas T. Tidball, who had recently taken command of the post. His journal provides the first description of many of the places he visited, and although most of the names have changed, his notes are so detailed that his route can still be followed. His force comprised fifty-seven foot soldiers with a string of mules to pack rations and other gear.

Most important to the expedition was its interpreter and guide, Merejildo Grijalva, who knew the country intimately. He was seven when he was taken by Apaches at Bacachi, Sonora. During his captivity he learned the language and customs of his captors and became acquainted with many of the Chokonen band. He had left the Indians in 1859 and, after interpreting for Agent Steck, had been with the army for two years before coming to Camp Bowie.

On July 10 the command left the post and followed the foothills for twelve miles to the east, to camp at a spring a mile up Little Wood Canyon. The next day they rounded Rattlesnake Point and camped in Wood Canyon, where Tidball noted ample, accessible timber for constructing more adequate housing for the post. So far the hike had been a picnic. They had marched short distances over easy terrain and camped near wood and water early enough to smoke a pipe before dark.

The third day's seventeen-mile march was tougher. With the San Simon Valley on their left, they skirted the foothills, intending to camp at a place Merejildo called La Cieneguita—probably Squaw Spring at Oak Canyon. Finding it dry, they crossed a low divide between the Nippers and Blue Mountain, and yucca-studded Whitetail Flat to water at the granite potholes under sycamores at the mouth of Turkey Creek Canyon.

Tidball's journal noted Merejildo's Spanish translation of the Apache name for the canyon as Tierra Blanca, or "White Earth." The journal was rephrased after the return to the post, and it's more likely Merejildo said Piedra Blanca, "White Rock"—in Apache, *tse-thligai*—for the light-colored tipi-shaped rocks on the north flank of Silver Peak, two or three miles up Turkey Creek from their camp. The mountain, visible from as far away as Stein's Pass and Doubtful Canyon, was known as White Rock Mountain until recent years.

On the fourth day out the command was divided and the pack train sent up Graveyard Canyon and down Silver Creek to Cave Creek, while the main party went past the white rocks and crossed over into Cave Creek Canyon south of Silver Peak. When they were reunited, probably at the junction of Cave Creek with its South Fork, they endured a saturating thunderstorm.

Merejildo's name for the creek was Río Ancho (*tu-ntelth-chinle*, "wide water emerging"), but he called the canyon Cañon del Potrero. A *potrero*, literally a colt pasture, is a Spanish term for a flat-topped, steep-sided spur projecting from a larger mountain mass, a place where livestock can be easily confined. Centella Point below Fly Peak and extending from it to loom over the basin in the head of Cave Creek, is such a feature.

The next day the soldiers climbed up to Centella Point on an Indian trail, a fourteen-mile hike involving a 4,000-foot gain in elevation.

The men were exhausted when they made camp near the cool water of Bear Wallow Spring in a grove of big spruce trees.

They had yet to see any recent Indian sign. They found in one spot "immediately upon a plain trail—in an old camp of the Mexican force which was up here in March last—a lance and bayonet; conclusive evidence that no Apaches had passed since." Five months earlier a large Sonoran military party had surprised an Apache camp in the Chiricahuas and had reportedly killed several men, women, and children.

After a cool night in the timber, the command moved out in the rain and dropped back down to cross the head of Cave Creek's basin on a course paralleling the scarp of the high mountain. They crossed several tributary streams to reach the main fork of the creek, which Tidball recognized as a major tributary to Ciénaga de Sauz (San Simon Cienega).

An hour after they made camp, the guard saw Indians going up a steep slope about a mile away. A sergeant with twenty men went in pursuit and climbed to where the Indians had been seen. They were hailed in Spanish "by an Indian from an almost perpendicular cliff about 100 feet above them. He said he was a warrior and a brave one, and commenced shooting arrows. After throwing a few arrows without effect he began to throw rocks. He struck Corp'l Bair . . . with a rock and bruised his arm severely." The soldiers returned fire and killed him. Merejildo recognized him as a chief named Old Plume, who "could easily have made his escape, but . . . halted to cover the retreat of his women and children."

Plume's death probably occurred in the cliffs on the south side of the main fork of Cave Creek Canyon. Their abandoned wickiups were discovered, either in Pine Park or Fossil Saddle, and were destroyed along with stores of dried mescal.

In the morning the soldiers found Indians down the canyon at the foot of Cathedral Rock. In a shouted exchange the interpreter tried to talk them down for a parley, but the Apaches were understandably leery. The capture of Cochise under a flag of truce three years earlier and the more recent treacherous killing of Mangas Coloradas were fresh memories, to say nothing of Plume's murder the day before. They refused to come down out of the rocks, so Tidball marched his men out into the valley and up into Horseshoe Canyon, where they "found several huts which had been occupied within a few weeks by a small party of Indians—but no fresh signs." There they rested until nightfall.

The captain, validating the Apaches' distrust, determined to return to Cave Creek to attack the people from the rear. After dark he moved his command back north to spend the rest of the night in Sulphur Canyon.

At daybreak he

> "directed Lt. Tápia to proceed leisurely down the trail to our old camp on the Río Ancho, and if the Indians showed themselves to attract their attention as much as possible. At the same time I started with Berriguildi and 20 picked men of my company up the mountain—hoping to get in the rear, or at least find them somewhere on the mountains. . . . I never passed over so rough and broken a region, or made so hard a march."

Tidball and his men had put in a brutally hard day. They went up Sulphur Canyon for four miles—the last mile or so through thick chaparral—to cross a saddle between Sulphur Peak and Horseshoe Peak, then dropped off into South Fork near Maple Camp. Then they climbed out of the canyon to the ridge below Snowshed Peak, where three days before they had found the Apache camp. There they were still three miles from bivouac. They hiked only about ten miles in twelve hours but over truly rugged terrain, climbing 2,500 feet, losing it, and regaining it. Anyone familiar with off-trail scrambling in the Chiricahuas will understand the brevity of the next journal entry: "Tuesday, July 19—Laid over. The stream had fallen somewhat and the water was very clear. Plenty of small fish show that this water is permanent."

Two days later they were making camp near the mouth of Tex Canyon when they saw two Apache men on horseback following their trail. When they were discovered, the Indians ascended a small volcanic hill and called out for Merejildo. The guide went out unarmed, and one of the two Apaches, leaving the other on the hill as a look-out, came down to talk. Merejildo recognized him as Ka-eet-sah, an old acquaintance, who told him that Plume's small band and his own were the only people in the Chiricahuas at the time and that Cochise was up on the Gila River. He asked why the soldiers had come back into Cave Creek after leaving it. Merejildo told him that the captain only wanted to try again to talk them into Camp Bowie for a palaver.

Ka-eet-sah wasn't eager for a treaty. He said they had recently made one at Fronteras with the Mexicans, who killed thirty of them. After a little more talk he said he would come to Bowie later in the month, and he asked for some tobacco, which he took up to his partner on the hill, where they rolled cigarettes before riding off. Merejildo was disgusted with his captain for not shooting Ka-eet-sah when he had the chance.

Tidball's patrol continued for eleven more days but never saw another Indian. They went up Tex Canyon and over into Rucker, then out into the Sulphur Springs Valley. Near Twin Buttes they found the broad, recently used trail made by Apaches bringing cattle north from Sonora, and in Gold Gulch, at the south end of the Mule Mountains, they found an old camp occupied the previous winter. The party continued across Escabrosa Ridge, down to the San Pedro River, then rounded the Tombstone Hills and crossed the Dragoons at Middle-march Pass.

On the last day out, they made a beeline for Camp Bowie, arriving at 9 A.M. The captain gave the troops the rest of the day off to soak sore feet in the cool waters of Apache Springs and to rinse out gummy uniforms. Although Tidball had earlier reported that the camp was a miserable collection of jacals with thatched or earth roofs, it no doubt looked better to him that day.

The campaign's mission of punishing Apaches was a failure. Light-footed and on home ground, the Indians easily avoided the soldiers for the most part while monitoring their every move. Still, it was a remarkable hike that added to the army's knowledge of the terrain. They had covered three hundred miles of rough country in twenty-three days with only two days of rest.

Apaches continued to peck at the edges of any military force, nick-ing a careless soldier or two and making it difficult for the army to maintain a string of saddle horses. Travel by civilians without a military escort virtually ceased.

In April 1865 there was another clash at Apache Springs between Chokonen and members of the garrison. But at the same time in a more significant event at Appomattox Courthouse, Virginia, Gen. Robert. E. Lee offered his sword to Gen. Ulysses S. Grant.

With the end of the Civil War, the California Volunteers were discharged, though some men stayed in Arizona or New Mexico. To fill the hole in the defenses, Governor Goodwin raised a regiment of Arizona Volunteer Rangers, and by June 350 men were enlisted. They were occupied almost wholly with defending the mines on the Verde and the Hassayampa Rivers from Yavapais and Tonto Apaches. Except for small settlements at Tubac and Tucson, that is where Arizona's population was in 1865. The entire white population east of the San Pedro River was at Camp Bowie.

During the Civil War, after Butterfield pulled out to operate on a northern route, no mail crossed Arizona, but in 1865 service from Mesilla to Tucson was restored by the Kerns and Mitchell Company, which carried the mail horseback. By August 1866, passenger coaches were running again, operated by Wells, Fargo and Company, which since 1852 had been engaged in banking and running stage lines in California.

Travel across Cochise's territory was still hazardous. His Apaches frequently attacked stages on the stretch from Mesilla to Tucson and raided isolated mines and ranches with such regularity that they could be maintained only by brave and reckless men.

One such man was red-bearded Captain Thomas Jeffords, who in 1866 was hired to carry the mail between Mesilla and Tucson. Raised in upper New York State, he'd been a seaman and a river boat captain before joining the rush to the placers in Colorado in 1858. By the time Denver City sprang up a few months later on the site of the diggings, he was on his way. He spent the next two years prospecting in the San Juan Mountains of northern New Mexico, then drifted south down the Rio Grande.

Jeffords was in Mesilla when the Confederates moved in. Not being of southern persuasion, he moved upriver to Fort Craig and fought at Valverde. He spent the war years as a courier between military units throughout the Southwest. Thus he knew the country and the route well when he signed on to carry the mail.

Even though the old Butterfield stations were refurbished and the route was operating again in 1867, the mail continued to be carried horseback throughout that year, and at considerable risk. In February mail rider Charles Fisher was killed between Camp Bowie and the San Simon station. In November, just west of Apache Pass, carrier John Slater was killed along with the lieutenant who rode with him, and another mail rider was shot off his horse northwest of Fort Cummings.

During that same year and the next, Apaches attacked Mowry Mine, raided ranches on the Santa Cruz, attacked an emigrant train in Cooke's Pass, killed mules in the stage company's corral at Fort Cummings, twice ran off the army's beef herd at Fort Seldon, north of Mesilla, and south of there raided a California-bound herd of Texas cattle. The Apaches also continued raiding for cattle in Mexico.

The Indians didn't have it entirely their way. In April 1867 soldiers from Chihuahua, disregarding the border, made a successful attack on a Chokonen camp in the southern Chiricahua Mountains, and in June troops from Camp Wallen destroyed a rancheria—probably in Rucker Canyon. A month later another Mexican unit, this one from Fronteras, wiped out a camp in the Perilla Mountains.

The army's resources for protecting settlers and travelers were stretched to the limit, but in August 1867 Fort Crittenden was established half a mile from the abandoned Fort Buchanan, and the following year the miserable quarters at Camp Bowie were torn down and a new post was built in a better location a few hundred yards away.

Such modest development did little to allay the danger. One estimate stated that in an eighteen-month period in 1868–69, Indians killed 750 in Pima County alone, though this was probably a journalistic exaggeration. Arizona's population in 1870 was less than six thousand. In May 1869 the post commandant at Camp Bowie, Capt.

Reuben F. Bernard, the same who as a sergeant had gone with Bascom in search of the Ward boy, reported that the Apaches threatened to drive the army out of the territory.

On October 5, Apaches attacked the westbound stage about three miles east of Dragoon, killing the driver, a passenger, and a four-man escort of soldiers. The passenger, John Finkle Stone, manager and part owner of the Apache Pass Mining Company, was trying, under severe difficulties, to get a mine into operation. Within the past few months his camp in Apache Pass and his wagon train bringing equipment and supplies from Tucson had been attacked.

The next day, near the scene of the attack on the stage, Cochise struck a Texas herd being trailed to California. A cowboy was lanced to death, and about two hundred head of cattle were taken. While some Indians drove the herd toward the Chiricahuas, others made a futile attack on an escorted government supply train. In the early evening, after a hard ride across the valley, a cowboy made it to Camp Bowie to report the loss of cattle.

Captain Bernard was away, but the senior officer present, Lt. William H. Winters, immediately left in pursuit with twenty-one cavalrymen and Merejildo Grijalva. In the Sulphur Springs Valley a messenger intercepted him with word of the attack on the stage. The tracks of the cattle were picked up and easily followed through a moonlit night. At sunup on October 8, they overtook the herd—probably in the vicinity of Castle Dome and Mud Springs. Though greatly outnumbered, Winters attacked. Merejildo recognized Cochise as the leader of a rear guard that engaged the soldiers in a running skirmish for an hour and a half while the main body of the Apaches abandoned the cattle and escaped north into the mountains. Two troopers were wounded in the engagement, but the lieutenant was pleased to have recovered the herd and to have killed an estimated dozen Apaches.

When Bernard returned, he left the post with sixty-one men and rode for two days down the east flank of the mountains to the scene of Winters's fight. With Merejildo ahead, cutting for sign, they followed fresh tracks up what is now Tex Canyon and across the divide into Rucker. From a ridge at the junction of Red Rock Canyon, they

were fired upon by a strong force of Indians who held their fire until
the soldiers were within arrow range. At the first volley two soldiers
were killed and another wounded. The troopers took cover and returned fire from behind trees and rocks. Both sides sniped at each
other until dark, when the Indians slipped away. The captain claimed
eighteen Apache dead.

Two days after returning to Camp Bowie, Bernard left again to
take up the fight, this time with seventy men. He expected reinforcements to join him from Camp Crittenden and Camp Goodwin. Again
he made the two-day march down the east side of the Chiricahuas
and over Chiricahua Pass into Rucker. Though he took some fire from
Indians high in the rocks above him, he was able to reach and bury
the now-ripe bodies of the two soldiers killed in the earlier battle.
With Merejildo interpreting, Bernard and Cochise had a long-range
talk but resolved nothing.

The next day, October 29, Captain Thomas Dunn, with nineteen
infantrymen, joined Bernard after making the fifty-mile hike from
Camp Bowie in twenty hours. Apparently piqued at the inadequacy
of his reinforcements and believing the combined strength still too
small to make a successful attack on the Indians, Bernard detailed six
cavalrymen to escort Dunn and his foot soldiers on a merciless return
to the post.

The following night Capt. Harrison Moulton and cavalrymen from
Camp Crittenden crossed into the head of Tex Canyon in the moonlight and ran into fire from the Indians. When the Apaches were in
turn harassed by fire from their rear, they scattered.

Sporadic fighting continued until November 2, when Bernard was
joined in Tex Canyon by reinforcements from Camp Goodwin. They
crossed back into Rucker and worked the side canyons, then scouted
the Swisshelms and Silver Creek without finding any more Indians.
Bernard declared the month-long campaign a success, claiming to
have killed thirty Apaches. The estimate was probably exaggerated,
though the soldiers apparently had forced Cochise to leave the Chiricahuas.

But not for long. Two months later the Chokonen and their Pinaleño allies, operating out of a base north of the Gila, ran off a herd of mules from Apache Pass. All that winter and into the spring of 1870, Cochise continued to raid on both sides of the Mexican border, but the American cavalry and Mexican troops as well followed him relentlessly, forcing him to keep moving.

Cochise had been at war for nine years and felt he had evened the score for the injuries received at the hands of Lieutenant Bascom at Apache Pass. Now he was tired, and in the summer of 1870 he showed up at Camp Mogollon, later to become Fort Apache, to make overtures of peace.

After Carleton's failed policy of extermination, the government had tried a blend of bribery and punishment to convince Indians to accept reservation life. A year before Cochise came to Camp Mogollon, the Chihenne under Loco and Victorio had been persuaded to settle in Cañada Alamosa in New Mexico. In September 1870 Cochise with some Chokonen arrived there on a visit. In October William Arny, President Grant's special agent to New Mexico's Indians, met with him. Both expressed a desire for peace, and Cochise agreed to bring his people to the Cañada.

Grant's "peace policy" included parceling out Indian agencies to various church denominations in the belief that men of God were best suited to convert and civilize the "savages." Some missionaries had a talent for administration, but many were disasters. An example of the latter was Orlando Piper, sent to the Apaches by the Presbyterians. On arrival at the Cañada, he decided the place wasn't suitable and that the Indians should be moved to Fort Stanton, near the Sierra Blanca of New Mexico. That hadn't been in the bargain, so Cochise took his people back to the Chiricahuas.

While at Cañada Alamosa, Cochise either began or renewed an acquaintance with Tom Jeffords. Jeffords hadn't stayed long with the mail, and for the past year or two he had prospected in southwestern New Mexico, where he came to know Warm Springs Apaches. In December 1869 he had obtained a license to trade with the Indians at Cañada Alamosa. Whether or not they had met earlier, Cochise and Jeffords knew each other there and shared a mutual respect.

The story of Cochise and Jeffords is one of many in frontier history in which documentary evidence and mythology become tangled. As a result of interviews with the reticent Jeffords a few months before his death at eighty-two, the story grew that he had gone alone into Cochise's camp in 1867 to protest the attacks on the mail carriers on the Mesilla–Tucson run, whereupon the Apache chief was so impressed with the Red-beard's spunk that he let him go unharmed and agreed to spare the mails.

Jeffords had a reputation not only for modesty but also for enjoying a joke. He may have been stringing along the Phoenix journalist who interviewed him, or his memory of events forty-five years in the past may have been rusty, or possibly the reporter confused the chronology of separate events that were related to him disjointedly. In the 1950s the interviews were embellished by a novelist who added a dubious ceremony of brotherhood involving the mingling of blood from incisions on both men's wrists and the marriage of Jeffords to a lovely Chokonen maiden. There is no doubt, however, that in 1870 at the Cañada the two men called each other *shikis*, "my brother."

The growing number of Americans in southern Arizona provided more targets for Apache attacks, most of them on the Santa Cruz River and in the neighboring mountains, where vulnerable mines and ranches were most numerous. But the Chiricahua Mountains weren't neglected. In January 1871 a party of fifteen would-be miners from Ralston in the Pyramid Mountains made a prospecting trip to the Chiricahuas, where they were ambushed on the east side of the mountains about thirty miles from Camp Bowie. Two men were badly wounded. (Thirty miles by trail around the foothills would have put them near the limestone hills between Turkey Creek and Cave Creek, very likely in Round Valley.)

Two men made their way to Camp Bowie to get protection for the party, and Capt. Gerald Russell with a company of the Third Cavalry went in pursuit. Russell was paralyzed on the left side from a horse fall, but he didn't let that interfere with his work, and he had a reputation as a hard-riding officer. He and his men looked for the attackers, but the Apaches had scattered.

At about the same time Apaches took a herd of horses from a corral
on the outskirts of Silver City, by then a burgeoning camp of eighteen
hundred. Capt. William Kelly from nearby Fort Bayard responded to
the alarm with a squad of soldiers. They were joined by a handful of
miners led by James Bullard, one of the town's founders. The plain
trail led them to the Gila River, then back through the Burro Mountains, across Lordsburg Flats and the Peloncillos, to the east side of
the Chiricahua Mountains, where they had a sharp fight—probably
in Horseshoe Canyon.

In 1870 Gen. George Stoneman was assigned to command the Arizona Military District. He had served with distinction since the Mexican War, but the increased complexity of a larger command spurred
him into a flurry of troop movement, closing some posts and opening
others and issuing orders only to cancel them. Many orders had no
strategic basis apparent to his officers, and in the confusion Apache
attacks increased.

In March 1871 frustrated Tucson citizens petitioned the general,
asking for protection for the three hundred settlers on the Santa Cruz
River. At the time Stoneman was building a camp on the north side
of the Pinal Mountains and hacking out the wagon road to supply it.
He replied sarcastically that surely such a large population should be
able to defend itself, ignoring the fact that the people were scattered
over hundreds of square miles.

In mid-April an indignant Tucson merchant, Sidney DeLong,
wrote to his friend Gov. Anson Safford for help to equip a militia,
citing nineteen killings by Apaches in the past two weeks. Safford, a
veteran frontiersman, would have been willing, but he was then in
Washington on territorial business. Before he could respond, strin-
gent measures were taken—measures remembered in sorrow, rage,
and shame for a century.

Jesús María Elías, scion of a pioneer Spanish family, with DeLong
and William Oury, Tucson's mayor, part owner of the *Weekly Arizo-
nian* and agent for the stage line, recruited townsmen, ranchers, and
Papagos to attack a rancheria near Camp Grant, at the junction of the
San Pedro with Aravaipa Creek, about fifty miles north of Tucson.

In the Indian camp were several hundred Aravaipa and Pinal Apaches who had come in to Camp Grant seeking protection and peace. The post commander suggested a campsite two miles from the post to separate the Indians from the sutler and the troops. Looking on the Apaches as prisoners of war, he authorized the butchering of a daily beef and asked headquarters for guidance. In nearly two months he still hadn't heard from General Stoneman. Tucson's self-appointed militia left town on April 28, the white men horseback and the Papagos on foot. Following the San Pedro downstream through groves of huge mesquite trees, they reached the Indian camp just before dawn on April 30, 1871.

Surprise was complete. Without losing a man or suffering a serious wound, in thirty minutes they killed eight old men and about one hundred women and children. There was little resistance, as there were no able-bodied men in the camp. The fleeing Indians were overtaken and their heads beaten in. Later President Grant, the unflinching commander at Cold Harbor, pronounced the massacre "pure murder."

A month later Brig. Gen. George Crook was assigned to relieve Stoneman as commander of the Department of Arizona—not because of the massacre at Camp Grant but in response to the citizens' lack of confidence in Stoneman's ability.

Crook was a quiet, unassuming officer, more comfortable in canvas pants and flannel shirt than with brass buttons up to his chin. His success as an imaginative and energetic field soldier in the Civil War and on frontier stations in the Northwest was a surprise to his classmates and instructors at West Point, where he had graduated near the bottom of his class. He arrived in Tucson like a whirlwind, having sent orders to his commanders to join him there for a council, then took to the field to scout the territory. He put out word that after a reasonable time all Indians not on reservations would be considered to be "hostile."

Crook's task was complicated by the ambivalence of U. S. Grant's administration. The iron determination of Grant the soldier had become complacency in the president. He appointed an unpaid "Board of Indian Commissioners" made up of philanthropists and religious leaders to advise him. The board gradually gained considerable influence on Grant and convinced him that feeding Indians on reservations would be more effective and cheaper than containing them by military action. The president allowed both the army and the Department of the Interior to deal with the Indians but didn't spell out the boundaries of their authority.

While Crook acquainted himself with Arizona's people and terrain and showed the Apaches he had the strength and will to force them to quit plundering, Vincent Colyer, secretary of the board, tried to tease the tribes onto reservations with prayer and the promise of beef every Sunday.

At Camp Bowie General Crook got word of Colyer's peace mission and went north to meet with him at Fort Whipple. Shortly after he left Apache Pass, the Apaches rustled thirty-eight head of cattle and killed two men within sight of the flagpole.

The army and the Indian Commission had the same goal. Both believed the only solution was the conversion of the native population to Christian husbandry. The differences were in how to go about it and who was in charge. Crook respected Apaches and treated them with firm fairness. He trusted them but impressed on them that betrayal of that trust would result in immediate punishment. Colyer, an artist and a humanitarian, thought that love alone would win the Indians over. A large and vocal part of the civilian population, tired of constant apprehension and preparedness, was convinced the only good Indian was a dead one. The newspapers were alarmed at Colyer's expression of admiration for Indians and called him a renegade.

In the fall of 1871, the still-vacillating government gave Crook authority to continue a vigorous campaign and admonished the superintendent of Indian Affairs to stay out of his way. Not all of Colyer's work was in vain. Some of the reservations he had negotiated were established, and one of his final accomplishments in Arizona was making peace with the Yavapais on the Verde River. A few weeks later the Yavapais killed six in an attack on a stagecoach near Wickenburg.

Responding to General Crook's announcement, Indians were flock-

ing to reservations at Camp Grant, Fort Apache, Fort Tularosa, and
Cañada Alamosa, but Washington hadn't given up on peaceful persuasion. Crook had just started his roundup when the War Department
ordered him to hold off for one more attempt to get the job done by
gentler measures. To replace the altruistic Colyer, they picked a military man, Gen. Oliver Otis Howard.

Howard was a distinguished veteran of the Seminole wars, was brevetted major general in the Civil War, earned the Medal of Honor,
and lost an arm. He was a devout Christian, had worked with the
Freedman's Bureau, and was founder and president of Howard University. Grant hoped his selection would satisfy both the war and the
peace parties.

In April 1872 Crook and Howard met at Fort McDowell, east of
Phoenix. George Crook, who felt his mission to be clouded and his
authority reduced by the special Indian commissioner's appointment,
didn't take to Howard, whom he found to be overly sanctimonious.
Howard, however, asked Crook to continue his operations against off-
reservation Apaches and to help arrange a meeting with Cochise at
Fort Apache.

Western Apaches were gathering at reservations in the White
Mountains and at Camp Grant on the San Pedro, and the Chihenne
were concentrated at the Tularosa Reservation in west-central New
Mexico. Cochise and some of his people were also at Tularosa and
the recently abandoned reservation at Cañada Alamosa but weren't
committed yet to reservation life. Many Ndenda and Chokonen still
roamed both sides of the Mexican border, and in May they killed
some settlers in the Santa Rita Mountains close to Tucson.

In August Howard went to Tularosa hoping to find someone who
could take him to Cochise. With him was his aide, Lt. Joseph A.
Sladen, a naturalized Englishman who had been Howard's enlisted
clerk during the war, was wounded, decorated, and commissioned.
He still served as the general's secretary, and he later wrote an account of the meeting with Cochise.

Army officers told Howard of Tom Jeffords and described him as
an unsavory character whose friendship with Cochise was based on

selling arms to him, a charge never substantiated. But he was told if anyone could arrange a meeting, it was Jeffords, who was presently guiding a cavalry unit looking for Apache holdouts reluctant to come to the malarial Tularosa Valley.

In a few days the cavalry returned. Sladen described his first impressions of Jeffords: "Riding by the side of the commanding officer was a tall, slender citizen with a long flowing beard of reddish hue, his face shaded by the broad brim of a drab slouch hat, but with a pleasant face lighted up with a pair of bright piercing eyes of bright blue."

That evening Howard asked Jeffords if he could persuade Cochise to come in to talk. The answer echoed what Crook had told him in the spring: "Cochise won't come. The man that wants to talk to Cochise must go where he is."

Jeffords agreed to take Howard and his aide, without any troops, to Cochise's camp. At the cost of a pony, they enlisted Chee, a handsome young relative of Cochise. Sending the general's wagon to Fort Craig by a different route, they left by horseback for the camp of a Warm Springs man Jeffords wanted to take along. Ponce, whom Sladen understood to be a brother-in-law of Cochise, was presented with a fine horse and agreed to help find Cochise, who was thought to be in the Chiricahuas. Leaving the horse with his wife, Ponce set out on foot to trot ahead of the horsemen, dressed only in moccasins, breechclout, and red flannel headband and carrying a bow and a few arrows.

In the north end of the Peloncillos, they found a group of about sixty Apaches led by an old man who told Ponce and Chee that Cochise was in the Dragoons. Howard sent his cook and the teamster to Camp Bowie with a message for the commander to explain his mission and request that troops be kept away to avoid arousing Apache suspicion.

The smaller party, consisting only of the general, his aide, Tom Jeffords, and the two Indians, crossed the Peloncillos by a faint trail, then descended into the San Simon Valley and to the foot of the Dos Cabezas Mountains. They camped after nightfall at a place where, as Sladen related, "we heard the welcome music of a waterfall as the stream came bubbling out of the rock and fell into the pool below." They probably were at the granite bluffs between Ninemile and Happy Camp Canyons.

The next day they crossed the Dos Cabezas, a tough climb by a trail known only to Ponce and Chee. It wasn't the easiest way to the Dragoons, but they were anxious to avoid any Americans. Cochise must surely know of their approach, and they didn't want him to have any reason to think they were in contact with other Americans. That night they intended to camp at Sulphur Springs, but finding a guard detail from Camp Bowie there, they went on to make a dry camp between there and the west side of the valley.

As they crossed Middlemarch Pass in the Dragoons, the two Apaches ranged right and left, looking for sign. On the west side the three Americans and Ponce rested in an oak grove near a spring while Chee rode out to find Cochise. A few hours later he returned with two boys who took them to a small rancheria in another canyon now known as Slavins Gulch. Cochise wasn't there, but they were told that he would come in the morning.

Rations were getting short, but at daylight Jeffords made a bannock in the frying pan. The Indians were crowding around to help drink the fresh pot of coffee when Ponce said in Spanish, "*Ya viene*" (He is coming). The people of the camp spread blankets on the ground for a seat and formed a circle. Soon a fierce-looking, spear-armed man with his face painted black and red rode full speed up to them and, reining his horse back onto its haunches, jumped off to embrace Tom Jeffords.

Jeffords quietly explained, "This is his brother, Juan."

While Juan was being introduced, Cochise, his silver-touched hair bound with a yellow silk handkerchief, rode up more sedately, followed by his wife, his sister, and his son Naiche, a boy of about fifteen. Cochise dismounted with dignity and greeted Jeffords warmly.

"General, this is the man," Jeffords said. "This is he."

After the chief interrogated Chee and Ponce to satisfy himself about Howard, they got down to business. Cochise quickly agreed to peace but demurred at a proposed removal to Cañada Alamosa, stating that many of his Chokonen would object to leaving their accustomed range.

"Give me Apache Pass for my people and I will protect the road to Tucson," he said. "I will see that the Indians do no harm." Many of his subchiefs were away, however, and he must consult with them. Howard must wait until he could call them in before any final decision could be made.

It was arranged that Howard, with Chee to guide him, would return to Camp Bowie to see that the army suspended aggressive operations until the conference was held. Jeffords and Sladen would remain in Cochise's camp. Thinking it was likely that the absent warriors were conducting raids and wouldn't be as inclined to peace as the older Cochise, Sladen was a nervous hostage.

Cochise led them to the camp of his own immediate family in the scattered oaks in the foothills just south of West Stronghold Canyon. General Howard and Chee rode off around the north end of the range for Camp Bowie. Jeffords and Sladen unsaddled and made themselves comfortable in the shade of an oak with a view across the broad San Pedro Valley.

Joe Sladen soon forgot his apprehension as he lost himself in lazy days of Apache hospitality. He learned to appreciate horse meat and to enjoy soup of mesquite beans and walnuts, baked mescal, and the refreshing, lightly fermented tulapai. He endured friendly ribbing when he and Tom joined the girls and young men in the evening social dances. The boy Naiche attached himself to him, taught him to make fire by friction, and the two traded Apache and English words. The lieutenant was much impressed with the laughter around him, the affection the group so obviously felt for each other and so easily displayed toward him also, and the sight of men and women brushing each other's hair.

Then Cochise suddenly moved his camp to an impregnable site in the rocks on a high ridge overlooking the valleys. There they stayed until they spied Howard's wagon returning from Apache Pass. They learned later that a returning warrior had reported a raid on a ranch on the Santa Cruz in which several soldiers had been killed. Cochise knew that retaliation could strike anywhere.

One by one, the leaders Cochise had sent for came in to the Stronghold and reported. Only Taza, his oldest son, apparently on a raid in Mexico, couldn't be reached. Cochise was grooming him to be his successor and was reluctant to proceed without him, but it had been two weeks since Howard had arrived in the Dragoons, and they could delay no longer.

During three days of discussions, it was agreed that Cochise would keep the peace and protect the Tucson road. The government would allot the Chokonen a Chiricahua Reservation with those mountains as its heart. It would extend from the north end of the Dragoons to the Peloncillos north of Doubtful Canyon, hence south to the Mexican border, west for fifty-five miles, then north along the west base of the Dragoons to the point of beginning. Tom Jeffords would be their agent and would draw supplies of food for the Indians until they could be self-sustaining through farming or stock raising. On October 11 Howard left for Tucson to report the results of the conference by the new telegraph.

Jeffords set up his agency at Sulphur Springs in a miserable adobe hut barely big enough to accommodate his bedroll, and sent word to his friend Fred Hughes at Ojo Caliente, offering him a job clerking for him. The two had been together at Fort Craig and the battle of Valverde and had known each other for years.

Fred G. Hughes, born in England, was brought to the United States as a child. At sixteen he went to California, where he joined the California Column and hiked with it to New Mexico. After the war he became *alcalde* of San Marcial, on the Rio Grande. When Apaches raided his village, he led a chase that ended at Cañada Alamosa, where he had a fight with the Chihenne chief, Loco. Later Hughes helped talk Loco and Victorio into Fort Craig for peace talks. He had known Cochise since the latter's 1870 visit to the Cañada.

General Howard was quick to get supplies freighted to the Sulphur Springs agency, where they had to be stored under tarpaulins. By early November Tom and Fred were feeding about four hundred Apaches. To be closer to the agency, Cochise moved his family across the Dragoons into the East Stronghold.

The reservation was quickly confirmed by executive order, but it wasn't universally applauded. Southern Arizona's citizens weren't pleased to have the Indians living athwart the Overland Road and had wanted them moved to New Mexico. General Crook believed that Howard had given away too much. The people of Sonora and Chihuahua saw the reservation as a safe haven from which Apaches could launch raids into Mexico. And it was.

Imuris, Sonora, was raided shortly after the conclusion of the treaty, and Governor Pesqueira protested to the U.S. consul. The Apaches were surprised to be admonished for the raids. They'd agreed not to bother Americans, but no mention had been made about Mexico. Undiplomatic Tom Jeffords was quoted in the Tucson papers that he didn't care how many Mexicans were killed.

Forty-five years of almost continuous warfare and his many wounds had aged Cochise. Years of running over deserts and mountains had stiffened his knees, and he was content to spend long days in the shade of a live-oak tree with a bottle of mescal in the crook of his arm, dreaming of the past. But his young men were impatient to test themselves and to know first-hand the thrill of a dawn raid. Their pasts were still in front of them. Nevertheless, Cochise saw the need to restrain his warriors.

In December Jeffords got word that the southern Ndenda in Chihuahua wanted to meet him in Pinery Canyon. Taking Fred Hughes with him, Jeffords rode east to where Pinery runs out onto a grassy flat in a string of sycamores, and there met Natiza and Juh with their bands. With them was Juh's first cousin, Geronimo, a fifty-year-old Bedonkohe Apache from the upper Gila who had been running with the Ndenda since his family was killed by Mexicans at Janos. Not himself a chief, Geronimo was credited with strong "medicine" and had a following as a war leader.

The Ndenda hadn't been considered when the army and the Department of the Interior were planning to put Apaches on reservations. They were Mexican Indians and Mexico's problem, but here they were. They wanted to get in on the rationing, and the agency took them in, about two hundred of them.

Juh, tall and heavily built, was about fifty. He stuttered badly, thus was no orator, but he was a brilliant tactician and he commanded a large following because of his outstanding success as a war leader. He took his band across the Chiricahuas to make a headquarters in the canyon that now bears his name (though with the spelling "Jhus").

In one respect the peace made with the Chiricahua Apaches was a success. Deaths resulting from Indian depredations in Arizona in 1873 dropped to less than a tenth of the number of the year before. But there were difficulties. It is easier for Congress to make appropriations for war than for peace, and feeding all those Indians was expensive. By this time an estimated one thousand people were drawing rations at the agency. It was imperative to get them on their feet and make them self-supporting.

Sulphur Springs barely put out enough water for domestic use and the stage company's horses. Farming the hard ground with the scant rainfall wasn't remotely possible, and it was intended that the Apaches be farmers. In September 1873 Jeffords moved his agency to the next valley east, where water at the San Simon Cienega was plentiful, even enough for a little irrigation.

Juh and his Ndenda didn't intend to farm. When government rations ran short, there was always Mexico. In between handouts of beef and coffee, they made lightning strikes at the ranches in Sonora and Chihuahua. Sometimes, despite their chief's warning, they were accompanied by some of Cochise's young men.

Not all the banditry was below the border. A California-bound family named Harris stopped at the cienega and were told by Indians hanging around the agency of a way over the mountains that would avoid the long way around through Apache Pass. They steered them up into the mouth of Turkey Creek. Where the canyon narrows at the foot of the hill now known as Harris Mountain, Juh or some of his men took the horses and a little girl, killed the rest of the family, and burned the wagon.

Cochise called a meeting at his camp in Goodwin Canyon near Apache Pass, where he had moved in the spring. Though it wasn't Apache tradition for him to speak for people not in his band, he gave out word that he would not tolerate raiding from his reservation, whether by Chokonen, Ndenda—or Chihenne, some of whom had recently drifted in from Fort Tularosa.

San Simon Cienega proved to be a poor spot for the agency. It wasn't centrally located, mosquitoes made it an unhealthy place, and the government hadn't supplied the seed and tools necessary for planting. Furthermore, Juh and most of his people left the vicinity and had gone to Mexico after Cochise's warning. After only a couple of months on the cienega, Jeffords moved his headquarters back across the mountain to a place between Pinery Creek and Bonita Creek.

By June 1875 Cochise, who had been failing for a year or more, was dying, probably of cancer but possibly from the bewitching suspected by the Apaches. He had moved back to the Dragoons, where Tom Jeffords visited his old friend for the last time. Cochise told him that he would be dead by midmorning the next day, and Tom agreed with him.

"Do you think we will ever meet again?" Cochise asked. "I've been thinking a good deal about it while I have been sick here, and I believe we will."

He was buried in a cleft in the granite before nightfall the next day, with his weapons and a favorite horse.

The Chiricahua Reservation was less than two years old when Cochise died, and it lasted only two years more. Of the several factors that led to its end, one was the success of the peace established by Howard and Cochise. Raiding in Mexico hadn't been completely halted, but southeastern Arizona became relatively safe. Many travelers replaced fear of Apaches with contempt for them and treated them with arrogance. There was a steady increase in population, and increased potential for friction, and some emigrants moving west through the reservation traded whiskey and firearms for Mexican livestock.

In May 1875, partly to prevent that trade and the trouble it could cause, Jeffords moved his agency to Apache Pass, into the adobe building abandoned by the Apache Pass Mining Company. He was on hand to take the Apache side of an argument when William Ohnesorgen, who had bought a herd of sheep in Chihuahua, drove them through the pass and attempted to water them at a spring that was used for domestic water. To keep the milling animals from fouling the water, the Indians threw stones at them, killing several. The sheepman sued the government, but Jeffords said the claim covered every head he'd lost since he'd left Mexico.

Ohnesorgen, irate that a white man should have to defer to an Indian, sputtered that Jeffords, "a tall, lanky fellow with a face full of hair . . . was a no-good, filthy fellow, lived right among those damn things," meaning the Indians.

Administration of the reservation had never been easy for Jeffords, and it became increasingly difficult. Added to the Ndenda who had flocked in, there were often small bands of Chihenne from Tularosa in temporary residence. Coyotero war parties heading for Mexico, or returning with plunder, crossed the reservation through the Sulphur Springs Valley or the San Simon, and their raids were frequently blamed on Taza, Cochise's son and successor. Sometimes they dropped by to get in line for a distribution of rations. The army and the newspapers attributed all of this to Jeffords's "coddling" of the Indians.

In the winter of 1875–76 a tight situation became worse when the beef purchase was reduced by 30 percent and there wasn't enough for the legitimate residents of the reservation, let alone the freeloaders. Jeffords suggested to Taza that the Indians scatter out and supplement the ration by hunting, and a number of them, including Taza, moved over to the Dragoons.

For several generations the game hunted by Apaches included Mexican livestock. It may have been Taza's attempt to prevent raiding that caused a quarrel in which three Indians were killed. Taza returned to Apache Pass, but several malcontents stayed in the Dragoons, using it as a base for forays into Sonora. They were led by Eskinya, chief of a southern group of Chokonen who had aspired to succeed Cochise. His resentment of Taza may have contributed to the fight.

In March 1876 the Dragoon bunch joined some Coyoteros on a raid and returned from Sonora with gold. Some of them took it to Nick

Rogers's Sulphur Springs stage station to spend for whiskey. During a wild binge that followed at their camp in the Dragoons, Pionsenay, Eskinya's brother, killed two of his own sisters. Somebody had to pay for their deaths, and he saw it as Rogers's fault for selling the whiskey. Pionsenay and others returned and killed Rogers and a man named Spence. They took some whiskey and a horse, and within the next few days some of the same men killed a rancher and took some cattle. Jeffords went with a detachment from Camp Bowie to corner them in the Dragoons, but the Indians could not be pried out of the rocks.

The Tucson papers were outraged, egged on by John Clum, agent for the San Carlos Apaches. At age twenty-two, Clum, a brash New York State farm boy, had been appointed through his membership in the Dutch Reformed Church. Shortly after he arrived in the territory, he became embroiled in a conflict with the army and didn't conceal his contempt for its officers, an opinion that was heartily returned. Arizona's civilians were more amused at his bombast than contemptuous. Clum had agitated for closing down the Chiricahua Reservation and removing its Indians to his San Carlos agency. Recent events put Clum, the Army, and the press in the same camp. They ballooned the • three white deaths at the hands of a handful of drunken Indians into a full-scale Indian war. In his memoirs Clum later wrote, "The Chiricahua Apaches were on the warpath—Southern Arizona was in terror."

Though not terrorized, those who had objected to the idea of the Chiricahua Reservation now had an excuse and made the most of it. Within a month Jeffords was suspended from office and Clum was instructed to move the Chiricahua Apaches to San Carlos. Before Clum arrived on the scene, Eskinya and some of his hard-liners had come into Taza's camp near Apache Pass, hoping to convince the chief to join them in resisting the move. Taza stood firm, but soon competition for the chieftainship, plus stored-up resentment, flared into a fight in which Naiche killed Eskinya. Six of the latter's men were also killed, and Pionsenay was severely wounded.

On June 12, 1876, with a cavalry escort and with the help of Tom Jeffords and Merejildo Grijalva, John Clum led a column of 325 Chokonen out of the pass on the Camp Grant road. Only sixty-one were warriors. One was Pionsenay, who believed he was about to die and had given himself up. Before the band reached the Gila, he apparently thought himself on the mend, for he slipped out of the wagon and escaped.

The reservation was officially abolished in October, but it wasn't the end of the Chiricahua Apaches. An estimated two hundred had slipped away to join the Chihenne in New Mexico. Geronimo and Juh left for Mexico with about four hundred and immediately started to raid on this side of the border from strongholds in the wild Sierra Madre.

## Chapter 6

# Galeyville

Arizona would be a desirable place to live if it had more water and a better class of people.
**Anonymous, perhaps apocryphal**

Three months after the Chiricahuas straggled past Camp Grant into exile, sixteen-year-old Henry Antrim drifted over from Silver City and found work waiting tables at Miles Wood's hotel just outside the post. A month later he stole a horse tied in front of the hotel. The horse was recovered but Antrim wasn't, and a warrant was sworn before Wood in his capacity of justice of the peace. In March 1877 the horse thief came back and boldly sat down at a table, but not too boldly for Judge Wood, who marched Henry to the guardhouse.

Antrim escaped, but he came back in August, got in a fight with Windy Cahill, shot him in the belly, and left Arizona, never to return. He had killed his first man.

A few weeks later Antrim and a companion were on the Río Mimbres, where they met a three-wagon train of immigrants and were invited to share a midday meal. The party was made up of the three Coryell brothers and their families. When the wagons headed west again, the two horseman continued on toward the Rio Grande. They had scarcely parted when Apaches attacked the train, and hearing gunfire, Henry and his partner rode back to join the fight. Faced with less favorable odds, the Indians rode away.

The oldest brother, J. L. Coryell, a machinist from Ohio, with his seven-year-old son, George, at his knee, extended his hand to Henry Antrim. "Give me a name to thank for our rescue," he asked. Henry adopted an alias he would use for the rest of his short life. "I'm William Bonney," he said. "They call me 'Kid.'"

There was no immediate stampede into southeastern Arizona following the removal of the Chiricahua Apaches to San Carlos, but a year later, in the fall of 1877, three families of pioneers were camped in the mouth of Seven Mile Canyon, east of Camp Bowie. The canyon was soon called Emigrant for the Reeds and the Riggses, who had come separately and from opposite directions in the search for a better stake.

Stephen Bayden Reed, a widower with two children, had spent the past year on the Gila, having come from California. Reed was born in Gasconade County, Missouri, to Leonard R. Reed and Rhoda Veach. He was nineteen early in 1848 when he left Independence with his father for Texas, which was advertising for families to settle its vast public lands. The Reeds had harvested one crop when they got the news of gold in California. It was widely believed that there a man could make his fortune in a jiffy, picking up nuggets from the streambeds. The Reeds were hardly settled in Texas. Home ties had been broken, so it was easy for them to keep moving. They joined a party of two hundred and left for California by way of Arizona.

For a year they worked along the Merced River, diverting stream water and shoveling muck into sluice boxes. Then, like most Forty-niners, they learned it was more profitable to provide goods and services to miners than to mine. For a time they cut timber and hauled logs out of the mountains with oxen, building such towns as Mariposa and Sonora. Stephen married Nancy Nestor and located in the San Joaquin Valley near Stockton and began to farm. They had a son, Wesley. After the Civil War Nancy died and Stephen married the widow Sanderson, who had an infant daughter, Lucinda Isabella. Stephen got the itch to move, and remembering favorably the grassy valleys and timbered mountains of Arizona, he pulled up stakes again in 1875.

In the spring of 1876, the Reeds reached Safford, where a small group of farmers had settled the year before. They arrived in time to clear land and get seed in the ground, and while their crop matured, the removal of the Apaches from the Chiricahua Mountains opened up that land for one more move. Apparently Stephen's second wife died on the Gila Valley farm, for in the fall of 1877 only three family members left the valley for Apache Pass: Stephen's stepdaughter in a bull-drawn wagon driven by Wesley, and Stephen driving a small bunch of cattle.

Brannick K. Riggs and his brother, James Monroe Riggs, and their families had moved to southeastern Arizona more recently. Brannick was a Confederate veteran born in Mississippi and raised in Arkansas. After ranching for a time near Bandera, Texas, in 1870 he and his brother had come west to the Purgatoire River (known as the "Picketwire") near Trinidad, Colorado.

For six years the brothers raised cattle, cut logs, and mined coal on the "Picketwire," then in the fall of 1876 moved to Safford, Arizona. When Brannick yoked up his oxen and strung out his herd for the move, he left behind his oldest son, Tom, who had a thriving business with his cousins cutting crossties for crews laying track for the Santa Fe Railroad. Brannick and Mary Riggs's oldest daughter, eighteen-year-old Rhoda, and son William, fifteen, helped with the cattle, and twelve-year-old Martha helped herd the younger kids.

In Safford in the fall, the Riggs brothers met the Reeds, and they all threw together to trek south for new homes on the now-open Chiricahua Reservation. When they got to Camp Bowie, they found they may have been lucky to reach it. They had been oblivious of danger, but disturbing news had reached Camp Bowie by the telegraph wires that had recently linked Bowie with Camp Lowell near Tucson, the new Camp Grant on the west side of the Pinaleños, and Fort Bayard, New Mexico. Apaches were loose again. Things hadn't been altogether quiet since Taza and most of his people went in peace to San Carlos. Some of those who had stayed out were still causing trouble. The preceding January Lt. John A. Rucker with units of the Sixth Cavalry from Camp Bowie had a fight with hostiles in the Pyramid Mountains south of Barney's Station. In May a gang of six renegades who had been harrying the area killed two mail carriers near Camp Bowie, and not long after that Lt. Timothy A. Touey, on a scout from the post, blundered into a force of fifty hostiles in the Animas Mountains.

While the Riggs and Reed families were on the road, Victorio and Loco and over three hundred of the Chihenne who had recently been forcibly removed from the New Mexico reservation to San Carlos left there and went up the Gila, headed for home. Pionsenay, up from Mexico, went with them as far as the Mogollons with a small following of Chokonen, then swerved south and returned to Chihuahua.

It seemed like a good idea for the three families to stay banded together near the soldiers until things settled down. Seven Mile Canyon had water and was far enough from Camp Bowie for good forage for their stock but close enough for security. It was also a source of basic supply, but more important, it provided work. Until their removal, Indians had cut prairie hay and hauled firewood out of the hills to Camp Bowie and the stage station in the pass. The Reeds and the Riggses earned a little by doing that work and by selling or trading butter and milk.

By November many of the New Mexico Apaches had been rounded up, or had given up, and were being held at Ojo Caliente, but throughout the winter there were loose bands of raiders making occasional strikes against isolated ranches or vulnerable travelers. In December Apaches out of Mexico under Juh attacked a wagon train in Doubtful Canyon, killing several men and getting away with all the livestock. By chance Lieutenant Rucker and a patrol stumbled into the raider's camp in the Animas Mountains, killed fifteen Indians, and recovered much of the stock.

In April 1878, to help police the border country, Camp Supply was established in White River Canyon and garrisoned with men of the Sixth Cavalry from Camp Bowie. In three months both the camp and the canyon were renamed Rucker after Lt. Tony Rucker died there while trying to rescue a man from the flooded creek.

Also in April Geronimo, who had been taken to San Carlos from Cañada Alamosa with Victorio's band, became discontented with reservation life and slipped away with a few followers. In May six men were killed and a number of horses and mules were stolen between Silver City and the border. In September a party of wandering Apaches were found off the reservation near Pinos Altos, and a couple were killed and some horses taken from them. The rest were chased down the Playas Valley to Mexico.

By late fall 1878 Stephen Reed had been a year in what he'd expected would be a temporary camp in Emigrant Canyon. Most of the recent Indian trouble had been on the New Mexico side of the Peloncillos, and a couple of dozen prospectors were now working in the foothills on the northeast flank of the Chiricahuas. He thought it was safe to move out, and the site he chose was Cave Creek Canyon, a choice that may have been weighted by the winter camp of a squad of Camp Bowie soldiers in the canyon's mouth.

The shortest trail from Emigrant hugged the foot of the mountains on Captain Tidball's route of fourteen years earlier, but Tidball had been afoot and Reed had a wagon. There was now a well-established road from Camp Bowie passing the mouth of Emigrant Canyon. It rounded Rattlesnake Point and struck out straight into the valley for the San Simon Cienega, then out Granite Gap to join the stage road near today's Lordsburg. From the cienega he could make his own road up the gradually rising plain to the canyon. He found the soldiers bivouacked at the narrows, and he camped close by, near today's ranger station.

At Stephen's camp the canyon pinched down to pass between cliffs and steep talus only a few hundred feet apart. Four miles upstream at the junction of two forks was a spring in a basin of open oak woodland, and there he found the spot he wanted to settle. There was good grazing for his cattle and a few flat acres of arable land near a supply of timber in the creek bottom. He couldn't get a wagon to the basin through the tree-choked, boulder-strewn canyon, but over the winter he made it possible.

During the winter Leonard Reed came from California to join his son on Cave Creek. He was getting old for pioneering; he was born while Lewis and Clark were making their famous discovery of the upper Missouri. His life had spanned the conquest of the West. This time he let his son break trail for him.

Still in his prime at fifty, Stephen could swing an ax. All winter he and Wesley cut through tangles of fallen timber and felled trees, leaving it to Leonard to manage the oxen to pull stumps and drag the heavy logs to the side. By spring they had a road and were able to move camp to what would be "the Reed place" for forty years.

Through the spring and summer of 1879, the men cut cypress, fir, and pine logs, squared them with a broadax, and raised the cabin walls. They dug out a saw pit and put up a frame for sawing lumber with a whipsaw brought from California. Thus they were able to frame doors and windows, make a board floor, and shingle a roof with pine shakes split out with a froe and put on with cut nails brought from Silver City, one hundred miles away.

Stephen Reed's was the first family to settle in the Chiricahuas. The second was only a few months behind. In the spring of 1879, Louis Prue, a soldier discharged at Fort Bowie (promoted from "Camp" to "Fort" in April), brought his wife, Annie, and his little daughter, Rosa, into the mouth of Bonita Canyon, only a dozen miles from Reed but a hard day's hike over the mountain. Prue was a French Canadian raised in New York State, a veteran of the Union army and three hitches with the Sixth Cavalry in New Mexico and Arizona. He was preceded in Bonita by a bachelor named Newton, said to have been an army deserter, who had a shack there for a short time.

It is possible that another single man was in the mountains by that time. In the early 1880s a market hunter, Alonzo Dionysius "Tex" Whaley, was living in what became known as Tex Canyon. Jesse James Benton, who bought Whaley's place at the mouth of Shake Gulch in the '90s, wrote in his memoirs that Tex moved there and built a cabin in 1872. It seems unlikely that the Chokonen would have permitted that, but it *is* possible that he risked it as early as 1876 or '77.

At about the time Prue moved to Bonita Canyon, Maj. William M. Downing, his wife, Elizabeth, and their grown daughter, Delia, settled on Pinery Creek nearby. Downing had gone to California from Kentucky and then to Colorado, where he operated a sawmill. In the spring of 1879 he freighted the equipment to Arizona and put it back together on Locust Flat in Pinery Canyon, about seven miles up the canyon, above the junction of the north fork.

Brannick Riggs's family was now alone in Emigrant Canyon, brother Jim having moved to the new mining camp of Dos Cabezas near Ewell's Station on the Butterfield road. Brannick wrote to Colorado asking his son Thomas, known as T. J., to come down and help them move. Mary had just had their tenth and last child, and they were ready to go.

Leading a pack horse, T. J. and his cousin, William, left for Arizona in June when the passes were free of deep snow. They rode the Santa Fe Trail to Albuquerque, then went west by way of Zuni and St. John. As a precaution in crossing Coyotero country in the White Mountains, they bedded down some distance from the campfire. They forded the Gila above San Carlos, crossed Santa Teresa Pass, and went on to Dos Cabezas, where they had a "sit-down" meal with Uncle Jim before going on to Emigrant Canyon.

In July the young men helped Brannick move his outfit over Apache Pass onto Bonita Creek, where he made his home about three miles below Louis Prue. His ranch became the center of "The Riggs Settlement," where many of his children's children's children live still. With the move made and the family settling in, T. J. and William returned to Colorado. For the protection of numbers, they joined the returning freighters who had delivered Downing's sawmill machinery.

With the Prues and the Downings close by, Brannick's location on Bonita Creek wasn't isolated. He was fifteen miles from Jim in Dos Cabezas and only ten miles from Fort Bowie by the trail over Bear Springs Pass. Close to the time of Brannick's move to Pinery, Joe Schaefer, his wife, and their three children settled their Bar ZZ Ranch at the west entrance to Apache Pass, only eight miles away. The Schaefers, coming from Missouri, had joined a California-bound train of emigrants in Texas and left it at Apache Pass. Another member of the wagon train to quit it and settle in Pinery was a young German bachelor, Christopher Grauer.

The Reeds also had neighbors. When Stephen and his children

came to Cave Creek, the cavalry's presence was brief, but Nicolas Hughes lived twenty-five miles away on the lower end of the San Simon Cienega. Hughes was born in Westmeath County, Ireland, and like many another Irishman, came west with the U.S. Army. He served at various posts in New Mexico and then married Josefa Armijo, of a prominent old Albuquerque family. He ranched and traded cattle at Ascención, Chihuahua, for a time before moving to the cienega with his wife and three children, probably in 1878. The San Simon Cienega, with its grove of black willows and cottonwoods and a meadow of sacaton so deep in places that a man on horseback could just see over it, was especially attractive to anyone who had crossed the glaring flat of a dry lake bed. When no water was standing in the cienega's many pools, a shovel could reach it quickly. In 1878 or '79 John McGill moved in a half mile below Nick Hughes. McGill had been in the Sixth Cavalry with Prue but chose a different side of the mountain after his discharge. And in '79 Alex Arnett with his wife and children located several miles below McGill at the north end of the cienega.

That same year Bill Stark and Al George camped three miles up the valley southeast of Hughes. William Achilles Stark, from southwestern Missouri, had been drawn to Leadville, Colorado, at the peak of its boom. He didn't find a fortune but he found a mighty cold winter, and he found a partner in Albert George, the "Kansas Kid," who had come up to the Arkansas River with a herd of Texas longhorns. They left that cold, snow-choked country for New Mexico, each with his own wagon and team. They crossed the San Agustin Plains, plodded by old Fort Tularosa to Silver City, and halted on the cienega, where the warm sun shown almost every day.

While those men and Reed were putting down roots, the handful of prospectors crawling over the brushy foothills was increasing. All the outcrops on the rough slopes of Harris and Davis Mountains, as well as the ridges between Whitetail and Turkey Creeks, were being explored by the optimistic, who chipped off rock samples and erected monuments, hoping to make a strike. The Mining Law of 1872 allowed a person to claim an area 600 by 1,500 feet. The area could be irregular in shape but couldn't exceed 90,000 square feet. The lingo spoke of "staking a claim," but rather than planting a post in bedrock, the usual practice was to erect a cairn of rocks at the corners. A tobacco can or a bottle was placed in one, with a witnessed location notice containing distance and bearing to a permanent datum point established by the government. The notice was recorded with the county. Directions were estimated or shot in with compasses that may or may not have reckoned on declination. Distances were often measured up and down hill by pacing, and the witnesses sometimes imagined. A yellow notice in a tomato can on one abandoned claim read, "Witnessed by God Almighty and my dog Juno." It is easy to see why there was confusion in areas with much activity, and contention if a claim proved to have any value.

To hold a claim, one had to do one hundred dollars of "assessment" work on it each year and post an affidavit attesting to it with the county recorder. That work could consist of the cost of dynamite and the labor, at the going rate, of building an access road and making holes in rock.

One way of prospecting was to find a promising site, then drill, blast, and dig down into it and follow a vein until it got rich enough to develop—or poor enough to abandon. Another approach was to stake as many claims as possible and still keep up the assessment work. The first method was most likely to produce ore, but the second might be more profitable. If someone else hit a bonanza in the vicinity, the undeveloped claims would immediately jump in value.

Whatever the method, few prospectors had the training to run a mining operation, and most preferred to look for a prospect than to mine it.

It was the lure of extractable minerals that brought to Arizona what small American population it had. (The term *American* is used advisedly. In that day those who had been Mexicans or were descended from Mexicans called themselves, without apology, *Mexicans*. Those who came west from the states or immigrated from Europe through the states were called *Americans* by everybody.) In the 1850s the mines in the Santa Ritas and the Patagonia Mountains attracted them;

in the early '60s it was the Prescott gold rush; and later, gold drew men to Ehrenberg on the Colorado River. Prospecting was the popular avocation of the time, and monuments marking the corners of undeveloped claims dotted Apache Pass. Among those who had staked them out were Captain Tidball, Tom Jeffords, John Finkle Stone, Sydney DeLong, and John Dunn.

Ireland-born "Captain" Jack Dunn had been prospecting in the mountains around Silver City when Apaches ran off with his horses. He was more angry than scared and tracked them alone until he ran the thieves to ground down near the border and stole his horses back. His resourcefulness won him a scouting job with the army. Returning from a scout in Mexico in 1877, he and Lt. Tony Rucker made camp at Iron Springs, at the south end of the Mule Mountains. The springs' foul-tasting, mineralized water led Dunn to look for a better source, which he found under Castle Rock. On his way back to camp, he picked up a promising piece of rock from an outcrop, which later assayed at twenty-two ounces of silver. He shared his find with Rucker, and they located the Rucker Mine.

On their way to Fort Bowie, the party ran into George Warren and grubstaked him to develop the claim. Before Warren reached the Mules, he stopped for a respite at Camp Huachuca, which had been established only four months before. He got drunk, gambled away his stake, and shared his knowledge as well. Others went in to jump the claims that, when developed, became the nucleus of the Bisbee mines. Warren, for his part, got a fifteen-year-long hangover. After his death the suburb for the elite of Bisbee was named for him. Dunn, like a good gambler, shrugged and continued to scout—and to prospect when he had time for it.

A month after Jack Dunn picked up that interesting rock in the Mules, Ed Schiefflin, who had come down to the San Pedro Valley from Signal in Mohave County, found ore in the Tombstone Hills, which was responsible for the birth of Cochise County a short time later. Returning to Signal with his specimens, he found one of them to assay an astounding two thousand dollars to the ton. Ed formed a partnership with his brother, Albert, and the assayer, and the three returned to the site of discovery. In the spring of 1878 Ed's pick knocked off a piece of ore that was estimated to yield an incredible twenty thousand dollars a ton. Within a year the town of Tombstone had been laid out, a post office opened, and an estimated one thousand people, mostly men, occupied the town and the hills nearby.

Soon every piece of the hills around Tombstone had been staked and recorded at the county seat in Tucson, and latecomers spread out to prospect outlying ranges. Even amateur geologists knew that mineral is often concentrated in areas of stress faulting. They recognized the Apache Pass Fault running from the south side of the Dos Cabezas Mountains, into the Chiricahuas on the west side of Cochise Head, across Whitetail and Jhus Canyons, and ending at the mouth of Cave Creek. Near its south end they found limestone that seemed to be the same as Tombstone's.

By the time the Reed cabin was roofed, there were a hundred or more would-be miners busy organizing the California Mining District only eight or nine miles from the door. They collected on the flat just below the mouth of Turkey Creek Canyon, on the right bank above the granite tanks in the creek bottom, optimistically calling their camp Chiricahua City. In a burst of enthusiasm characteristic of western expansionism, one of them wrote to the *Daily Arizona Citizen* in Tucson:

> A new camp with a boom is springing up and a town is being laid off. The people in camp commenced to take and improve lots as fast as marked off. It is located on a beautiful mesa or plateau of land . . . slightly undulating toward [the] San Simon Valley. The rush for lots became a stampede. Tents went up every fifteen minutes; fence poles, wickyups, hockells [jacals] and all kinds of cheap improvements. . . . From Turkey Creek, nearby, brush and posts and rail and house logs were being brought on wagons and carts, on horseback and on foot. The new town of Chiricahua City . . . looks . . . some like Rio Janeiro . . . having a large plaza. . . . A. C. Rynerson & Co. are going to move their store on to the northeast corner; the Dickson House will adorn the southeast.

A prime mover at Chiricahua City, a boomer looking for the main chance, was John H. Galey. In 1859 Galey was teaching school in

Titusville, Pennsylvania, when the first oil well blew. He took notice and within a year had a gusher of his own. Described as slight and unobtrusive, he had a modesty that masked a keen and inventive ambition of more than one kind. He was married three times, and years later a son wrote of him: "He was pretty handy with the ladies and admired beautiful women."

John Galey got to Tombstone late in 1879 and drifted to Turkey Creek, where he arrived in the middle of the excitement and decided to get on board. He bought the Emma Bryant, the Icicle, and the Keystone mines, and in October 1880 bought a major interest in the Texas Mine from Samuel Wessels for ten thousand dollars.

Jack Dunn hadn't lost the itch and had been prospecting out of Fort Bowie, supporting his habit by tending bar for Sid DeLong, the sutler. He called the mine he located in the head of Pinery Canyon's north fork the Hidden Treasure, but everybody else referred to it as the Dunn Mine. To raise capital to develop it, Dunn had sold interests to John A. Duncan and Thomas Burns and had been hand-sorting ore and packing it out on mules. Wessels arranged to buy the Dunn and the adjacent Mayflower for ten thousand dollars, then resold them to Galey, retaining one-quarter interest.

Galey organized the Texas Consolidated Mining and Smelting Company with Wessels and Sam's brother-in-law Joseph Bowyer as partners. They ordered machinery from San Francisco and cut a wagon road through the greasewood to San Simon in time to greet the Southern Pacific Rail Road, whose tracks reached that point in the summer of 1880.

By October the four-horse stage of R. R. McLeod's California District Stage Line met the trains and brought passengers and mail to the thriving camp. By December the partners had driven an eighty-foot shaft in the Texas Mine and had started a tunnel to intersect the Dovetail, another of their claims. Fifty men worked in the mine in three eight-hour shifts and built a five-hundred-yard road to the site of a proposed smelter. Others cut wood and made charcoal for smelting. Across the creek the Rough and Ready Mine had a sixty-foot shaft, and nearby the Washington and the Tame Buck were beginning to sink shafts.

Although there were two hundred men in the canyon, Chiricahua City was dying only three months after it was born. In January 1881, to be closer to the work, the Galeyville Townsite Company laid out a new town across the creek on a bench less than a mile upstream, near the Texas Mine and the site of the proposed smelter. Everybody flocked to Galeyville. The *Tombstone Epitaph* reported it to be "a flourishing town, containing a Post Office, fourteen stores, seven saloons, four meat markets, three blacksmith shops, two corrals, one doctor's office, and about forty houses and tents." The reporter may have exaggerated the number of mercantile establishments but was probably close to the mark in the matter of liquor dispensaries.

A few weeks later "F.W.C." for the *Arizona Weekly Star* wrote of Galeyville:

> The continued clatter of the hammer and saw is a convincing argument that the boom is getting . . . more substantial, and there is not . . . a doubt that the near future will show up Galeyville one of the best mining towns in Arizona. . . . The new smelter . . . is expected daily and as soon as running will be the means of giving a further impetus to mining.

Sam Wessels, while waiting for the smelter, which was to be his particular responsibility, did a little moonlighting, as the *Star* explained:

> Another of those delightful hops for which Galeyville is getting famous took place last week. Mr. Weasles [*sic*] new and commodious lodging house tent was engaged for the occasion, where the beaus and belles of the town assembled to trip the light fantastic and enjoy themselves generally. The tasty and elegant costumes of the ladies was particularly noticeable and, right here, it would not be an injustice to the other towns of the Territory to say that, for its size, Galeyville can more than hold its own for the number and beauty of the fair sex that adorns its society. The dance and lunch which was gotten up in style at the Cosmopolitan Hotel was greatly enjoyed by all.

Jim Hancock arrived on the scene just in time for that sparkling soiree. Unlike nearly all the others who made Turkey Creek such a lively place that day, Hancock didn't leave. He died there fifty-six years later.

James Covington Hancock was born in Indiana and was thirteen when his parents took him to California, where he went to work for Harrison Gray Otis as a "printer's devil" on the *Santa Barbara Press*. In the fall of 1880 he rode with his stepfather in a mule-drawn hack to Tucson and went right to work as a delivery boy for the Pusch and Zellweger butcher shop on Mesilla Street. Two months of that was enough, and with two others for company, he made his way to Galeyville. Although the camp was still mostly in tents, frame houses of lumber freighted around the mountain from Major Downing's mill in Pinery were going up fast. Hancock soon had a job in a butcher shop.

Al George rode a nervous bronc by the shop one day. The butcher carelessly waved a piece of paper, which spooked the horse, nearly dumping the Kansas Kid. Al drew his pistol and fired a shot at the ground near the butcher. It didn't have a calming effect on the horse, but it caused Jim's employer to sell out and leave the camp. Jim then hired on with A. G. Higbee, "General Merchandise." In three months Higbee closed up and moved back to Silver City, and Jim began clerking for Frank McCandless in his store and post office.

Other general stores were C. S. Shotwell's and A. C. Rynerson's. Specialty shops included Thomas Vaughan's bakery and that of Israel Burdick, shoemaker. The Foster & Blake Brewery was in operation early in 1880, with two German immigrants, Albert Fink and Jacob Strohl, making beer. The names of five of the seven saloons have come down to us: Nick Babcock's, Holterman & Hollings, McCarthy's, J. H. Tomlinson's, and S. W. Waring's. Stephen Reed found a ready market at several eateries for produce from his large garden. A black couple, "Snowball" and Rosa Johnson, ran a restaurant, and meals were also served at three hotels: the Dickerson House, the Cosmopolitan, and Tom Whitehead's Miner's Boarding House.

Whitehead had been a very young guerrilla in the southern cause in Missouri during the war. With the war's end he had found his social environment unfriendly and had moved to Prescott and the more relaxed life of a hotelier.

The *Arizona Silverbelt* of Globe advised the readers of its January 29, 1881, issue: "We are in receipt of the first number of the *Ari-*

*zona Bulletin*, published at Galeyville, Pima County. . . . It contains 28 columns of instructive editorial, spicy local items and well-selected clippings, as also a fair share of advertisements." Unfortunately, no copy of the *Bulletin* is known to exist.

Galeyville news was also reported in the *Weekly Arizona Citizen*: "Provisions are reasonable. Starr's 'extra' flour is only $6 per one hundred pounds, and other supplies in proportion. The blacksmith shop of Bostick & Bro. is supplied with two skilled workmen . . . where work is done at eastern prices: horses shod all around at $2.75. . . . Freighting from the San Simon station is $12.75 per ton to this camp."

The same paper in its issue for February 13, 1881, reported that the Texas Mine had almost doubled in size in the past two months: "[It] is still being developed as rapidly as men and money can accomplish it, and is becoming more valuable daily. The main shaft is now down 140 feet, with drifts at 65 and 100 feet."

By May the company had thirty thousand bushels of charcoal on hand and hundreds of cords of wood stacked for making more. Tons of ore were stockpiled when Wessell's smelter was hauled out from San Simon. It was a small water-jacketed furnace: an iron shell thirty-six inches in diameter, encased in a hollow metal jacket in which water flowed—a type popular with western miners, as it was relatively portable and could be bolted together to stand on four six-foot pillars. Crushed ore was shoveled into limestone flux and charcoal, the furnace was fired, and air was blasted up from the bottom through the column of material. Melted ore was drawn off through taps near the bottom, and the slag—a lighter froth—through a couple of spouts placed a little higher.

Although the assay was high, averaging two hundred dollars, the first run was disappointing. The ore from the Texas Mine was in a limestone matrix expected to be the flux, but it wasn't "self-fluxing" and the mineral couldn't be separated from the gangue (the worthless matrix). Experimentation with other fluxing rock revealed that mixing one part limestone from a mine in Granite Gap, across the valley, with two parts of Galeyville ore worked fine.

The Granite Gap Mine was owned by Harry Elliott, a strapping young graduate of the University of Tennessee and a junior member in a Silver City law firm. Elliott was more interested in prospecting than in law, but he had neither a smelter nor capital and was glad to lease his mine to the Galeyville company. Ore from the Texas Mine piled up, but before another run could be made, Granite Gap ore had to be mined and stockpiled, and fifteen miles of road laid out to freight it to the smelter on Turkey Creek.

Sam Wessels applied himself to those matters while John Galey took stage and train to Pennsylvania to raise money. The company had spent about a quarter of a million dollars but hadn't sold any bullion yet. By early summer Galeyville had a life of its own beyond the Texas Mining and Smelting Company, with a population in 1881 estimated at four to six hundred, with perhaps as many as a thousand if people in the surrounding area who traded there were included. Among the latter were three Irishmen, William W. Shanahan and the brothers John and Mike Keating—all ranchers. The Keatings lived between Whitetail Canyon and Wood Canyon at a spring in the mouth of the short canyon that now bears their name. Shanahan located in the mouth of Whitetail Canyon and built a cabin in the sycamores.

Another to settle Galeyville's outskirts in 1881 was John Augustus Chenowth, a rebounded Californian who, like Hancock, stayed in the country. In 1854 Gus had crossed Arizona on the southern route and for a decade had logged on California's Feather River. He came to Arizona with his fleet of wagons and eight-horse teams to haul goods from the terminus of river transportation at La Paz to the growing camp at Prescott and carry lumber back with him to the placers of La Paz and Ehrenberg.

In September 1868 Chenowth was at La Paz when a peaceful party of thirty Yavapai Indians came to town. Some of the women and children begged at a store for flour, but after a while they all withdrew to the town's outskirts to camp. After several hours of whiskey, patrons of the La Paz saloon concluded that the Indians were about to attack the town. At 3 A.M. Chenowth led a party of teamsters to the camp and fired into the sleeping Indians, killing half of them and wounding most of those who escaped.

Capt. William Price, charged with the protection of the Prescott–
San Diego road, sent troops to investigate, but it was nearly two weeks
before they arrived and arrested a local man for taking part in what
the captain termed a "cold-blooded cowardly murder committed by
low-lived, drunken cowardly villains." The U.S. district judge turned
him loose.

The incident at La Paz wasn't random. Miners had been subjected
to horse stealing and petty theft for some time and held Indians to be
vermin. Chenowth and his men had the approval of most of their fellow citizens. A man had recently been killed by Indians (though not
necessarily the same ones), and Irrateba, the chief of the Mojaves,
had warned the whites of impending trouble. Irrateba may have had
his own objectives. The Yavapais, as well as the white men, were in-
fringing upon Mojave territory.

In 1869 Chenowth moved to the Salt River Valley, where he helped
build the first dam and canal. He put in a farm of his own and became one of the founders of Phoenix. At the same time he kept his
wagons rolling, and his route became a triangle with apexes at Prescott, Phoenix, and the new port of Ehrenberg—La Paz having been
left high and dry by a shift in the river channel.

Maricopa County was formed in 1871, an eventful year for Gus. In
the first marriage in the new county, he was wedded to twenty-year-
old Mary Murray, a pious girl who was fond of handing out religious
tracts. He attended the Democratic Convention, was nominated for
sheriff, and shot and killed his opponent.

As superintendent of the Salt River Canal, Chenowth had been at
Maricopa Wells on business. When he returned he heard that the Republican candidate, "Whispering Jim" Favorite, had campaigned in
his absence, telling people that he and Gus had agreed that the win-
ner of the race would appoint the loser to be chief deputy. Gus hadn't
made such an agreement, so he went to Jim's ranch to ask him about
it and found him at the corral. Favorite denied making the alleged
statements and refused to make a retraction.

Precisely what was said by whom, and in what tone of voice, was
known only to the two of them, but Chenowth had a reputation of

being quick to anger. At any rate, at some point Jim grabbed a shotgun and let fly at Gus, incredibly missing him. Jim threw the shotgun aside and vaulted into the corral as Gus was drawing his pistol. As Favorite ran for the opposite side of the pen, Gus poked his six-shooter between the poles and shot him.

The community accepted Chenowth's claim of self-defense when he exhibited the hole burned in his pocket by the smoking wad from Jim's shotgun. But Gus, having eliminated his opponent, felt the appropriate thing to do was to remove himself from the race. In 1879 the Southern Pacific tracks reached Maricopa, twenty miles south of Phoenix, forecasting a downturn in the need for horse-drawn freight, and Chenowth looked for another field beyond the end of steel.

Driving a small bunch of cattle, he left Phoenix with Mary, three-year-old Ivy, and their infant son, Charles, and went south to the prairie on the east side of the Huachuca Mountains. He found work for his teams freighting lumber from the new Chiricahua mills in West Turkey Creek.

The previous summer Philip Morse had set up his steam saw and planing mill on Saulsbury Flat, on the Ward Canyon fork of West Turkey Creek. He cut pine and fir logs on the west slope of Fly Peak (then called Turkey Mountain) and chuted them off the slope on a skid road of parallel logs, traces of which can still be found high in North Ward Canyon. After Gus hauled a few loads of lumber to Tombstone from Morse Canyon (as West Turkey Creek was known for many years), he freighted lumber from Major Downing's mill in Pinery around the north end of the mountains to Galeyville. There he met a man who offered him the temporary use of his jacal of adobe-plastered pickets at the upper end of the San Simon Cienega. Gus moved his family in, and his benefactor presumably never returned to reclaim his shack.

The lifeblood of Galeyville was mining, but its stores and saloons also attracted a swarm of drifters whose means of support were obscure and whose disdain for decorum was notorious.

The unelected leader of this element was a good-looking young cowboy named William Brocius, who had come into the country as a legitimate cowboy helping to move a herd of Texas cattle to San Carlos. Now, though, when he worked at all, it was to steal cattle for a ready market. Known as "Curly Bill" for his head of thick, black, curly hair, he was a big, muscular fellow with a mercurial temper. Friendly enough, even jovial at times, in his cups he could be morose, mean, and dangerous.

Curly Bill is suspected of being the principal actor in this story in the *Weekly Arizona Citizen* for June 5, 1881:

> It is said the cowboys put Mr. G. L. Upshur through a primary course in singing on the train from Tombstone to Galeyville recently. . . . Upshur was "taking in" the forward car where the boys were, when they requested him in language more forcible than polite, to sing for their amusement. Considering discretion the better part of valor, Mr. Upshur favored the audience with his best, but not entirely to their satisfaction, for the boys, with many a "G-d D—n you, open your mouth wider when you sing," forced him to exert himself to his utmost. When they had pumped him dry they permitted Mr. Upshur to retire to the sleeping car, where he staid for the rest of the journey. If this really occurred then it is a shameful outrage on a peaceable passenger, and if it did not, it is a libel upon the cowboys.

Galeyville wasn't well equipped to regulate antisocial behavior. James Goodman, known as "Webfoot" for his Oregon origins, was town marshal. A miner who followed the surge from Signal down to Tombstone, he wasn't a professional lawman. The only court was that of the justice of the peace, G. W. Ellingwood, whose qualifications were equally flimsy.

Several cowboys rode into Galeyville one day in May and commenced to get liquored up. Among them were Curly Bill and Jim Wallace, a veteran of New Mexico's Lincoln County War. As Bill began to feel his liquor, he started baiting Jim, and to prevent things from getting serious, his pals took Bill's pistol and separated them. Wallace went to the corral, saddled his horse and led him to the front of McCarthy's saloon, dropped the reins to "ground-tie" him, and then stepped up on a little porch in front of the door. Jim Hancock later described what happened.

Hancock was talking with Milt Hicks in Higbee's store, seventy-five feet away. He asked if Milt thought Jim would ride off before there was trouble. Milt, a friend of Curly Bill's, had just said he hoped so when they heard a shot. Brocius, who was in a saloon across the street from Babcock's, had seen Wallace on the porch and started over to him. Jim waited until Bill was in the middle of the street, then shot him with a pistol. Men came pouring out of buildings, and those who earlier had tried to keep the peace now began to choose up sides. Before war broke out, big Harry Elliott stepped out in the street with a rifle.

"Hold on, boys, let's keep it quiet and talk it over," he said, "I'll kill the first one to make a crooked move."

Curly Bill was alive, but with a bad wound through the neck. Deputy Sheriff Billy Breakenridge, who was in town on county business, arrested Wallace. Judge Ellingwood's log book entry for the next day, May 19, 1881, reads: "Territory of Arizona vs James L. Wallis. Charged with attempt to murder Wm. Broshie [Curley Bill]. Charge dismissed on the ground of self defense."

Wallace had more to fear from Curly Bill and his friends than from the law. He left camp immediately. Breakenridge met him in San Simon the next morning and bought him lunch, but he was never heard from again.

Galeyville had no jail and little citizen concern, so Ellingwood kept things as simple as possible. A week after Wallace's case was dismissed, Y. M. Purien, "charged with an assault with a revolver with intent to do bodily harm," pled guilty to a misdemeanor and was fined thirty dollars. A couple of months later, in his capacity as acting coroner, the judge presided over a jury inquiring into the death of Jonathan Barton. The verdict was that he "came to death by disuse of the heart."

Often the citizenry handled things themselves without resorting to law. Dick Berry, a dimwitted fellow who swamped for the saloons, had a yen to be one of the outlaws. In good-natured ridicule, Berry was called "Shoot-'em-up Dick" or "Prairie Jack." He came into camp one day riding an old horse and leading a burro. Curly Bill, recogniz-

ing the animals, demanded that Dick return them. With a mixture of
anger and contempt, he told him, "If you can't do better than to steal
from a busted down old prospector, get out of the rustling business."

One of the group of ne'er-do-wells that infested Galeyville was
would-be badman John Rogers, nicknamed "Cherokee Jack," who
demonstrated his ineptitude for outlawry to Gus Chenowth. Shortly
after Gus was settled down at the cienega, he had to go to the county
seat in Tombstone on business. (He likely thought he was a citizen of
Arizona. It would be two years before the state line was surveyed, re-
vealing that his home was almost a mile into New Mexico.) A cowboy
who'd been staying with the Chenowths had a fine, blooded horse. He
suggested Gus take his horse rather than his own common broomtail,
saying, "He'll give you a better ride, and he needs the exercise."

So Gus was well mounted when he topped the divide at the head of
Jhus Canyon in a drizzling rain. There he met Rogers, who had come
up from the west side of the mountains, headed for Galeyville. They
chatted a bit, then Jack pulled his pistol.

"Well, stranger, I guess I'll trade horses with you," he said as he
stepped off and started to untie his cinch.

Huddled in his yellow oilskin slicker, with rain dripping from his
beard, Gus seemed docile enough, and the rustler carelessly put his
gun away. Reaching under his slicker, Gus pulled out the pistol tucked
in his belt, and Jack whirled around when he heard the click as the
hammer was pulled back.

. "Now put the saddle back on your horse and get out of here, or I'll
let the daylight through you," Chenowth commanded. Cherokee Jack
responded with such alacrity that, as he rode away, Gus called after
him, "Son, you'd make a good soldier. You take orders real good."

That is the way his son, Charlie, wrote the story after hearing Gus
Chenowth tell it to his family many times over Sunday dinner, and it
has the ring of authenticity. It was the seed of more elaborate versions
that have become part of the local folklore. In one of those accounts
Gus dismounted as ordered, but he pulled a rifle from the boot under
his stirrup leather as he did so. Keeping his horse between himself
and the outlaw and pointing his buffalo gun from under the horse's
belly, he disclaimed any interest in trading horses but pointed out

that his saddle was getting old and beat up and that he'd be happy to swap saddles.

In his later years Gus was quite religious, possibly through Mary's influence because no such bent is recorded for his earlier years. Though not ordained by any denomination, he was a lay preacher and would read a few verses or come up with a prayer at the drop of a hat. Hence the most frequently told story of his encounter with Cherokee Jack: Gus is ordered to give up his horse *and* saddle and pleads, "You wouldn't take an old man's bible would you?" The outlaw allows him to rescue the bible from his saddlebag, but instead of a bible, Gus pulls out a pistol, wheels, and shoots Jack in the brisket. The "old man" (he was forty-seven) then calmly lashes the dead body across the outlaw's saddle and leads his horse into Galeyville, where the next morning he conducts a proper burial service over his grave.

In a variation of the last account, Gus has offered to say a prayer for the sinners in a Galeyville saloon, and one of the patrons with a skinfull baits him to the point where Chenowth's notoriously short fuse burns out. Gus kills him with a single blow of his fist—and, of course, with the victim unable to protest, preaches a sermon over his grave. There is no coroner's report of either of these last two killings on Judge Ellingwood's handwritten record.

Tales like these, told with such relish, may be as important to the understanding of the times as what really happened. They reveal what it is people *want* to believe—and that may say more about us than simple facts.

Cherokee Jack wanted to be taken seriously. He had failed to get Gus Chenowth's horse, but he was still trying to be a badman. At gunpoint in a saloon, he ordered an old miner to sing for him, then he pistol-whipped him about the head. He picked a fight with a burly miner, Pat O'Day, in Shotwell's store one summer day in '81, but once again—and for the last time—he fumbled it. Someone got his pistol and Pat got him down. While they were rolling around on the floor, Pat grabbed a new three-pound single jack and began to work him over. "Don't kill him in here, Pat. Drag him outside," Shotwell called out.

When Pat pulled him out into the street, bystanders started to intervene but then thought better of it. Nobody really wanted Jack around anyway. Pat borrowed an army-issue Springfield that stood by Shotwell's counter and dragged the inert body down to the slag heap by the Texas smelter, from where, moments later, a shot was heard.

"What was that shot?" someone asked in mock surprise. Cherokee Jack Rogers was found sprawled on his back and his head blown open. A makeshift coroner's jury quickly reached a verdict: "Death from gunshot wound at the hands of someone unknown to the jury." The body was rolled in an old tarp and buried next to the road downstream from camp a little way.

Judge Ellingwood's court procedure itself made the news when a Galeyville correspondent signing himself "Clipper" wrote this account for the *Arizona Weekly Star* on September 19, 1881:

EDITOR OF THE STAR: Permit me to give a brief history of a trial before a border justice of the peace. . . . David Estis [Eustis in Ellingwood's records] was one of two men who robbed a game of about four hundred dollars at the midnight hour in the town of Galeyville. . . . Estis entered the front of the saloon in which the game was being played, armed with a Winchester and six-shooter, his "pal" passing in at the rear of the house armed in a similar manner. They ordered the players to throw up their hands and surrender all their cash. This accomplished Estis proceeded to the corral of Babcock and Co. and . . . confiscated a valuable horse, making the total clean up about $500. Estis was subsequently arrested by Deputy Sheriff Goodman and tried . . . and discharged. His honor ruled in the examination of the witnesses that they could not testify to the taking of the money (ordered by the bandits to be left on the table) unless they . . . knew to whom a particular parcel of the money belonged. This could not be proven as all the occupants of the room were commanded to absquatulate instantly. . . . Thus you see, a single *pair* in Galeyville wins $500.

While the tending of cattle was a respected trade in Arizona of the 1880s, the word *cowboy* was more often than not a derogatory term, indicating a lawless ruffian. There is some historical basis for that.

## Chapter 7

# Cowboys and Indians

This whole territory is peopled by a community of gamblers, thieves, robbers, murderers and adulterers. . . . I intended to bring my family . . . but now I would rather be burned alive, than suffer them to live in such a society.

**W. F. Hall**

There had been cattle in Arizona since the late 1600s in small herds, providing for a sparse population of settlers and a smaller number of priests and soldiers. Drovers brought Texas herds across Arizona to California in the 1850s, and in the '70s cattle were driven back from California to feed troops stationed in the territory and Apaches on reservations. Then in the late 1870s the new towns of Globe, Bisbee, and Tombstone created new markets.

A California contractor who supplied beef on the hoof was New Hampshire–born Col. Henry Clay Hooker. In 1872 he established his Sierra Bonita Ranch in the north end of the Sulphur Springs Valley to fill some of his government contracts.

Still, for several years most of the cattle slaughtered in the territory were steers raised in California or increasingly in Texas, and not much breeding stock was brought in. Two factors altered the situation: isolated ranches were safer from Apache threat, and the arrival of the railroad made it easier to ship to distant markets. By 1880 several large cow ranches were established in southeastern Arizona. The Babocomari Ranch, near old Camp Wallen north of the Huachuca

Mountains, ran 3,600 head; John Slaughter had a herd of 2,500 in Mule Pass; and Hooker's herd, wearing his Crooked H brand, had expanded to 5,500 head.

Moving a herd from Texas took a dozen or so cowboys for an average drive of 1,500 to 2,000 head. Most of the men were laid off after delivery. Even the cattleman bringing cows in to start a breeding ranch didn't need as many men to take care of them as it took to get them to the new range, so the population of out-of-work cowboys increased. A large established ranch might use twenty men at roundup, but what made a range cattle operation possible was free grass and low overhead. A cowboy was overhead.

It took twenty-four three-year-old fifteen-dollar steers to pay a hand's wages of thirty dollars a month for a year, and a few more to feed him. After a roundup, crews were whittled down to half a dozen for the rest of the year. Cowboys tended to be strong farm boys from sixteen years old to the midtwenties who had a yen for adventure and no other prospects. With so many young men feeling invincible and left with time on their hands, it is little wonder that many got into trouble. Not every man who was in trouble was a cowboy, but enough were that a troublemaker was often dubbed "cowboy."

In a country where more cattle were eaten than were produced and more horses ridden down than were raised, horse stealing and cattle rustling presented employment opportunities, as this story in the *Weekly Arizona Citizen* for December 11, 1880, illustrates:

> For some time the settlers and ranchmen of the San Simon Valley . . . have been subjected to a regular course of theft, which resulted a short time ago in the murder of a man named Martin. On the night of the 22nd of November seven head of horses and mules belonging to Turner and Lindeman, were run off by a band of four outlaws whose headquarters were in a portion of the valley. . . . A party of six settlers immediately armed themselves and started in pursuit . . . and after following them into Cloverdale District, about 60 miles distant into New Mexico, succeeded in recapturing the stock, together with eight head which had previously been stolen from parties in Shakspeare [*sic*]. The stock was brought back to the ranch of Turner and Lindeman, which is

on the road from the San Simon station to the new California Mining District. . . . The ranchers are organizing to . . . protect themselves, and we may expect to hear of some neck-tie parties soon in the valley.

George Turner wasn't so lucky when a few months later, with a government contract to furnish beef to Fort Bowie, he went into Sonora to buy steers. He and his partner, Galeyville butcher John McAllister, came across a herd that seemed to be unattended and started driving it north without benefit of a bill of sale. They were overtaken and killed, and their bodies were later recovered with the purchase money intact. It probably didn't occur to the vaqueros who nailed them that they were there to *buy* cattle. Turner's ranch was evidently on San Simon Creek, about where the Portal–San Simon road crosses it.

None of the small ranchers had the capital to build up much of an operation, and most of them, like the Apaches, looked to Mexico as a source of supply. Turner had been a kind of banker for rustlers, as he paid cash for stolen cattle to fill his contracts. A few of the rustlers, like those who ran off the Turner-Lindeman horses and like Curly Bill Brocius, for whom the Arizona Stock Association offered a thousand-dollar reward, didn't care who they stole from, but most of them only rustled Mexican ranges, a socially acceptable activity.

One of the ranches in the Animas Valley, no more than a shack and a picket corral, belonged to Mike Gray, a realtor in Tombstone, who bought the place for three hundred dollars from Curly Bill, who then moved a bit south and made another headquarters. Mike was seldom at the ranch himself, leaving it to his nineteen-year-old son, Dixie, who was sometimes joined by his older brother, John, when the latter could be spared from his duties at the Tombstone post office. There is no evidence that the Grays were directly involved in rustling, but their location twelve miles north of the border made them neighbors to several who were.

The boys were just rolling out of bed when a neighbor rode in before sunup from his camp in Double Adobe Canyon, eight miles north, looking for help. During the night Mexicans had taken one hundred head of his cattle. John and Dixie grabbed a couple of left-over biscuits and saddled up. They found four more cowboys at Billy Lang's at Cienega Spring, where thirty-two years earlier Mangas Coloradas had braced the party of Forty-niners. They followed the trail east, overtaking the herd on Deer Creek, on the east side of the Animas Mountains. The Mexicans were bluffed off with no loss of life. As the cattle were driven back the way they had come, the Gray brothers came to realize that they had helped retake cattle that had earlier been stolen below the line.

If theft of Mexican livestock was regarded complacently, stealing horses from neighbors was not. Major Bill Downing went out to his corral on Pinery Creek one morning to find the bars down and a team of mules gone. He followed their tracks several miles up the canyon and found the animals tied to an oak tree. A few feet away lay Dick Berry, fast asleep. "Prairie Jack" was still aspiring to be a horse thief. Downing quietly secured Berry's rifle and slipped the pistol from the sleeping man's holster. He then got him up and used the thief's own saddle rope to hang him from the tree he slept under. He led his mules back to the ranch and rode to Tombstone to notify the sheriff.

An attempted robbery in the San Pedro Valley in March 1881 had a bearing on activities in and around Galeyville. Bound for Benson from Tombstone with twenty-five thousand dollars in silver bullion under the care of the Wells, Fargo Express Company, the Tucson and Tombstone Express Line's stage labored up a sandy rise six miles north of Contention City. Bob Paul, the "shotgun messenger," had just taken over the ribbons from Eli Philpot, the regular driver. At the top of the hill, three men stepped out of the mesquite and opened fire, killing Philpot and a passenger. The frightened horses bolted into a run, but Paul was able to bring the coach and its treasure safely into Benson.

By first light Sheriff John Behan was on the trail of the bandits, as was a small posse led by Wyatt Earp, the deputy U.S. marshal, who was also a Wells, Fargo detective. Riding with Earp were his brothers, Virgil and Morgan. Four days later, after making a loop of more than a hundred miles, the combined posses ran Luther King to ground not far from the scene of the crime. King confessed to having been a horse holder for Harry Head, Jim Crane, and Bill Leonard, who, masked and on foot, did the dirty work.

Wyatt Earp was particularly interested in finding them, certainly for the twelve-hundred-dollar reward that was offered for their living or expired bodies but also, according to some suspicious citizens, to silence the witnesses. The rumors were that he had foreknowledge of the robbery and that his close friend, unemployed dentist and professional card player John Henry "Doc" Holliday, had been on the hill with the other three and was responsible for one of the murders.

Wyatt Earp, by virtue of having outlived most of his contemporaries and through good press, has become the model of the frontier lawman standing against the forces of evil—an almost mythological hero. His reputation among the people he left behind when he quit Arizona wasn't quite so glowing. He was raised in Iowa and had been a freighter, a buffalo hunter, and a policeman in Kansas towns along the westward-pushing railroad before coming to Tombstone. He aspired to be sheriff of the newly created Cochise County but was edged out by Behan. He listed his occupation in the county register as "salonkeeper," but his main source of income was gambling.

Not long after the ineffectual holdup, the three fugitives—Leonard, Head, and Crane—stopped by the Grays' and, tacitly admitting their part in it, told John the enterprise had been masterminded by Wyatt Earp. Little is known about Harry Head, but Slim Crane was a middle-aged cowboy and teamster in the Tombstone area. Bill Leonard was a watchmaker from New York City who had come west for a cure for tuberculosis. He had stopped for a time in Las Vegas, New Mexico, where he opened a jewelry store and became acquainted with Holliday, who practiced dentistry in the same building. Leonard was handy at intricate work, and while he and his two companions rested at the Gray ranch, he remodeled a rifle for John, accepting as pay a dog-eared copy of *The Life of Bill Hickock*. He spent hours reading the adventures of Wild Bill to his spellbound partners.

Meanwhile, sometimes in a bunch and sometimes split into smaller groups, the Behan-Earp posses made their way into the San Simon and Animas Valleys on the trail of the highwaymen. Frank Leslie, deputized by Wyatt Earp for the search, rode up to Grays' and was invited to step down and eat a bite. Known as "Buckskin Frank" for his accustomed fringed deer-hide shirt, he was tidying himself at the wash bench outside the door when Jim Crane rode in on a stolen army mule.

They sat down to dinner in the cook tent behind the cabin, Jim with his rifle across his lap. He knew that Leslie was looking for him, and no doubt the deputy recognized his fellow guest. It is possible that Buckskin Frank didn't want to abuse the Grays' hospitality, but he also knew that Jim Crane had him at a disadvantage. After finishing his beans, he pushed back his chair and walked out to tighten his cinch and ride away.

While posses continued to spur tired horses across dry lake beds and stony mountain passes without overtaking them, the three fugitives, who were well known in the country, made no strenuous effort to elude them.

On June 11 Leonard and Head picked a fight with Ike and Bill Haslett in Eureka, New Mexico, on the northeast side of the Little Hatchet Mountains, thirty miles from the Gray ranch. We don't know now what the two had in mind, perhaps a last effort to gain a reputation or to pick up a little spending money by robbing the Haslett store. An eyewitness suggested that it was on behalf of their friends, the Grays, who wanted the Haslett range.

At any rate, the two outlaws drunkenly bragged they were going to kill the Hasletts, so the latter ambushed them from behind a stone wall, killing Leonard instantly. Harry "Kid" Head, reportedly still suffering from wounds received at the stage robbery, was hit again but lived long enough for Morgan Earp to get to Eureka to take his dying confession that only he, Crane, and Leonard were involved in the killing of Philpot and his passenger. Unfortunately, nobody unrelated to Wyatt was present to hear his exoneration.

The outlaws were a loyal bunch and thought they owned the country, as indeed they came close to doing from the Chiricahuas into the Animas Valley. Curly Bill, Jim Crane, and John Ringo, a hard case from Galeyville, wanted revenge for the deaths of Head and Leonard, and they rode for Eureka. On the way they stopped at the Gray ranch, where Gray dissuaded Crane from compounding his felonies, but Brocius and Ringo rode on, banged into the store, and killed both of the Hasletts.

It is unclear exactly when, but sometime in the early summer Curly Bill led a sortie into Mexico and came back with three hundred head of stolen cattle. With him were Alex Arnett, John McGill, Milt Hicks, and Jake Gauze of Galeyville, and an Animas Valley rancher, Charles Snow. Brocius and Snow cut out their shares near the border, and the rest of the herd was driven north for another cut at Double Adobe Creek. From there Arnett and McGill continued north, aiming to take their cattle to their ranches on the San Simon Cienega via Cowboy Pass, while Milt Hicks angled off to the left, intending to drive his bunch to the canyons near Galeyville. The two parties were still in sight of each other when pursuing Mexicans swept in from the south, intent on recovering their livestock. They headed first for Arnett and McGill, who, seeing they were outnumbered, abandoned their herd and loped over to join Hicks, who then took flight as well. It couldn't have been easy to turn the tired cattle around to retrace their route—they had been moved fifty miles with little time to rest or graze—but the vaqueros took them back to the west side of San Luis Pass, south of the Animas Mountains, picking up an extra two hundred head from the Green and Thomas ranch on the way.

Hicks and Arnett found Curly Bill resting from his labors, but he pulled his boots back on to join the chase. The three picked up several recruits: Joe Hill, Jim Hughes, Tall Bell, and John Ringo. Charles Green and Charles Thomas, who had just lost some cattle, also fell in. They caught up with the exhausted cattle in the pass dividing the San Luis and Animas Mountains. Now the odds were closer to even, and while the footsore stock bawled and scattered, the cowboys chased the Mexicans off, killing several of them. The Thomas-Green cattle were cut out, and the rustled Mexican cattle taken to the Brocius ranch, where a few days later Newton H. Clanton bought them for fifteen dollars a head. "Old Man" Clanton, as he was called, was not known to have *raised* cattle, but he had been dealing in stolen cattle for years on the Gila and on the San Pedro.

Hard on the heels of this chousing of cattle back and forth across the border, early in the morning of August 1, a party of about a dozen Mexicans with a string of pack mules made its way from the east down Skeleton Canyon, on the west side of the Peloncillos. Coming from Chihuahua with cash, they were headed for Tombstone to buy goods to take into Mexico without paying duty. Waiting for them at a narrow place in the trail was an ambush. The surprise was successful. Four of the would-be smugglers were shot out of the saddle, and several mules were killed. Four thousand "adobe dollars" taken in the robbery were packed to a cabin occupied by Al George at the spring in the mouth of Cave Creek Canyon, and there the loot was divided.

There are several accounts of the affair—none by anyone who took part. The number of men said to be involved varies. Some put Old Man Clanton in command, and others claim Brocius was in charge, but the most reliable sources say that neither was there. Reuben Haddon of Galeyville knew them all personally, and years later he named the participants: Ike Clanton, the old man's son; Ike's younger brother, nineteen-year-old Billy; Joe "Hill," an alias for Olney, wanted in Texas for grand theft and murder; Jim Hughes, from the San Simon Cienega; and three more Galeyville men, "Rattlesnake Bill" Johnson, Jack McKenzie, and another whose name Haddon couldn't remember. Jim Hancock filled in the roster with the name of his friend Milt Hicks.

To be in place at the right time, the robbers had to have had information about the smugglers' plans, and Nick Hughes's son, Jim, was vital to their success. Raised in the vicinity of Janos, he had only recently moved with his father and Mexican mother to the San Simon Cienega and still no doubt had many informative contacts in Chihuahua. If Haddon and Hancock had it right, those seven had almost six hundred dollars apiece for a day's work—maybe a day and a half with travel time. A salvaged pack mule may have been used to get the 150-pound load of pesos to Cave Creek for the cut.

Latter-day romanticists, dreaming of buried treasure, have grossly exaggerated the money the mules carried. Myth has the robbers either unable to carry it all away or, overcome by fear or guilt, caching their loot somewhere and then forgetting where they put it. It isn't credible that those self-reliant men didn't find a way to get that money spent. Hancock reported that "they had Galeyville flooded with new Mexican silver dollars that looked like they had just come out of the mint." There may have been some new hats and a few pairs of boots, but it's hard to believe that saloon keepers, faro dealers, and prostitutes didn't have most of the "treasure" by Thanksgiving Day.

That assessment doesn't discourage the true believers, one or more of whom can be seen almost any day in the year combing Skeleton Canyon with a metal detector. The statement of Milt Hicks is enough to keep alive the dream: "The Mexican leading the heaviest packed mule got away, and us a-shootin' at him."

John Gray didn't find his government job too demanding, for after a short tour of duty at the Tombstone post office, he took another leave of absence to help his brother get the Animas ranch on its feet. Traveling horseback, he went over the Chiricahuas via the recently abandoned Camp Rucker and Tex Canyon, crossed the grassland of the San Simon Valley, and entered Skeleton Canyon, fifteen miles from the ranch across a pass in the Peloncillos.

In Skeleton, through a cloud of flies, John saw the bloated carcass of a mule wearing a pack saddle. A mile farther into the canyon, his horse shied from a dead horse with a saddle sporting the flat pommel of a Mexican tree. The two dead animals and their rigs spoke of a running fight involving Mexicans, and he uneasily pushed on to the ranch. Dixie knew nothing about any battle.

John stayed over to hold down the ranch while his brother went into town for a haircut and other pleasures, but because of what he'd seen in Skeleton Canyon, John suggested that Dixie not take that direct route, especially alone. If there had been trouble there, the Mexicans might come back for revenge and they wouldn't care which gringo got in the way. Dixie knew that Billy Lang planned to move a herd from his place on the border to Tombstone, and he knew his help would be welcome. He decided to join the drive for the safety of numbers.

Old Man Clanton had a buyer for his Mexican cattle in Billy Lang's father, who had a Tombstone butcher shop, and he had agreed to help the younger Lang deliver them. From Tombstone Charlie Snow, who was in on the initial rustling of the cattle out of Mexico, joined them, along with Billy Byers, a young cowboy from Kansas. Upon reaching the Lang ranch, they found Harry Earnshaw of Tombstone there, looking for milk stock to buy, and they enlisted him to help with the drive. On the evening of August 11, Jim Crane, still eluding posses and riding chuck line up and down the valleys, rode into the Lang camp in time for supper. The Grays had been trying to talk him into giving himself up to the law, and when he learned of the trail drive, he decided to go along. While eating dust, he would mull over whether to surrender to Sheriff Behan or turn back at the edge of town.

At daylight on the twelfth, the cattle were strung out headed west across the valley. It was an easy job for five cowboys, with Old Man Clanton to drive the wagon. The herd was small and was trail broken from all the summer's movement in and out of Mexico. By dusk the men had made almost fifteen miles to the mouth of Guadalupe Canyon. They made camp in the first open space, a few hundred yards southeast of Monument 73 marking the border common to Arizona and Sonora, in a spot surrounded by three small hills.

Dixie Gray, not knowing the exact date of departure, arrived late at Lang's place and found it deserted. He set out to follow, but being several hours behind, he was still in the mountains when dark caught him, so he hobbled his horse and stretched out on his saddle blanket in the canyon bottom.

Early in the night the cattle spooked at something and ran back up the canyon the way they had come. Dixie woke as the cattle ran by him, and he saddled up to help the cowboys bring the runners back to the bed ground. For the second time that night he threw his blanket down, this time next to the wagon.

At first light Clanton was up rattling pots and pans, preparing to fix breakfast. He started a fire and was building a pot of coffee when Harry Earnshaw and Billy Lang got up and started to pull on their pants. Charlie Snow, who was riding night herd, rode up to the cook fire, hoping coffee was ready. Lang sensed that the cattle seemed nervous. "Charlie, get your gun," he said to Snow. "I think there's a bear out there. If so, kill it."

Snow pulled his rifle from its boot under his leg and rode up one of the hills into a volley of gunfire that also rained down onto the camp. Though hit, he stayed in the saddle for a half-mile run before his pursuers knocked him off his horse and riddled his body on the ground. Old Man Clanton was killed instantly and fell face down across his fire. Jim Crane and Dixie Gray were killed in their blankets.

Billy Byers was still in his bed, clothed but bootless, when the firing started. Having overheard the talk of a bear, he first thought that the boys were shooting one, and he jumped up to reach for his Winchester just in time to see Clanton fall. Not immediately finding the rifle, he grabbed for his revolver and started running blindly and barefooted. He hadn't gone forty feet when he took a bullet through the body, and in a few more steps a shot in the arm knocked the pistol from his hand and he went down. Just as he hit the ground, Earnshaw and Lang passed him, running for shelter in the canyon. Earnshaw ran across gravel and thorn with a boot in each hand.

Both men dropped down behind the sketchy cover of a clump of brush, then ran for it again. In a few strides Lang was shot through both legs and brought down, but he rolled over and opened up with his six-shooter. His covering fire allowed Earnshaw to escape with a bullet scratch across the bridge of his nose. Billy Lang's were apparently the only shots fired in defense. He killed one and wounded another of the attackers before he, too, was killed.

Byers saw riders coming in from the direction Lang and Earnshaw had gone, wearing his companions' hats. Others were stripping the bodies of Clanton, Gray, and Crane. He made himself less conspicuous by undressing, even to his finger ring. With as little movement as possible, he hid his clothes under him, and played 'possum. Several times the attackers, bent on plunder, walked by, ignoring his naked and bloody body. Just before they pulled out, a vaquero rode by and fired several rounds at him. One grazed his head, and others kicked dirt over him. He lay still, and the Mexicans rode off with weapons, saddles, clothing, and all else they could carry, driving the few saddle horses and cattle that hadn't scattered too far for them to gather quickly.

An hour or more passed after the last rider had disappeared before Byers dared to move. Finally he crawled back to where he had dropped his pistol, and as he picked it up he heard the sound of a horse approaching. He pulled back the hammer, determined to kill a Mexican, but the rider proved to be an American rancher who had heard the firing and, after a safe interval, had ridden up cautiously to investigate. He helped Byers up onto his own horse, led him to a shady spot in the canyon, and left him there, promising to return with a horse for him in the evening.

Harry Earnshaw kept on running but stopped when he was out of range to pull on his boots. It may have been terror that caused him to lose his way, but when John Gray saw him stagger in to the ranch at dusk, he thought him a tenderfoot not used to open country. Harry had hiked miles farther than necessary and stumbled onto the ranch only by lucky accident. He had seen Clanton fall but didn't know the fate of John's brother or the others. Harry was used up, so John rode alone through the dark across the north end of the Animas range to the little mining camp of Gillespie for help. The miners quickly responded, and soon twenty-five of them were mounted and heading for Guadalupe Canyon. They stopped at Gray's for a team and wagon, then hurried on through the night over ground muddy from the summer rains to reach the campsite as the rising sun lit the grisly scene. The nude bodies of Clanton, Crane, Lang, and Gray were found where they had fallen and were loaded onto the wagon. It took a while to find Snow a half mile away. His body had already begun to bloat, so they buried him on the spot. On the return up the canyon, they came upon Billy Byers, who, in a delirium, had wandered five miles from where the rancher had left him. They dressed his wounds and put him in the wagon with the corpses.

In addition to John Gray, the cleanup party included John Ringo, Charlie Green, and Rube Haddon. The attackers were assumed to be a force of Sonoran militia from Fronteras led by a Captain Carrillo. The Mexicans had little concern for the smugglers bushwhacked in Skeleton Canyon, if indeed they even knew about them, but rather were hoping to discourage cattle rustling.

Ten days after the killings in Guadalupe Canyon, the Warm Spring chief, Nana, returned from two months of raiding through the Black Range and slipped by Gillespie to enter Chihuahua in the vicinity of Antelope Wells. With few losses he had taken two hundred head of horses and mules and killed thirty-five Americans. Old Nana had become the leader of these hostile Chihenne Apaches after Victorio and some seventy-five of his people were killed by Mexican troops the preceding October.

The killings by and among the outlaws that started with the attempted holdup of the Benson-bound stage didn't end with the *matanza* in Guadalupe Canyon. Billy Clanton, who had participated in the Skeleton Canyon robbery, was killed along with others by Morgan, Virgil, and Wyatt Earp and Dr. Holliday in a shooting on a Tombstone street on October 26. Two days later Virgil Earp was badly wounded by would-be assassins wielding shotguns. As soon as he was well enough to travel, he went to California for his health.

Except for the local people directly involved, all the rustling and hijacking had no effect on daily life and business in Galeyville. By December enough fluxing limestone had been hauled from Granite Gap to the smelter to make another run. Rube Haddon, who had helped set up the smelter and had worked on the disappointing run the past spring, returned from Gillespie for the new one. The result was encouraging. In ten days the company smelted 100 tons of ore to produce about 80,000 pounds of lead and 190 pounds of silver.

The smelter operated for several weeks but shut down in January 1882. The company's total production since its inception was said to have been valued at less than twenty thousand dollars, a fraction of what had gone into its development. John Galey hadn't succeeded in raising more capital in the East and didn't return to oversee the company's dissolution. Like the gambler he was, Galey lost this hand, but he borrowed a stake and got into another game and became a major player in the Spindletop oil field near Beaumont and the Cushing field in Oklahoma.

To Rube Haddon, who as a nine-year-old boy had seen his parents killed in the Mormon attack on the Fancher wagon train in Utah, the loss of his job was only another wrinkle in a hard life. He went back to mucking out Turkey Creek prospect holes.

On March 18, 1882, Morgan Earp was shot through an alley window while playing billiards in a Tombstone saloon. He died within minutes. Wyatt, who was present at this shooting, thought he knew the killer and went after him. Five days later he cut Curly Bill Brocius in two with both barrels of a shotgun at Iron Springs in the Whetstone Mountains—at least he later claimed he did. Some doubters think the man Wyatt killed was someone else, but Brocius, under that name, never appeared again in Cochise County. Running out of brothers and time, Wyatt, too, left the country for Colorado.

On July 14 John Ringo was found sitting against a sycamore tree in West Turkey Creek with a bullet hole in his forehead. The jury assembled for a coroner's inquest and, in the best position to assess the evidence, called it suicide. But some doubters claimed to have seen Buckskin Frank Leslie following him with blood in his eye, and Wyatt's widow many years later stated unequivocally that her husband had slipped back secretly and dispatched him with a rifle shot. However he died, not many mourned him.

Several years later Frank Leslie was convicted of killing the dance hall girl he was living with and did time in the Yuma penitentiary. About 1900 he revisited his old ranch in Horseshoe Valley, by then known as Leslie Canyon in his honor.

Luther King, the horse holder at the abortive stage holdup, escaped from jail and slipped away to Mexico, doubtless glad to be out of the way. Alex Arnett repaired quietly to his family on the San Simon Cienega, and his son, also Alex, who was a year-old baby when his daddy was running Mexican steers, grew up to become a well-known lawman in Greenlee County.

After regaining some strength, Billy Byers, with a bullet in his belly, drove the Clanton wagon into Tombstone, where the townsmen marveled at the thirty bullet holes in its sideboards. He didn't stay long but went back to Kansas to nurse his wounds. Six months later he received this letter from Ike Clanton, who had neatly stepped out of the shooting that killed his brother:

Charleston, Arizona
Feb. 14, 1882
Billy Byers
Leavenworth

Dear Billy
  Your favor of the 8th duly received. Was truly pleased to hear from you. Everything is running satisfactory this way. I have got the Earps on the hip and am going to throw them good. Jim sends his kind regards. Frank has already gone to Oregon. Jeff Lewis address Colorado City, Texas.

Complements and all those kinds of things.
Ike Clanton

Ike was a little ahead of himself. On the very day that letter was dated, as a deputy with Sheriff Behan, he was to accept the surrender of Dr. John H. Holliday and the two remaining Earps, Morgan and Wyatt, for the murder of Ike's brother and his companions the previous October. The accused showed up on time with a large band of armed friends. The judge, after sizing up the crowd, denied having jurisdiction and dismissed them. Ike drifted away from the immediate area but not from his occupation. Five years later he was killed by a posse chasing rustlers in Apache County.

John Gray and his father felt too exposed in that no-man's-land of the Animas Valley, and they were a long way from their occupations in Tombstone. They sold what is still known as the Gray ranch to California capitalists for a reported twelve thousand dollars and used the money, or some of it, to buy out the holdings of Norton and Stewart, the sutlers at the recently closed Camp Rucker. They ranched there successfully for several years.

It isn't known if Harry Earnshaw ever found enough milk stock to start a dairy. He faded away and was lost to history. If he ever had any grandchildren, he had a story to tell them.

Billy Byers came back west to homestead in Colorado, where he *did* tell his story to his grandchildren.

While Mexicans and Americans were so energetically running each other's cattle back and forth across the border, a tense situation was developing on the San Carlos Reservation. Except for the remnants of Victorio's Chihenne under Nana and Kayatenae in the Sierra Madre, all the Chiricahua Apaches were now on the San Carlos Reservation along with Coyoteros—Western Apaches—and a few Yavapais. Several groups not used to living with each other were jammed into an area not suited for so many.

The crowding, the disruption of a way of life, and the fraudulent practices of agency officials all made the people ripe for the teachings of a wraithlike, charismatic old White Mountain Apache shaman who prophesied that the whites would disappear; Mangas Coloradas, Cochise, and Victorio would be reborn; and the old ways would be restored. He taught special songs that would enable all this to happen.

The agent and the soldiers at Fort Apache feared religious fervor would become war fever, and in August 1881 they tried to arrest the shaman at his camp on Cibecue Creek. The effort was botched, and in an ensuing fight seven soldiers were killed along with an unknown number of Indians, including the medicine man. The army poured in troops, and the Indians went into the remote regions of the reservation to avoid reprisal.

The Chiricahuas had been outnumbered by Western Apaches in the Cibecue scrape, but they expected the army to blame them alone. On September 30 Juh, Naiche, and Geronimo led seventy-four of them out of the Gila Valley toward Mexico.

They attacked a ranch, a telegraph-repair party, and a wagon train on the road from Fort Thomas to Fort Grant, killing eleven men. While they were busy stripping the bodies and looting the wagons, a body of troops under Capt. Reuben Bernard—still chasing Apaches after twenty years—came upon them, pushed them into the hills, and pinned them down in the rocks, losing a trooper and a number of horses in the process. After nightfall the Indians slipped away in the dark and went on south.

To cut off the Indians before they reached the border, Capt. Henry Wagner led troopers and Walapai scouts out from San Simon. They camped the night of October 7 on Turkey Creek near Harris Mountain and the next day rode south to San Bernardino, but the Indians had already crossed the Chiricahuas and gone to Mexico.

The fight at Cibecue and Juh's departure for the Sierra Madre caused a lot of recrimination in the army. Gen. Orlando Willcox, commanding the Department of Arizona, preferred charges against the commandant at Fort Apache, who had been the responsible officer at Cibecue. But Sherman, General of the Army in Washington, had little confidence in Willcox and ordered Gen. Ranald Mackenzie to step in from his command in New Mexico to straighten things out.

Galeyville hadn't worried much about Indians. Victorio's and Nana's recent depredations had been east of the Peloncillos, but this last outbreak and the position of the Chiricahua Mountains between the two main trails from San Carlos to Mexico moved the action west again. At a public meeting the citizens organized the Galeyville Militia Company and elected Civil War veterans George Roberts and George Montgomery to be captain and lieutenant. To equip the volunteers, Frank McCandless and Joe Bowyer went to Tucson and got twenty old .50-caliber Springfield rifles and five thousand rounds of ammunition from acting governor John Gosper, out of a shipment from the secretary of war for just such a purpose.

During the winter the hostiles, mostly Ndenda and Chokonen, sent emissaries north to the reservation to induce Loco, who had become leader of most of the Chihenne, to join them. When he was young, the Mexicans called him Loco for his crazed behavior in battle, but now he was nearing sixty. He hadn't gone with Victorio on his final campaign, believing peace the better course. He ignored the appeals from Mexico. In January 1882 Juh sent another message. "We're coming up to bring you with us."

In New Mexico, at Cañada Alamosa, elements of the Fourth Cavalry were preparing for trouble, and new recruit Neil Erickson looked forward to it. Neil had a special interest in fighting Indians. His father had come to the United States from Sweden to make a stake before sending for his family. But in 1874, while working on a track gang in Dakota Territory, he was killed by the Sioux. Wanting revenge for his father's death was a part of Neil's decision to join up. After two weeks in New York, he was sent by train with other recruits to Jefferson Barracks, Missouri, where the new men stood in formation on the parade ground to hear General Ranald Mackenzie ask for volunteers for the Southwest. Private Erickson stepped forward.

He was at Ojo Caliente before Christmas 1881 and was assigned to Capt. C.A.P. Hatfield's Company E, Fourth Cavalry. In March 1882 the post was closed down and the company joined the rest of the regiment at Fort Craig on the Rio Grande.

Later in March Al Sieber, scouting for the army, ran across Indian sign in the Peloncillos that he correctly interpreted as the tracks of Juh's hostiles making their way north to keep their promise to Loco. On April 19 with about sixty men, Naiche and Chato, a young warrior beginning to gain prominence, slipped into Loco's camp near the subagency at Camp Goodwin on the Gila. Word of their presence reached the agency at San Carlos. The chief of police, Albert Sterling, rode into the night for Camp Goodwin with a single Apache policeman. They were intercepted and Sterling was killed. Two months earlier he had broken up a tulapai party, and maybe it was for revenge that his head was cut off and used as a football.

Loco's fear that he would be blamed for Sterling's death convinced him he would have to go. Although some families escaped to the north, Loco took with him about six hundred Chihenne, including seventy-five warriors. Apaches had experience at quickly catching horses, bundling up what belongings it was practical to carry, and counting children before hitting the trail.

The Gila Valley was no longer Indian country. In the past six years many white families had settled along the river, and freight wagons rumbled through eight communities on a well-traveled road connecting Globe and Silver City. The road and most of the settlement were on the south side of the river, so after looting a freight train near Fort Thomas, the Indians crossed the river and moved east along the north side to avoid trouble.

While Loco shepherded his women and children up the valley, Juh, Naiche, Chihuahua, Geronimo, and their warriors from Mexico ranged out, striking freight wagons, ranches, and parties of prospectors to gather what guns, ammunition, and livestock they could. In the first two days out of Camp Goodwin, they killed an estimated fifty people. Telegraph wires were hot, and alarmed newspapers all over the Southwest railed at the army.

Private Erickson's company at Fort Craig was ordered south to Fort Cummings to join the rest of the regiment. At Nutt Station on the railroad, thirteen miles east of the fort, they were met by the regiment's commander, General Mackenzie, who informed them that Lt. Col. George A. Forsyth and four other companies had left by rail. E Troop was to join them. Greeting Captain Hatfield, Mackenzie said, "These are nice looking men you've got here, Captain, but they are awfully dirty."

They were going to get dirtier. They loaded the horses into boxcars, and the men got on top for a cold night ride to Stein's Pass, arriving at midnight on April 22. Reveille was at 3:30. There was no water at the station, but Forsyth had ordered a tank car from San Simon. It had only two faucets, so it took two hours to fill canteens and to water the horses from buckets.

Forsyth was convinced he could catch Loco on the Gila, and the next morning he marched north with six troops of cavalry. Near Doubtful Canyon his scouts made contact with Apaches, who fell back to a strong position in the head of Horseshoe Canyon, about six miles north. After a long-range firefight that kept the soldiers at bay, the Apaches slipped over the crest. The cavalry had six men killed and four wounded. The Apaches lost two.

Forsyth sent the wounded to Lordsburg by road and took the regiment back to Steins, arriving at 9 P.M. The tank cars were a welcome sight. On only a few pints of water apiece, the men of the Fourth had ridden seventy-eight miles, some of it at a hard gallop, and been in a fight of several hours. It was learned later that the warriors had been fighting a holding action to allow the noncombatants to escape.

During the night of April 23, while Forsyth was moving toward the Gila, Loco led his people out of West Doubtful Canyon into the San Simon Valley. They had acquired a few horses on their way up the Gila, but most of the people were afoot. They crossed the railroad near Vanar, six miles west of Steins, and with warriors riding out on the flanks for protection, struck out for the Chiricahuas at Rattlesnake Point. The fugitives got water and a short rest six miles north of Galeyville—probably at Squaw Spring on Keating Creek, on the north side of Blue Mountain.

With the closing of the Texas Mine, everything had gone downhill in Galeyville. Many of the miners had already left to look for other holes to gopher into, but Galey's partners, Wessels and Bowyer, were still in town. After breakfast on April 24 the two, with another miner named Ayres and storekeeper Cyrus Shotwell, left camp to inspect some mine properties in Whitetail Canyon. They rode down canyon two miles to where the Josephine Trail left the creek to climb a low ridge separating Turkey Creek from Jhus Canyon. In the divide they could see across Jhus onto the yucca-studded Whitetail Flats, where a small party of Apache horsemen a mile away were chasing a lone white man. While Wessels and his companions watched in horror from the shelter of the oaks, the Indians overtook the fleeing man and pulled him off his horse and stoned him to death. Knowing that Loco had left the reservation, the three were armed, but they were too far away to help and were badly outnumbered to boot. They discreetly withdrew to Galeyville, where they raised the alarm.

The few women and children gathered in an adobe building for safety while the men patrolled the outskirts. The Indians approached Galeyville from down canyon and tore up a tent and ran off a few loose horses, but were turned aside by a few shots. They crossed the low divide into Round Valley and went on to cross Cave Creek. From near the mouth of Horseshoe Canyon, they crossed the valley again to go up Skeleton Canyon into the Animas Valley.

The next morning several citizens went out to bury the mutilated body of the victim, who turned out to be Deputy Sheriff Jim Goodman. They buried him between Jhus Canyon and Mackey Wash, near the trail. It is ironic to consider that Juh may have been in the bunch that did the killing so close to the canyon that, unknown to him and with a confused spelling, bore his name.

As fast as the Indians moved, the news of the breakout moved faster by telegraph. Southeastern Arizona and southwestern New Mexico were just short of a state of panic. The depredations of the Indians were severe enough, but the reports exaggerated them several times. The *Phoenix Herald* blew the killing of Webfoot Goodman into this report of a "Galleyville Massacre": "LORDSBURG, April 25. A report, which is reliable, just received from Stein's Pass, says 173 Indians attacked Galeyville and killed thirty-five whites. The Indians are all south of the railroad headed for the Chiricahua mountains. General Forsyth is close on them, and a fight may be expected tonight or early in the morning." The ranchers on the San Simon Cienega were on alert, and the danger was brought closer when, before the action in Doubtful Canyon, warriors roving in advance of Loco's vulnerable band killed a railroad track walker west of Stein's Pass.

On the morning of the twenty-fourth, Alex Arnett put his wife and two-year-old son in the wagon and drove up the valley to join the Hughes family and several of the bachelor stockmen on the cienega at the Chenowth place. Out in front of Gus and Mary's house was a large round adobe corral with walls chest high, a relic of some unrecorded Spanish presence in the valley dating from half a century or more earlier. By prearrangement, the settlers gathered there for mutual protection. There were at least four women: Nick Hughes's wife and their nearly grown daughter; Mary Chenowth with three small children and five months pregnant with a fourth; and Mary's sister, Eula. The women cooked on fires built against the inside walls while the men watched for suspicious movement from the surrounding willows.

There was scant shade thrown by the wall at the south side of the corral, and it was warm enough for flies. The corral held not only a dozen or so people but most of the settler's best horses. It wasn't discomfort so much as boredom that caused some of the men to become restless toward sundown. Nothing had stirred, and some of the men thought the danger, if it ever existed, was past and that it was unnecessary to hunker down in the corral all night. Gus gave it as his considered opinion, based on twenty-five years in Indian country, that it was best to stay put a little longer. The women's safety lay in the number of their protectors. Scattering was folly.

These were independent men, and it was natural that a couple of them gave a glance sideways at Chenowth and proceeded to gather up their possibles. Gus cradled in his arm the large-bored rifle that had ridden against the wagon seat through many miles of freighting. "The first man over that wall, I'll shoot him where the suspenders cross," he said. He sounded like he meant it, and everyone settled down to spend the night.

The evening of the day after they had swept past Galeyville, the Apaches crossed the border and went onto Mexico's wide Llano de Carretas. There was much military activity in their wake. Colonel Forsyth got onto the trail again west of Steins, followed it across the valley, and lost it again. He guessed the Indians would be heading for Turkey Creek, so he made for Harris Mountain and camped two miles from Galeyville at 10 P.M., having marched forty miles. At that time Loco and his band were entering Mexico, having gone more than sixty miles without rest. Forsyth recruited a couple of civilian guides at Galeyville and early on the twenty-sixth struck out on the regained trail of the Apaches. He was two days and one hundred miles behind them.

Capt. Tullius C. Tupper was closer, having left Galeyville twelve hours ahead of Forsyth with a troop of the Sixth Cavalry from Fort Bowie, forty-five San Carlos Apache scouts, and Al Sieber. He had been at San Simon Station on the night of the twenty-fourth when he heard that Loco was at Galeyville. He left for that camp immediately and arrived at daylight on the twenty-fifth to learn that the Indians had recrossed the valley, heading southeast.

Albert Sieber had scouted for the army in Arizona for ten years. He spoke Apache and had intimate knowledge of the country. Tupper took his advice and laid over for the day to take up the trail in the evening when the Indians couldn't see them coming. By midday on the twenty-sixth, they neared the border in the Animas Valley. At the first dim light on the twenty-seventh, Tupper got on the broad track and followed it until after dark. Then Sieber's scouts, working ahead of the column, found the Indians camped at a little cienega at the west foot of Sierra Enmedio, fifteen miles into Chihuahua. They had been there two days, resting from the forced march. Chihuahua, Juh, Naiche, and their raiders had joined Loco's larger band and were celebrating with a dance.

Tupper prepared a dismounted attack at daylight, but surprise was foiled by an early-rising mescal-gathering party from the hostile camp. However, after scouts on the hill above poured a hail of fire down on the Apache camp, the troopers charged, and a detachment drove off the Apaches' horses.

The Indians suffered a few casualties at the first volley but quickly took cover behind boulders at the foot of the hill. They couldn't escape without abandoning the women and children, but neither could the cavalry and scouts pry them out of the rocks. After several hours of firing, the soldiers were almost out of ammunition and Tupper was forced to retire. He pulled back to camp eight miles away, estimating that they had killed fourteen to seventeen warriors and seven women.

According to Apache accounts, three women were killed and four people wounded, including Loco, who suffered a slight leg wound. But when night fell, they were scattered all over the hillside and had lost their horses and gear.

In the evening Forsyth caught up with Tupper and took command of the combined force, now comprising seven companies of cavalry and three of scouts. Forsyth had orders to stay out of Mexico, but believing that Tupper had hurt the Apaches, he determined to hit them again. He hoped that in that wide-open country the Mexicans wouldn't know he was there, and at daylight on April 29 he took up the pursuit.

In the dark the Apaches gathered themselves and headed south again. Through the night and the next day, they straggled to the low pass into the valley of the Río Bavispe. With the troopers behind them, most of the warriors hung back to protect the rear. It was mainly women and children, then, who blundered into a devastating ambush by Mexican infantry under Col. Lorenzo García, who had seen the dust of their advance. Although the Apaches took cover and fought back desperately, within minutes seventy-eight were killed and thirty-three women and children were taken. The rest eventually found refuge deep in the Sierra Madre.

Still a day late, Forsyth met Colonel García, who pointed out that the Americans were trespassing on Mexican soil and asked that they leave. However, the colonel courteously showed Forsyth and his officers around the battleground.

A Mexican lieutenant also guided some of the Americans around the field and showed them a deep arroyo filled with bodies, and scrambling down onto the pile, he fired his revolver into the breast of one still breathing. He pointed out the body of an old gray-haired Apache who, from behind a yucca, had killed eight Mexicans before he lost his own life.

Pvt. Neil Erickson was one of those who surveyed the gruesome scene and shared his rations with Mexican soldiers who hadn't eaten in two days.

Tupper was brevetted for his action at Sierra Enmedio, but to avoid admitting he was illegally in Mexico, the citation read that the fight had been in the Hatchet Mountains of New Mexico.

After Loco's flight a unit of the Sixth Cavalry established Camp Price in Price Canyon in the Chiricahuas, both named for the recently deceased Col. William R. Price, who had ordered the investigation of Gus Chenowth's massacre of Yavapais in 1869.

General Willcox wasn't solely to blame for the Cibecue incident, for Loco's leaving for Mexico, or for the failure to overtake him, but the Tucson and Prescott newspapers called for blood, and Willcox was the scapegoat. He was replaced by General Crook, in whom the army and the citizens had more confidence. Crook came to Arizona in September 1882 and made an inspection trip, after which he expressed his wonder that *all* the Indians hadn't defected, so abysmal had been their treatment by the agents.

Crook had always believed that only an Apache could catch an Apache. He recruited five more companies of Apache scouts and put Lt. Charles B. Gatewood, Sixth Cavalry, in charge, Al Sieber as chief of scouts, and Archie McIntosh as assistant. Felix Martínez (now known as Mickey Free), whose kidnapping from the Ward ranch in 1861 had triggered the "Bascom Affair," was hired as interpreter. Gatewood, nicknamed "Beak" or "Long Nose" by the Indians for that prominent feature, was a Virginian and a West Pointer. In October Crook sent Gatewood to Cloverdale with his scouts to patrol the border. He and they were to play an important role in the containment of the Apaches during the next few years.

## Chapter 8

# Geronimo's Time

> I know plenty about him [Geronimo]. I know that he and others like him were
> the cause of the death of my mother and many of my relatives who have been
> pushed around the country as prisoners of war. I know we would not be in our
> present trouble if it were not for men like him.
> **Sam Kenoi, Ndenda Apache**

Nobody remembers now why Stephen Reed and his father argued so
bitterly in the summer of 1881 that Leonard stormed out and walked
down the canyon to the valley to stay with Gus Chenowth. He was
hot, dry, and still angry when he arrived at the cienega. It was too
much for his eighty years, and he suffered a heart attack and stroke
from which he didn't recover. Before he died, he asked to be buried
at the entrance to Cave Creek Canyon, the prettiest place he'd ever
seen. Gus put the old man's body in the wagon and did that, breaking
the rocky ground on the bench above the creek where the Reeds had
camped three years before.

Stephen Reed had been single for several years when he was married to his fifteen-year-old stepdaughter, Isabella Sanderson, by Par-
son Chenowth, later recording their action with a justice of the peace
in Lordsburg. Their first child, Lula Lee, was born in November 1882
at Soldier's Hole, a stop on the southern road to Tombstone.

Loco's breakout had nothing to do with it, but by May 1882 enough
of Galeyville's population had left that the post office closed. The few

stayers had to go to San Simon to pick up their mail. The California District Stage Line went out of business, and Chenowth bought the coach to use as a family conveyance.

When the McCandless store closed, Jim Hancock lost his job and threw in with Tom Whitehead, whose hotel was empty. In January 1883 the two of them explored the valley for likely ranch sites and made separate camps at two springs, intending to run cattle together. "We were lords of all we surveyed from the head of the cienega to the Mexican line, nearly a hundred miles of territory," Hancock wrote fifty years later. "We could claim it if we wanted to as there was no one to dispute our right."

In those recollections Jim described the places as about four miles apart, twenty-five miles south of the cienega. A year later Walter Neil of the General Survey Office mapped the eastern part of the county, and his map indicates a "house and spring" three miles east of Pothole Peak and another three-and-a-half miles to the southeast and about nineteen miles south of the Chenowth ranch. These are likely the spots Jim and Tom claimed. Because of the threat of Indian trouble, the partners camped together most of the time, and that trouble wasn't long in coming.

The Apaches in the Sierra Madre had more freedom and dignity than they'd had on the reservation, but they hadn't improved their lot economically. By 1883 the old way of life, which had gradually become more difficult, became impossible. A living based on gathering acorns, mesquite beans, and mescal and hunting deer and rabbits required a wide expanse of country. The Chiricahua Apaches had lost nearly 90 percent of their area when they were stuffed into the already crowded reservation. Even when they supplemented venison with Mexican cattle, the meat supply was only barely meeting the demand.

It wasn't only for meat that the Apaches were dependent on industrialized society. A steer hide could cover a wickiup or make moccasin soles but couldn't make shirts or skirts. They needed cloth but didn't grow fiber or weave. They had ceased to make clay pots and stone knives and found rifles more efficient than bows and arrows. It wasn't possible to gather enough piñon nuts and mescal to trade for kettles, knives and axes, firearms and cartridges. Even if they were willing to go back to the old ways, the wild environment of the Sierra Madre wasn't big enough or productive enough to support the five to six hundred Apaches now living there. Raiding had become essential to their life.

In March 1883 Geronimo led a party out of the mountains toward the west to replenish meat supplies from ranches in the Yaqui and Sonora Valleys. While Chihuahua, aided by Chato, Benito, and a couple of dozen others, headed north to acquire arms and ammunition, they embarked on one of the most remarkable guerrilla campaigns in western history. It is most often referred to as Chato's raid, and that energetic young warrior undoubtedly played an important part, but the sixty-year-old chief, Chihuahua, was the real leader.

The raiders crossed the border southwest of the Huachuca Mountains and cut a swath through southeastern Arizona and adjacent New Mexico, sometimes splitting into two or three parties to reassemble at prearranged points. Not many saw them and lived to tell about it. The Apaches first struck a camp of charcoal burners in the Canelo Hills, where they killed four men. Warned by gunfire, the men at a nearby camp drove the Indians off, killing one of them. One party swept as far west as the Empire Mountains and killed three miners at the Total Wreck Mine. They killed one man at "Willow Ranch" in the Sulphur Springs Valley, probably at Willow Springs at the mouth of John Long Canyon. Not far away, Frank Leslie repelled an attack on his 7UP Ranch near the Swisshelms—at least, so Leslie said.

At Ayres Camp, below the forks of Pinery Canyon, three men loaded mine timbers onto a wagon, then went to camp to cook supper. Soon several men came down from a mine in the North Fork to warn them that "at least 1,000 Indians" were moving down the San Simon Valley. Nineteen-year-old Jack Fife saddled a mule, rode down the canyon to warn the people at the Riggs settlement, and spent the night at the Fife ranch.

His father, William Nicol Fife, had been on Pinery about two years, having arrived only eighteen months behind Brannick Riggs. He had converted to Mormonism in his native Scotland and had emigrated to Utah, where Brigham Young delegated him to lead a party from Salt Lake City to southeastern Arizona. Most of the party settled on the Gila or the San Pedro, but Fife and his two wives homesteaded on Fivemile Creek, his brother David about a mile north of him. Fife Canyon and Fife Peak are named for them.

The next morning Jack rode back to work despite his parents' pleading, and his partners, older prospectors Tom Frenoy and Fred Lobley, came down from the mine where they had gone for refuge. They finished loading the wagon, stopped at the creek to water the mules, and set off. All three were on the wagon seat, with Fife in the middle, when Frenoy shouted, "Indians!" One Apache was directly in front of them, and several horses were on their right. They jumped down, unhitched the team, and turned it loose, hoping that taking the horses would occupy the Indians for a moment. Lobley was unarmed and decided to run for it, but he made only a few paces before an Apache rose up in front of him and shot him down. While his killer was beating in Lobley's head with a stone, Frenoy ran up a shallow arroyo coming into the canyon, and Fife on a ridge alongside. From his vantage point Jack saw five Indians ahead of Tom and shouted a warning just as the older man was shot. The Indians immediately stripped his body.

Jack went on up the ridge, and when an Indian arose from the brush just above him, he dropped to one knee to take aim. Before he could fire, the Apache winged him, but Jack's shot was truer, and the Indian's body rolled down the hill to rest against the boy's leg. He fired twice more and believed he had scored two hits, but his cartridges were gone, and he crawled into some heavy brush. The Indians fired the brush to smoke him out, and when the fire got close to him, he bolted for the canyon bottom, where the smoke was settling. Although he was seen and fired at, a bullet striking the sole of his shoe, he was followed up North Fork only a short distance, and he made it to the mine, weak with loss of blood. Later Frenoy's coat was found on a dead Apache.

The hostiles were operating in a country full of soldiers. In addition to elements of the Sixth Cavalry at Fort Bowie and Colonel Forsyth's

Fourth at Camp Richmond on the Gila, General Crook was gathering mules, troopers, and Indian scouts in Willcox for an expedition into the Sierra Madre. Somehow the raiders managed to elude them all, and by riding horses to death and stealing others, they rapidly struck widely separated places.

They crossed into the San Simon Valley and down that to the Gila, where in two attacks they killed ten men near the York ranch between Duncan and Clifton. From Pueblo Viejo the Apaches turned east through the Peloncillos at Ash Springs Pass and into New Mexico, crossing the Burro Mountains south of Silver City.

Judge Hamilton C. McComas of Silver City had mining interests in the Pyramid Mountains, south of Lordsburg. March 28 was a pleasant spring day, and when he left town for an inspection trip to the mine, he combined pleasure with business by taking Mrs. McComas and their five-year-old son, Charlie, with him. They planned to visit an older son that evening. The judge's hack crossed the sandy draw in lower Thompson Canyon to start climbing to the divide at the south end of the Burros when Apaches fired on them from the cover of the oak trees.

The moment of terror was short. Though wounded, McComas whipped up the team in an attempt to get away, but one of his horses was shot and the wagon turned over. The Apaches shot McComas four times, killed his wife with a single shot to the head, and stripped the bodies. They cut the remaining horse out of the traces and headed for Mexico, taking Charlie with them.

The stage driver from Silver City came upon the scene shortly after the killing and careened on to Lordsburg, fearful of meeting the Indians. Colonel Forsyth and five troops of the Fourth Cavalry were in Lordsburg at the time, and at daylight they went out to retrieve the bodies and took up the trail of the Apaches. They came across the corpses of two young men from the Hachita mining district who had been on the road in a wagon when they were jumped and killed with stones. Neil Erickson later recalled that Troop E followed the tracks south into the Animas Valley as far as Double Adobe Creek before they turned back from a cold trail. The Leitendorf Rangers from the mines in the Pyramids, Reuben Haddon among them, made a loop and also found a few tracks but, like the cavalry, failed to make contact.

The raid had been a success for the Apaches. They had killed about thirty, taken many horses, and added arms and ammunition to their arsenal, losing only three men: a warrior killed on the San Pedro, another in Pinery, and Tsoay, who left the raiders to return to San Carlos. When they recrossed the border in New Mexico's boot heel, they had traveled four hundred miles in eight days.

Although Jim Hancock and Tom Whitehead knew of the Apache raid and had kept their eyes open, they weren't touched. They had been in possession of their domain in the San Simon Valley for only about three months when a Texas cattleman, James W. Hall, made a deal with them to quit-claim their squatters' rights to him. With a view to controlling the valley, Hall also bought out Al George and his partner, Bill Stark, reportedly for five thousand dollars. Stark moved around the mountain into the Riggs country, married Brannick Riggs's daughter Mary, and set up a ranch. Al George drifted away. Hancock and Tom Whitehead, after looking around awhile, settled in the mouth of Wood Canyon.

Hall may have been an agent for Clabe Merchant, Jim Parramore, and the latter's brother-in-law, Hugh Lewis, for the three arrived in the valley on his heels and bought him out. Nick Hughes also sold to them and moved his family to Shakespeare. Jack McGill may have sold his place too, as he disappeared from the record. At about that time Joe Hill's short, violent career came to an end when he was thrown from a bronc and killed. His camp, to which he had no title, was forfeited to the partners. Four other small ranches established in the past two or three years along the eight-mile stretch of the cienega—those of Jesse Roscoe, J. M. Black, W. B. Moore, and B. F. Dunn—were also apparently gobbled up. Arnett at the lower end of the cienega and Chenowth at the top held out and refused to sell. The Keating brothers also stayed put in the canyons draining the east side of Cochise Head, and Bill Shanahan didn't budge from Whitetail.

The partners quickly stocked the range with longhorn cattle shipped to San Simon by rail from their ranches near Abilene, then driven to water at the cienega with the cowboys that came with them from Texas. The Stark and George cabin, three miles north of Chenowth's, served as headquarters for the newly formed San Simon Cattle and Canal Company. Lewis, a banker and a partner of Parramore's in a ranch between Abilene and San Angelo, was a financial backer of the enterprise and was soon bought out.

Claiborne W. Merchant, the son of a veteran of the battle of San Jacinto, had raised a company of Texas Cavalry in 1861. He ran a store in east Texas before the war and after it, until about 1870, when he brought a herd of cattle up the Colorado River to start his 74 Ranch in Callahan County, Texas.

James H. Parramore was raised near Gonzales, Texas, where he grew up horseback with a rope in his hand. He served in the Eighth Texas Cavalry and survived Shiloh and Chickamauga. After the war he took several trail herds to Kansas and in '79 established himself on a ranch in Runnels County. Clabe and Jim were friends from the time they were both involved in the founding of Abilene, and they remained friends for life.

On their new Arizona ranch they branded H Lazy H H on left shoulder, ribs, and hip, or 7 Lazy H H. The outfit was sometimes referred to as the San Simon but most often simply as the H's or the Seven H's.

The San Simon wasn't the only big outfit in the valley. The MOK preceded it by a few months when Edward and William Munk, both attorneys, established a ranch in Railroad Pass, at the south end of the Pinaleño Mountains. The brothers were ambivalent about their name, sometimes spelling it Monk. When they arrived, except for a few small ranches, the San Simon Valley was open for one hundred miles from the Gila to the border.

Brothers Austin and Jonas "Stub" Shattuck from Erie County, Pennsylvania, arrived on the heels of Parramore and Merchant in August 1883. The Shattuck boys grew up raising cattle and for the past five years had trailed steers from Texas to Kansas. Foreseeing the end of open range on the plains, they were looking for a place to land. With Jim McNair and other investors from Pennsylvania, they bought up small ranches in the south end of the Sulphur Springs Valley and organized the Erie Cattle Company. From two camps, at Mud Springs and at Double Adobe (not to be confused with the Double Adobe Creek in the Animas Valley), they controlled Whitewater Draw to the border, as well as the Pedregosa end of the Chiricahuas. Their Tumble T cattle also used the malpais country on the divide between the San Simon and San Bernardino drainages and thus bordered the H's on the south.

On May 1, 1883, General Crook left San Bernardino Springs and entered Mexico to bring in the hostiles. He first paved the way by visiting Mexican officials, who, though they didn't have the authority to allow his operation on Mexican soil, were as eager as the Americans to contain the Apaches. They indicated that if Crook was discreet, they wouldn't interfere.

Most of the force that made its way south were the 193 enlisted scouts—Western Apaches with a few Yavapais and Chiricahuas—led by Capt. Emmet Crawford and Lt. Charles B. Gatewood. Also in the party were a troop of the Sixth Cavalry, Crook's personal staff, and Al Sieber.

Tsoay, who had deserted from Chato the month before, agreed to lead Crook to the Apaches in Mexico. On the upper Río Bavispe, "Peaches," as the soldiers called Tsoay because of his clear complexion, was able to take them to the camp of Chato and Benito. Miraculously, they saw the hostiles before they themselves were detected. It was Crook's intent to talk, but the Coyotero scouts had come to fight; several Chiricahuas were killed and the hostiles scattered before the scouts were restrained. One of those who died in the melee was Charlie McComas.

Hauzous, a boy of about thirteen, was fleeing with his mother, Nah-ke-de-sah, and his aunt when they came upon the McComas child, who had been badly beaten with stones in the attack. He was still alive, and they called to him using his Apache name. He responded

weakly, and Nah-ke-de-sah wanted to take him with them, but her
sister convinced her that the boy was so badly injured that he would
die soon and that the soldiers would blame them for his death.

The general learned from captured Indians that the camp was part
of a larger rancheria of Chihuahua's band. Crook loaded one of the
captured women with gifts and sent her back with the message that
he wanted peace, that the attack was a mistake made by the scouts,
and that no soldiers were involved.

Three hours after the woman left, Chihuahua sent word that he
would come in for a parley if Crook would return a horse and saddle
taken in the recent attack. The horse and more gifts were sent back,
and the next day, preceded by about twenty women and a few warriors, Chihuahua loped into camp on his white horse with ribbons
streaming from its mane and tail. He dismounted and shook hands
with Crook, but he was angry. "If I wanted to make peace with someone I wouldn't raid his camp and shoot his relatives," he said. One of
the dead was his aunt.

Nevertheless, Crook and Chihuahua seemed to trust each other.
Geronimo and many warriors were away on a raid, and he wouldn't
speak for them, but Chihuahua said he would return to the reservation. Two days later, on May 20, suddenly Geronimo, Naiche, and
the returning raiders showed up on the hills above camp. The meetings over the next few days were marked by guarded joviality but also
suspicion. It was a delicate predicament demanding the aplomb and
psychology that few but Crook could have mustered. On the twenty-
third Nana came in and all the leaders agreed to return to San Carlos,
but first they had to round up their people who were still scattered
throughout the mountains.

The situation was still ticklish. Crook was worried that Mexican soldiers might blunder in. An attack would blow the agreement and be
an embarrassment to Crook as well. He had exceeded the conditions
of his permit and was in Mexico only by courtesy of a knowing wink.
And further, though they had left Bernardino with sixty days' rations,
feeding all the Indians had made serious inroads on the supplies.

On May 26 Loco came in. He hadn't wanted to go to Mexico in

the first place, and he quickly agreed to go back north, but he needed more time to find all his people. On the twenty-eighth Crook could delay no longer, and he got underway with 384 Chiricahuas. To avoid Mexican patrols, they took a trail north through the mountains and crossed the Bavispe-Janos road, where the previous year Colonel García had killed so many.

When they reached the border where they had entered Mexico forty-one days before, they had five Mexican women with them and a babe in arms, captives taken by Geronimo on his recent raid, but they didn't have Geronimo, who was still out with Naiche rounding up "strays." Six months later, with eighty-five of their people and 350 head of Mexican cattle, Geronimo showed up at San Carlos. On his way north he had sold a number of cattle for ten dollars a head to Mike and John Gray to stock their Rucker Canyon ranch.

He left a few Apaches still roaming the Sierra Madre and adjacent valleys. They killed three Mexicans at Bacachi in June and two more near Oposura in December, and in February 1884 they stole some horses and killed and butchered a cow near Bavispe.

The following summer, in June 1884, the Fourth Cavalry was moved from New Mexico to Fort Huachuca. The regimental commander, Major Mizner, detailed Sgt. Neil Erickson to drive the wagon of Miss Emma S. Peterson, his family's cook and housekeeper. Neil and Emma, the thirty-year-old daughter of a Swedish army officer, began an acquaintance that was to last almost fifty years.

The San Simon and the Erie companies got a new neighbor to the south in 1884, when John Slaughter moved his outfit from the San Pedro to San Bernardino Springs. That *aguaje* had been the site of an Indian pueblo in the 1400s, had refreshed centuries of travelers, from Apaches to Forty-niners, and more recently had been a base camp for Crook's Sierra Madre expedition. Probably Geronimo had watered his cattle there on his way to San Carlos only shortly before Slaughter arrived.

John Slaughter was born in Louisiana, but he grew up in the Republic of Texas helping his father gather mustang cattle. He spent much of the Civil War as a Texas Ranger helping to protect frontier settlements from the Comanches. For some time he ranched in partnership with his brothers and trailed steers to markets in Kansas and Colorado. He was in business for himself on the Pecos River in New Mexico for a short time before moving his cattle to the Mule Pass side of the San Pedro Valley in 1878.

Though only five and a half feet tall, Slaughter wasn't diminutive in any other way, and his calm, self-confident demeanor commanded respect. His confidence stemmed from self-knowledge. He knew he could do what had to be done. He was in no way a belligerent man but had killed when it seemed to him that killing was called for.

Slaughter's new ranch, which spread over one hundred square miles of the San Bernardino Valley, had been established by Ignacio Pérez in 1822 but was abandoned in the 1830s because of depredation by Apaches. A claim to the grant was still in the hands of a Sr. G. Andrade of Guaymas, who sold it to Slaughter. It covered the country from a little north of the springs on the border down to below the confluence of the Arroyo Guadalupe in Sonora.

Most of the sixty-five thousand acres was on the Mexican side of the line, but a deed to the springs and the cienega surrounding them was all the base needed to lay claim to the use of the valley from the Perilla Mountains on the west to the Guadalupes and Peloncillos on the east, and north to the low, volcano-studded divide between the valleys of the San Bernardino and the San Simon. Parramore Crater was the mutually acknowledged boundary of the ranges of Slaughter, the H's, and the Erie.

In late 1884 or early in 1885, Parramore and Merchant were challenged at the north end of their range when the three Ruch brothers laid claim to the lower end of the San Simon Valley between the railroad and the Whitlock Mountains and established a headquarters on the west side of the creek five miles northwest of San Simon Station. They branded inverted triangles on the left ribs and both hips.

In 1885 the pioneer California miner-capitalist George Hearst, owner of the *San Francisco Examiner*, extended his ranching interests when he and two partners formed the Victorio Land and Cattle

Company. Branding Diamond A, they laid claim to about eight hundred square miles of the Animas Mountains and the Animas Valley, an area that included the ranches once owned by the Grays, Newton Clanton, Billy Lang, and the Haslett brothers.

Hearst did things in a big way. Not satisfied with a share of a big ranch, in 1887 he acquired a *latifundia*, a vast area of 1,350 square miles in the Babícora basin of Chihuahua, a property held by his son, William Randolph Hearst, until 1953.

These were the days of open range. The railroad wasn't fenced, nor was the divide of the San Simon and San Bernardino watersheds, so it wasn't unusual for Triangle cattle to drift south into the north end of the Chiricahuas or for H cows to wander north of the tracks. When an outfit worked cattle, representatives from neighboring ranches participated in the roundup. If the H's were branding at the cienega, an Erie cowboy or two would be on hand, and Slaughter would have a man there to make sure that the calves following any Z cows that had drifted north got burned with the Z brand. When the Ruch brothers planned to gather the flank of the Peloncillos for a shipment of steers by rail, it was the courtesy of the time to alert Parramore so he could have a "rep" there to make sure that H cattle didn't get loaded and to ease any strays back up the valley.

Another large outfit represented at San Simon Valley roundups was the Chiricahua Cattle Company of Thomas White, J. V. Vickers, and James C. Pursley, with a headquarters at the mouth of Rock Creek. They claimed the Sulphur Springs Valley north of the Erie and west of the Riggs family's range. The CCC cattle were far from home range in the San Simon Valley, but longhorn cattle were great travelers. There were still many small ranchers on the fringes, but by the mid-1880s the well-capitalized partnerships dominated the business, and it was they who brought in the huge herds that overcrowded the ranges. The cattle population of the territory had soared from an estimated five thousand head in 1870 to almost a million in 1885, when the Erie was credited with forty-three hundred head and the CCC with sixty-one hundred.

A severe drought that year made this crowding even more apparent, and stockmen organized to protest the importation of more Texas cattle. Until then the market for local beef was mostly within Arizona, but the oversupply forced the price of a three-year-old steer down from thirty-five to ten dollars, and ranchers began to ship feeder cattle to ranges in California and Montana.

Crook settled the Chiricahua Apaches in the pines on a different Turkey Creek, about twenty miles south of Fort Apache on the White Mountain Reservation, under the charge of Lt. Britton Davis. After two years there, on May 17, 1885, thirty-four men, eight boy apprentices, and ninety-two women and children bolted for Mexico one last time. The Indian Bureau blamed the outbreak on the army's poor control of the Chiricahuas, while the army claimed that the Indians were incited by civilians, but the cause may have been simply that many Apaches weren't ready yet to subject themselves to the white man's will.

It was Geronimo who spurred the exodus, and later many Chiricahuas blamed him for their eventual fate. He told Naiche and Chihuahua that he had had Lieutenant Davis killed and that the Americans would take revenge on all of them. After it was too late to turn back, they found he had arranged for a murder that hadn't come off. Mangas, son of Mangas Coloradas and Naiche's maternal uncle, was an ally of Geronimo in the flight. Eighty-five-year-old Nana left too. Most of the Apache leaders were at an age when old soldiers usually settle back to tell stories to their grandchildren. Juh, Geronimo, Chihuahua, and his brother Ulzana were all in their sixties. So was Loco, but this time Loco stayed put, as did Benito and Chato, who had been made a scout and had become attached to his commander, Britton Davis.

The hostiles didn't stampede in a bunch but scattered and raised hell in all directions before reassembling below the border. Chihuahua took a party up the San Francisco River as far as Alma, New Mexico, with Gatewood's scouts and two companies of the Fourth Cavalry a day behind them, then swung southeast past Silver City. A battalion of Tenth Cavalry "buffalo soldiers," newly arrived in Arizona, left San Simon to intercept them, but the Indians had scattered in the Mogollon Mountains.

On June 4 a small band of Chiricahuas were headed toward the border when they exchanged a few shots with some cowboys in Doubtful Canyon, then crossed the valley at nightfall within a couple of miles of the San Simon Station. Soldiers of the Sixth Cavalry under Capt. Gilbert E. Overton took up their trail the next morning, but at Cave Creek he judged the trail to be cold and further pursuit futile.

While Overton was riding back to San Simon, another party of Apaches was seen crossing the tracks just west of San Simon. They went up Wood Canyon in the dusk, bypassing the Hancock-Whitehead ranch, and camped near the junction of Cottonwood Canyon. A man named Lindsay lived up Wood Canyon above where the Indians had stopped. He was unaware that they were near until he went out the next morning to walk down his horse and came upon several head of cattle skinned and partly butchered. He promptly went up the side of the canyon and hid in the rocks. After dark he made his way out to the Cross J in the mouth of the canyon, where he found Tom Whitehead. The two went on to San Simon that night and got Captain Overton to take up the trail again.

The Apaches had been in the canyon two nights and a day, had killed seven head of cattle, and had gone over the mountains with twelve horses by the time Overton got there. The soldiers camped at the head of the canyon, where a tributary to Wood still carries the captain's name. Coming down out of the canyon the next day, June 8, the soldiers broke into the Hancock-Whitehead house and made off with some canned goods and two pairs of Jim's new eight-dollar shoes.

Troops and scouts were now deployed from the Chiricahua Mountains to the Rio Grande and north to the San Agustin Plains. From the Fourth Cavalry's new station at Fort Huachuca, Capt. Henry W. Lawton was ordered with three troops to Guadalupe Canyon to guard the Animas Valley and San Bernardino approaches to Mexico. After setting up camp, he split his command, taking two troops to Lang's ranch at Cienega Spring in the Animas and sending Captain Hatfield of D Troop to Skeleton Canyon. He left a sergeant and seven men to guard the camp and forty horses.

A cattleman brought word to Hatfield that the night before, a party of hostiles had taken all the horses from a corral about twenty miles north. The captain crossed the valley in the night and at dawn, with the help of some cowboys, began to cut for sign along the foot of the Chiricahuas between Squaw Mountain and the mouth of Jack Wood Canyon.

While D Troop looked for tracks, Captain Lawton reached Skeleton Canyon and sent orders to Hatfield to work south along the foothills, then cross into Rucker by way of Tex Canyon. When Hatfield arrived at Mike Gray's in Rucker, another courier caught up with him with word that the hostiles' trail had been found in the Animas Valley headed toward Guadalupe Canyon, and that he should backtrack to San Bernardino Ranch. There the next day he received another order to proceed to the supply camp. Before he could get there, he learned that with all the marching and countermarching by the cavalry, Chihuahua, as a parting shot, had slipped in and killed the sergeant and two privates, burned the tents and wagons, and gone into Mexico with the horses and thousands of rounds of ammunition. General Crook reported that the Apaches had left seventeen dead settlers behind them before they reached the border.

A few days later, with the backing of General of the Army Philip Sheridan, Crook sent Capt. Wirt Davis, Fourth Cavalry, down the east side of the Sierra Madre in Mexico, and Captain Crawford, Third Cavalry, down the west side on separate expeditions to find and bring back the renegades. Frank Leslie was with Davis as a courier. Although three or four Indians were killed and a few women and children retaken, the campaigns had no result other than to drive the Apaches deeper into the sierra.

In July, while Davis and Crawford were in Mexico, Crook kept small parties of the Fourth Cavalry at key water holes near the border, including Mud Springs, Skeleton Canyon, Guadalupe Canyon, and the San Bernardino Ranch. Later in the month a handful of hostiles, holed up in the Mogollon Mountains since May, made a dash for the border with a herd of horses in front of them and Captain Hatfield and Troop D of the Fourth behind them. With the soldiers was another civilian frontiersman, Jim Tevis.

After his time at Pinos Altos in 1860, Tevis had served the Confederacy at Valverde and later accompanied the retreating Sibley to Louisiana. After the war he had moved to St. Louis, married, and run a bakery and candy store—tame occupations for a man with such an adventuresome past. Too tame, apparently, for in 1880 he came back to Arizona and opened a trading post in the structure he'd helped put up in Apache Pass for the San Antonio to San Diego Mail. He prospected, and he homesteaded at Teviston (now Bowie) just in time to sell land to the new railroad. Tevis stayed with the Fourth Cavalry for several days, rode to Chihuahua with them, and then returned with dispatches for Crook.

Despite the pressure on their Sierra Madre refuge, the runaway Chiricahua Apaches eluded the soldiers. On September 28, four months after leaving the reservation, twenty warriors returned to Arizona to replenish supplies. Entering the United States at Guadalupe Canyon, not far from the Fourth Cavalry vedette, they went to the north end of the Chiricahua Mountains, where they killed Mike Keating and an unknown prospector, then crossed the range to Morse Canyon, where they robbed and wounded a rancher. Gatewood and Wirt Davis, who had just returned from Sonora, were immediately sent on their trail, but the hostiles evaded them. After leaving the Chiricahuas, the hostiles crossed over into the Dragoons, then went down the west flank of those hills, crossed the Mules, and returned to the San Simon Valley.

Bob Gilbert and Jim Barnes were alone at a camp on the cienega, cutting hay under contract for the army at Fort Bowie. Their three partners had left the day before to deliver wains of hay to the post. The hay camp was a thatched-roofed adobe house with a single door facing east, a picket corral behind the house, and a fenced enclosure for stacked hay. During the night the camp dog yapped continuously, so when Jim went out to water the horses in the morning, Bob cautioned him to watch out for Indians. Jim discounted any danger and went out into the dawn.

Bob was just pulling on his boots when he heard shots from the direction of the corral. He grabbed his rifle and ran out to see Jim stagger toward him and fall dead.

Indians ran toward him from his right, and Bob whirled to throw a couple of shots at them, forcing them to take cover while he bounded inside and barred the door. The only other openings were ports in the south and north walls, through which he fired alternately, hoping the Indians would think there were two of him. After return fire ceased, hoping the Indians had left, he cautiously unbarred the door and stepped into the doorway.

With the door partly open, he was hit in the belly and knocked to the floor by a shot that ricocheted off the iron rod used to bar the door. The Apaches had posted a man forty feet in front of the house who, thinking he had killed Bob, stood up and walked toward the door. Bob was able to prop himself up for a kneeling shot and hit the man in the head, killing him instantly. Bob Gilbert thought his hip had been broken, but in great pain he dragged himself to his feet. As he re-barred the door, he smelled smoke and heard the crackle of flames. The Apaches had fired the tule thatching of the roof, and pieces of it were falling into the room. He buckled on an ammunition belt, picked up two Colt pistols, and again carefully opened the door to peer out from the threshold. By now it was well into the afternoon. The sun shone past the north side of the house, backlighting an Indian whose shadow fell in front of the house.

The smoke was making it impossible to stay inside. Despite his pain, Bob sprang out toward the corner with a pistol in each hand and fired them both into the Indian's middle just as the latter raised his rifle to fire a round that passed over Bob's shoulder, so close that the muzzle blast burned his ear and deafened him. Luckily, there was no one posted at the opposite corner, and he staggered out into the dense cover of the cattails, where the Indians prudently declined to follow.

As he made his way, Bob felt the bullet fall out of his wound and down his pant leg into his boot. When he felt safe, he looked at the wound and found that his large intestine was protruding out of a ragged hole in his abdomen. He gingerly pushed it back in and plugged the hole with a piece torn from his shirttail.

At dawn the next day he cautiously crawled back to dry, open ground. Barnes still lay where he had fallen, his body stripped, but Gilbert was too weak to bury him. In addition to the pain of his wound, he was hungry, having eaten nothing for thirty-six hours. The fire had burned itself out, but there was nothing to salvage. He pulled a few carrots from the small garden they had put in. He desperately needed help, but having no idea when the partners would return, he decided he must hike for it. He fashioned a canteen, cut a yucca stalk for a cane, made a turban out of his shirt sleeves to replace his hat, which had burned in the fire, then left for Fort Bowie.

The hay camp was only three miles from the Parramore ranch, but the cowboys were all out on fall roundup. Gilbert was unaware of Chenowth's place six miles south or Arnett's an equal distance to the north. Galeyville wasn't much farther. So he made a hot, dry, hungry, and painful hike through the greasewood for twenty miles before he met a horse wrangler loose-herding army horses not far from Fort Bowie. In his condition it took him two days.

By the time they left the cienega for Mexico, the raiders had covered more than two hundred miles in a bit over three days, much of it in rough country. Forced to avoid the settlements, they'd had little success and their horses were worn out, but they made a compensating haul close to where they had killed Mike Keating.

The H's roundup wagon was on Whitetail Flats. There was floor space in William Shanahan's house in the mouth of Whitetail Canyon, so rather than sleep in the open, the cowboys unrolled their beds inside. No cattle had been gathered yet, and the boss hadn't put out a night herd but instead had hobbled the remuda a quarter mile from the house. In the morning the cowboys were afoot, but the Apaches were well mounted for their return to the Sierra Madre. A day late and on the wrong side of the mountain, Troops E and H of the Tenth Cavalry from Fort Grant arrived in Bonito Canyon to set up a small camp to guard against such a raid. Many years later Captain Hatfield, referring to this raid, would write: "No Indians in the Southwest but the Chiricahuas could have accomplished this feat. It was done by great mobility in a rough country, extreme daring and good luck."

There was to be one more Apache raid in Arizona, one of incredible endurance. Around the first of November 1885, Ulzana, Chihuahua's older brother and right-hand man, crossed the border at Tres Hermanas south of Deming, New Mexico, and went into the Black Range north of Hillsboro with nine warriors. For almost two months, evading cavalry patrols, they attacked miners, ranches, and freight wagons from the wilderness of the upper Gila and its tributaries between the Mogollons and Fort Apache.

They created a furor of fear and frustration. The newspapers in Albuquerque, Tucson, Phoenix, and Prescott raged at the army and demanded Crook's removal from command for his inability to protect the citizens. Crook knew the difficulty of intercepting a small body of men in a big country and stuck with his belief that it would take Indians to find them and that it was necessary to deny their Sierra Madre refuge to them. From Fort Bowie he sent Captain Crawford down below the border.

On Christmas Day Ulzana gathered fresh horses at the mining camp of Carlisle, near the Arizona line, and headed south. On the twenty-seventh Gus Chenowth was crossing Whitetail Flats, returning from Turkey Creek with a load of lumber salvaged from Galeyville's empty shacks. As he passed the point of Blue Mountain, a party of Apaches approached him on horseback. Gus raised his rifle in warning and the Indians veered off to Turkey Creek.

Deputy Sheriff Casper Albert and Bill Reese weren't so lucky. Driving a wagon into Turkey Creek about two miles below Galeyville, where the road leaves the bench to drop into the creek, they had only a moment to be startled as Indians rose up from below the rim and fired. Albert, a veteran prospector, fell over his team, shot through the head. It took two or three shots to kill Reese, the last casualty of Ulzana's raid. After cutting the horses out of the traces, the warriors disappeared.

Although four troops of cavalry out of Fort Bowie combed the mountains and its flanking valleys, they lost the trail in a three-day blizzard. The Chiricahuas reached Mexico, having covered twelve hundred miles, killing an estimated thirty-eight on the way. They had

250 stolen horses and had lost one man. Coyotero scouts from Fort Apache had caught up with one on Eagle Creek and cut off his head to take back to the post.

During Ulzana's raid Stephen Reed lost several horses. Weeks later a black SR horse returned to Cave Creek with a sore on his side from a tight surcingle. For many years the Reed children rode him, calling him "Old Indian."

On January 9, 1886, Crawford's scouts made contact with the hostiles south of Oputo. Early the next morning, after a grueling night march, they attacked an Apache camp near the Río Aros. All the hostiles escaped but lost their horse herd. Later that day a woman came into camp with a message from Geronimo. He wanted to talk, and Crawford agreed to meet with him the next day.

At daybreak on the eleventh, when Crawford's outfit began to stir, a line of armed Indians approached them. No alarm was given. They were taken for Geronimo's men coming in for the parley. It was mistaken identity all around. The men coming through the morning mist were Tarahumara Indians from Chihuahua in a loosely organized militia under Mexican officers. The Mexican force mistook Crawford's Coyotero scouts for hostiles and opened fire. Before the officers could stop the exchange of fire, the Mexicans had suffered casualties, and three Coyoteros and a packer were wounded. Crawford was struck down with a wound from which he died seven days later.

After making uneasy peace with the Mexicans, Gatewood's second in command, Lt. Marion Maus, took over and moved his camp. From a high vantage point, the Chiricahuas had enjoyed the sight of their enemies shooting at each other, but later two women came in from Geronimo to say that, in view of the Mexican presence and the gunfire, he hesitated to come in to talk. Apache tradition says the women may have been Chihuahua's sister-in-law, Dahteste, and Lozen, a famous medicine woman and sister of Victorio.

On the fifteenth Maus met with Geronimo, who agreed to discuss terms with General Crook in two months' time in Cañon de los Embudos, twenty miles southeast of San Bernardino Springs. Maus slowly made his way north with six hostages as Geronimo's guarantee to meet. They included a pregnant woman and two children who may have been a burden to the Apaches anyway.

By mid-March Maus and his scouts were camped just below the narrow slots in Cañon de los Embudos, which gave rise to the name Funnels Canyon. The Apaches made their camp a half mile away, across a steep, brushy gulch, on a rocky hill with a view in all directions: the hills in the east that fed the canyon, distant mountains across the San Bernardino Valley, Portal Peak in the Chiricahuas, and the Sierra Madre, which darkened the southern horizon. They made precautionary rifle pits behind rows of lava stones and watched the approach of General Crook's small party coming in from San Bernardino Springs.

Crook and his two aides, Capts. John G. Bourke and Cyrus Roberts, and Roberts's twelve-year-old son, Charley, had come down from Fort Bowie to camp on Whitewater Draw below Camp Rucker. The next day they passed Frank Leslie's ranch and camped with E Troop, Fourth Cavalry, near the Erie's Mud Springs ranch. Crook had brought the wives of some of the hostiles with him, and Neil Erickson, now 1st Sergeant, was detailed to escort Nana's wife to him by an army ambulance. Just before they left Mud Springs, Camillus Fly drove in from his Tombstone studio with a hack load of photographic equipment. He'd heard rumors of the upcoming conference and asked Crook's permission to take pictures.

On March 25 and again on the twenty-seventh, Crook met with Naiche, Geronimo, and Chihuahua. The upshot was that they agreed to surrender, understanding that after two years of prison they could return to Turkey Creek in the White Mountains. The general agreed to those terms. He reported to General Sheridan, "After my talk with them it seemed as if it would be impossible to get any hold on them except on condition that they be allowed to return to the reservation on their old status."

Crook and his party returned to Fort Bowie on the twenty-eighth, leaving Maus to follow at a necessarily slower pace with the scouts and his still-armed "prisoners," many of them women and children on foot. They camped just below the border that night. During the evening Bob Tribolet, one of a family of butchers in Tombstone, set up a tailgate saloon not far away. He sold the better part of a barrel of liquor and told the Indians that they would be turned over to an Arizona court for trial and hanging. By morning Geronimo, Naiche, eighteen other warriors, thirteen women, and six children had lit out for tall timber in the rain.

It must have been a bitter irony to Naiche to know that the same Americans who had loathed and feared his father, Cochise, then honored him by naming their county for him, now wanted to hang the son.

Maus followed their trail nearly to Fronteras before turning back. Two of the men who had bolted thought better of it when they were sober and turned themselves in to him. Meanwhile, the escort with the remaining eighty, including Nana, Chihuahua, and Ulzana, crossed the border to Slaughter's ranch, where a pack train of rations awaited them. By the time they reached Fort Bowie in a sandstorm on April 2, a telegram had arrived from Sheridan with word that President Cleveland wouldn't honor the terms of surrender. Crook asked to be relieved of his command.

On April 7, 1886, all those who had surrendered (and stayed surrendered) boarded a train at Bowie Station to begin the long ride to Florida, from which they would never return.

Tribolet's liquor prolonged the conflict, but not everyone regretted it. Some Arizonans were ambivalent in their feelings about the Apaches. The large presence of the army was an economic plus for many. Tribolet, who held an army beef contract, had important backers in the "Tucson Ring," a loose-knit group of contractors who would be sorry to lose a profitable business.

Brig. Gen. Nelson A. Miles assumed Crook's command at Fort Bowie on April 12. Though a brave and able officer, Miles was very different from Crook. Ambitious, jealous, and conscious of his splendid appearance in full uniform, he was convinced that the way to advancement was through political leverage.

Miles made some immediate changes. First he pulled back the Indian scouts, convinced that the proper way to bring the problem to a successful conclusion was to confront the hostiles with regular troops. He believed that anything an Indian could do a soldier could do better. This proved to be difficult. Although Miles had five thousand soldiers to draw on, 25 percent of the entire U.S. Army, it was relatively easy for Naiche and Geronimo, with only thirty-six Chiricahuas altogether, only seventeen of them full-grown men, to elude a confrontation.

One innovation of the new commanding general's proved to be extremely useful. That was a chain of heliograph stations linking the military installations of southern Arizona and western New Mexico so completely that a message could reach them all, given four hours of sunlight. The station on Bowie Mountain, behind the fort, had a direct link with five other stations: Bowie Station on the railroad, Stein's Pass, O'Reiley's ranch between Pinery and West Turkey Creek, Whitewater Draw at the north end of the Swisshelm Mountains, and Antelope Springs in Mule Pass. Relays from those points could make contact with Fort Huachuca, Tubac on the Santa Cruz River, and Fort Bayard in New Mexico. Telegraph from Bowie could reach Fort Lowell and Phoenix.

Before all of this could be put in place, Geronimo and Naiche came up into the Santa Cruz Valley on a raid that resulted in a number of deaths, none of them among the Chiricahuas.

On May 5 Miles dispatched Captain Lawton from Fort Huachuca to find the hostiles. Lawton, assisted by Surgeon Leonard Wood, led a small force composed mostly of soldiers. By Mile's instructions he took only enough scouts to be able to pick up a trail. Lawton was tough and energetic and had proved himself a hard-driving, competent officer in a campaign against Comanches in the Texas panhandle a few years before. Wood, a recent graduate of Harvard Medical School, had no experience but was chosen for his enthusiasm, energy, and outstanding physical strength.

On the same day Lawton went into the field, Capt. Thomas E. Lebo with Troop K, Tenth Cavalry, ran into some Indians in the mountains of northern Sonora, where he lost one man killed and

another wounded, with no loss to the Apaches. Shortly after, part of
Troop K under Lieutenant Kennedy was sent to the east side of the
Chiricahua Mountains to establish a temporary camp complemen-
tary to the one set up the previous fall in Bonito Canyon. The tented
camp, named for Capt. Emmet Crawford, was on a bench near the
junction of Onion Creek and Turkey Creek, at the foot of Silver Peak
—a site still known as Soldier Flat.

On May 15 Captain Hatfield had two men killed and two wounded
just south of the border. The same little bunch of Apaches showed
up shortly after that on the White Mountain Reservation, where one
of them, Kayitah, turned himself in. On June 6 a troop of the Fourth
Cavalry had a brush with Geronimo in the Patagonia Mountains, and
on the thirteenth Lt. Robert Brown with a group of Coyotero scouts
captured some of his horses but didn't get an Indian, either dead
or alive.

Lawton and Wood held up well under extremely grueling conditions. The average trooper, however, couldn't match those officers in
stamina, and the cavalry couldn't begin to equal their adversaries.
They couldn't even find them. In spite of his rivalry with Crook and
dislike of his methods, Miles was able to recognize his own mistakes,
and by summer he reverted to his predecessor's tactics and the use
of Apache scouts. In July he sent Lieutenant Gatewood into Mexico
again.

At Fort Apache Kayitah, a cousin of Yanosha, who was one of
the hostiles, and Kayitah's cousin Martine volunteered to accompany
"Long-nose" Gatewood. Kayitah, a Chihenne who had been wounded
in the fight with García in 1882, believed that it was in the Apaches'
best interests that they all come in. He knew their hiding places and
thought he might talk them into giving up. Martine was a Ndenda
who had been an apprentice warrior under Juh. He, too, knew the
country well.

With these two Chiricahua guides, Gatewood went to Fort Bowie,
on the way picking up George Wratten, who as a boy had clerked in
a store at San Carlos, where he rapidly learned the language, made

many Apache friends, and developed a sympathetic understanding of their ways. For several years he had served the army as interpreter, packer, scout, and guide.

At Fort Bowie Gatewood added three mules and a packer to his small party but was unable to get the mounted escort he wanted. As they passed Tex Canyon on their way south, Alonzo "Tex" Whaley, an old Galeyville hand, joined them at his ranch as a courier.

In the first week of August, on the Río Aros two hundred miles south of the border, Gatewood met Lawton's exhausted column, which had floundered without effect for two months across rough mountains and dry deserts. Acting on a rumor that Geronimo was in the vicinity of Fronteras, Gatewood headed there with his own party and ten of Lawton's troopers. There he heard that two Chiricahua women had been in town and left again. He got on their trail and followed it with caution and a flour sack tied to a mescal stalk as a sign that he was on a peaceful mission.

Martine, who had gone ahead with Kayitah, met Gatewood at the junction of the San Bernardino and the Río Bavispe with word that Geronimo was camped in the mountains four miles away. At great risk to their lives, the two scouts had approached the camp, where Kanseah, standing guard, gave the alarm. Geronimo gave orders to shoot the scouts, but Yanosha recognized his cousin and argued that they should be allowed to come into camp. Giving in to the opinion of several of his men, Geronimo agreed to talk with Gatewood. Kayitah stayed with him as hostage while Naiche sent a message to the lieutenant guaranteeing his safe conduct.

At the ensuing conference Gatewood made it clear that General Miles would insist on surrender and imprisonment in Florida. Geronimo at first said he would come in only if he was allowed to go back to the reservation, but after hearing that Chihuahua and those who had surrendered with him in March had been sent to Florida, he agreed to meet General Miles in Skeleton Canyon to discuss terms. Unknown to both parties, President Cleveland had told Miles that Geronimo was to be treated as a prisoner, "if we cannot hang him which I would much prefer."

Lieutenant Gatewood and Geronimo's small following went up the San Bernardino Valley. Lawton's troops traveled separately because the Chiricahuas distrusted the soldiers. They camped one night on Arroyo Elías and another in Guadalupe Canyon and then went on to wait for General Miles in Skeleton Canyon. They waited several days while messages went back and forth between Gatewood in Skeleton and Miles in Tucson.

Geronimo was getting nervous, and with good reason. Miles sent veiled suggestions to Lawton that Geronimo and Naiche might be killed while escaping, and he stayed in Tucson to attend a dinner before he entrained for Fort Bowie. Then he went by horseback on the foothill trail from the post and spent a night at Gray's in Rucker Canyon. The general asked John Gray for a guide, and Bob Beale, a visitor at the ranch, volunteered. After the long delay, Miles was now in a hurry and demanded a "bee-line" route with no dawdling. Beale took him over the mountain at a furious pace, making a rough trip of it.

After several meetings Geronimo, speaking for the Chiricahuas, accepted the terms that Gatewood had spelled out for them days before. At daylight on the morning of September 5, Miles left for Fort Bowie by mule-drawn ambulance. Not taking chances on another bolt, he took Naiche and Geronimo with him.

The team was fresh, and they made good time. By midday they had reached Chenowth's on the San Simon Cienega, where they halted to water and rest the mules. Miles asked Mrs. Chenowth if she could feed them. It was short notice, but Mary scratched up a hasty meal. While she was busy at the stove, the soldiers and their prisoners went out into the kitchen garden to fetch several watermelons for themselves. Before leaving the ranch, General Miles told his hostess that it was "a mighty poor meal" but that he'd pay fifty cents. He refused to pay for the watermelons, however. At that Geronimo pulled a little buckskin bag out from under his belt and paid Mary Chenowth in Mexican pesos.

While Miles and his principal prisoners made it to Fort Bowie in one day, the rest of the party, many of them afoot, took three-and-a-half days for the hike. On the second day they lunched on Cave Creek and camped for the night at Galeyville. The third night was spent ten miles east of the fort near the KL Bar Ranch, on the north side of Rattlesnake Point, a place acquired earlier that year by Jim Hancock and Tom Whitehead to work with their adjacent ranch at Wood Canyon. That night seven of the captives—four men, two women, and a child—slipped away, but when Lawton's party arrived at the post early on September 8, 1886, they were short only six prisoners— a baby had been born on the way from Skeleton Canyon.

Whitehead and Hancock were working around the corrals in Wood Canyon the next day when Lt. C. B. Johnson of the Tenth Cavalry rode up with a few scouts and asked if the ranchers had seen any signs of the missing Indians. They hadn't, but they volunteered to help. Sign was picked up a mile above the ranch and followed up a tributary gulch leading down from the back side of Dunn Springs Peak. The lieutenant followed it down into Sonora without result.

During their layover at Fort Bowie, while they waited for the rest of their people to arrive, Naiche and Geronimo were the objects of much curiosity. Emma Peterson, no longer housekeeper to an officer's family, was running a bakery at the post. She was one of those who shook Geronimo's hand and found him, in her words, "a perfect gentleman."

There was no dawdling at Fort Bowie. The entire bunch was put in wagons, taken to Bowie Station, and were soon on their way by rail to prison in Florida. The day before, all the Chiricahuas on the White Mountain Reservation, including those who were peacefully trying to farm, were rounded up and headed north for the railroad at Holbrook, also bound for Florida.

Another who escaped imprisonment was a Chihenne man, Massai (Máhsee). A member of Loco's band, he had been hostile from time to time but had also served as a scout for the army and had been discharged only about four months before being rounded up. Massai rode the train from Holbrook to a point a bit west of St. Louis, where he slipped away during a brief stop. His absence wasn't discovered until the next head count hours later. Equipped solely with a butcher knife one of the women had slipped him, he made his way undetected through settled farming country in Missouri and Kansas and across the Staked Plains. In the Sierra Blanca of New Mexico, he stole a Mescalero woman and took her with him into the Black Range south of Ojo Caliente to live off the country.

Henry Lawton and Leonard Wood both earned Medals of Honor for the "capture" of Geronimo. The grateful citizens of Tucson presented Miles an inscribed ceremonial sword at a gala reception. Gatewood earned his general's jealous resentment. Martine and Kayitah, whose efforts were largely responsible for Gatewood's meeting with the hostiles, earned imprisonment when they were bundled onto the train with the others at Bowie.

Two or three years after Geronimo had eaten watermelon at the Chenowth's on his way to prison, Mary Chenowth heard the house dog barking wildly at something outside. "See what that dog is barking at," she called to ten-year-old Charlie.

The boy went around the corner of the house and saw an old Apache man standing under the cottonwoods, looking toward the house but obviously afraid to come closer because of the dog. He was in worn moccasins, dirty cotton breechclout and ragged coat, and he looked hungry.

The Indian lingered about fifty yards from the house until the men came in from work and Gus went over to talk to him in broken Spanish. They fed him and Gus told him to move on. But in the morning they saw the smoke of his fire not far from the house, and Gus thought it would be well to take him to the sheriff to be returned to the reservation. Al Farr, a drifter staying at the ranch, volunteered to take him to Lordsburg.

By noon Farr returned from what should have been about a sixty-mile round trip. He pulled off his saddle and went to sleep against the barn. At dinner he was asked about the Indian.

"He won't never hurt anybody," Al assured them.

Riding one and leading one up Market Street in Paradise, circa 1903.

:iting for the arrival of the stage at the Hayes Hotel in Paradise in 1906. The stage office is low building on the left.

Susan Wilson Sanders in about 1904, after her divorce from Joe and before her marriage to George Coryell. With her are her children, Emma and Lizzie (rear), and Willy and Myrtle.

Samuel F. "Jack" Maloney at about twenty years of age, just before he left Texas for Arizona.

Alejo Bedoya, proprietor of the Monte Cristo Saloon in Paradise.

John Wethered, M.D. (left), who gave up medicine to work for the Forest Service, with Ranger Neil Erickson at the Barfoot Ranger Station around 1910.

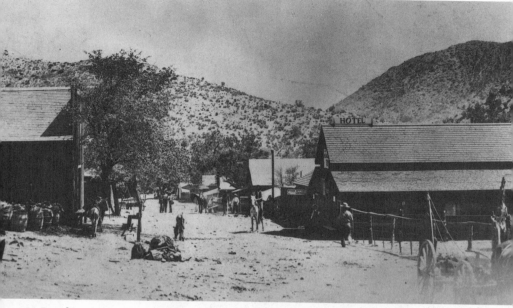

A Paradise street scene in 1906, looking north. The Hayes Hotel is on the right, and woodcutters' pack saddles are stacked against the wall on the left.

The Moore and Coryell stage in Graveyard Canyon on a return trip from Rodeo to Paradise.

Howard Pinckney Chenowth, college student. This studio photograph was taken about 1900, not long before his shooting spree in Silver City, New Mexico.

Loyola Agnes "Ola" Chenowth, cowgirl, schoolteacher, and daughter of pioneers.

Chamberlain and Hawkins' store on the east side of Market Street in Paradise. The post office was also located in this building.

Stephen Reed, Cave Creek's first permanent settler, with Alice, Claudie, Walter, and Bill, and John Hands in about 1907.

The San Simon Cattle Company headquarters near Rodeo, New Mexico, about 1912.

Rodeo in about 1920, looking north past, at left, the railroad depot, the water tank, and the pump house.

Albert Fink brewed beer in Chiricahua City and Galeyville in 1880 and then mined until his death. He is shown here at his Silver Creek camp.

Charles T. McGlone, supervisor of the Chiricahua Forest Reserve, at Crystal Cave, which he actively promoted as a tourist attraction. This snapshot was probably taken in 1907.

Will Noland (left) and two prospectors at "Eagle City" in 1906. Eagle City was a camp on Whitetail Flats for miners who worked Doran's Eagle Nest Mine, the Ajax Mine on Blue Mountain, and the mines of the Scanlon group on Harris Mountain.

Clowning at Faraway Ranch around 1905. In the rear (left to right) are Lillian Erickson, her fiancé Ed Riggs, Marvin Hudson, and Ana May Stafford. In the front are Charles McGlone and Pansy Stafford.

The first year of the Paradise school, 1906. In the back row are Maggie Bendele, Ola Martyr (teacher), Gertrude Chamberlain, Tom Hawkins, Jim Hancock, Laura Hancock, Eva Morrow, Rosaline Morrow, Holly Sweeney, W. K. Morrow, and Harry Chamberlain. In the front row are a Bendele baby, Carson Morrow, Erle Hancock, an unknown child, Bertha Bendele, Mart Moore, Jerry Chamberlain, Chester "Bally" Morrow, Irene Hancock, Ralph Morrow, and Dottie and Ted Chamberlain.

Henry and Gertrude Chamberlain in front of their yellow-painted Paradise home on the hill behind the store, circa 1908. The children are, left to right, Ted, Jerry, Bill, and Dottie.

Seamstress Hollis "Holly" Chamberlain Sweeney modeling one of her creations.

Henry and Susanna Buckalew in a studio pose with their youngest children, Audie Buckalew and Maude Noland, around 1910.

Frank and Will Noland at the Buckalews' adobe bunkhouse at Squaw Spring about 1907.

Patrons of Joe Wheeler's saloon, circa 1909. Frank Hawkins is in the white jacket, and Carson Morrow is the boy with the baseball bat.

James H. Parramore and his 7H cowboys at the cienega ranch in the mid-1920s. Parramore is the man with a white beard at center. Frank Noland is standing fourth from the left, and Joe Wheeler (scratching his head) is at his boss's left. Bill Shugart and George Franklin are second and third from the right.

John Lee (left) and Albert Fink with the "auto-stage" on the Portal bridge in about 1915. This suspension bridge was a few feet downstream from the present concrete bridge.

George "Ironfoot" Coryell in the early 1920s when his stage had gone out of business and he was raising goats and hogs.

William Wesley Sanders, home from the war in 1919.

After the hey-day. Judge James Ha▯
(left) and a friend in front of Parad▯
"Federal Building" in 1933.

Cowboy Manuel Domínguez, a former Villista
revolutionary *soldado*.

Apple trees in bloom at the Sierra Linda Ranch in 1942.

## Chapter 9

# The End of the Frontier

This part of Arizona was God's own country until the Curse of Civilization hit it.

**Leonard Alverson**

After a five-year hitch, 1st Sgt. Neil Erickson was discharged in April 1886, between Geronimo's two "surrenders." He pursued odd jobs around Fort Bowie, and he pursued his countrywoman, Emma Peterson. In January 1887 they were married in the Cosmopolitan Hotel in Tucson and went to Volcano, a new mining camp six miles north of Steins, to open a restaurant.

At 3 P.M. on May 3, 1887, the dinner crowd fed and the kitchen cleaned up, Emma was leaving the house when the ground beneath her feet began to wave alarmingly. She saw the proprietor of the drugstore across the street dash down his steps, looking back as though he expected the store to come after him. The ground continued to wave like a blanket for about three minutes.

The Safford stage rolled toward Bowie Station on a level road. Ten miles out of town, suddenly the dusty track whipped violently from side to side. The cantering horses lost their balance and fell to the ground in a jumble of harness and trace chains. The coach, piling into the frantically thrashing horses, tilted precariously but stayed upright.

In San Simon a brick chimney collapsed. In Cave Creek Stephen and Isabella Reed felt the ground move and heard the roar of wagon-sized slabs of cliff crashing down the talus a mile or so down the canyon. In Rucker Canyon John Gray heard rocks rolling and later saw fires in the mountains. Two adobe buildings at Slaughter's ranch fell into rubble. A long crack appeared in the Sulphur Springs Valley, and artesian water burst forth in several places. At other spots springs ceased to flow.

Closer to the epicenter at Batepito, Sonora, thirty-two miles south of Slaughter's, the damage was more severe. The town of Bavispe was nearly all laid on the ground, and a seven-foot fault ran for miles along the foothills west of the Sierra de los Embudos and across the arroyo a few miles below where Geronimo had sat with General Crook fourteen months before.

Two other events that year weren't earthshaking but were relevant to the region's social history. One was that John Slaughter, impatient with the general outlawry that prevailed, allowed himself to be elected sheriff of Cochise County. The second was the arrival of twenty-one-year-old John Hands in Cave Creek.

Edward John Hands, one of six boys, was born in Kings-Weston, near Bristol, in the west of England. At eighteen he sailed to New York to seek his fortune and found work in a greenhouse. After a year Hands went to San Antonio, Texas, and worked as a farm hand. There he met two young brothers from Arkansas, George W. and Joseph W. Walker, and the three became partners in the ownership of a team and wagon, with which they crossed the plains, drove across New Mexico, and passed through Granite Gap. They camped midst the debris of Galeyville on Turkey Creek, where they dissolved the partnership.

The Walker brothers went to work for the H's, where George eventually became a hotshot roper who brought wild cattle out of the mountains at so much a head. Parramore and Merchant had only four year-round cowboys in 1887, with Jess Henley as foreman, but they took on six or seven extra hands for the spring and fall roundups. That year they branded 4,193 calves.

John Hands went over to Cave Creek and moved in with Stephen Reed to do odd jobs for board and shelter. He was still at Reed's a year later when his brother, Frank, showed up. Four years older than John, Francis Henry Hands immigrated in 1888 and took the train for San Simon, Arizona Territory. When Frank stepped off the car into the white glare at the San Simon Station on June 17, no one met him. The temperature must have been a shock to one so fresh from British mist.

The Galeyville stage had not run for six years. The station agent pointed out the Chiricahuas shimmering behind the heat waves, and Frank picked up his portmanteau and started to make footprints. It was late at night when he arrived, footsore and hungry, at the mouth of Cave Creek Canyon, where a prospector took him in and fed him at his campfire. The next day he limped up the canyon to Reed's and joined brother John.

Reed's family was growing. Wesley was now a young man. Six-year-old Lula had a baby sister, Claudie, and Isabella had another baby started. It was a crowded cabin, and Stephen suggested that John and Frank find a place of their own.

Just below the mouth of the canyon, the boys picked a spot in the hackberry and cottonwood trees and dug a shallow well at the south end of the cienega at the foot of a low limestone ridge. The winter of 1888–89 was one of heavy rains, but they occupied Al George's abandoned rock-lined dugout in the bank of the talus while they built a more substantial cabin. Stephen helped square logs and whipsaw boards for flooring and roof. In the spring, with the house completed, the Hands brothers began to roam the hills to prospect for promising rock.

The wet winter made a good start for spring growth, and the valley was yellow with Mexican poppies when the San Simon branded 5,416 calves. To fill a contract with a Montana buyer for breeding cows and stocker steers, they sent notice to all the neighboring ranches that the '89 fall roundup would start early at the craters in the head of the valley. The gather slowly worked north, with men spreading out at first light each day to work the canyons in the Peloncillos and the Chiricahuas while others moved the growing herd down the middle of the valley. When the roundup finally reached the San Simon Cienega, the wagon went north to work the country from the railroad back south.

The participating cowboys estimated that when the cut began, there were between twelve and fifteen thousand head in the herd. The Erie Cattle Company, Slaughter's cowboys, the Munks, the Ruch brothers, and the Diamond A's from the Animas Valley had the most stray cattle to cut out, but owners or their "reps" from a dozen or more smaller outfits cut out stuff wearing their brands. Stephen Reed, Bill Shanahan from Turkey Creek, and John Keating from a bit north of him were among the smaller owners who took part, and from farther up the valley came John Gray, as well as John Cush, who had taken over Whaley's cabin in Tex Canyon the year before. Jim Hancock was there without his partner. Whitehead had sold his half to Jim to return to the hotel business in Tombstone.

The H bulls and cows with calves, some three thousand head, were cut back and thrown into a large fenced holding pasture on the cienega. The eight thousand head remaining from the cut, mostly two- and three-year-old steers and heifers, were driven to the pens in San Simon and loaded on cars for shipment.

Both Parramore and Merchant were probably present for this large working, but neither had given up his ranching interest in Texas and neither became a permanent resident on the ranch. It was Parramore who took the most interest in the Arizona outfit and who did most of the buying and selling. For the first few years he spent much time on the place, and thereafter he kept close tabs during whirlwind visits from Abilene. He left the routine operations to his wagon boss, Jesse N. Henley, whom he'd brought with him from Texas.

A tragic postscript to the roundup was the unexplained death of an H cowboy, Judson S. "Comanche" White. After the cattle were shipped, White was alone at a horse camp on Skeleton Wash. John Gray and two Diamond A cowboys, Joe Taylor and Bunk Robinson, found his bullet-riddled body there when they were drifting the cuts of their brands back to home ranges. It seemed White had been killed in the morning while walking down his stake horse. The camp was stripped of everything.

The year of that big roundup, 1889, was the company's sixth year, and they had steam up. Cowboys drifted in, worked awhile, and moved on. Forty-three men drew some pay that year, though there were probably never more than half that many around at any one time. Not all was cow work. One man dug a twenty-five-foot well at $1.25 a foot and set fence posts at 7½ cents each. Another contracted to plow seventy acres for three dollars an acre. The remuda held seventy-five head, and the horse breaker drew forty-five dollars a month. In later years an ordinary cowboy could earn an extra five to ten bucks per horse for breaking colts. Next on the wage scale were two windmillers who worked year-round to keep nine mills pumping. A cowboy drew thirty dollars and found. (One H cowboy said, " 'Found' is all you can eat if you aren't hungry.") A man could earn a little extra when the wagon was out by giving up sleep to night-herd.

For the convenience of those who couldn't wait for payday or get to town, the company kept a small storehouse with basic supplies. A tot was entered in a notebook, to be taken from his wages. He could get a pound of tobacco or a wool felt hat for 55 cents, a saddle for $28, a pair of leggings for $5.50, a suit of clothes for $18, or a pair of blankets for $6. Boots went for $4.50 to $14, depending on the quality. A pistol with holster and belt was $12, and a box of cartridges was a dollar. Judging from the amount of .45-caliber ammunition that went on the books, jackrabbits, roadrunners, and quail either became scarce or, through natural selection, developed strains of agile dodgers.

Before her marriage to Neil Erickson, Emma Peterson had visited Camp Bonita on picnics from Fort Bowie, and she fell in love with that canyon. When the army abandoned it, she bought the cabin that was its nucleus with her meager savings. Built by a man named Newton, rumored to have been an army deserter, the cabin was currently owned by J. Hugh Stafford, whose place was just up the canyon a rifle shot away. A year after their marriage, Emma and her husband homesteaded the site but continued to operate the restaurant in Volcano to increase their grubstake. Neil worked at day labor for a dollar or less at any job he could pick up in Lordsburg, Separ, or Deming. In 1888 they moved onto the ranch, but Neil continued to work out wherever he could. But he was home one May morning in 1890, working with his brother John, hauling away spoil from a recently dug well, when Stafford's hired girl, Mary Fife, came running up, skirts flying.

"Indians are coming down the canyon," she cried.

Stafford had gone out to a small trap to catch up his horses to take a load of produce from his truck garden for sale at Fort Bowie. He found the fresh track of a big moccasin and returned to the house and sent Mary to warn the Ericksons.

Erickson sent John horseback a mile and a half down the creek to warn the Prues while he stationed himself outside the stone cellar with a .45-70 and a belt of ammunition to watch for Indians. He was at his post when Mrs. Stafford came to the house with her two small daughters and told him her husband hadn't seen an Indian, just moccasin tracks. She stayed with Mary, Emma, and the Ericksons' two-year-old daughter, Lillian, while Neil went to join Stafford in checking out the sign.

One horse was missing from Stafford's trap. A single set of tracks showed that the Indian had tried to catch up a mare also, but she had evaded him. They followed the sign to where it was joined by a smaller footprint, apparently a woman's. Indications were that the two Indians had watched Stafford from there until he went back to the house. Then the man had put the woman on the horse and followed her up the canyon. Cautiously Erickson and Stafford followed the tracks a mile through thick brush and over fallen logs, then went back to their wives and children. John hadn't returned.

When John Erickson reached Prue's, he found that Louis already knew about the Indians. The day before, Jim Phillips and his half-brother, Malcolm Barfoot, who had places in Pinery Canyon, had taken their families on a Sunday visit to see sister Jennie's new baby. When they returned, they found the Phillips cabin ransacked. Moccasin tracks told the story. They sent a message to the Fort Bowie commandant, and at daylight troops from the post passed Prue's to head up Pinery shortly before John Erickson arrived.

John set out after them to tell them the Indians were now in Bonito. The green shavetail in charge hadn't looked very skillfully for tracks, assuming that the thieves had headed up Pinery to cross the mountain at Hands Pass (then known as Dunn Pass). By the time John could catch up, the Indians had topped out and were going down White-tail on the east side. It was evening by the time the detail made camp back at Prue's, and it was dark when John returned home.

In the morning the lieutenant dismounted half his men and, with Prue and Erickson to guide them, followed the tracks up Rhyolite Canyon. A short distance under the top, by a large boulder, they found where the two Indians had broiled a lot of beef over a fire, more than they could eat or carry, for there was much cooked meat left on the rocks. The officer wouldn't let his men eat the meat, suspect-ing it was poisoned, but Neil and Louis ate their fill. Prue wouldn't have found it so tasty if he had known, as he found out later, it was a fat cow of his own. They found where the man and woman had gone down the east side of the range, but with the Indian's lead, it was use-less to pursue them.

From a window of his stone cabin in the mouth of Whitetail, the old miner John Sullivan saw the Apache couple go by, but he was wise enough to keep his head down. If John Erickson had not persuaded the lieutenant to come back into Bonito, the soldiers might have over-taken them the day before.

Stafford's horse was later found in Stockton Pass in the Pinaleño Mountains, and the word from San Carlos was that Massai had turned up there with his pregnant wife for her delivery. Erickson believed he recognized the print of "Bigfoot" Massai, whose tracks they were fol-lowing, and the rocky prominence above the head of Rhyolite Canyon is still called Massai Point. However, Apache accounts of Massai's ac-tivities imply that his *queréncia* was in New Mexico's Black Range. His wife's people were Mescaleros. It would have been unusual for her to be taken to strangers of a different tribe. Another bronco Apache at large in 1890 may have been the one involved in the incident.

An Aravaipa Apache named Ski-be-nan-ted, the son-in-law of Chief Eskiminzin, was trained as a scout by Al Sieber in 1882 and had been with General Crook's Sierra Madre expedition the next year. In '87 a brawl occurred at a tulapai party near San Carlos, and Sieber sent Ski-be-nan-ted to restore order. The scout found that his own father had been killed, and instead of arresting the man responsible, he executed him—an action consistent with the traditional Apache code of justice.

When he returned, Sieber had him disarmed and arrested. A flurry of misunderstanding and disagreement ended with Sieber getting shot in the foot and Ski-be-nan-ted taking flight. Later the scout came back in, believing Sieber could be made to understand. But Al's foot was sore and so was he. He jailed him.

In November 1889 Ski-be-nan-ted was convicted of murder and sentenced to seven years in Yuma. During his transportation, he and other Apache prisoners overpowered their guards, killed the sheriff and his deputy, wounded the stage driver, and escaped.

For the next eight or nine years, Ski-be-nan-ted, known thereafter to Americans as "Apache Kid," ranged between the White Mountains and the Sierra Madre, living off the country and what he could plunder. No specific killing was ever proved to be his work except the stabbing of the man he blamed for his father's death. Though he was undoubtedly guilty of some, he was likely to be credited with any unsolved murder.

John Gray had frequent visitors at his Rucker Canyon ranch. On one occasion in 1890, the same year that Massai, if it *was* he, was in Bonito Canyon, Gray had two paying guests, a Dr. Haynes of Los Angeles and his patient, Robert Hardy, a lawyer from Toronto. The two were hunting one morning about two miles above the ranch when Hardy was shot. Suspecting careless hunters, Haynes ran to him but then saw Indians in the oaks a short distance away. He ran back to his horse and rode hard for the ranch. Gray attributed the killing to Apache Kid.

Apache Kid was particularly hard on Indians. On more than one occasion he kidnapped a woman from the reservation and took her with him to the Sierra Madre. He was said to have cut the Achilles tendon of one to prevent her escape and to have killed another who had tried to. Massai and Apache Kid were contemporaries, roaming the same general area, and it's possible that they sometimes ran together, but they seem to have usually been independent of each other—and of anyone else. Their identities were often confused, and the crimes of one were blamed on the other.

In 1907 some cowboys killed an Indian near Chloride, New Mexico, claiming he was Apache Kid, but his woman escaped with her children and returned to Mescalero. Their descendants know him to have been Massai.

The end of the real Ski-be-nan-ted isn't so clear. In 1894 cowboys from the San Simon horse camp came across a young Indian woman in the valley west of the mouth of Skeleton Canyon, riding a little brown pony branded 76 Quarter Circle. She told them that she had been in the Sierra Madre witl the Kid, who was very sick, was dying, and had let her go. The cowboys took her to camp, fed her, and sent her on her way with food for the ride to San Carlos. Squaw Mountain's name is a memorial to the incident.

A killing some have attributed to Apache Kid is that of Alfred Hands, who emigrated from Scotland sometime between 1893 and '95 to join his older brothers, John and Frank, on Cave Creek. The three had a small herd of goats, and it was Alfred's job to stay home to tend the livestock while the others prospected. In the early spring of 1896, John was working in the new gold-mining town of Pearce in the Sulphur Springs Valley, and Frank was working the Dunn Mine at the head of Pinery's north fork. On March 28 Frank rode down Jhus Canyon and over to Cave Creek, intending to spend the weekend with Alfred. When he rode up, he saw the door standing open and the yard strewn with white feathers from emptied pillows. Without dismounting, he called Alfred's name. He got no response, but he saw moccasin tracks on the ground in front of his horse. He cautiously circled the cabin and found Alfred's body two hundred feet from the cabin on the path to the dugout storeroom that had been their shelter the first year on the place. He had been shot in the head, and his face pounded in with stones.

The signs seemed recent, and when out of the corner of his eye Frank saw the movement of a horse disappearing over the hill east of the house, he left. He knew that Stephen Reed had been to Solomonville for supplies and was planning to spend the night at Bill Shanahan's Redtop Ranch. Hoping to find him there, Frank struck out for Turkey Creek, six miles north.

Stephen was just unhitching when Frank arrived. Concerned for the safety of his own family, Reed hooked up again and they both rode the wagon back to Cave Creek and up the canyon with Frank's exhausted horse tied to the tailgate. The next morning they went down the creek to bring back Alfred's body.

Frank returned across the mountain to his camp in Pinery Canyon, and since Fort Bowie had been closed in 1894, he sent word of the incident to Fort Grant. When Lt. Sedgwick Rice came to Pinery with a handful of Indian scouts, Frank rode over to the Cave Creek Cienega with the party. At his cabin they picked up the cold trail and followed it to the border.

At the San Bernardino Ranch John Slaughter and his foreman joined them. A couple of days into Mexico, they came upon a small Apache camp in the mountains. Their approach had been detected only shortly before they arrived, for fires were still burning. In the Apaches' hasty flight, a two-year-old baby girl had been left behind. The child was wearing a skirt made of a cloth election notice taken from the Hands cabin door. The shirt she had on and a shawl found in the wickiup were identified as belonging to Eliza Merrill, who was killed with her father in December 1895. Merrill had been taking a load of grain from his farm in Pima to Clifton when they were attacked on the road. Frank Hands recovered a stolen horse, and John Slaughter took the little girl home to his wife, Viola, to raise.

While Frank trailed the Apaches, Stephen Reed and Rube Haddon made a coffin of two-by-twelves from the ceiling of the Hands cabin, and they buried Alfred on the hill above Reed's, beside Stephen's son, Wesley, who had died not long before.

At some time in 1896 or '97, Walter Birchfield of the Diamond A's tipped off John Slaughter that he believed Apache Kid was camped in the Animas Mountains. Slaughter is said to have tacitly admitted that he and an off-duty army captain named Benton then picked up Apache Kid's trail and tracked him to a cave in the Pilares de Teras, northwest of Nacozari, Sonora, where they shot him. He was alone. This account has been questioned.

The deaths of Alfred Hands, the Merrills, and Hardy may be laid to Apache Kid or Massai, but it is equally possible they were the work of a small bunch of Apaches never brought in from Mexico who continued to eke out a hardscrabble freedom in the Sierra Madre west of Casas Grandes until 1935, when the last man was killed and his children raised as Mexicans.

Of greater concern to Cochise County cattlemen than the forays of Massai and Apache Kid was the weather. Following fairly plentiful fall and winter rains, the spring of 1891 brought a bumper calf crop. Parramore family tradition says that in its best year the San Simon branded fifteen thousand calves. It is likely that in '91 all that hair was burned, but many of those calves were never marketed. The summer rains were short, and it was dry all through the next year. The lack of stock water was as serious as the shortage of feed. Scant snowfall in the mountains and unreplenished groundwater caused springs and wells to go dry. Live streams became dusty arroyo beds. The H's shipped four thousand steers to a Nebraska buyer in the fall of 1892.

By the time a meager rain fell in the summer of 1893, a great die-off was underway. Jim Hancock figured he lost 50 percent of his cattle. That fall he helped Fred Ruch with a drive of Triangle cattle. Forty years later he wrote:

> When we got the cattle throwed together on the round-up ground, some of us rode over to the creek to get a drink of water, and it was a sight, dead cattle all along up and down the bank, some lying in the water. It didn't look any too good so we rode up a little way to where the chuck wagon was to see if the cook had any water that was drinkable; he said he had some that he had strained through a barley sack and said he thought he had got all the *cresas* [maggots] out of it.

Another old cowboy, remembering the 1891–93 drought, said that for a quarter of a mile out from the dried-up water holes one could leap from one carcass to the next and never step on the ground. Starvation Canyon in the Peloncillos was named for such a condition. The cattle population of Cochise County went from 82,000 in 1892 to fewer than 40,000 mighty poor cattle in '93. The cattle on Arizona tax rolls went from 720,940 in 1891 to 432,292 in '94.

Depression and unemployment in the East reduced the demand for that lean beef. The better steers in 1893 brought $10, but the average two-year-old went for only $8.50. Rather than let them die at home, the Ryan brothers in the Sulphur Springs Valley sold off most of their breeding cows for six bits a head.

The southwestern ranges never fully recovered from the scorching of those three years of brutal sunshine. Although there have been more severe droughts since, the range was never again so overloaded. Colonel Hooker, who had twenty good years on his Sierra Bonita Ranch, said the ranges were never half as good as they were in the years preceding the drought. Hooker had predicted disaster when he saw the dangerous overstocking that followed the laying of the Southern Pacific tracks. His neighbor Joseph Munk, the first president of the Cochise County Stock Growers Association, also warned "no range can safely carry more cattle than it can support in the poorest year."

As confusing as the identities of Apache Kid and Massai were those of three white outlaws operating in and out of Cochise County in the 1890s. All were known as Blackjack.

Will and Bob Christian were big enough to be working for their own bed and board when the family made the 1891 "run" in Pottawatomie County, Oklahoma, but the boys were viewed by their neighbors as likable good-for-nothings. Not bad, but headstrong boys who didn't give a damn. Before long they both were wanted for bootlegging and stealing.

In April 1895, when Bob was twenty-six and Will two years younger, a deputy sheriff tried to serve a warrant on them. They resisted and the deputy opened fire. Bob shot back and killed the officer. They were quickly convicted of manslaughter, but with smuggled weapons they broke out of jail, and as they got away, one of them shot and killed the chief of police.

With two slain officers and an escape on their heads, they were genuine outlaws now. Honest work in Oklahoma was out of the question, so they held up a couple of stores and a train for ready cash, then went to Arizona in time for the 1896 spring roundups. They rode for the San Simon, the CCC, and the Erie outfits, Bob as Tom Anderson and Will as Ed or Frank Williams.

Will's congenial nature soon made him widely known and well liked in cow camps. A big man, he was known in the Sulphur Springs Valley as "202" for his weight, then as "Blackjack" for his complexion. He had more than heft and friendliness going for him and was known on both sides of the Chiricahuas as a good man to turn a bronc into a manageable animal. He broke a string of work mules for Jim McNair, then broke horses for Pete Johnson at the foot of Nipple Peak (now College Peak).

Under their assumed names, the Christian boys weren't threatened by the law, and they had work they were good at. They didn't have to turn to robbery, but the wild days in Oklahoma had given them a taste for excitement that branding calves didn't satisfy. In early July 1896 Blackjack got in touch with Bob, who was working for the Wagon Rods on the old Boquillas Land Grant on the San Pedro. On July 20 the two of them and three like-minded companions held up the store at Separ, east of Lordsburg. They rode off with $250 and some groceries, tobacco, and cigarette papers.

The Christians' companions included two fugitives from rustling charges in eastern New Mexico: George Musgrave, who had been working for a ranch on the San Pedro as Jesse Williams, and Code Young, who had ridden under the name of Cole Estes for the Diamond A's. The fifth member of the gang was Bob Hayes, wanted in Texas for horse stealing. The boys became known as the "High Five" and were well regarded by all who knew them except the sheriffs of Grant and Cochise Counties and the U.S. marshal.

Although the name Blackjack was first applied to Will, when brother Bob rode into the 7D Ranch and went to work, the foreman, Leonard Alverson, called *him* "Black Jack" and said he was a "good hand and a willing worker." Shortly after he left, Alverson heard of the bungled Nogales bank robbery.

On August 6 two of the outlaws held the horses while Musgrave and Hayes drew pistols, entered the International Bank in Nogales, and held up the cashier. The fifth member of the gang followed them in with a rifle just as the president made a bolt through the door. The rifleman chased him into a store next door. While Musgrave was scooping money into a sack, a customer came in, diverting the robbers' attention long enough for the cashier to snatch a pistol from under the counter and fire a few ineffective shots at them.

By this time local citizens were firing on the horse holders, and those inside ran out both doors, front and back. Musgrave tripped and dropped the money bag before he could reach his horse and didn't take the time to pick it up. The High Five pounded out of town in a hail of bullets without any profit. They'd left thirty thousand dollars on the steps. The only casualty was an innocent bystanding horse.

Sheriff Bob Leatherwood of Pima County got up a posse and took out after them. He was joined by Cochise County Sheriff Camillus Fly, who ten years before had photographed Geronimo in Embudo Canyon. They followed a trail across the Swisshelms and the south end of the Chiricahuas and blundered into an ambush in Skeleton Canyon. One of the posse was killed, and a cowboy of John Slaughter's was wounded in the neck and hip and had his horse shot from under him. After the initial volley there was a desultory exchange of gunfire from behind rocks until dark, when the pursued men withdrew.

Will Christian and George Musgrave rode chuck line around the San Simon Valley for a while, and the other three were seen in Deming not long after. The five got together again in late September to hold up the Atlantic and Pacific train at Rio Puerco, east of Belen, New Mexico. Their ineptitude equaled that displayed in Nogales. Code Young got himself killed by a U.S. marshal who happened to be a passenger. No longer the High Five, the others left in a hurry, without a dime.

The bandits had made $250 in two months, fifty bucks less than they would have made without much risk and fewer horse tracks if they had just continued to punch cows.

Brighter men might have learned that crime doesn't pay well, but the four remaining members of the gang rode east across the Rio Grande and picked up some pocket money in a stage holdup. While they were in New Mexico, Musgrave went over onto the Pecos River to murder George Parker, a man he had a grudge against.

On their way back to Cochise County, the four separated. On October 27 the Christian boys, in the habit now, went into Dave Wickersham's Teviston store and post office at Bowie Station. Waving pistols, they collected about twenty dollars from the till. A few miles south of the railroad tracks, they hobbled their horses and slept on their saddle blankets in the greasewood. At daylight they rode up to Joe Schaefer's house east of Apache Pass and politely asked Mrs. Schaefer if she could fix them breakfast.

That same day the truly mean members of the gang, Musgrave and Hayes, went back to have another whack at Separ. They got some small change at the station and then went into the combined store and post office. The take from the store's till was about a hundred dollars—less than it had been three months earlier. Angered at the measly $5.50 he was able to get from the post office window, Bob Hayes viciously beat the postmaster about the head with his pistol. Then he did the same to a Mexican customer who was slow to empty his pockets for him. The two badmen loaded their saddlebags with tobacco and whiskey to make up for the small amount of cash.

Grant County's sheriff got on their trail with three deputies and made camp in the Peloncillos north of the railroad. During the night the sleepers awoke when they heard a noise in the mesquite and opened fire, fatally wounding the deputy who was standing guard.

While the sheriff and his remaining deputies were ruefully packing the body back to Silver City, the two pairs of the gang reunited to hold up T. R. Brandt's store in San Simon, where the post office yielded $80.53. Then they crossed the road into the station to clean out the till. Agent Langlotz protested, so they beat him up and took his brand-new mail-order coat.

Again they split up but this time in a different combination. On November 6 Bob Christian and Bob Hayes held up the post office at Central, near Fort Bayard. They netted $138.98, which was almost nine dollars more than Will and George got the next day from the express agent at the Lewis Springs railroad siding, which served Fort Huachuca.

The four reassembled at Triangle headquarters, north of San Simon, where they talked things over. As long as they could steal canned peaches and tobacco from country stores, they could get by, but the slim pickings from cigar-box tills weren't profitable. And it was getting riskier by the day. The country was swarming with sheriffs' posses from three counties, plus postal inspectors, U.S. marshals, and Wells Fargo detectives.

The outlaws could evade the law easily enough by avoiding settlements. Cowboys and ranchers weren't likely to turn them in. Mrs. Nicolas Hunsaker of Leslie Canyon said she'd rather have them visit than the posses. They were always polite and wiped their boots, while the courthouse hangers-on the sheriff hired came in the house with their spurs on and dripped tobacco juice. Still, the gang risked discovery if they took honest work, so they went to Mexico to lie low for a while.

On their way south, on November 14, they stopped at Steins long enough to hold up the store and the foreman of the track gang. Then they rode south up the Animas Valley and hid out in the hills near a cabin on Horse Camp Wash, thirty-five miles south of Steins and six miles north of Diamond A headquarters. Before coming to Arizona, George Musgrave had been wanted for rustling in Eddy County, New Mexico, but he wasn't wanted badly enough to hunt for until Parker's murder. Now Sheriff Les Dow with two deputies joined the Grant

County sheriff in Separ, where they got a tip that their quarry was on the Diamond A, watering at the horse camp well. They rode all night, getting to the camp just before daylight on November 18, 1896.

Walter Birchfield, the Diamond A boss, and some cowboys were working that part of the country at the time, bunking in the small shack. The officers joined them for breakfast and kept a lookout through the window. Someone spotted four men on horseback in the junipers on the ridge above the camp. Dow went out with his deputies, Fred Higgins and Charles Ballard, to take positions behind the cover of a screen of trees between the shack and the corrals. The Grant County men declined to follow.

Two of the riders stayed on the ridge, and two rode down toward the water. Before Blackjack and Bob Hayes reached the trough, Dow stepped out and ordered them to throw up their hands. They responded by firing at him. Blackjack's horse started to buck, making it impossible for his rider to get off an accurate shot but also making an evasive target. Hayes's horse was killed and the outlaw wounded, but he got to his feet and fired several shots at the officers before one of their rounds was fatal.

Meanwhile, Dow emptied his pistol at Blackjack, and his last shot dropped the horse. Blackjack rolled the dead horse over, slid his rifle out of the scabbard on the underside, and with covering fire from his brother and Musgrave, climbed the hill on foot. The surviving three of the High Five went into Mexico.

It is intriguing to speculate that Blackjack and Apache Kid may have been in hiding not far from each other on Diamond A range at the same time in November 1896. It was Birchfield, who sat quietly sipping coffee in the cabin during all the gunfire outside, who had reported the Kid's presence in the Animas at about that time. There could be no question that he knew most, if not all four, of the outlaws. If not in sympathy with them, he surely figured their activities weren't his business.

Birchfield, from Uvalde, Texas, had come to the Animas Valley about ten years earlier. In 1887 he was on the H payroll, and the next year he worked for the Chiricahua Cattle Company in the Sulphur

Springs Valley. While he was riding for the CCC, he was charged with shooting three Mexican sheepherders but wasn't indicted. Early in '96 he was foreman for Fred Ruch's Triangles. He had been general manager for the Victorio company for just a few months when Bob Hayes was killed.

Sheriff Les Dow had to get back to his duties in Eddy County, but he left Higgins and Ballard to continue the hunt. Shrugging off the niceties of jurisdiction, the two went into Sonora with Scott White, sheriff of Cochise County. White, a long-time cowboy for the H's, undoubtedly was personally acquainted with the desperadoes but was unable to run them to ground. They had looped back to hide out in the High Lonesome and Rustler Canyon country at the south end of the Chiricahuas.

In February 1897 Blackjack's reduced gang recruited new members and made another abortive try at train robbery near Grants, New Mexico. That failing, they stole a little cash and new suits of clothes from the store in Cliff and hid out in a cave on Rousensock Creek north of Clifton and east of Rose Peak, where happy-go-lucky Blackjack began to unravel. Suspecting betrayal, he killed one of his new companions, then was informed on by another, with the result that he was killed by sheriff's deputies sometime in April 1897. Bob Christian and George Musgrave retreated again to the Chiricahuas to let the dust settle.

Among the many on the trail of Blackjack's gang was an experienced lawman, Jeff Milton, appointed in July as deputy U.S. marshal, specifically assigned to arrest or eliminate the gang. Milton brought in an old friend, George Scarborough, to help him. The two had punched cows together in Texas, and both had been lawmen in El Paso, where Scarborough had killed a notorious badman, John Selman. He was currently range detective for the Grant County Cattlemen's Association, working out of Deming.

Milton suggested that he hire on as a cowboy on one of the ranches, where he could, from under cover, keep his eyes and ears open. Scarborough was well acquainted with J. D. Parramore, so in August 1897 he rode up to H headquarters, where Holmes Maddox and Bill Shugart were shoeing horses in cottonwood shade, and asked for the boss. Jess Henley gave him a job, and a few weeks later Scarborough's son, Edgar, joined the crew.

Milton then hired four deputies and spent weeks combing the Chiricahuas for traces of Christian and Musgrave, sometimes in a bunch, more often split into two parties. For a time Jeff and Billy Stiles camped in a cave not far from Stephen Reed's ranch. On at least one occasion they stopped in for an evening of the old man's stories of the olden days. They got plenty of exercise and ate a lot of deer meat, but they didn't find an outlaw. While Milton was still searching the canyons, checking out the springs, and asking questions, Bob Christian and Musgrave slipped out and went north. Then on November 6 they succeeded where Will Christian had failed. Aided by one other man, they blasted open the express car of the eastbound A&P train east of Grants and made off with an estimated ninety thousand dollars, possibly the biggest haul ever taken in a train robbery.

"Tell them Blackjack has come to life," they called to the fireman as they left the train.

They had enough to retire and tried to. They rode back to the Chiricahuas, but the once-friendly ranches were no longer safe. The reward money on their heads put too much temptation on their old acquaintances. So in late November they crossed the border east of Bisbee and rode through La Morita to Fronteras, where they felt safe enough to celebrate. There they tied one on and shot up the town, terrorizing the citizens. They got so roaring drunk, they were easily taken and thrown in jail. They were found with nine thousand dollars in bills among them.

Word reached Bisbee of their capture, and U.S. authorities made plans for their extradition, but on December 9, 1897, before formalities were concluded, they were turned loose. Some of the money that *wasn't* taken from them when they were arrested may have played a part in their release.

Bob Christian disappeared into Mexico forever. Thirteen years later George Musgrave was picked up and tried for Parker's murder but was acquitted, and he, too, went south to disappear in Latin America.

Between the April 1897 death of Will Christian and his brother Bob's exodus into Mexico, Susanna Buckalew brought her family from the Blue River side of the White Mountains down to the east slope of the Chiricahuas.

Elizabeth Susanna Allen was born in an Amish community near Allentown, Pennsylvania. Her parents died when she was a little girl, and a neighboring couple took her in. She was fifteen when her foster parents packed their wagon and hooked up with a party making up a wagon train bound for the Rocky Mountains with Martin Noland to guide them. He had made his way to California and back and knew western ways and the route across the plains.

At fifteen Susanna was a buxom young woman. Martin, a widower, was much older, but the two were the only single adults in the expedition, and in 1879, somewhere on the grassy Kansas prairies, they were married. They set up housekeeping in Arkansas Valley, where Martin went to work for the track-laying crews of the Atchison, Topeka and Santa Fe Railroad and Susanna did her part by doing laundry. In 1881 their first child, Mary Margaret, was born.

The following year they moved to Trinidad, Colorado, still railroading and washing clothes. They pastured a small bunch of Durham cows on the middle fork of the Picketwire River, just north of town, and as soon as Susanna could travel after the April 1883 birth of their second daughter, Katie, they moved again.

It was slow going. With a baby and two-year-old Maggie to look after, Susanna handled the team while Martin kept the little herd of red cows bunched and moving. They eased south and west from one patch of grass to the next, looking for a spot of unclaimed land where they could elbow themselves a place of their own. They were sixteen months making it to the San Agustin Plains west of Magdalena. Near Horse Springs they camped long enough for Susanna to give birth to their first son, Will.

They moved through scattered yellow pines to the headwaters of the San Francisco River, where settlers had just established the small community of Luna, named for Don Salomón Luna, who, until he lost his footing and drowned in a tank of sheep dip, was a big rancher and a prominent politician. South of Luna, on the Dry Fork of the Blue River across the Arizona line, they stopped on a little tributary still known as Noland Canyon.

Together they built a one-room log cabin. Ulzana's raid had reached within twenty-five miles of the place the year before, and Geronimo was still at large, so they took the precaution of digging a cellar below the floor, a place of concealment for the children in case of attack. They moved into the cabin in time for the birth of Albert Franklin, or "Frank."

Over the next five years, three more children were born in the cabin on the Blue. One day in late September 1893, Susanna and Martin left the smaller children in Maggie's care and rode out to work cattle on the canyon rim. Fall comes early in the high country, and the children built up the fire in the stone fireplace by using fat pitch pine, which was ordinarily saved to use, a sliver at a time, as kindling. They overdid it and the roaring fire that shot up the chimney set the shake roof on fire.

Smoke rising above the timber alerted Martin and Susanna, who rode to the edge to see the cabin in flames. They suspected that Indians had set the house ablaze, and Martin, fearing for his children, recklessly plunged down the steep slope. In a quick glance he accounted for five children, but two were missing, and he suspected that they had taken refuge in the cellar. He jumped down at the cabin door and ran inside. As he raised the trapdoor, he was overcome by smoke and heat and was barely able to stagger outside before collapsing.

The children were all safe; Maggie had taken them to the willows by the creek. But Martin never recovered. The severity of his burns and the smoke inhalation that damaged his lungs brought on pneumonia, to which he shortly succumbed.

Susanna and her children lived through the winter in Luna, and eight months after his father's death, Susanna's eighth child, Tom, was born. She built a new cabin in the summer of '94 with the help of neighbors.

Henry Buckalew, a cowboy working on one of the big outfits on the San Francisco, took to riding by to visit Susanna and to lend a hand. Another visitor may have been Will Christian, who passed that way to and from his attempt to rob the train on the Río Puerco in September 1896. If not then, it isn't unlikely that he and Susanna Buckalew—for she and Henry were married in November—became acquainted sometime between February '97, when Blackjack went north for his last try at train robbing at Grants, and April, when he was shot to death. His last hideout was only twenty miles southwest of the ranch on Noland Creek.

Whether or not she was acquainted with Blackjack Christian, there is no doubt in the Noland family that she was a good friend of Curly Bill Brocius, whom she knew as a neighbor called William Graham, or "Old Cack," who also ranched on the Blue. There is reason to credit Susanna's assertion. Jim Hancock and Jim Hughes of Galeyville, Billy Breakenridge, and Melvin Jones, all of whom knew Brocius well, stated that he had left the country nearly ten months before his alleged killing by Wyatt Earp in 1882. Several contemporaries identified William Brocius as an alias for William Graham.

Some believed that after his wounding by Jim Wallace in May 1881, Brocius went to Mexico or Texas, but Jones claimed to have met him on the San Francisco River near what is now Reserve, New Mexico, in the summer of '81. According to Jones, he rested on Negrito Creek to heal his wound and then went north. Although Hancock maintained that Graham and Brocius were two different men, he stated that Graham ranched on the Blue for several years before going to Montana. Frank Noland, who was seven years old at the time, believed Graham to be Brocius.

"Bill Graham was the biggest hearted and most liberal man on the river," Noland told his children.

He helped us many times after the death of my father and not only us but anyone else he thought was in need. His hair was long and curly and he wore it down to his shoulders. He used to play the harmonica, and when we heard the music we knew that Bill was coming and would soon be at the ranch.

Before he came to the Blue, Buckalew had worked the ranges of Cochise County, and he liked that country of easier winters. He convinced Susanna that it was time to move again. Only months after their wedding day, they packed the wagon and, with the three older children to help, started the cattle on a drive of 160 miles down the San Francisco, across the Gila, and up the San Simon to camp at Squaw Spring under the bare, jagged rocks of Cochise Head. Once more Susanna made her home in a tent, just in time to bring daughter Audie Lee into the world.

While the High Five were operating, Leonard Alverson moved with a little bunch of cattle and a partner, Bill Warderman, to Tex Canyon. It isn't known if they bought their stock with money saved from their cowboying wages or if they happened on unbranded calves with no identifiable mothers. They moved in with John Cush in Alonzo Whaley's old cabin, where Pine Gulch comes into Tex. Cush, who also went by the name of Vinredge, had a few cows, as well as a saloon in Pearce. The surrounding Erie Cattle Company range—Box Canyon, Rustler Canyon, and High Lonesome—was a favored rest area for the outlaws, who were always made welcome at the Cush-Alverson-Warderman cabin.

The Christian gang, though they seldom picked up much spending money from the little stores they knocked over, always helped themselves to chuck. Salt pork, coffee, baking powder, and flour were easily packed into the hills for basic staples. No doubt a dry cow sometimes furnished camp meat, but the boys were careful not to antagonize the ranchers, and there was plenty of game—whitetail deer in the brushy country, mule deer in the more open foothills, and antelope on the grassy prairie. Parrots and turkeys fed in the pines of the higher country, and the numerous Harlequin quail on the oak-juniper slopes were easily taken.

In the fall of 1897, while the remnants of Will Christian's gang were slipping away to their train holdup near Grants, another gang moved into the Chiricahuas. The Erie manager, Bob Johnson, was aware of their presence but wasn't disturbed by it. Leonard Alverson called them the "Snaky Four," and thought them a poor substitute for the High Five. It wasn't generally known that Will Christian had been killed, and some people thought it was *his* gang that was still frequenting the Pedregosas. Soon the leader of the new gang was also being referred to as "Blackjack."

The new Blackjack was Thomas E. Ketchum, new to the Chiricahuas but not to crime. He was born in San Saba County, Texas, where he indulged in antisocial activities that caused him to come west— for freedom, if not for health. He was a cowboy in the Pecos Valley of New Mexico when his older brother, Samuel, joined him, and soon the two were robbing stores and stages. After killing a storekeeper during a robbery in June '96, they looked for a still healthier climate farther west.

Sam went to work for Gene Rhodes on his horse ranch in the San Andrés Mountains. Tom rode farther west to the San Simon Valley, where he made contact with Will Carver, an Erie cowboy whom he had known back home. Carver, from Coryell County, Texas, had been a partner of Sam's in a Bandera saloon.

After a few months of ranch work interspersed with long periods of rest, Ketchum and Carver went back to Texas. There they picked up two more old acquaintances, Dave Adkins and Bud Upshaw. In May 1897 they stopped a train and blew up the express car safe to salvage some forty-two thousand dollars. Then Ketchum, Carver, and Adkins rode west to recruit Sam from the Rhodes place.

(Five years later Gene Rhodes moved to New York State and became famous for his literate western fiction. It was rumored that his involvement with the Ketchums forced his move, a rumor he was careful not to deny. It is just as likely he moved because his eastern wife wanted to see an occasional rain.)

The Snaky Four rode north, and on September 3 they used fourteen sticks of dynamite to blow up the express car of a night train in

Folsom, New Mexico. The take was only two to three thousand dollars. Within three weeks the four were back in camp near the head of Tex Canyon.

In the spring of 1897, a man known in Texas as John Hespatch cooked for the San Simon wagon as Ed Cullin. He earned a derisive nickname when a Chinese restaurant owner in Lordsburg asked him to pay for his dinner. Ed, thinking to bluff him out, said, "Don't you know who I am? I'm 'Shoot-'em-up-Dick.' "

The proprietor pulled a six-shooter from under the counter, leveled it at Ed, and told him, "I 'Shoot-'em-up-Sam.' You pay."

Cullin was cooking at the Erie's Double Adobe headquarters on Whitewater Draw when Stubb Shattuck, one of the owners, asked him to fill the pitcher for the wash bowl. "Get it yourself, you bald-headed son-of-a-bitch," Ed growled.

This exchange possibly had some bearing on Ed's being unemployed in late November, when he began to hang out with the Ketchums.

In the liberal, populist, working man's West, the railroads were the public's enemy, owned by such piratical capitalists as Jay Gould, C. P. Huntington, and the Vanderbilts. To many they were fair game, and train robbers got some sympathy and, if not overt protection, at least a blind eye. If it weren't for George Scarborough's undercover job with the H's, the lawmen probably wouldn't have learned that a holdup was planned.

By the first week in December, in addition to Jeff Milton's posse, a swarm of U.S. marshals, sheriffs' deputies, and detectives employed by the railroads and Wells, Fargo Express Company patrolled the tracks between Willcox and Lordsburg. Even so, in the early evening of the ninth, Dave Adkins, Sam Ketchum, and Ed Cullin appeared at the cluster of buildings at Steins, where they shook down the postmaster for two dollars and the express office and station agent for a few more before they were joined by Tom Ketchum and Will Carver, who had been snipping the telegraph wires.

They forced the agent, at the point of his own .44 Winchester, to signal a stop to the Southern Pacific Flyer. The train crew was quickly taken under control, but when the express messenger and his two guards were commanded to come out with hands up, the response was a shotgun blast from inside the car. The robbers, highlighted by a bonfire they had built, had to take cover. Two of them climbed on the tender to pitch a charge of dynamite through the open door of the express car, but busy shotguns inside that door hampered their efforts. Shots had been exchanged for a half hour when Ed Cullin leaned forward to reload his pistol. A shotgun charge took off the top of his head. All the gang had received light wounds by then. They left Cullin where he lay and called it quits.

The telegraph line running west hadn't been cut, and word reached Bowie Station while the shooting was still going on. One posse left Bowie before midnight to head for Skeleton Canyon, where a tip indicated the robbers were headed. Another posse, including Milton and Scarborough, loaded horses into stock cars by moonlight and arrived in Steins before sunrise. At daylight they were bemused at watching a raven picking at gobbets of Cullin's brain on the roadbed. They followed a trail up the valley to San Simon headquarters on the cienega.

Some of the posse thought H cowboys had made the horse tracks they'd followed, but Scarborough was able to vouch for them. A confusion of tracks around the ranch made it difficult to pick up the trail again. It was the morning of December 12 before Milton's men got on the outlaws' trail leading up Tex Canyon. There they met the posse led by Cochise Sheriff Scott White, who had found nothing in Skeleton Canyon. The two parties followed horse tracks up the canyon to Tex Whaley's old place, where they found Leonard Alverson, Bill Warderman, and Walter Hoffman, a cowboy who was also known as Fatty Ryan.

Hoffman had a fresh bullet hole in his leg that the officers thought sufficient evidence for arresting the bunch, even though the men had made no attempt to escape. Even under forceful "interrogation," Hoffman maintained that his wound was the result of a drunken accident.

While questioning was underway, two Erie cowboys rode in, Tom Capehart and Henry Marshall. Even though they had seen the posse's horses tied by the corral and could have easily turned away, Milton took them into custody. Capehart received a gratuitous pistol-whipping in the process.

The officers didn't have clear evidence but were determined to make somebody pay for four days of hard riding without bed or breakfast. Hoffman was known to have killed a man over by the Swisshelms the previous August, and they had no doubt that the rest had guilty knowledge. The sheriff took them to San Simon in a wagon while Milton and Scarborough continued to try to flush out the Ketchums. They scooped up John Cush and found the gang's vacated camp in Shake Gulch. The Snaky Four, who had watched the activity from the rim of the canyon, then drifted off to Texas to rob two more trains.

In February the six men taken in Tex Canyon stood trial in Silver City for attempting to rob a mail car. John Cush used his Tex Canyon ranch and two hundred head of cattle as collateral to raise cash for a lawyer. The jury deliberated long enough to smoke a cigar and found them not guilty. Capehart, Marshall, and Cush were freed and they returned to the Chiricahuas. Cush, under the name Vinredge, joined the San Simon's fencing crew, and the other two went back to the Erie. But Alverson, Hoffman, and Warderman were held, tried, and found guilty of robbing the Steins post office. In September they began ten-year terms in Santa Fe for stealing two dollars that none of them ever saw.

While Alverson and his partners were taking the fall, the gang split into pairs. The Ketchums rode chuck line across New Mexico, stopping at William French's WS Ranch near Alma on the San Francisco River long enough to pay for the hospitality by running off with two blooded horses. By late October the four were reunited in Wyoming. It is likely that it was there that they met Butch Cassidy and "Elzy" Lay, who had been associated for several years in a series of horse thefts and holdups from South Dakota to Utah. Soon the six of them were wintering in Cochise County, where Cassidy as Jim Lowe and Lay as William McGinnis were hired to ride for the Erie.

Presumably, the Snaky Four wandered about their old haunts in the mountains that winter of 1898–99, but they were a less congenial gang. "Blackjack" Tom Ketchum was a more successful train robber than his namesake, but he was a hot-tempered, morose, and unsavory person. He picked on Dave Adkins, whom he blamed for a loose mouth, until Dave left them.

French's foreman, Clarence "Tip" Tipton, had married and set up a place of his own, so French sent for an old employee, Perry Tucker, now a straw boss on the Erie. In February 1899 Perry arrived on the WS, weeded out cowboys he didn't want, and sent for Lowe and McGinnis. Lowe enlisted three other Erie cowboys: Clay McGonagill, Max Axford, and Jim James. Tom Capehart showed up soon, and French had seven ex-Erie hands on the payroll. French was pleased with them. Rustling decreased and the operation benefited from a shakedown.

In May Tom Ketchum and his two remaining men helped themselves to Erie horses and left the shelter of the Chiricahuas to ride east. They may have stopped at the San Simon Cienega on the way, and this may have been the time told of in Chenowth family history that Gus Chenowth recognized the brands and threatened Ketchum with death if he didn't take his stolen horses out of the old adobe corral near the house.

In June Will McGinnis told French he wanted his time. The horses were all gentled, and there wasn't enough excitement to hold his interest. The captain, who found him an excellent hand as well as a "paladin among cowboys," didn't want to see him go. McGinnis joined his old companions, including Tom Capehart, who had come up from the WS. Tom may have been an honest cowboy whose treatment at the hands of Milton's posse and time in jail convinced him that if he was tarred with the badman's brush he might as well be one, but some chroniclers of the "Wild Bunch" claim Capehart was really Harvey Logan, a long-time member of Butch Cassidy's robber gang. At any rate, the gang held up the same train near Folsom twice. Sam Ketchum was fatally wounded by a posse, but before he died, he exonerated Alverson, Cush, and Warderman of the Steins robbery.

McGinnis and Tom Ketchum were also taken. Will McGinnis went to trial first, and in October at Raton he was sentenced to life without divulging his true identity as Ellsworth Lay.

The Blackjacks in all their characters were out of business, but the Chiricahuas weren't through with outlaws. After the capture of McGinnis/Lay, Capehart and Carver made their separate ways west again. At least for a time Capehart was on the WS, and Will Carver may have returned to the Chiricahuas. Somewhere between eastern New Mexico and Cochise County, he seems to have picked up tall, lean Ben Kilpatrick, on the dodge after helping stop a train in Wyoming the past June.

In February 1900 two men held up a bank in Las Cruces and got away with three thousand dollars. It was strongly suspected that Tom Capehart was one of them. Carver or Kilpatrick may have been the other. Sheriff Pat Garrett tracked them as far as the Mogollon Mountains, but they got away and their identities were never learned.

George Scarborough's cover was blown after the Steins holdup, but he still doggedly combed the area for rustlers and holdup men. He was in Deming on April 2, 1900, when he got a wire from Walter Birchfield, now foreman for the Triangles. He had come across the carcass of a freshly killed Triangle beef. The number of tracks indicated more men than he wanted to tackle alone.

Scarborough took the next train to San Simon, where Birchfield met him with a horse, and they immediately left for the kill site, about a dozen miles down the San Simon River below ranch headquarters. They reached the spot after dark and had to wait until daylight for enough light to pick up tracks.

They followed the trail about thirty miles south across the railroad and to the Chiricahuas, which they reached at midday. In the mouth of Triangle Canyon, they found where the men they were after had recently boiled coffee in a lard can. The coals were still warm. They split the lukewarm dregs and followed the tracks on up the south fork of the canyon. The trail then circled to the right and crossed a low ridge to a spring in the north fork.

It was obvious they couldn't drop down onto the outlaws' position undetected. Birchfield suggested a route over a divide into the south fork of Wood Canyon to escape an ambush. He said later if he'd realized at the outset that a gang of outlaws had killed the steer rather than honest rustlers, he'd have let them have the beef. But Scarborough insisted they go down to confront the men they'd been trailing.

A couple of hundred yards from the outlaws' position on top of a small hill below them, the two opened fire, which was immediately returned. No shots were effective, and everyone took cover behind boulders and waited for somebody to make a move. After half an hour Scarborough, hoping to bluff the quarry, determined to ride away as if giving up the fight. His real purpose was to find a better position.

They had gone three hundred yards when the outlaws fired on them, hit the lawman in the thigh, and knocked him off his horse. Birchfield jumped down, but his spooky horse pulled away and ran off before he could pull his rifle. He crawled to the unconscious Scarborough and got the rifle from his horse, which was standing ground-tied. In a hail of bullets he managed to get behind a sycamore, picking up a ricochet in the shoulder in the process.

Scarborough came to and worked his way to Birchfield's tree. It was scant cover. About thirty yards away a pile of boulders offered better protection. Birchfield crawled to it, built a fort, then got his partner to its protection. After dark he covered him with his coat and rode the detective's horse for help.

He rode thirteen miles through falling snow and sleet to H headquarters on the cienega to find that the wagon and the whole crew had left for San Simon to start the spring roundup. There was nothing to do but ride on to town, getting there at three in the morning. He found Holmes Maddox in a poker game with two other cowboys. The four borrowed a buckboard and got back to Triangle Canyon at daybreak.

They found Scarborough alive but cold and thirsty. Birchfield was tired and hungry. In twenty-four hours he had gone forty-five miles horseback, had a gunfight, and ridden twelve miles or so in the wagon, all on little more than coffee grounds. At San Simon they were met

by Scarborough's son, Ed, and a doctor. Also there was Sheriff Ed
Beeler of Apache County, who had been on the trail of men he be-
lieved to be the same outlaws suspected of killing two possemen near
St. Johns. George Scarborough died the next morning.

The spring in Triangle Canyon where Scarborough caught up with
the men who killed him is now called Outlaw Spring, but the identity
of the outlaws is unknown. Most authorities place Tom Capehart and
Will Carver on the scene, as well as Ben Kilpatrick. Scarborough's bi-
ographer, Robert DeArment, names T. C. Hilliard as a fourth man. A
year later Ed Scarborough arrested Hilliard but had to release him
for lack of evidence. Will Carver helped rob a train and a bank before
a Texas sheriff killed him in 1901. Ben Kilpatrick was killed several
years later trying to rob a train. Capehart was thought to have gone
across the border—unless he was the Harvey Logan look-alike who
was killed after a 1903 train robbery in Utah.

Tom Ketchum waited a year in a New Mexico prison for his trial
in September 1900. In the interval he had a little fun with a gullible
lawman. He gave a sheriff the precise directions to a juniper tree in
Tex Canyon where his plunder was buried and was gleefully satisfied when the man scuttled off to Cochise County to dig in vain for
a nonexistent treasure. He dictated a statement admitting the Steins
robbery and denied that Alverson, Hoffman, and Warderman had any
part in it, but out of characteristic malice, he implicated a Diamond
A cowboy, Bill Walters, who wasn't there either.

He went to his hanging under his own name, still unable to convince reporters that he wasn't the original Blackjack Christian. That
hanging was most spectacular and ensured his place in history. The
seven-foot drop jerked his head off.

## Chapter 10

# Paradise

It is a certainty that the foothill circle in the Chiricahuas constitutes a mining camp today with the broadest prospects.
***Douglas Daily Dispatch*, 1906**

Galeyville's death as an active camp didn't end the prospecting. A dozen or so veterans of the 1880s boom hung around the California Mining District badgering holes between Whitetail Canyon and the mouth of Cave Creek. Among those who stayed were Rube Haddon, Albert Fink, Dave Doran, Chris Grauer, and Belgium-born Peter Fervent. John Sullivan had built his "Rock House" in Whitetail Canyon, and the Hands brothers in partnership with another British pair, Edward and Paris "Pete" Boyer, worked the old Dunn Mine just across the divide in Pinery's North Fork.

Confidence that a bonanza lay under the next ledge kept prospectors climbing steep hillsides and driving steel with a four-pound hammer. Others were motivated more by love of independence than by hope. Though there were hot days and cold nights and grueling labor, a man could shave or not, kill a deer if he was hungry, sell enough ore to buy a little powder, and could call his own shots.

By the turn of the century, with the panic of 1893 over, the economy was booming again and the mines with it. America's electrification brought a demand for copper wire. Increased production and inadequate smelting facilities in Bisbee prompted the Phelps Dodge

Copper Company to find a location for a new smelter for its Copper Queen Mine. They found that spot twenty-five miles east, where the Aguaje de Agua Prieta overlapped the border on a spacious flat where John Slaughter, the Erie company, and others were accustomed to holding roundups.

James Douglas of Phelps Dodge, John Slaughter, Lem Shattuck, and four other early birds, as the International Land and Improvement Company, laid out the town site of Douglas. The first lots were sold in January 1901. Tents went up on corner lots, ground was broken for a smelter, and crews started laying railroad track from the mines headed for El Paso. The El Paso and Southwestern Railroad, with Phelps Dodge as principal shareholder, planned to build a railroad that could take ore to the smelter and reach lines that could take copper cathodes to eastern markets and bring coal and coke from their mines in Dawson, New Mexico. Boosterism was general.

In June 1900 twelve men in four camps were scattered along Turkey Creek from Galeyville to the site of old Camp Crawford. Rube Haddon had a shack at the fork of Graveyard Canyon and Turkey Creek. Another camp held two old-timers who also had been in the country since the demise of Galeyville: Owen C. Davis, known as O. C., and Louis H. Scanlon, who had been working recently in the gold mine at Pearce. Three Hannon brothers from New Jersey, two Phelans from Texas, and George A. Walker and George Myers camped under the rhyolite cliffs of White Rock Mountain upstream from Haddon.

Running water isn't common in southern Arizona, and to sweating travelers who had reached the sycamore-shaded stream after crossing sunstruck greasewood flats, Turkey Creek seemed like heaven. They named the camp Paradise, despite the lack of women. Except for one widower, they were all bachelors.

George Walker had come west to Phoenix with his parents as a boy. An avid reader, he grew up with a spirit of adventure and inquiry and became a part of the rush to the Klondike, where he failed to make his fortune. He left Yukon Territory still tantalized by gold and came south with another sourdough, George Myers, to look over Pearce, Arizona's most recent boom town. There the Commonwealth

Mine was chewing up a small mountain, but by the time they arrived, Pearce's boom had peaked. They both knew there was no future in mucking for someone else, and they were readily recruited when Lou Scanlon suggested they join him in starting their own rush in the Chiricahuas.

While Scanlon looked for mineral around Harris Mountain, Myers and Walker prospected in Indian Creek under Cochise Head, then drifted over into Turkey Creek, where they staked out lead-silver prospects across the creek from their camp. They optimistically called one of their claims the Leadville Mine, for the fabulous bonanza in Colorado that was currently staging a resurgence.

Another miner attracted to the district was Ulrich Rieder, born in Switzerland. "Ully" came to Whitetail Canyon in 1900 and camped with John Sullivan until he could put up a shack of his own nearby. He immediately started to erect monuments around his Eagle claim, high in Mackey Canyon above Sullivan's Eclipse Mine.

In the spring of that year, a Mississippi-born locomotive engineer from San Simon, George "Dad" Colvin, a weekend prospector, with his fifteen-year-old step-grandson, George Hall, staked out the Turkey Creek and the Comet claims on the north slope of a hill overlooking Chiricahua Flats. Dad Colvin's nickname may have derived from a bizarre genealogical tangle. He had married young George Hall's grandmother after being made a widower by the death of the daughter of his current wife's first husband's first wife. He was his new wife's stepson, his deceased wife's—and his *own*—stepfather-in-law.

His household in San Simon included his wife, Nancy, her daughter, Annie Rodgers, who was teaching school, and a couple of grandchildren. Later in 1900 Colvin left the railroad and moved into the mouth of Whitetail Canyon below Rieder and Sullivan, where he continued to prospect and record claims—the Ju, the Patty Mack, the Tip Top, the Saturn—along the ridge dividing Jhus and Whitetail Canyons.

In the spring of 1901, Colvin was joined by his stepdaughter, Henrietta, her husband, Robert Davis Hall, a railroad construction worker in San Simon, and their children, Charles, Fred, and Nannie. Infected by his father-in-law's enthusiasm, Hall lost no time placing monuments around his Last Chance mining claim, following it in short order with the Manila and the Morning Star.

Henrietta Hall wasn't as interested in mining as in taking care of her children. Agriculture seemed a surer way of putting food on the table, and she urged her husband, "R. D.," to file for a homestead straddling the creek immediately downstream from Dad Colvin's, just under Split Rock, a monumental formation at the mouth of the canyon. She bought a small bunch of cattle and the Z-T brand from Edward W. "Will" McCarty, who gave up his cattle business to punch 7H cows.

The spot the Halls picked for their homestead was probably the location of William Shanahan's first cabin. The old Irish bachelor, who had been running his longhorn cattle on Whitetail Flats and in the valley since 1880, had built himself a new place. Sometime after Ulzana's raid in 1885 he moved to the edge of a sacaton meadow where Turkey Creek emerges from behind Harris Mountain and put up a four-room puddled adobe house split by a dogtrot. He roofed it with ungalvanized corrugated iron, which soon rusted, and it came to be called the Redtop. Though rapidly deteriorating, it still stands today—after the Reed cabin in Cave Creek, the oldest structure in this part of the county.

In 1900 San Simon had a population of fifty-two, which included twenty children, nine married women, a widow who ran a boarding house, and one young unmarried woman (who must have been an object of attention from the fifty or more single cowboys within a thirty-mile radius). Thus, even in what passed for civilization in eastern Cochise County, men outnumbered women by almost three to one. Out of town, the ratio was ten to one.

There were few women or children in the mountains or on the valley ranches. Mary Chenowth had six children at home down on the cienega, though daughter Ola, at eighteen, was no longer a child. The thirteen men at 7H headquarters were all single. Cave Creek's population totaled only ten. The only woman was Sarah, the wife of Mitchell Pentecost, an immigrant prospector from England who camped in the mouth of the canyon.

Stephen Reed's six children up the canyon were now motherless. Just the year before, as Isabella rode out of the corral, ten-year-old Grover closed the pole gate behind her too soon, hitting the horse in the rump. The filly skittered out from under her, and she caught a foot in a stirrup and was dragged to death. In the winter following his wife's death, Stephen boarded his family for schooling in San Simon, where the older girls, Lula and Claudie, cared for the younger ones.

Before the Colvins moved up from the valley, there were no women in Whitetail except old Mary Bridger above Sullivan's, where her husband, Tom, prospected the canyon's highest reaches.

From the railroad south to Rattlesnake Point and along the foothills to Whitetail Creek, there were three solitary prospectors and six ranches with a woman on each. The total population on that stretch was thirty-three, fifteen of them children. One of the six women was Laura Wood Hancock in Wood Canyon, the daughter of the same Judge Miles Wood who had arrested Billy the Kid some years before. Laura had ridden from Bonita to a dance at Apache Pass, where she met Jim Hancock. They were married in 1898.

Another of the women was Susanna (Noland) Buckalew at Squaw Spring on Keating Draw. She now had seven children at home, though Maggie, at nineteen, must be counted as a woman, a fact not overlooked by Lee Eaton, a cowboy from Willcox.

During the fall and winter, increased activity on Turkey Creek focused on a group of claims on the ridge dividing Jhus Canyon from Turkey Creek. The property had been located several years before by Thomas "Cap" Burns, a Canadian Irishman who had prospected the vicinity since Galeyville days. His partners were John McClellan, recently arrived in the Chiricahuas from Cripple Creek, Colorado, and John A. Duncan, who had been in the area since selling his interest in the Dunn Mine to Galey in 1880. (He's not to be confused with John W. Duncan, who came into the country shortly afterward to work for the San Simon).

It's one thing to clamber over rocks to locate a promising ledge and recognize its mineral content. It's a different thing to make it into a mine. Development takes a lot of money, and raising capital requires vision, energy, and the ability to interest those with the spondulicks to risk. John Duncan was such a man. He believed that there was strength in unity and that, if the independent-minded prospectors would bunch their claims, they would have a better chance of attracting capital.

In 1901 a loose consortium was born, the exact composition of which is unclear. Men joined and dropped out and the officers changed. Myers and Walker joined Burns and Duncan at the start; the Hannon brothers sold out their claims to the group; and at one time R. D. Hall had a stake in it. Professional credentials were lent to the cause by S. S. Badger, a mining engineer.

The population of the California Mining District grew. In anticipation, Walker and Myers laid out a twenty-acre town site on the west side of Turkey Creek with lots measuring 25 by 100 feet lining both sides of Market Street paralleling the creek. They were their own first customers. Walker opened a small store, and Myers, putting first things first, opened a saloon. Both enterprises started out in tents.

With the optimism of a promoter, George Walker renamed White Rock Mountain, giving it the more romantic name of Silver Peak. He was in a romantic mood because of his acquaintance with Stephen Reed's oldest daughter, Lula Lee. They were married in Bowie before the summer was over, and one source credits their state of bliss with the selection of the name for the Paradise post office, which was established in October with George as postmaster. However happy the couple, the camp had been called Paradise for a year already.

Lula's happiness was interrupted at brief intervals when she was terrified by drunken cowboys galloping down the road not twenty feet in front of her canvas-covered home, whooping and firing their pistols. As soon as possible, George built her a frame house on a lot at the southwest corner of the town site, and at the same time he replaced the tented store with one of lumber. With Lula's marriage, it became fifteen-year-old Claudie Reed's job to keep house for her younger brothers and sisters in San Simon that fall and winter.

John Duncan's salesmanship was rewarded when, in late 1902, he interested the Calumet and Arizona Company in the Turkey Creek claims. The C & A was largely owned by Michigan investors attracted to Arizona when copper production on the Keweenaw Peninsula began to flag. In Bisbee the C & A was the Copper Queen's biggest rival, and in fact, it had just blown in its new smelter in Douglas ahead of Phelps Dodge's. The C & A became the major shareholder in the newly organized Chiricahua Development Company in Paradise, providing most of the capital.

In 1902 a factor adding to the attraction of Turkey Creek's mines was the El Paso & Southwestern Railroad. Built to connect Bisbee and Douglas to El Paso, its tracks in the San Simon Valley passed within fifteen miles of Paradise. The railroad drilled a well where engines took on water for the pull into Antelope Pass and the Animas Valley. The surveyors picked a spot a mile or so south of a broad flat where the H's were in the habit of working cattle, and they gave the new station the appropriate name of Rodeo. Rodeo's first resident was "Pop" Bond, who, anticipating the route, had claimed a tract lying athwart the right-of-way, forcing the railroad to buy him out.

It was increasingly difficult for the big cattle spreads to operate, depending as they did on free grazing. For some time the Erie had been able to hold its range through bluff and control of the limited water, but the numbers of settlers pouring into the country, filing homesteads, digging wells, and helping themselves to company beef became a lot to contend with. The first year of the new century was to be the Tumble T's last. The absentee stockholders sold off their cattle, steers bringing thirty-five dollars a head, sold their patented holdings to the Ryan brothers' Double F, and dissolved the company.

Among those who had crowded the Erie were Charles and Jennie Barfoot Gardner, the same who had barely missed Massai's pass through Pinery Canyon and Bonita Canyon in 1890. Charlie Gardner was raised southwest of San Antonio, Texas, but by 1900 he'd been working cattle for twenty-five years from there into southeastern Arizona. The Gardners hadn't tarried in Pinery. Charlie had tried to keep a little place of his own where he could brand a calf now and then, but he'd had to drift from ranch to ranch for the wages he could make. By 1900 he was back in the mountains as a partner of his brother-in-law, Josiah "Joe" Glenn.

It was a reunion of sorts. When he was only a boy, Charlie and Joe had made a trail drive to Kansas together. Now they were running cattle in High Lonesome Canyon, south of Rucker and just north of the Bar Boot Ranch of Englishman Bill Lutley, who had preceded them by a year or two as an interloper on Erie range.

The Gardners arrived in that country early enough to become acquainted with some of the free and easy men who frequented that end of the Chiricahuas. One of them was Clay McGonagill, whom Charlie had known in New Mexico. McGonagill and Charlie's nephew, Joe Gardner, were hired for the spring works by Bunk Robinson, Walter Birchfield's successor as manager of the Diamond A's. Though only eighteen, Clay had the reputation for being a hell of a cowboy. When he was shown a horse that nobody could ride, he averred that *he* could—and backward. Stakes were collected, and the blindfolded horse was saddled with the cantle over his withers and was held by the ears until the rider was seated. The horse was turned loose and Clay rode him to a standstill.

McGonagill was one of the Cochise County cowboys taken on at Captain French's WS in Alma by Butch Cassidy/Jim Lowe. There is no reason to believe that he was ever involved in the criminal escapades of either of the Blackjacks or the "Wild Bunch" or that he ever stole a horse. Cattle are different. Local oral history says that McGonagill used the short canyon under Hummingbird Spring southeast of Portal for holding 7H cattle until he could market them. If it is true, it is equally true that he wasn't burdened by feelings of guilt.

Arriving first, the big cattlemen had done as they pleased for seventeen years, but by 1900 their grip was slipping. The ranges had never recovered from the abuse of the 1880s and the drought of 1891–93, and as the grass diminished, demand for it increased. The ranges of the 7H, the Erie, the Triangles, and the CCC were ringed and riddled by independent ranchers. Not only did the "nesters," as the company men called them, compete for grass and water, but many of them got their breeding stock by branding company heifers.

Jesse Benton in Tex Canyon was one of the small competitors. He was only thirteen when he made his first trail ride to Kansas with a herd of Texas cattle. He'd worked on Arizona ranches since 1882, mostly above the Mogollon Rim, and by the '90s had a butcher shop in Pearce with a partner, Ed Wolfe. Benton became acquainted with the Tex Canyon ranch when he bought slaughter steers from Leonard Alverson and John Cush. The latter had hired a lawyer to defend them from the charge of robbing the train in Stein's Pass, mortgaging the ranch to him in lieu of a cash fee. Alverson went to the pen, Cush went to work for the 7H, and the lawyer sold the ranch and cattle to Benton and Wolfe for fifteen hundred dollars.

San Simon cattle were used to watering at the head of Tex and were ruining the grass, so Benton and Wolfe built two miles of fence across the mouth of the canyon and threw the 7H cattle out into the valley below. The company foreman, Jess Henley, retaliated by attempting to keep Benton and Wolfe off the valley range. At roundup he denied them permission to join the wagon or to cut their cattle. It was only in the face of a shotgun in the crook of Jesse Benton's arm that Henley backed down.

The range was open, and Benton believed he had as much right to a piece of it as anyone. Henley took the stand that the country belonged to whoever got there first with the most cattle. The disagreement—and the confrontations arising from it—might have become serious had Clabe Merchant not gotten wind of it. He'd known Benton back in Texas, and he called his foreman off. Probably the events were unconnected, but 1901 was Henley's last year with the H's. After working for the outfit for at least fifteen years and ramrodding it for most of that time, he'd had enough. Oscar Cochran took over.

Such contests as that between Benton and Henley were multiplied around the fringes of the surviving large ranches, which had greater resources than any of their contestants but were outnumbered by the aggregate and began to shrink. The chief victim was the range itself. The smarter ranchers realized that the heavy stocking of the 1880s had put too much pressure on the semidesert savannas. Col. Henry Hooker was one of the forward-looking stockmen who advocated lighter use. One of the first to introduce pure-bred bulls to his *corriente* longhorn cows, he saw more profit in one fat steer than in two poor ones.

However, recognition of a problem doesn't solve it. The land-hungry settler looking for a toehold on water and grass where he could establish his family knew that if *his* cow didn't eat that bunch of grass, his neighbor's would. Benton and Wolfe had about five hundred head of cattle competing with the 7H's ten thousand, probably more than most of the settlers in the valley. But by 1900 a score of brands were nibbling at the edges of what the San Simon Cattle Company thought of as *their* grass. The crowding may have been one reason the San Simon bought a 1,500-section ranch forty-five miles east of Carlsbad in 1897, stocked it with five hundred cows from the Arizona place, and called it, too, the San Simon. In 1902 Clabe Merchant sold out his ranches near Abilene and moved to the eastern division of their joint holdings to give it his entire attention.

With Clabe's move, the two old friends split their partnership. Merchant took the eastern ranch and turned over his share of the 7H and two thousand dollars' boot to Parramore, ending a business association of many years—one based on total trust. It didn't end the friendship, however, and years later after his old partner's death, Clabe said that Jim "was in the cow business with me for twenty-six years and he was just too good a man to talk about."

Trust was a common way of doing business in those days. From the beginning, the San Simon sold their cattle through A. E. De-Riegles of Denver, who for the first two years came down to inspect the cattle. He learned he needn't bother. One of the partners would write to tell him how many cattle they would sell and their condition, and he would write back to tell them what he could pay. Those letters constituted a "contract," and DeRiegles estimated that over a period of twenty-two years he'd bought seventy-five thousand head of cattle from them.

One year when prices were high, an unusual number of speculative buyers were scouting for cattle. One of those "in-and-outers" approached Clabe to inquire about the 7H calves and was told they were already sold.

"If it's a fair question, what did they bring?" the would-be buyer wanted to know.

"I don't know," Clabe told him, " 'Dee' hasn't written me yet."

Paradise was booming in 1902. No count was made, but the population must have increased tenfold since the 1900 census had listed eleven men. The Chiricahua Development Company, under the superintendency of James Hoatson from Michigan, ordered mining machinery delivered by rail to Rodeo. Getting it up the hill to the mine in the saddle wasn't easy. The straight-line distance from Market Street in the bottom of the canyon was only two-and-a-half miles, but the elevation to be gained was one thousand feet.

Workmen hacked out a road, with the last mile a series of sharp switchbacks. An eighteen-foot boiler for generating steam power, added to the sixteen-mule hitch, was too long for the tight curves. A special wagon was constructed with a tongue and swinging axle on a king bolt at each end. Bypasses were cut to continue beyond the switchbacks far enough for the rig to clear the bend. The outfit was taken to the end of the bypass, where the team was unhitched, brought around to the rear of the wagon, and rehitched. What had been the lead axle was locked in place and the rear axle unlocked so the load could be hauled to the next switchback, where the process was repeated.

To support the mine and miners, an even larger population of men and a few women flocked in to provide the various services required. William "Dad" Hayes, a locomotive engineer with the SP in San Simon, left the railroad and with his wife, Emily, opened the Paradise Hotel, complete with restaurant and bakery. George Walker retained the office of postmaster and some mining interests, but to concentrate on selling real estate, he sold his store to Dick Brown and Joe Slater. Why Walker retained the post office isn't clear. It was no more than a cubbyhole in the corner of the store where the mail sack from San Simon was sorted. His compensation for 1903 was $59.22.

Another general store was opened by John Rock and Frank H. Christy. Rock was an Apache who, as an infant, had been taken by soldiers after an attack on his people's camp and had been raised by a white couple.

A third store was a combined lumberyard and hardware store owned by Edward F. Sweeney with his sons, Ed and Jack. The Sweeneys came from the logged-off forests of northern Michigan and now had a lucrative trade as the town converted from tents to frame buildings. Their source of supply was the sawmill at the head of Pine Canyon, only seven miles by trail but closer to sixty by any road you could get a loaded wagon over.

Old Brannick K. Riggs's middle boy, B. B. Riggs, had bought Major Downing's Pine Canyon sawmill several years before. The growth of Pearce across the Sulphur Springs Valley made a ready market for lumber, and to meet the need, he moved the mill up Pine into uncut timber at the Rattlesnake Canyon fork. About 1900 he moved the setting a second time, to the head of the canyon, where a few years earlier Malcolm Barfoot had grown potatoes in an open meadow. Two years later Riggs sold a share in the mill to J. W. "Will" Sanders and Ed Boyer. Since 1884 Sanders had been cutting and hauling logs for Downing and later for Riggs. Boyer had also been in the mountains since coming from England in 1887, but his interests had centered around mining and he was still partner with the Hands brothers in the Dunn mine.

Some buildings in Paradise were set on solid footings of mortared stone, but the common practice was to set out, at eight-foot intervals, rows of short stubs of cedar logs on flat stones to support the floor joists. These piers were cut just long enough to keep the floor off the ground. To conserve lumber, joists, framing, and purlins were set at wide intervals. Sheathing, and sometimes roofing as well, was of wide boards and battens. Occasionally Douglas fir was split into shakes, but more often rolls of paper covered a roof. The more up-to-date and affluent builders roofed with sheets of corrugated iron.

The sawmill had no planing equipment, and consequently, all lumber was rough sawn, and it drank up paint so fast it was often left unpainted. The demand for lumber was so great there wasn't time to season it, and it was common for a completed structure to be occupied while pitch still oozed from knots and the smell of turpentine perfumed the air.

At first everybody dipped buckets of water from the creek, an unreliable source for the growing population and, with the proliferation of outhouses, not a safe one. A few wells were dug, but many citizens found it convenient to keep a water barrel at the back door and buy water from Frank Barfield, who delivered it for two bits a barrel.

Early in 1902 Paradise was a town of tents, most of them pitched over board floors with sides of slabs. It's probably significant that the second "permanent" frame structure in the camp was the Cock-a-too Saloon, owned and operated by Scotty Cobaugh and Jim Coachman. It was shortly followed by Joe Larrieu's Mineral Park Saloon, which sported a billiard table, and by Ben Milam's, operating under the straightforward handle Boozer's Place. Soon after his opening across Market Street from the hotel, Milam hired Jack Cross to manage the saloon and concentrated his own efforts on the operation of a less elegant establishment across the creek known as Madge's Place, for his wife, a semiretired "professional woman" who handled several girls who were still working.

Similar businesses joined Madge's on the east side of the creek, and soon the expression "the other side of the creek" was used with a wink and a leer to refer to "the district." A predominantly male society with a shortage of refined ladies and their civilizing influence entertained itself mostly by drinking and playing cards. The combination frequently became boisterous, interfering with a hard-working miner's rest.

Paradise wasn't incorporated, but it was big enough to attract the county's notice, and the sheriff appointed Luke Short (not the famed gunman of an earlier time) to serve as deputy and constable. Short

had little crime to deal with, but he often had to restrain obstreper-
ous drunks by shackling them to a logging chain stretched between
two oaks by the creek at the upper end of the street.

In one morning's small hours, Luke attached one pitiably inebriated miner to the chain, and before he passed out, the man vomited.
With the new day Luke had more pressing business than tending to
his prisoner. The sun was beating down on the open "jail" before he
was unlocked and let go. Without taking time to clean up, the fellow
started hiking up the canyon to work at the Chiricahua Mine, but he
collapsed on the way and slept the rest of the day in the shade of a
cedar. Screw worm flies laid eggs in the vomitus in his nostrils during the morning, and by the following day maggots had eaten their
way up his nasal passages. The poor fellow, whose name is no longer
known, was said to have always been "a little funny" thereafter, and
Luke Short was blamed for being derelict in the care of his prisoners.

The saloons of Paradise couldn't have survived if they hadn't been
able to draw clients from farther afield than the mining camp alone.
Widow Ruch, the Triangles owner, had remarried, and her new husband, Oscar Roberts, enjoyed a good time and a game of poker. In
1902 there was a lot more action in Paradise than in Bowie or San
Simon, and he liked to bring his cowboys to town from time to time.
Shanahan was gone, and his empty house at the Redtop made a convenient overnight shelter for them.

Not all the miners who came to Paradise in 1902 came to work
for the Chiricahua Development Company. Some were lured by the
prospect of a strike of their own. Among them was Clarence "Cappy"
May, a trained mining engineer from Kentucky. After a fling at business in Louisiana, he'd drifted from one Colorado mine to another,
finally to camp in Round Valley with his Canadian wife, Isabel, and
their ten-year-old son, Clarence.

Another boomer for whom Paradise was the last rush was Joseph S.
Sanders. Born in Georgia and raised in Texas, Joe Sanders came west
for the first time in 1862 at eighteen, landing in Pinos Altos at a time
when Cochise and Mangas Coloradas were making any arrival prob-
lematical. For more than twenty years he mined and prospected from

Silver City to the Santa Ritas and back to the Black Range camps at Hillsboro and Kingston.

"He was a mountain man," his son said of him, somewhat ruefully. "He was in this country early enough to have anything he wanted, but he didn't want to see a neighbor's smoking chimney. Then it was all settled up and there was no place to go."

After nearly a quarter century of drifting, Joe went back to Texas to visit and in Brownsville met and married Susan Wilson. He stayed only long enough for daughter Lizzie to be born and to squeeze the last old cactus thorn from his hide before the West called him back. Susan's father and her fifteen-year-old brother, Fitch, accompanied them, first to El Paso, where a daughter, Emma, was born, then on to Solomonville on the Gila River. There in 1890 Joe filed on a homestead not far from that of Merejildo Grijalva, whom he may well have known in his Pinos Altos days.

Joe Sanders had roamed too long to put down roots, and he continued to wander, coming home often enough, in the words of one family member, "to get Susan pregnant and spend what money she had, then go away again." By 1902 Susan had two more kids, Myrtle and Bill. Joe packed them all with him this time and brought them to Paradise. He moved into an abandoned house on the left bank of Turkey Creek at the granite tanks where Captain Tidball had camped many years before. Susan had had enough of the poor provider. She got a divorce and took in miners' washing.

At Stephen Reed's suggestion, Joe moved over to Cave Creek about a half mile below Reed's hay field and made himself a shelter by digging a cut into the foot of the talus. He closed off the front with logs, roofed it with poles and earth removed from the cut, and went to trapping.

It was chance that brought Samuel "Jack" Maloney to the country in 1902. In later years he implied that he was run out of Texas, saying, "The people hated to see me leave. The sheriff followed me to the state line, just begging me to come back." In reality he was punching cows for the Matadors in west Texas when he heard the rumor spreading through the West, from south Texas to Montana, that Argentina still had free range where a man could start a spread of his own. Jack drew his wages and headed south.

When he got to El Paso, he found a wide-open town with a saloon and poker parlor on every corner. In the process of taking in the sights, Jack depleted his travel money in a game of faro. In a rare moment of discretion, he went to the depot, and at the window he plunked down his remaining change—two silver dollars, a quarter, a nickel, and two pennies—and asked for a ticket.

"Well, where do you want to go?" the agent asked him.

"Two dollars and thirty-two cents worth out of here, in any direction," Jack answered.

The agent consulted his tables and said, "That could take you to San Simon, Arizona, and leave you two cents to spend foolishly."

"That's just where I want to go," Jack told him.

When the train slowed for a stop in San Simon the next day, there were thousands of head of cattle being loose-herded on both sides of the tracks, waiting for cars. Jack went right to work for Oscar Cochran, helping to load 7H steers, then on to the cienega to put in the rest of the year.

Jack said of the San Simons that "it don't take long to spend the night there," but they gave their cowboys Sundays off when the work could spare them. It may have been on a sporadic trip to the Paradise saloons that Jack met Emma Sanders. It is more than likely that it was eighteen-year-old Lizzie who caused him to stop off at the Sanders place to see if breakfast was ready, but it was thirteen-year-old Emma who sized him up.

She was in the pole corral for the morning milking of a skittish cow. The old thing wouldn't stand and kept trying to put her foot in the bucket. Emma rapped her across the rump with the handle of a hay fork and the cow tried to jump out of the pen, couldn't make the height, and got hung up with her front legs between the two top poles of the corral.

"All right, you darn fool," Emma said, "I've got you now. You'll stay there until I'm through milking."

Watching the act from outside the corral, Jack guffawed in amusement tinged with approval. Emma had nothing to say to him, but from the corner of her eye she admired the big, handsome cowboy. She said forty years later, "He's the only man that ever laughed at me and got away with it."

The Sweeneys weren't able to get lumber into the yard as fast as they could sell it. They needed a road off the mountain from Barfoot Park through Turkey Park to Paradise to avoid the long trip around through Apache Pass. They didn't want to build a road for a sawyer who might sell to a competitor, so Ed bought out Sanders and Boyer's share before joining B. B. Riggs in hacking out a road. By 1903 it was possible to drive a wagon across the mountains on a track that was referred to as Riggs Road on the west side of the mountain and Sweeney's Road on the east. It had a steep pitch, and drivers often had to get down and roll a rock out of the way.

Ed Boyer and Will Sanders didn't dissolve their partnership when they went out of the timber business. They moved down into Paradise to open a wagon yard and livery stable, and to soothe the dry throats of the growing community, they built and stocked the Midway Saloon—"first class in all its appointments." Unconcerned about competition in the liquor business, they allowed Hiram Fisher to put up a stall in the corner of the wagon yard where one could buy a bottle of beer and a bowl of chile and beans.

Hiram, one of the older pioneers, was in Paradise to recuperate his body and fortune. With nine other cowboys he'd attempted to drive a herd of cattle from Stein's Pass to the Yukon, but by the time they reached northern British Columbia two years later, most of the cattle were lost and they were broke.

It was largely the payroll of the Chiricahua Mine that supported Paradise, but other outfits with fewer employees were driving tunnels and sinking shafts. David J. Doran, a veteran of Galeyville, had a crew tunneling into the east end of Blue Mountain, and another old-timer, Lou Scanlon, punched holes all around Harris Mountain. Their miners lived between the two mountains at the east end of White-tail Flats in a tent camp ambitiously called Eagle City, after Doran's Eagle Nest Mine.

Archie Stamps had a camp at Iron Springs in the Horsefall Canyon tributary to Pinery. Although it was on the west side of the range, Paradise was its post office and the closest saloon. For a while the old trail to Jhus Canyon over the saddle where Gus Chenowth had bested Cherokee Jack was called Stamps Trail.

Typical of the many young bachelors who were drawn to Paradise in search of a living, if not riches, was Otto Duffner, from Beaver Dam, Wisconsin. His first lessons in prospecting came from old Tom Burns. Burns wasn't content with his success in selling his shares in the Chiricahua Mine and was now exploring a new claim between Split Rock and the Nippers on Whitetail Flats.

Edward F. Epley was a bachelor when he first saw the Chiricahuas and had prospected around the Southwest for several years when Paradise got underway. But at twenty-eight he wanted to settle down and went back to Texas for a girl he'd known before. The newly married couple came by train to Rodeo and rented a buckboard and team. The bride, Ann Elizabeth, known as "Bee," said years later that, coming down Graveyard Canyon to the sycamores and walnut trees, she looked up at the timbered mountains and thought it the most beautiful place she'd ever seen. She wanted to spend the rest of her life there.

The increase in mining activity called for an expansion of support services. The first thing that came to the mind of a prospective entrepreneur was the liquor business. John Bendele and his wife, Maggie, opened another saloon "across the creek" in Paradise. Despite his Texas birthplace and his German parents, Bendele was known as "Swede." Alejo Bedoya came up from Solomonville with his wife and three kids to open the Monte Cristo Saloon in a tent on the mesa west of the creek bottom. Joe Wheeler and his nephew, "Little Joe," from Texas by way of Magdalena, New Mexico, opened still another. Joseph J. Wheeler had worked cattle for Parramore in Texas before

coming to Paradise to run a saloon and dance hall with rooms in
the back.

Not all the new businesses involved barrels and bottles. Kentuck-
ian G. B. Richardson, physician and surgeon, provided medical care,
and for a while a patient could get a second opinion from Dr. George
Nye. For a short time in 1904, a Dr. Hitchins ran a dispensary for the
Chiricahua Mine. German-born Alfred Hoch, who had been windmilling for the 7H's, set up a blacksmith shop where he fitted wagon
tires and shoed horses. The Chiricahua Mine had its own smiths to
keep tools sharpened. W. W. Saddler built Hooligan's Tonsorial Parlor, where one could also get a bath, and he built a home for himself
and his wife, Margaret, on the mesa west of the Monte Cristo and
across the road from it. John Heron, another barber, may have had
his own shop or perhaps had a chair at Hooligan's. Theodore Waugh-
tel's assay office was a vital facility for a mining camp. The 1904 Great
Register for Cochise County also lists a shoemaker, a plumber, two
carpenters, a stone mason, and Hen Bass, who played the banjo and
fiddle for the delectation of saloon customers.

The only Asian in Paradise, Gin Ah Quong, opened a small res-
taurant, and Joseph P. Wagner, a professional cook from Prussia and
"one of the best-known caterers of the Southwest," offered German-
style cooking in his Star Restaurant. Jim Hancock sold his KL Bar and
Cross J Ranches to T. J. Riggs and moved to Paradise, where he and
Laura built the two-story Arcadia Hotel at the upper end of Market
Street. Jim retained an interest in some cattle in the valley, and it was
Laura who paid particular attention to the operation of the hotel.

W. K. "Bill" Morrow had banged around quite a bit and wasn't so
rhapsodic as Bee Epley, but Paradise promised opportunity, and he
*did* spend the balance of his life in the vicinity. Bill was born in
Texas near Fort Worth but moved with his divorced mother to New
Mexico's Pecos Valley. In 1894 he married Eva, daughter of Martin
Corn, a big sheep rancher on the Pecos.

Bill went into partnership with Charles Ballard, the husband of

Eva's older sister, in a cattle ranch on Salt Creek north of Roswell. Ballard made a good partner. He was three years older than Bill and for eight years had run the wagon for cattleman J. C. Lea, whose home ranch became the nucleus of Roswell.

The larger share of the ranch work fell to Bill, owing to Ballard's job as deputy to Lincoln County Sheriff George Curry. It was during the period of his partnership with Morrow in 1897 that Ballard was involved in the fight with Blackjack Christian and the killing of Bob Hayes in Diamond A country.

During their four years on Salt Creek, Eva and Bill Morrow had three sons: Carson, Ralph, and Chester, also known as "Bally" for Bill's partner, Ballard. And in that same period Bill's brothers, Archie and Sam, took to stealing cattle, which led to bigger trouble. Sam became associated in a peripheral way with Tom Ketchum and then got in on a train robbery with someone else. He evaded the law under the name of Henry Sears until a "friend" gave him away.

Ballard was away for the last two years of the nineteenth century, serving in George Curry's company of Rough Riders. Bill Morrow had to mortgage his share of the ranch to put up bail and pay for Sam's defense. Sam was convicted and sent to the pen in Santa Fe.

In a postscript to Sam Morrow's short criminal spree, family ties and friendship paid off. Charles Ballard had become very close to his old employer, Sheriff George Curry, during their service together in Cuba. Curry had made a favorable impression on Teddy Roosevelt, who, when he became president after McKinley's assassination, appointed him to the governorship of New Mexico Territory. Charlie Ballard became Curry's chief of staff and arranged that Sam Morrow be made a trusty. Sam served the rest of his term living on the grounds of the governor's mansion as handyman and gardener. He was so appreciative that after his release and marriage, he named his first son George Curry Morrow. He later joined Bill in Paradise and worked as a carpenter.

In an unrelated act of generosity, Roosevelt pardoned Leonard Alverson, who returned to Arizona to find his old Tex Canyon ranch occupied by Jesse Benton. Alverson landed in Douglas and got an appointment as deputy sheriff.

Bill Morrow's support of Sam had cleaned him out but for a salvaged team and wagon and bit of cash, so he lit out for Telluride, Colorado, with Eva and their four children. He worked one winter in the Smuggler Union Mine high on the side of the mountain overhanging the town, but in the spring the miners struck and he was out of work. They moved again, landing on Eagle Creek, thirty miles north of Clifton, where Bill took up a little ranch near the Double Circles, but after barely a year he went to the Mexican border with a string of horses.

Morrow got a contract to grade the streetcar roadbed from downtown Douglas to the Copper Queen smelter. This made him a stake, which he invested in a share of an Agua Prieta saloon, but prosperity eluded him. Thieves ran off his horses, and through their loss, he lost his contract. He packed up once more and went to Paradise—his last move. Arizona Rangers followed the horse tracks across the border, but if they recovered any of the stock, Bill didn't. He later saw his brand on a horse dragging logs to the sawmill in Barfoot. The teamster had a bill of sale from an Arizona Ranger, and Bill was convinced the law had bilked him.

On his arrival on Turkey Creek, Bill housed his family under canvas and opened a saloon in partnership with Charles Randolph, a lean Texan whom he'd known on the Pecos. When they opened up for business, there were at least seven saloons ahead of them, but there were no butcher shops. Morrow saw in the meat trade a field less cluttered with players. He sold his share in the saloon to Randolph and built an adobe shop with a slaughter yard in the rear. An inventory of supplies and equipment on the bill of sale to his partner in the saloon included six beds and mattresses.

In mid-1902 an event of great importance to the history of the region slipped in quietly and for a time was scarcely noticed. The government created the Chiricahua Forest Reserve. The timber and range resources of the mountains, which had been free to the first or the strongest, were now to be managed for the public good by the Department of the Interior's General Land Office. There had been forest reserves in Wyoming and Colorado since 1892, but it wasn't until '97 that Congress authorized the hiring of employees to manage them. Roosevelt was an ardent conservationist, and when he became president in 1901, he added over 150 million acres to the country's reserves.

The Chiricahua Reserve was only a paper concept for six months, until the appointment in early 1903 of Forest Ranger Charles T. McGlone with an office in Willcox. He had a big job for one man. On the land under his care, three sawmills were operating, and dozens of citizens grazed cattle, goats, and hogs and cut fence posts, mine timbers, and firewood. Doing the paperwork of sales of permits would have been tough enough, but McGlone had the more daunting task of convincing a population of rugged individualists that they must ask for permission to pick up stove wood that had always been free for the taking.

Most of the cattlemen were at first amused, then incensed, at being told they must apply for permission to graze the canyons and ridges they'd been using for years. The 7H management, perhaps more in tune with the way the world was changing, made application to graze three thousand head on the slopes facing the San Simon Valley and settled for one thousand.

McGlone had worked on the Pecos River Forest Reserve near Mora, New Mexico, but he was untrained. Forestry was a new profession, and the jobs were filled, as post offices were, with political appointees. With the bureaucratic hierarchy of the future still to come, he was responsible directly to the land commissioner in Washington, to whom he wrote in May asking to be allowed to hire a helper. Anticipating a favorable reply, he built a two-room house near the sawmill in Barfoot Park for a fire guard to occupy in the summer.

McGlone got two men. Ex-sergeant Neil Erickson reported for duty on July 8 to start a second career of public service, and Eddie Riggs, grandson of old Brannick, signed on just for the summer season. Rangers provided their own saddle horses and were required to equip themselves with "pocket compass, camp outfit, axe, shovel, and pick or mattock." They were paid sixty dollars a month and got Sunday off unless "reserve interests would be injured by postponing the work until the following day." With two rangers to supervise, McGlone was promoted to forest supervisor.

One of the many prospectors who swarmed over the faulted limestone between Cave Creek and Apache Pass was Frank Caldwell, known as "Banty" for his short stature and cocky demeanor. Caldwell lived with Steve and Jennie McComas in Whitetail Canyon, near John Sullivan's place, but he was in the habit of spending several days at a time camped at his prospect in Jhus Canyon.

One July evening in 1903, returning horseback from work on the claim, he topped out on the trail that climbed out of Jhuṣ Canyon's wash to skirt the oak-clad hills to the mouth of Whitetail and was shot between the shoulder blades. At the shot Caldwell fell off his horse, landing in such a way that his head hit the point of a short miner's pick that he been carrying on his shoulder. The pick was driven through his skull, but he was surely already dead.

Henry Buckalew and his stepsons, Will and Frank Noland, were a mile away riding across Whitetail Flats, and at the single shot they rode over to investigate. It wasn't necessary to check for a heartbeat. From a distance they could see that the man on his back with a pick in his head was beyond help. They checked the ground, where the tracks told them that a man had tied his horse in the mesquite, walked to the body, turned it over, walked back to the horse, mounted, and ridden away. For several afternoons running, Buckalew with one or both of his boys had seen tall, skinny, one-armed Jim Gould at that spot and had seen him that afternoon riding toward the place where the shooting occurred. But for a time they kept their information to themselves.

Caldwell's friends and neighbors were planning to roll his body in a tarpaulin and bury him with little ceremony where he fell, but Steve McComas objected to the lack of respect. Frank had a good suit of clothes at the house that he could be dressed in, and they found lumber at Tom Burns's mine at the Nippers for a decent coffin. They buried him on the side of a low hill about fifty yards from where he was killed.

Paradise had no magistrate, so Deputy Luke Short sent to Teviston (as Bowie was known in those days) for Justice of the Peace James H. Tevis to come to hold a coroner's jury. "Captain" Tevis, at sixty-eight, was still going strong after fifty years on the frontier. At his court in Paradise there was testimony about a rivalry between Caldwell and Gould, and it was widely suspected that it was for the affections of Steve McComas's wife, Jennie. Ninety years have passed and all the principals are long gone, but the children of some of their contemporary neighbors still talk about them. A rumor has persisted that the object of Gould's and Caldwell's attentions was actually Susanna Buckalew and that Henry Buckalew was well shed of both of them.

The most telling fact was that Gould had skipped. Judge Tevis found that Caldwell had met his death at the hands of James M. Gould, who "on the 26th of July, 1903, did then and there deliberately, willfully, and unlawfully, and of his malice aforethought, kill and murder F. P. Caldwell by shooting said F. P. Caldwell with a gun."

It wasn't generally known by his neighbors—it was a time when questions were asked carefully—but Jim Gould was familiar with trouble. He headed for familiar country in the timbered hills northeast of Silver City. As a twenty-year-old cowboy known as "Kid Allen," he'd come there from San Antonio in 1886 with a drove of cattle belonging to a Captain Rabb. The cattle delivered, Jim ran off with part of the boss's remuda and used it to steal more horses in Mexico. With a couple of like-minded youths, he indulged in little holdups until a posse surprised them asleep in camp. After a trial in Las Cruces, Jim served time in the pen.

After a short time Gould came back to Paradise and gave himself up. He readily admitted he shot Caldwell but claimed it was in self-defense. Caldwell had fired at him first but then reined his horse around to run away just as Gould returned the fire, hitting him in his back.

Jim had several supporters, including Dad Colvin, Joe Wheeler, and Steve McComas, who all pitched in to go his thousand-dollar bail. At the December trial when the prosecution sprang the testimony of the heretofore close-mouthed Henry Buckalew and Will Noland, Gould's case of self-defense crumpled. He was found guilty of first-degree murder and sentenced to life imprisonment in the territorial penitentiary at Yuma.

Because the sentence was so specific, Jim Gould served only five years. In 1909 the prison was moved to Florence. They couldn't move Jim, who was sentenced to "Yuma," and they couldn't keep Yuma open just for Jim. They had to turn him loose. A number of years later Gould was grubstaked by Cliff Darnell to homestead on Deer Creek on the west slope of the Peloncillos. About once a week he came down on foot to Darnell's ranch with a burlap bag to load what food he could cadge before trudging back to his cabin. He would visit long enough to drink a cup of Lillie's coffee while little Sally, knowing he was a jailbird, peeked at him from a safe distance. In his dotage Jim lost his grip on reality and was committed to the state hospital in Las Vegas. This time he served out his term.

Paradise experienced its greatest surge of growth in 1904, its population swelling to an estimated three hundred. Of course, the community wasn't incorporated and had no legal boundaries, and that number wasn't confined to the two sides of Market Street. It included people from Cave Creek to Whitetail who drew their mail in Paradise and bought their horseshoe nails there.

The Chiricahua Mine got a new general manager in James H. Knowles, another Michigan copper miner. Knowles deepened the main shaft to over four hundred feet and extended hundreds of feet of drift, exploiting veins that produced up to 2 percent copper. Lou Scanlon's old partner, O. C. Davis, employed a number of men to begin developing the Cochise Group of claims east of Turkey Creek and on the north side of a low mountain that became known as Davis Mountain. There was good reason to expect Paradise would soon rival Clifton, Globe, and Bisbee, if not, indeed, Leadville, Cripple Creek, and Butte.

Several new businesses followed the increased mining activity. Inevitably, some of them were saloons. Frank Witt opened one, and Pat Walsh, a stubby, fat Irishman, another. Dentist T. B. Porter set up shop to pull a tooth or drill one with a machine powered by a small boy peddling a stationary bicycle. McGlone moved into a tented summer headquarters in Paradise; Daniel Moseley opened a new hotel; and Lemarcus J. "Mart" Moore began daily stage service to and from Rodeo.

Moore had moved over from across the mountain, where he had a place in West Turkey Creek. In April 1899, shortly after he and his first wife separated, his eighteen-year-old son, Teddy, was shot and killed by rustlers. Early one morning a sheriff's deputy had stopped by the Moore ranch and asked Ted to guide him to where Tom and Bill Halderman were staying. He had a warrant for their arrest. The boy led the deputy down the canyon to a ranch where the Haldermans were just sitting down to breakfast. The officer showed them his warrant but allowed them to finish their meal while he waited outside.

After they finished eating, Bill Halderman came to the door. The deputy asked if they were ready to go, and he swung into the saddle. His back was turned to the house when Halderman fired from the door, hitting him in the back of the head. Ted was mounting his horse when the shot was fired. As his right foot found the stirrup, he was hit in the back as he rode away but stayed in the saddle to die at home two hours later.

It was the next morning before Sheriff Scott White arrived from Tombstone to lead a posse including Mart Moore, which tracked the killers up Morse Canyon, over the mountain, and out Cave Creek Canyon. They were run to ground at the Hill ranch near Lordsburg and were hanged in Tombstone eighteen months later.

Mart Moore then married a sister of Alejo Bedoya's wife and moved to Paradise so the two sisters could be together.

Another positive addition to the Paradise population was Renwick White, who set up a press in a shed at the north end of Market Street and started weekly publication of the *Paradise Record*. White was born in Highlands, North Carolina, where he learned the printer's trade on the *Highland Star*, and he contributed squibs for local papers while attending college in Middleton, Connecticut. In 1898 he came to Arizona, and while serving as the acting postmaster in Douglas, he contributed freelance articles to the *Douglas International-American*, the *Bisbee Review*, and the *Naco Budget*.

To print the *Record*, White bought 24- by 36-inch newsprint from the Western Newspaper Union in Denver. It came to him already printed on one side with two pages of filler—old news of a national flavor, thunderous editorials, advertisements, and bad jokes. The *Record*'s editor (reporter, printer, and salesman) printed the back of the sheet with his own material and folded it down the middle to make a four-page paper, the front and back of which was local news, gossip, and advertising.

On a clear spring day Henry Chamberlain stepped down from Mart Moore's mud wagon. It was two in the afternoon and he was hungry. He'd taken the morning train from Douglas and boarded the stage in Rodeo with no time for lunch. Paradise's boarding houses and restaurants weren't serving at that hour. He went into the Brown and Slater store, where an open cracker barrel stood by the stove and a wheel of cheese sat on the counter. For fifty cents a customer could have a slice of cheese and a handful of crackers.

As Henry ate a lunch that would have cost fifteen cents in Douglas, he poked around and checked prices. He found them outrageous. He knew the mercantile business, and he knew he could halve the prices and still turn a profit. He caught the next stage back to Rodeo and the next train to Douglas, determined to come back soon.

Henry S. Chamberlain was raised in San Saba, Texas, and after attending San Saba College for a time, he worked in a store and post office. In 1899 he married Gertrude, the daughter of the San Saba County sheriff, farmer Andrew Jackson "A. J." Hawkins. When Henry's father-in-law was defeated for re-election, the two of them joined in buying out a local general store.

Henry had bronchial asthma and had been advised to go west to a drier climate. When he was offered a job in Clifton, Arizona, he took it, and A. J. decided to go with him. The two families made a large party when they struck out with several wagons in August 1901. It included Henry and Gertrude with their year-old baby, their parents, Gertrude's sister, Daisy, and two younger brothers.

They made their way west to the Gila River, where Henry and his father-in-law rented a farm near Duncan and had the ground ready to plant by the spring of 1901. They had a good harvest the first year, but the next year lost a potentially bumper crop to a flood. Then came the severe illness of one of the Hawkins children and the death of Gertrude's mother. A happier event was the birth of the Chamberlain's daughter, Dorothy.

Henry wasn't a farmer, and hearing of the Douglas boom, he moved there and went to work clerking for Ben Goldman's Douglas Mercantile Company. But his situation wasn't improved. The two smelters in Douglas were making breathing difficult and painful for him.

The store manager, George Reay, was counting the day's receipts one evening when he was shot during an attempted robbery. He wasn't seriously hurt, but needing time to mend, he went to Paradise to stay with his brother, Jim, who was working in one of the mines. Reay returned to Douglas to find Henry in misery, scarcely able to breathe. He suggested an immediate trip to the cool, pure air of Paradise.

Chamberlain returned from the mountains and told Goldman he wanted to go into business for himself in Paradise. His boss encouraged him and arranged credit for him with wholesalers in El Paso with whom he did business. Only two months after they had come to Douglas, the Chamberlains moved again, and Henry housed his family in a tent. In April 1904, with Gertrude's brother, Tom, they opened Chamberlain and Hawkins Mercantile in a rented building on the east side of Market Street.

Gus and Mary Chenowth provided their nine children with a family environment that taught self-reliance and piety. It also included complete familiarity with the use of firearms, a strong resistance to being pushed around, and at least as far as the boys were concerned, a knowledge of distilling. Gus, by example, was seldom taken advantage of, was known to have killed without apparent reluctance, and would open a prayer book at the drop of a hat or cuss word. His plot of corn on the cienega was primarily for the making of whiskey, which was widely acclaimed. Some of the precepts instilled into the Chenowth children came into play, though piety wasn't in conspicuous evidence, when at twenty-three, devil-may-care Howard Chenowth senselessly murdered two acquaintances and seriously wounded a good friend.

Howard was a good cowboy. He was roping calves from horseback when he was ten and had gone to work for the H's when he was only sixteen. From constant practice and the expenditure of quantities of ammunition, he was a crack shot with rifle and pistol. None of this was unusual for the place and time, but what wasn't usual was that he had the equivalent of a high school education from New Mexico State Normal School in Silver City.

Training and education don't automatically guarantee maturity. In 1903 Howard asked for a job with the Diamond A's, but Jim Block, the general manager, thought he looked a little wild and wouldn't hire him. He tried again the following year, and his friend Pat Nunn, who was the foreman, vouched for him and assured Block that he could handle the young man.

One Saturday in August, Nunn had business in Silver City and rode into town from the Diamond A's Cow Springs ranch, taking with him Howard Chenowth and another cowboy, Mart Kennedy. While the foreman took care of his affairs, the two young men had a few drinks, and they were having too much fun to quit when Nunn was ready to go back to camp. He indulged them for a while, but sometime after midnight, determined to get them out of town, he teased them out of the saloon and onto their horses by promising to buy a bottle they could tug at on their ride to the ranch.

Trying to talk one drunk into anything can be difficult, and Nunn had two on his hands. He got them both horseback and went back into the saloon for the bottle, but Mart got off his horse and followed him in, and while Nunn was trying to get him back out, Howard rode his horse in after them. Finally the foreman got the two jovial cowboys outside again, but Mart bowed his neck and refused to get back on his horse. Nunn had had enough.

"Take off your saddle," he told him. "You're through."

Mart Kennedy angrily untied the cinch, pulled off his saddle, and started to remove the headstall.

"Leave the bridle until I can get a rope on him," Pat said. It was a Diamond A horse, and he wanted to lead it back.

Mart responded with some disparaging words, and Nunn thereby lost the last vestige of patience. He was standing in front of the Palace Saloon. Kennedy was across the street. City ordinance required visitors to check their firearms on coming into town. Nunn had retrieved his some time ago when he prepared to leave town, but both his cowboys were still unarmed. When Kennedy cursed him, Nunn unbuckled his gun belt and laid it on the curb, strode across the street, knocked Mart onto his back, and put his foot on his chest to hold him down.

The racket brought Deputy Sheriff Elmore Murray to the scene, and he tried to restore peace. Howard, still sitting on his horse observing the scene with dispassionate amusement, felt it was time to take a hand in the game. He stepped off, pulled Nunn's six-shooter from its holster, and with good humor and accuracy, shot his friend in the chest. A second shot went wild as Nunn dodged for the door of the Club Saloon, and a third grazed his eyebrow, blinding him with blood. Luckily, the first bullet hit the watch in the foreman's vest pocket, which saved his life.

A single shot on a Saturday night didn't cause excitement in Silver City, but three shots were the accepted fire alarm, and soon several citizens came into the street. Murray and another man were trying to disarm Howard when former constable Perfecto Rodríguez stepped out of a building next to the Club Saloon. Howard raised his pistol and unhesitatingly drilled him in the heart from sixty feet, showing the value of practice—too drunk for good sense but not too drunk to hit what he was looking at.

Another who responded to the supposed fire alarm was unarmed City Marshal W. H. Kilburn. As he approached the struggling four-

some, Kennedy said, "There is Kilburn—shoot the son-of-a-bitch."
Casually, Howard pointed his pistol and did so with a single shot. Kilburn wasn't killed instantly, though he died a week later. As he lay paralyzed in the street, the two cowboys walked by him and he heard Howard say, "Ain't I the brave one?"

Kennedy went back to the Palace for another drink, where he was easily taken into custody. Howard ambled around the corner, and when confronted by a constable with a shotgun, he waved his pistol. The officer, nervous from all the shooting, let go, pinking him in his face with bird shot. The blast sobered Howard enough not to face down a second barrel, and he surrendered. In March he was convicted of second-degree murder and sentenced to fifty years— an easy sentence for creating two widows and leaving ten children fatherless. But he never served it.

On Christmas evening 1905 the night guard at the Grant County jail was confronted by a man who stepped out of the dark with a black hat pulled down over his eyes, the lower part of his face covered by a red bandanna. He had a six-gun in each hand. "Throw up your hands. I mean business," he said.

At gunpoint the unarmed jailer, at the gunman's request, took him to Howard's cell.

"Howard, I've came after you," the masked man said.

"Well, if you have I guess I'll have to go," Howard said, putting on his coat.

The jailer was locked in the vacated cell, and it was an hour before he could attract attention and raise the alarm. The next day the *Lordsburg Liberal* reported: "From the tracks in the snow about the court house it is thought that there were two men engaged in the plot . . . only the one, however made himself known, the other evidently remaining in hiding until after the escape was consummated."

The various Chenowth family accounts agree that Howard's younger brother, Hale, was the masked man who broke him out of jail, but there is disagreement about who helped. One has sisters Frances and Ola backing him up, but when she was over eighty, Ola, not known for modesty, didn't claim a part in it. She said that Charley waited at the door and their older sister, Ivy, held horses for them. The Chenowths are unanimous in agreement about what happened afterward.

A mile west of the Chenowth cienega ranch is a broad alluvial fan where the waters of Turkey Creek and Round Valley join, slow, and spread out on the flat ground. Heavy rains in the mountains flood down to settle there and produce lush wild tobosa grass, which Gus cut, baled, and stacked at the ranch. He removed bales from the middle of the pile to make a small bay that could be quickly closed off with a bale of hay. Howard lived there for months, until the hunt cooled and he could quit the country.

Not everybody was moving *into* Paradise in 1904. At least four left. Lee Eaton and Mary Margaret Noland were married and set up housekeeping near the present corrals at the Portal ranger station.

At the end of the shift one day at the Chiricahua Mine, Jack Maloney, who was working underground between roundups, climbed up the vertical ladder out of the shaft with a man, known now only as Judd, behind him. Moisture seeping out of the walls had made the rungs of the ladder slippery. Jack heard Judd yell as he lost his grip and fell over a hundred feet to the bottom of the shaft. Jack went back down, put Judd on his back, and climbed out with him, a feat of strength that became part of his legend. Judd survived to reach daylight but not much longer. His body was taken a half mile up the gulch now known as Graveyard Canyon and buried there, the first in the Paradise Cemetery. They might have put the grave a hundred yards to the north in soft alluvial soil, but they dug their hole up the slope, where there is a scant six inches of soil above bedrock—a more suitable resting place for a hard-rock miner. A hundred years of gravediggers who followed them have not blessed them for that.

In 1906 Alexander Wills got drunk and lay down to rest behind Joe Wheeler's saloon and froze to death. He was buried next to Judd.

## Chapter 11

# Portal

A deal was consummated in Douglas early in the present week by which Harry Alexander and O. C. Davis, the well known Chiricahua District promoters, acquired the entire tract of land on which the embryo town of Portal now stands, being located between Cave and Silver creeks at the mountains and in the heart of the most promising mining district.
***Arizona Republican*, January 15, 1906**

Cave Creek emerges from the mountains through a break in an uptilted ridge of limestone at the southeast end of the Apache Pass Fault. The northeast-facing gap in the ridge is a scant mile across. At the foot of the rock on the east side is a strong seep, Cave Creek Cienega, or Cienega Spring, in a grove of willow and hackberry. It was there that people of the ancient cultures and their successors lived for centuries. A reliable water source when the creek was dry, it was later a stopping place for Apaches and troopers on the trail between Apache Pass and San Bernardino Springs. And it was here that the Hands brothers built the cabin where Alfred was killed in 1895.

Upstream from the cienega the canyon opens into a basin of about three-and-a-half square miles, bordered on the east by the bulk of Bear Mountain, now Portal Peak, with the gabled facade of Cathedral Rock at its foot, and on the west by White Rock Mountain, which by 1904 was beginning to be known as Silver Peak. Shaded by sycamore, walnut, and oak, the creek hugs the east side of the basin, flowing through a bottom a quarter-mile across. Near its upper end a ledge of bedrock in the creek bed forces water to the surface of the boulders in a year-round spring.

About four hundred yards above that spring, Emmett and Melissa Powers and their eighteen-year-old daughter, Blanche, built a camp and claimed a homestead of four quarter-sections running north toward Silver Creek. Missouri-born Emmett had started in his teens punching cows in the Texas panhandle. The Lee Eatons lived less than a mile above them, and in the spring of 1904, William H. Pratt filed for appropriation of the water from South Fork and from the main channel of Cave Creek, probably for farming in the vicinity of Sunny Flat. These locations were possible because initially the Chiricahua Forest Reserve took in only the higher, timbered country. The lower elevations were still public domain. Hugh "Dutch" Mouser was camped with his wife and two children at Cienega Spring, and Ed Epley moved over from Turkey Creek to prospect Limestone Mountain. Ed and Bee camped at a spring midway between Mouser and Powers.

Farther up Cave Creek, in its north fork above Reed's ranch, Ed Estes had a year-round wood camp. With the help of his sons, Marshall and Glick, and a fluid roster of Mexican axmen, he cut oak cordwood and packed it on burros two and a half miles over a low pass west of Silver Peak to Paradise. Marshall and his wife, Ora, built a house above a little spring a half mile below the pass and ran a few cows.

In the winter of 1904–05, G. E. Buxton and Frank Kelsey set up a larger commercial firewood operation in Cave Creek in a camp about a half mile west of Estes, and with a crew of *leñadores* packed wood to camp with burros. It was also taken on wagons to a siding in Rodeo, then on flatcars to Douglas. José Pacheco had a smaller wood camp in the South Fork of Cave Creek. Although some people in Douglas and neighboring Agua Prieta burned coal, most kitchens used firewood. Over the next twenty years those men—and a few years later A. B. Rodman, cutting in Horseshoe Canyon and Sulphur—packed out thousands of cords of oak and juniper. The Chiricahua Mine had its own woodcutters to keep its boilers hot.

In 1904 mining operations expanded east of Owen Davis's Cochise Mine and closer to Cave Creek when Chicago investors formed the Savage Gold Mining Company with Francis Wajtalewicz, president, and J. A. Lewandowski, general manager. Lewandowski soon had a dozen men sinking a shaft high on the side of a hill above the eastern exit from Round Valley. The Chiricahua Mine was in full operation. The company sent in another Michigan man, Fred Hoar, to manage it, and by the year's end he had a 385-foot shaft with over 2,400 feet of drifts.

Estimates of the population for the period vary widely with the amount of country being considered. If Paradise is defined as the area served by its post office and stores, there may have been three to four hundred people between Cave Creek and Whitetail and from the sawmill in Barfoot Park to San Simon Cienega. Those clustered around Market Street were probably not more than a third that many, but enough of them were children that their parents took steps to get them educated.

There had been a school in San Simon for several years, but people who lived too far out or who couldn't board their kids in town, as Stephen Reed did, often had to try to do the teaching themselves—or let it go. Mary Chenowth wouldn't let it go, and a year after settling at the cienega, she got her sister, Eula Lee Murray, to come down from Phoenix to tutor her older children. In 1884 Brannick Riggs hired Eula away to teach his children on Pinery Creek. In 1885 the Chenowths hired a young bachelor from Georgia to teach the three R's to their children.

Public education came to Paradise in 1905, when Cochise County established the Paradise School District and provided an annual teacher's salary of $720, leaving it to the local people to furnish a building. Henry Chamberlain, Jim Hancock, and Bill Morrow were appointed to the board and immediately went to work canvassing for funds and material. Chamberlain had built a new store building with an attached warehouse for hay and grain and a yellow-painted home on the hill behind the store for his family. He was free to turn his attention to civic affairs. George Walker, who had been sorting mail in a cubbyhole in the Brown and Christy store, relinquished his post-mastership to Frank Christy to devote full time to real estate and mine promotion. His daughter, Georgia, wasn't of school age yet but soon would be. Looking ahead, he offered to donate any vacant lot of the board's choice, but instead, a spot on open public land was chosen on the mesa a quarter mile west of the Chamberlain and Hawkins store. So Walker contributed to a fund for windows, doors, and equipment, and the Sweeneys donated lumber. Childless Joe Slater made a particularly generous cash contribution.

Volunteers helped put up a board-and-batten structure on a concrete footing—a single long room with a raised dais on one end for the teacher's desk. A sheet-iron wood-burning stove at the other end of the building had a stove pipe running the length of the room. Two single-seater outhouses were set on the bank of an arroyo a hundred feet north of the school, desks were purchased, and all was ready for a fall opening.

Miss Maud McDonald had her hands full with eight grades to teach. The first grade alone included three Mejía kids who didn't speak English and had pupils ranging in age from six-year-old Ralph Morrow to Charlie McComas, twenty-one (no relation to the boy kidnapped by the Apaches in 1883).

The new school was five miles by the woodcutter's trail from Stephen Reed's, too far to walk. Reed had been boarding his kids in San Simon for school, but he found hiring a tutor more convenient. He hired Miss Ida Hiveley from Arkansas and built a lean-to attached to the side of his cabin to house her. He put together a small frame schoolhouse, then turned over to her his five remaining children, from Claudie, seventeen, down to William, seven. He paid her a cowboy's wage, thirty dollars and found.

Mart Moore's daily runs with the stage to Rodeo, a round that took him from 8 A.M. to 6 P.M., left him little time to take care of his horses, maintain the harness and mud wagon, and do a little road work. When George Coryell moved to town from Pearce, Mart took him on as a partner.

Like Mart, Coryell was from Missouri. He was an eight-year-old boy when his father took his family to Silver City, and it was they who were helped out of a scrape with Apaches on the Mimbres River by Billy the Kid. J. L. Coryell was a machinist and easily found mechanical work to do for the mines. When Deming was born at the tip of the advancing railroad, the Coryells moved to that burgeoning community, where J. L. first worked for the Southern Pacific and then went into business for himself erecting and maintaining windmills.

As a youngster, George had a crippling accident. His mother had shaved a bar of soft yellow soap, scattered it over the floor, and sluiced it down with hot water. She was on her knees, scrubbing, when George burst into the back door and ran across the room, slipped on the soap, fell, and skidded into the wall, dislocating his leg. It was several days before he could be taken to a doctor, and by then the leg was stiffened and couldn't be straightened. He walked with crutches until his father made a prosthesis of iron straps. George, known as "Iron-foot" Coryell, grew up windmilling despite his handicap.

In the mid-1880s George took his mechanical skills to the mining camps of Courtland, Gleason, and Pearce, where he lived by his wits and a deck of cards. He had a flair for figures. When five players around the table had five cards each—two face up—George knew immediately what the odds were that the fellow with a pair of treys had a third one buried. For a time he had a saloon in Pearce, where he presided at the poker table. In one unusual thirty-day period, he was ahead by forty thousand dollars. Sometimes Coryell dabbled in other pursuits. Two years before coming to Paradise, he was arrested in Charleston with two others by an Arizona Ranger. The charge was "theft and unlawful handling of cattle" when they "feloniously" bought fourteen head of cattle from a man they knew didn't own them, but a jury found them not guilty.

With Coryell handling the stage run to Rodeo, stocky, energetic Mart Moore started making improvements. The road to Rodeo via Graveyard Canyon and Silver Creek was a wheel-busting trail in the creek beds for the first five miles to Ed Epley's camp on Cave Creek. Mart prevailed upon the law to serve the public cause and incidentally advance his own business interest.

Constable Luke Short often found it necessary to confine roistering drunks for their own safety and the peaceful sleep of the community. Paradise now had its own justice of the peace in James Williams. Mart easily persuaded "Bigfoot" Williams that sweat was the best antidote for booze, and the judge cooperatively sentenced the inebriated to hard labor on a road gang under Short's supervision. Paradise businessmen supported the arrangement. The new road made it easier for the growing population of Cave Creek to trade in Paradise than in Rodeo.

With the improvement of the Silver Creek road, Ed Epley found himself at a busy road fork. Buxton's wagons, returning to camp from loading cordwood at the railroad, often stopped at his little spring to water the teams before following the creek up the canyon. "The Rocking Stage," as the citizens called the Moore-Coryell conveyance, made a similar stop going to and from Rodeo. Epley noticed that the wagoners and the stage passengers were often as thirsty as the horses.

Fifty feet from the spring stands a large sycamore, its trunk almost ten feet in diameter and hollow through rot. Ed placed a keg of whiskey in the hollow, nailed a board across the open front for a counter, and was prepared to offer refreshment to drivers and passengers while the horses watered. From this modest beginning, Epley expanded to open the Midway Store up on the bank behind the spring, operating in a tent until he could erect a frame building. He chose the bench because the bottom land, narrowing at this point, had flooded earlier in the year. He turned his liquor business over to John McManus who pitched two tents nearby, one to house himself, his wife, Carrie, and their daughter, Minnie, the other for a saloon.

Another who moved into the canyon in 1905 was Chester "Fitch" McCord. McCord had known the Powers family in the Texas panhandle, but it wasn't Emmett and Melissa he came to visit. Blanch Powers was the attraction. The two were soon married, and they filed on a quarter section of the wooded creek bottom just below the Powers homestead.

Powers and his son-in-law also became partners in a valley ranch six miles below the mouth of Triangle Canyon. The place was known as the Hot Well Ranch for a drilled well that produced water almost too hot to drink. When he wasn't taking care of their cattle, Fitch prospected, and between Fox and Triangle Canyons he located and developed the Willie Rose Mine, named for his baby daughter.

When James C. Reay came out from Douglas to work for the Savage Mine, his wife, Minnie, kept house for him and their six-year-old son, Francis, in the mine's tent camp in the greasewood under the hill. Jim, born on England's Scottish border, was twelve when his parents immigrated to Georgetown, Colorado, where the father worked in mines above timberline. In 1881 the family moved to the silver mines at Kingston, New Mexico, in time to huddle with other townspeople in a large hall for protection from Nana's raid.

When Kingston began to play out, Jim followed the boomers to Douglas, where he and his brother, William, opened the Star Livery Stable. There wasn't enough in the business for two families, so he left it to William and came out to the Savage Mine as tool sharpener. Jim wanted a better environment for his wife and child than the rough camp on Savage Wash, and he homesteaded on Cave Creek where Silver Creek joins it.

Out in the valley four miles southeast of Jim Reay's, Frank Sanford claimed a homestead on Anderson Seep, a little cienega fed by drainage off Portal Peak. Benjamin Franklin Sanford was born in Sweetwater, Texas. His widowed father brought him and his brothers to Clifton in 1891, and at fifteen Frank went to work for the Double Circles, a large outfit that ranged between Eagle Creek and the San Francisco River. When Frank caught smallpox, a young cowboy, August English, took him to his home in Clifton, where August's sister, Nancy, nursed him back to health.

After his recovery Sanford went south of the Gila and rode for the Triangles, worked in the mines at Dos Cabezas and Bisbee for a while, and in 1902 joined the drift toward Paradise, where he drove a team freighting from Rodeo. In Rodeo he ran into Nancy English again, who was cooking in the Prather Hotel, and they were married. She continued to cook, and Frank worked for the San Simon while they raised a stake to start their own place.

The San Simon Cattle Company had a new foreman in Tim Blevins of Austin, Texas. J. D. Parramore had him move the 7H headquarters from the middle of the San Simon Cienega, where it had been for over twenty years, to a spot three miles south of Sanford on another *ciéneguita* on Sulphur Draw. There he built an adobe house big enough to house and feed a crew. The new location was more central in the range and was only three miles from the telegraph office and railhead at Rodeo.

On a Sunday afternoon one of a bunch of cowboys lolling around the new ranch commented that they might play a game if only they had a deck of cards. Straws were drawn to determine who would ride to Rodeo to get one. Jack Maloney lost the draw, saddled a horse, and was jogging toward town when he saw the smoke of the El Paso–bound train from Douglas approaching from the south. The track gang had left a pile of ties along the side of the tracks, and Jack dragged a couple of them across the track, pulled his bandanna up over his nose, waved his pistol to signal the engineer to stop the train, and boarded the smoking car.

"I don't want your money or your watches, boys. Just a deck of cards," he told the startled passengers.

A drummer obliged. Jack thanked him, jumped off the steps, mounted his pony, and waved as he rode for the ranch. He'd saved four miles and made a more profitable haul than Blackjack Ketchum had at Steins.

German-born Albert Fink, who had come to Galeyville to make beer and stayed to look for a mine, moved over from Turkey Creek and built a shack in Silver Creek at a good spring about halfway between Paradise and the new settlement on Cave Creek. Now sixty, conscious of being an old-timer, Fink told newcomers, "Ven Rube [Haddon] und me vas here, dere vas *nobody* here."

Otto Duffner, with his younger brother, Max, who joined him from Wisconsin, had been camped up Cave Creek for a year mining crystals from Crystal Cave behind Reed's ranch. Forest Supervisor Charles McGlone took a great interest in the cavern and called it to the attention of Chief Forester Gifford Pinchot in Washington. Under Pinchot's orders, McGlone brought suit against the Duffners "for destroying a natural wonder." Judge F. M. Doan dropped the suit with the provision that the Duffners cease their operation. The two then moved to Whitetail to work claims near the Nippers.

Hugh Rowe homesteaded a few hundred feet west of Ed Epley, and a few other prospectors whose names are lost joined the budding community on Cave Creek. By June 1905 there were about fifty people living on the creek or within easy range of Epley's little store. He applied to the postmaster general to open a post office called Cave Creek. He got his post office but had to pick another name. His first choice had been preempted fifteen years earlier by a little place in Maricopa County of such insignificance that nobody in the Chiricahuas had heard of it. Ed asked for suggestions from the loafers' bench in front of the store. Jack Thomas, a miner from Oregon, suggested Portal because it was the gateway to Paradise and the portal to the mines. The fact that it was also the entrance to Cave Creek Canyon was only incidental but made the name triply suitable.

When Emmett Powers and Fitch McCord filed on homesteads on Cave Creek, they had more in mind than farming. In the latter half of 1905, they became part of a group of enterprising men who were betting that the mines on the northeast side of the Chiricahuas were destined to rival those in Bisbee and Clifton. Obviously there was no room in the narrow confines of Turkey Creek for the kind of expansion that they expected. Portal would become the residential area for the Paradise industrial complex, as Warren was for Bisbee. O. C. Davis, the concept's prime mover, had found two partners with access to potential investors in Pittsburgh, Pennsylvania: Harry Stone and Harry F. Alexander.

Those three had acquired the Ajax Mine between the Nippers and Blue Mountain, just north of Whitetail Draw from "Cap" Tom Burns, who typically found a mine and sold it. Davis and his new partners leased the Doran and Gallagher mine on Blue Mountain and operated it, the Ajax, and the Cochise Mine, on the side of Davis Mountain north of Round Valley, as the Cochise Consolidated Copper Company. A post office named Pittsburgh, in deference to their backers, was established at their headquarters at the Cochise Mine, but it was rescinded in four months.

Davis, as an individual, also provided some backing for the Duffner brothers, who had worked in his Ajax Mine. He grubstaked them to explore the south side of Limestone Ridge, and they moved their camp to Silver Creek, where they built a small adobe house just above Albert Fink's shack.

Powers, McCord, Davis, Alexander, and Stone then formed the Portal Land and Improvement Corporation, with Alexander as president and Stone as secretary. What followed was a complex series of transactions that, ninety years later, is hard to sort out.

Not long after Powers and McCord had recorded their homesteads on Cave Creek, Congress extended the boundaries of the Chiricahua Forest Reserve to include the mouth of Cave Creek Canyon, making those homesteads inholdings within the forest. By executive order, President Theodore Roosevelt traded 160 acres of the reserve now lying north of the Powers and McCord homesteads to the Santa Fe Railroad for a piece of the "checkerboard" north of Flagstaff that had been granted to the railroad by the government as an inducement to lay tracks across the continent. The Santa Fe sold the Cave Creek acres to Hugo and Lottie Seaberg of Raton, New Mexico. The Seabergs sold the quarter-section to Fitch McCord. McCord quit-claimed it to the Portal company.

The fact that the sequence of those events wasn't in that order is evidence that the entire scenario had been carefully drawn up well in advance. Although they had been occupying the ground for several months, it wasn't until January 11, 1906, that Emmett and Fitch formally filed on their homesteads. Six days later they bought five lots of the Portal town site between Silver and Chiricahua Streets. The next day the town site was surveyed. Two months later, in March, the Seabergs sold the 160 acres to McCord. Three weeks later McCord deeded it to the Portal corporation on a quit-claim deed (having already bought lots from them). The company immediately hired prospectors Charlie and George Jowell to grade the streets and then named Jewell [*sic*] Avenue for them as partial payment. The town site wasn't "dedicated" until May.

Other lots were sold in May and June. One went, as his fee, to Albert Sames, a Douglas lawyer who had drawn up the articles of incorporation. Ed Epley got seven lots that included the spot where his store already stood, and Hugh Rowe "bought" the lots in the creek bottom on which he'd been living for several months. On August 18 A. D. Boswell was deeded the five lots on the corner of Cave Street and Alexander Avenue where a few months previously, without title, he'd built a saloon of lumber to compete with McManus's tent. The day after the "sale" to Boswell, the Santa Fe Railroad was granted title to the land that they had sold to the Seabergs five months previously.

While these real estate machinations were getting underway, in the early morning of March 1 an evening of revelry at Boswell's saloon was winding down. Boswell was an even-tempered and well-spoken gentleman, but somehow in persuading his customers to break up the binge and go home, he managed to rile one L. B. Reed, who went to his camp for his rifle and came back to threaten the bartender. Boswell reached under the bar for a pistol and shot him dead.

Reed was buried in an unmarked grave on the east side of the creek just upstream from the ford. Luke Short arrested Boswell and took him to the justice of the peace in Paradise. Williams had been replaced in the office by a carpenter, H. A. James, who bound Boswell over to the grand jury. A bond of three thousand dollars was posted by Dutch Mouser and by the Gardner brothers employed at Buxton's wood camp. The trial was quick. The district attorney didn't have his heart in it, and on April 26, without missing but a day or two of work, Boswell was found not guilty by reason of justifiable homicide in self-defense.

Two weeks after Boswell bought his lots, Powers and McCord bought the eight lots across Davis Avenue from his saloon. Since April they had been doing business there as "Powers and McCord, General Merchandise, Hay and Grain, Mine and Ranch Supplies." They had opened the completed building on April Fools' Day with a feast and dancing until sunup to the Bass boys' banjo and fiddle. It may have been the proximity of the saloon and the killing there a month earlier that resulted in the Powers and McCord deed, and all subsequent sales, containing the restriction "shall not permit to be used or occupied said premises or any part thereof for the assemblage of men and women for lewd or immoral purposes, or for public places or saloons where women are allowed to sing or dance, or indulge in drinking or serving wine, beer, or spiritous liquors, or for places where intoxicating liquors are sold or dispensed whatsoever." Apparently it wasn't unseemly for *men* to sing and dance.

Emmett Powers didn't sell liquor in his store, but having no well, he hauled water to the place in barrels. When someone wanted a bottle of whiskey, he bought it at one of the saloons or stores that had a license. The saloons bought most of their booze in barrels from which they filled bottles to use at the bar. The empty barrels were in great demand for holding water, and Powers and McCord had just acquired one that stood empty on the porch until someone got around to knocking out the top. Several men were gathered one summer afternoon in the shade of the north-facing porch, exchanging misinformation. One of them, sitting on the barrel, casually reached down and knocked out his pipe against the barrel, inadvertently dropping a few live coals into the bunghole. There was a "boom" when the volatile remnant alcohol let go, and every man hit the dirt, not knowing which direction the firing was coming from.

The new mining excitement rekindled interest in abandoned claims. Fred A. Bernoudy and a partner cleaned up the old adit of the Rough and Ready Mine across Turkey Creek from the site of Galeyville, and a new flock led by Carl Rice from Michigan's Upper Peninsula arrived to look over the ridges between Jhus and Whitetail. Rice and two partners bought claims from R. D. Hall, Ulrich Rieder, and Joe Wheeler, blocked out twenty-three new claims at the head of Mackey Canyon, and formed the Manhattan Mining Company, hiring Fred Hoar away from the Chiricahua Mine to manage it. Although their properties were mostly in the Whitetail drainage, they were more easily reached from Manhattan Camp at Smith's Spring in Jhus Canyon, where they soon had a dozen miners.

The first miners in Cochise County were Anglos. Welshmen and Cornishmen were recruited from the coal and tin mines of southwestern England, and the proud Celts refused to work underground with "foreigners." They put up with Prussians or Swedes, allowing them to be fellow countrymen by proxy, but the courtesy wasn't extended to Mexicans. The latter were tolerated as woodcutters, well diggers, or for moving ore and gangue once it was on the dump, but "Cousin Jacks" were known to walk off the job if asked to work side by side with them at the stope. That occupational separation was beginning to break down by 1900.

The prejudice extended to social and political activities. The county register for 1904 listed 120 voters in the Paradise precinct. Only F. Valenzuela had a Spanish surname. Registered voters in Bisbee in 1912 were 23.5 percent foreign born, but few were Mexican. Knowing that Chihuahua Hill and Tin Town in Bisbee were teeming with Mexicans, one would suspect that they weren't encouraged to vote. Mexican immigrants, however, were less likely to become naturalized citizens than immigrants from Europe. It is probable that many intended to go back to Sonora.

Alejo Bedoya's Monte Cristo saloon was the social nucleus for Mexican males in Paradise. Four of Alejo's customers broke in after hours one spring night in 1906 and made off with much of the stock. They drank enough of it to make it easy for Constable Short to round them up and attach them to the logging chain. It was one of Short's last official acts. He resigned shortly after and left town. It was said his departure was encouraged by an irate husband. Mart Moore assumed his badge.

With the opening of the Powers and McCord Mercantile, Ed Epley closed his store but leased lots near the Silver Creek road, moved his post office to that location, and built a small hotel or boarding house, which Bee took care of while he devoted his time and efforts to mining. For a year or more, with the backing of George Walker, he'd been running a drift at his Virtue Mine into the side of Limestone Ridge, about a mile northwest of the town site. With several million years of sedimentary deposits standing on a forty-five-degree angle, he reasoned that a mile of tunnel could perforate the mountain and intersect every potentially ore-bearing formation through the Permian into the Precambrian. Somewhere in there must be a rich lode.

By midsummer the California Mining District was fairly bouncing with optimistic energy, and plans were made for a spur line, the Arizona Copper Range Rail Road, from Rodeo up to Paradise. The Savage Mine now had three 100-foot shafts and 340 feet of tunnel and had twenty-eight men in camp. Portal's future as the commercial and residential center for the more industrial activities in Turkey Creek seemed assured, as reported in the *Arizona Republican* for January 15, 1906:

> Portal is the most favored site in the Chiricahuas, not only is it the key to that extensive and promising mining district but the location is an ideal for a summer resort for this vicinity. An abundant supply of water is at hand, a stream of mountain water running through the center of town. An abundance of timber is available with short hauls to bring it into town and the promoters of the company who have the development of this site in hand were not slow to recognize the exceptional value of this location.

It was that abundance of timber that was the cause of another flurry of railroad excitement reported by the *Paradise Record* on April 6, 1906:

> The Record has learned from a reliable source that a railroad will be built into the Paradise district . . . by the Phelps-Dodge Co. The road will leave the main line of the El Paso and Southwestern System at Rodeo, and the end of the line will be at the head of Cave Creek. The object for building the road is to afford means of transportation for 50,000,000 feet of mining timber from the Chiricahua forest reserve to the Copper Queen mines. . . . The road will pass through Portal and will run within three miles of Paradise, that being the distance from here to the ranch of S. B. Reed, on Cave creek, the nearest point on the proposed line.

The editor's "reliable source" was probably Forest Supervisor Charles McGlone, who had met representatives of the mining company in Rodeo and brought them to Portal to take them over the proposed route and into the timber to be exploited. The stage had a full load of passengers when it reached the ford at Cave Creek just below the modern bridge. Warm weather and spring rain had swollen the creek with melted snow, and Coryell eased his team into the freshet. As the horses struggled for footing in shifting stones, the coach began to slip sideways from the force of the water. A tobacco drummer on his way to Paradise with his sample cases excitedly tried to get out the door on the downstream side, and his weight tipped the rig perilously.

"Ma" Brown, who owned a "house across the creek" in Paradise, grabbed him by the coattail and jerked him back. "Sit down, you damn fool, or you'll drown us all," she told him. He did, and the stage crossed safely.

Though surveying for the railroad was confidently expected to start within a few weeks, it didn't. Anyone who spent the expected profit the road would bring to the district was premature, because the company found other sources for stull timber or other means of getting it out.

In February 1905 the Forest Service had been taken from the Department of the Interior and put into Agriculture, which was more exacting in its requirements. Supervisor McGlone went with the transfer, but he came under closer supervision than before. This may have dictated his giving up the office in Willcox and moving his headquarters into the woods. The framed ranger station near the sawmill in Barfoot Park was too far from a communication center, and the tent in Paradise was inadequate.

Ranger Neil Erickson had been busy scaling timber, measuring ricks of cordwood, and setting out Apache pine seedlings at the Barfoot station. But his boss found time for him to build a frame ranger station on Soldier Flat, the site of old Camp Crawford. During slack periods Neil built five miles of trail from Barfoot around the head of Rustler Park and the west side of Fly Peak to Ranger Park, as Cima Park was then called. While Erickson was thus employed, McGlone applied himself to paperwork and romance. After a long leave of absence, he returned with a bride and built a house between the school and the Chamberlains and across the road from the Saddlers.

Margaret Saddler was actually living alone now. The barber was "away on business," as she put it. It was a lengthy trip, and Mrs. Saddler was taking in washing to make ends meet. Gertrude Chamberlain, with whom the woman spent much time, was sure that Saddler had left for good.

Miss McDonald taught only the fall term in Paradise. Mining man Jim Knowles was an insistent suitor and married her in the middle of the school year. The year was finished by Alma Jones, who left in the spring to go back to school himself. His place was taken by Gus and Mary Chenowth's second daughter, Loyola Agnes. "Ola" had recently married a San Simon cowboy, Bob Martyr, and they had filed on a homestead just a mile west of her father's place on the Arizona side of the line.

The McDonald/Knowles wedding was followed later in the year by that of Jack Sweeney to Miss Hollis Chamberlain, Henry's sister. Henry had made a quick trip back to San Saba to see family there. When he was leaving he said offhand, "Come go with me, Holly." Holly flew up the stairs, threw some things in a portmanteau, and did so. A striking looker with a lively air, she was a skillful seamstress and was soon taking in sewing. Jack Sweeney, who had just bought out B. B. Riggs's remaining interest in the sawmill, didn't give her much time for needlework before they were married.

The year of 1906 ended with a bang following a protracted post-Christmas celebration at Boswell's Saloon in Portal. In the early morning hours of December 30, A. D. closed up and went to bed in the back room. George Jowell, who had been one of his best customers during the evening, wasn't ready to quit. Just before the daybreak he returned for more and banged on the door. Boswell yelled at him from his bed, telling him to go away. Jowell, prepared for refusal, had come back armed with a large-caliber rifle with which he shot off the lock and part of the outer stile, and he went into the bar. Boswell could see that the man really wanted a drink, and he resignedly got up, lit a lamp, hung it on a hook suspended from a ceiling joist, put out a glass, and picked up a bottle. Jowell wasn't content with the bartender's compliance—or just liked noise. As the saloon keeper poured him a drink, Jowell shot out the light. Boswell ran back into his bedroom, returned with a shotgun, and blew him down.

Jowell was buried in an abandoned prospect hole near the Virtue Mine. Boswell got considerable local sympathy. He wasn't charged for two weeks, and then only at the insistence of the dead man's brother. Charles Jowell signed a complaint before James C. Hancock, now the precinct's justice of the peace. Bill Morrow, George Walker, and Jess Henley put up bail, and many of his neighbors made depositions in Boswell's behalf. The case was dismissed without trial, but having found it necessary to kill two men within nine months, Boswell lost his taste for the business. He closed up and moved to Rodeo.

There can be few regions that swing so quickly from Elysium to limbo and back again. When the creek runs and grass is green and the air is soft on the cheek, beneficence seems likely. It takes little imagination to see waving fields of grain, trees laden with pendant fruit, and a rose-covered cottage in the shade of sheltering cottonwoods. One forgets that in the previous year at the same time, the cloudless sky glared white-hot, the relative humidity stuck in a range between 2 and 12 percent, the mesquite began to shed its graying leaves in midsummer, paint blistered on the sheathing, and boards shrank to let sand blow through the cracks. When the black widow spiders in the wood box shrivel and die, it is hard to believe that it will ever rain again.

The winter of 1906–7 was an unusually wet one. Wet enough to keep the creek running full and clear. Hugh Rowe plowed and planted his lots near the Powers and McCord store, filed a claim on Cave Creek water, and dug the ditch to carry it, possibly seeing a vine-covered cottage in his future.

Mrs. Charles McGlone wasn't happy in Paradise. The amenities she was accustomed to are not recorded, nor are the specific complaints about her new situation. The new house may not have suited her—the privy on the bank of the wash, the nearness of the schoolyard, or the thirteen saloons within shouting distance—whatever the reasons, her dissatisfaction spilled over onto her husband. In June 1907, less than a year after the completion of his new headquarters on Soldier Flat and a little over a year after moving into his house in Paradise, McGlone went into Douglas to make arrangements for moving the office of the Chiricahua Forest Reserve—and his wife—into town.

The supervisor's absence didn't leave the forest totally unprotected in the middle of fire season. Several employees had been added to the staff. Forest Assistant Harry A. Burrall was left in charge at Paradise, aided by Assistant Rangers Murray Averett and Walter Edwards. Ranger Casper was stationed in Price Canyon, and Guards E. A. Blevins and William A. Stuart at Barfoot Park and Rock Creek, respectively. The mainstay, though, was Neil Erickson, who was allowed to keep his headquarters at his ranch in Bonito Canyon; he was used as a sort of "roving ranger."

Field employees were required to keep a daily log in which they recorded what work was done, places visited, and miles traveled. Erickson's journal has survived, and it indicates the extent of his patrolling. For example, one day might find him riding from the ranch over the mountain into Jhus Canyon to inspect a dozen mining claims, spending the night at Manhattan Camp; the next day riding up Indian Creek to check the road Duncan McDonald was building to his mine at the head of that canyon, returning to Eagle City and the Ajax Mine; the following day riding with Susanna Buckalew from her ranch into Keating Canyon to see the proposed site for a new tank, then on to Wood Canyon to look into a reported trespass, and riding over Emigrant Pass to put in a couple of days of surveying before returning home by the way of Buckhorn Basin.

On June 17, 1907, on one of these sashays, he left home early and rode southwest to intersect the old Cavalry Trail. This route led up Witch Creek and Fife, crossed Fife Saddle, went down Crook Canyon, and crossed Rock Creek. There was "heavy thunder" and some rain in the high mountains as he went down Turkey Pen Canyon into West Turkey Creek (then still known as Morse Canyon). He talked to a woman regarding the trespass of her hogs in a cornfield on Rock Creek, then spent the night at the Smith ranch. The next day he spent with Gabe Choate inspecting the range and discussing with him his application for a permit to graze hogs on the reserve. He commented on much afternoon lightning in the north. On the twentieth he rode up Mormon Canyon to the foot of Round Mountain (now Chiricahua Peak) and followed the "Summit Trail" along the crest to Barfoot and then down to Paradise and the station at Soldier Flat.

He left the next morning for Tex Canyon, where Martínez and Bracamonte were cutting cordwood, but in passing the mouth of Horseshoe Canyon, he spotted smoke curling up from behind Pothole Peak. He found the fire midway up Horseshoe's North Fork, but by midafternoon it was moving faster than he was. He rode out to Rodeo for help and returned to the fire with nineteen recruits.

The fire was burning grassy country with scattered oak, juniper, and sotol on steep and rocky hillsides. Through the night and the next day, the men cut fire line to keep the flames from the timbered high country. Shortly after sunrise they thought the fire was contained, but by early afternoon smoke had boiled up again and the fire crossed Horseshoe and found richer fuel on the more heavily wooded south side of the canyon. On the twenty-third Erickson recruited more men in Rodeo and got in touch with Supervisor McGlone, who came out from Douglas by train the next day to give logistical support and free Erickson to fight the fire.

Despite twenty-five fresh men hired in Agua Prieta, on the twenty-fifth the fire went up Red Mountain between Horseshoe and Jack Wood Canyon. Ranger Averett and Frank Sanford kept it from burning higher into the mountains. By the twenty-seventh the fire and most of the crew were on Red Mountain, and the next day A. D. Boswell brought a crew over from Horseshoe to join them. McGlone showed up with more men from Douglas, and with fresh men they were able to get ahead of the fire and to set backfires. By midnight for the second time the burn was declared controlled. With a few men on patrol, most of the firemen curled up in the ashes and slept.

In the morning McGlone went back to Rodeo. Erickson found water in Two Weeks Spring Canyon, and with four men draped with canteens, he hauled water for mop-up. On the thirtieth he patrolled the entire burn, and finding no fire, he sent home all but a skeleton crew. Again it was too soon. An east wind in the afternoon of July 1 fanned up a blaze in Jack Wood Canyon. Erickson sent one of his few men into Rodeo to get provisions and, if possible, to get men to return. He and his firemen, red-eyed and stumbling with fatigue, fought fire until daylight. A stand was made farther up Jack Wood Canyon. That line held. On the evening of Independence Day, for the fourth time, Erickson declared the fire to be controlled and everybody went home.

In mid-July Supervisor and Mrs. McGlone moved themselves and the reserve headquarters to Douglas. He was interviewed by a reporter about the reasons for the move, and though he may not have been quoted accurately, the printed story was mainly a complaint about the quality of life in a small mining camp in the mountains where the stores carried little but stale bread and moldy ham. The papers reached Paradise the day after publication.

September found Erickson at the north end of the Chiricahuas mapping and surveying the boundary of the reserve. His camp for several days was at the junction of Josephine and Emigrant Canyons, a short distance north of Hell's Half Acre. He hadn't been home much that summer. He had no one to talk to and plenty of time to dream. He called his campsite Camp Far Away, a name he later applied to his ranch in Bonito, and in the back of his notebook one evening, in lonely reverie, he wrote:

> The sunny smiles, the fond embrace,
> The fervent kisses, the blushing face,
> The round hills of alabaster
> Each capped with the bud of a rose.

While the ranger put in long days climbing the rough hills, shooting angles with his compass, and drawing neat contour lines on his maps, and spent long evenings thinking about other contours, his boss's thoughts were of an impending inspection.

Chief Forester Pinchot intended to upgrade the Forest Service and, when necessary, to replace unqualified political appointees with trained foresters. He sent selected men to inspect each of the reserves. Therefore Forest Inspector A. O. Waha's visit to the Chiricahua Reserve was probably routine, but in the course of it questions arose about McGlone's performance. Waha met the supervisor in Rodeo, where they caught the stage for Paradise. As they reached the stage office across the road from the Chamberlain and Hawkins store, loiterers on the porch recognized Charlie McGlone and recalled his comments in the newspaper. "Stale bread and moldy ham. To hell with the Forest Service," one of them called out, following with a wild hoot.

During Waha's inspection McGlone complained about Erickson's performance. In September the chief forester in Washington asked Erickson to respond to his supervisor's charges, indicating that there would be an investigation. Erickson's reply through channels, thus through the hands of his accuser, must have been delayed. By letter on December 15 McGlone requested Erickson to resign and turn his equipment over to Guard William Stuart. Before he complied, the ranger got a telegram from Washington: "Erickson suspended from Dec. 18th pending investigation."

By December 1907 Emma Sanders, the girl who had admired Jack Maloney out of the corner of her eye, had turned eighteen and had caught the eye of Jack Maloney. At the beginning of the Christmas season, Jack and Emma were married at her mother's home on Turkey Creek, with a lively soiree attended by most of the people living between Oak Canyon and Sulphur, as well as all the H cowboys. The couple were officially spliced by Judge Jim Hancock. The best man, Will McCarty, and the maid of honor, Hugh Mouser's daughter, Irma, were themselves married not many days later. The inseparable Noland brothers, Will and Frank, were there with their sister, Kate, who would shortly marry another in attendance, Carl Washburn. Other singles at the affair who would follow Jack and Emma's example were John Costin and Nancy Hall, Robert and Henrietta's daughter.

That afternoon after the service, a party of nearly thirty saddled up and went to Rodeo for a dance. A faded and blotched photograph of the happy couple horseback shows Jack in a suit with a flower in his lapel, new black Stetson typically uncreased. Emma is sidesaddle in a black dress with light-colored cable stitching around the yoke. She is wearing a white silk handkerchief around her neck, a flat sailor hat with a flower on the brim, a pair of gauntleted buckskin gloves, and a satisfied smile. Jack is grinning broadly.

The inflated accounts of two-hundred-dollar-a-ton ore, rhapsodic stories of the coming of the railroads, and starry-eyed predictions of a new metropolis didn't diminish with the beginning of the year in 1908. Not many local people knew it, but nationwide events in the preceding fall had already begun to dampen those happy prospects. Following a time of excessive unregulated speculation in railroad, banking, and mining stocks, a run on the Knickerbocker Trust Company of New York City and the failure of the Westinghouse Electric Company resulted in the October Panic of 1907.

Copper was hit the hardest. Between May and September the price dropped from 25 to 15½ cents a pound, and by October it couldn't be sold. Cananea Copper Company shares slipped from $10 to $1.50, and the mine temporarily shut down. At Big Bug, in the Prescott district, the Consolidated Arizona Smelting Company went bankrupt.

The depression didn't impose immediate hardship on ordinary people. Unemployment was negligible and agriculture wasn't affected, but investors became cautious and tighter with dollars needed for development work. The well-established, well-financed companies were secure enough if they weren't overextended, but the mines in the Chiricahuas were still in the developmental stage and hadn't shipped enough ore to pay for getting it out. Calumet and Arizona, the large grubstakers for the Chiricahua Development Company, cut their losses and backed out. Early in 1908 the Chiricahua Mine, Paradise's largest payroll, closed down.

Most residents of the area viewed the shutdown as temporary, and the laid-off miners went deer hunting. A few, closer to the sources of money and power, could read sign better. Owen Davis and his partners, Alexander and Stone, divested themselves of their interests in the Ajax Mine and the Doran and closed the Cochise down, leaving Charles Welch as watchman. Their names don't appear on subsequent documents of the Portal Land and Development Company. Not waiting for the dedication of Portal's railroad depot, Davis sold his new white clapboard house in Paradise to Henry Chamberlain and moved to Douglas.

C. A. Overlock, one of the incorporators of Douglas, its first postmaster and its first mayor, replaced Harry Alexander as president of the town-site company for a short time, perhaps expecting lightning to strike twice.

By 1908 the struggling two-year-old Portal town site had sold only 46 lots of the 1,184 platted—those few to just eleven buyers. Only a store, a small combination hotel and butcher shop, and a saloon comprised the commercial center; thus there was no compelling reason to buy residential lots. Anyone who wanted to live in the vicinity could use the unclaimed land that lay on three sides. Powers and McCord themselves lived on their homesteads to the south. Hugh Rowe homesteaded 160 acres just across Silver Street, the north boundary of the "town," and sold his newly plowed lots to John Frederick Finnicum.

For Fred Finnicum this was a third shot. He'd tried farming in Texas, where he married Emma, then joined one of the land rushes in Oklahoma, where his three daughters were born. Somewhere along the way he picked up blacksmithing, and when his dry-land farm in Indian Territory played out, he came to Paradise to sharpen miners' picks and drills. But farming was his true occupation. Blacksmithing brought in a little cash, and he fed his family from a kitchen garden on Rowe's town-site lots. Meanwhile, Finnicum homesteaded east of Rowe's new location on a place that would become El Portal Ranch.

In April Neil Erickson's fortunes took an upturn. Only a month after Neil's December suspension from duty, McGlone himself was fired. Guard William Stuart served as acting reserve supervisor from his headquarters in Rock Creek until the April appointment of Arthur W. Zachau.

The new supervisor, born in Prussia, was an educated, able man of affairs who had come to the job from Albuquerque. Zachau wasted no time. On April 15 he reinstated Erickson, appointing him deputy forest ranger, and the next day he started a three-day meeting of all his guards and rangers at his Douglas office, where he asked questions and made decisions. Within two weeks he'd moved his office to Rodeo, inventoried the government property on the forest, and made many horse tracks. He had Erickson guide him over the mountains, on one day riding from Paradise into Rucker Canyon and back.

Zachau believed his place was on the reserve. In mid-May he met Erickson in Portal, and they rode up the canyon a little over a mile — in the words of Neil's journal for that day — to "examine the house and grounds of Lee Eaton with the view to purchase same for an administrative site." Lee and Kate Eaton actually had sold the place to Frank Hagerty and moved into the valley near Apache, but Hagerty was willing to sell. Erickson estimated the value of the lumber in the 14-by-28-foot house to be $73.40. The house was all there was to sell; the land was forest property. Zachau offered Hagerty $100 and they shook hands on it.

Neil Erickson was in his element. It was good to be back riding the forest trails. And after a day in Cub Park (now known as Old Headquarters) to assess its suitability for a summer work camp, it was also good to be "at home all day eating strawberries and cream," as he wrote one Sunday.

Emma Maloney's father, Joe Sanders, had a nice location on the creek, with a piece just below Stephen Reed's hay field that was level enough to plow if one could dodge the boulders. Joe wasn't a plowman, but he invited Jack and Emma to move in with him. His living quarters were limited to his little dugout, so the Maloneys pitched a tent under the sycamores until something better could be arranged.

Jack cleared that ground and put in an orchard with cuttings from apple trees old man Reed had planted a quarter century before. Emma had a little garden of corn and turnips and cooked for the two men, who kept her well supplied with deer meat. She didn't really "keep house" for both of them, because her Dad didn't sleep inside. He sat around the stove and smoked his pipe after supper and then went out to roll up in his sugans on the ground, using his dugout only when it rained or snowed. When the weather was cold enough for fur to set, Joe ran a trap line for foxes, ringtail cats, bobcats, and skunks. Emma helped him boil down the skunks to render the fat for harness oil.

Supervisor Zachau, whose duties were expanded in July when much of the Peloncillo range was added to the newly designated Chiricahua National Forest, had a site for his new headquarters above Portal, but Lee Eaton's two rooms were inadequate for the purpose. Zachau wanted them out of the way and, knowing Jack's situation, told him if he would haul the house away he could have it. Jack knocked it down, piled the boards on a wagon, and reassembled them fifty yards north of his father-in-law's camp.

Somehow Jack acquired a small bunch of cows that wore his N Lazy E Connected brand. It's possible the seed stock were 7H sleepers that Parramore's cowboys had failed to gather from the high country, but years later, when asked if he hadn't swung a pretty wide loop in his youth, he denied it. "Naw, I never needed to. When Emma and I moved up here, I bought six springing heifers, and do you know, ever' one of 'em had twin heifer calves that done the same thing!"

Mavericking, putting one's own brand on unbranded, weaned cattle of unknown parentage, was legal. If mavericking was practiced on "sleepers" running with a bunch all wearing a single brand, it was frowned on, and, of course, putting your brand on a calf that was sucking a cow wearing another's brand was out-and-out stealing. There were nuances to the definition of cattle theft. Taking a calf following a 7H or Diamond A cow owned by a rich man in Texas or by anonymous stockholders in California wasn't quite as heinous (and not as risky) as branding a neighbor's calf. Strangely, an upright man who would shrink from running his brand on another man's calf might butcher and eat that same calf.

Will and Frank Noland were close in more than age. Less than two years separated them, but Frank had looked up to his older brother ever since, as little kids, they had helped their mother and stepfather move their cattle down from the Blue. The Buckalews had taken out homesteads in the valley opposite Skull Canyon in the Peloncillos, where they were staying with the younger children. They left the two older boys, twenty-one and twenty-three, and their nineteen-year-old brother, Martin, to take care of the old place at Squaw Spring. Sister Kate stayed to cook for them in the rock ranch house, and the boys slept in "the butcher shop," a small frame house with an adobe addition where meat was cut. The boys took turns doing the chores in the morning. When it was one's turn to bring in the horses, the other two had the privilege of staying in bed until Kate called them to breakfast. But Will didn't wake up easily. When it was his turn to wrangle, Frank and Martin were often up and about and sometimes did his chores for him so they'd be ready to ride when they'd had their coffee and biscuits.

On the morning of September 17, 1908, it was Will's day to roll out to do the chores. Frank and Martin went to the house and had a cup of coffee. Frank went back, looked in the window of the bunkhouse, and saw Will on his cot across the room under another open window—on his back, still sound asleep. To wake him up, Frank aimed his six-shooter at the opposite open window and fired. Will woke at the click of the hammer being pulled back, and he sat up in bed just in time to get shot in the head.

Frank, in a welter of grief and horror, saddled Will's wrangling horse and rode furiously up to the pass between Blue Mountain and Split Rock and past the closed Ajax Mine, across Whitetail Flats, and up Turkey Creek to find Dr. G. B. Richardson. His horse was foundered from the run, so Frank rode back behind the doctor's buggy on a borrowed horse. Neil Erickson, who was in Paradise that morning, rode escort to Judge Hancock and to assist Kate, who was alone with her dead brother. Martin had taken to his heels in fright.

When the white-winged doves returned and the mesquite bloomed in the spring of 1909, the Chiricahua Mine still hadn't reopened. The Cochise remained shut down, and the Ajax and Doran's were in a holding operation. Miners had drifted out in such numbers that Bill Hayes and Dan Moseley closed their hotels, and Fred Christy and

John Rock shut their store. Christy bought out his partner and moved the stock to Globe, which promised more stability. The Star Restaurant shut its doors, as did several saloons, including the Milams' place and Joe Wheeler's. Joe landed on his feet. The San Simon's wagon boss, Tim Blevins, wanted independence. Recently married to Maude Miller, an Oklahoma girl from Chickasha, Tim left to homestead up in Price Canyon. Joe Wheeler, who had worked for Parramore in Texas, got his job and went back to work for his old boss.

Paradise was in the doldrums, but another mining operation in the Chiricahuas was just getting underway. In the latter part of 1908, John G. Kerr, for the Arizona Marble Company, established a small camp in the head of McIntosh Canyon not far from old Fort Bowie. A Denver consortium organized and financed the company after purchasing a claim staked by two soldiers shortly before the post was shut down. The first access was by way of the Josephine Trail and Bear Springs Pass on a crude road that was too steep for a loaded wagon.

By February 1909 Kerr had men building a road up Emigrant Canyon to the camp. The construction required making two cuts through a granite narrows, bridging several arroyos, and installing culverts in smaller washes. While road building was underway, four wells were drilled, pipelines laid, and the construction started on a large mill next to the site of the quarry. The steam-powered mill was to operate machinery for drilling, sawing, and hoisting rock and for pumping water. It was fueled at first by juniper and oak from the upper basin of the canyon, which was nearly denuded, and later by coal brought in fourteen miles from Olga siding, about halfway between Bowie and San Simon. An office-storehouse, a cook shack, and a combined machine and blacksmith shop were erected, as well as residences for Kerr and his business manager, Dana Miller. Two dormitories were built, but many of the crew lived in a tent camp a hundred yards down the canyon.

By midsummer the Chinese chef at Bowie's Southern Pacific Hotel had been enticed away to cook for the crew. Fong Doo had a soft spot for miners and often grubstaked prospectors with his poker winnings, at one time lending seventeen hundred dollars to Cap Burns, the prime mover behind the Chiricahua Mine.

By the year's end there was talk of applying for a post office for "Marble, Arizona"—an event that never transpired, but McIntosh Canyon was thereafter Marble Canyon.

Supervisor Arthur Zachau had Ranger Erickson sketch plans for a ranger station at Portal. He had no money to build it but didn't intend to manage a forest from the open flats. He put up a tent over a board platform at the new site and used it for an office.

If his headquarters were primitive, in other ways the operation was thoroughly modern. In 1909 a grounded telephone line was strung from Portal to Paradise and up the logging road to Barfoot. Telephones powered by dry-cell batteries put Zachau in instant touch with his rangers—except when they were horseback or during high winds, lightning storms, or heavy snows. Private citizens were encouraged to purchase their own phones and tie into the government line, and many did.

John and Frank Hands had homesteads in the North Fork of Pinery where Horsefall Canyon joins it—places where they had been living for many years and from which they pecked away at their claims around Jack Dunn's old mine. They needed cash to buy a box of giant powder from time to time, and John hired out to help Neil Erickson and the supervisor's brother, Walter, string telephone wire from Barfoot Park down the crest of the mountain to Cima and around the shoulder of Ida's Peak into Pinery and Neil's Bonita Canyon headquarters.

More pine seedlings were put out in the heavily logged area around Barfoot, and piñon seedlings were planted in the head of the north fork of Cave Creek and on Onion Creek where cutting firewood, fence posts, and mine timbers had bared much ground. Seedbeds were laid out at the Portal station to produce more seedlings. Much of this work fell to Neil Erickson, still spending most of every week away from his wife. Neil jotted another note in the margin of his daybook: "Great men are nourished by the elements; woman is an element—all the elements in one: earth, air, fire and water, met together in a rose."

If Paradise still suffered from a setback, it wasn't dead yet. Ironfoot Coryell, still a bachelor at forty-six, married the grass widow Susan Sanders and acquired a ready-made family. He continued to drive the stage, but he moved into Susan's house at the Turkey Creek tanks, below the site of old Galeyville, and became a man of more substance when he invested in a herd of Angora goats, which he grazed in the foothills.

Portal continued to grow slowly. Kentucky-born Ribern and Mary Justice and their four children settled on Silver Creek about a mile northwest of the Powers and McCord store. Ribern dug a well, put in a futile kitchen garden, and did a little carpentry. Their older son, twelve-year-old Noble, rode a burro over to Paradise on publication days to clean type for the *Paradise Record* and to learn to set it up.

Jim Reay's brother Steve joined him from the Kingston mines with his pregnant wife, Martha, and their two children. Housing was tight at the Reays' but they put up a tent over a lumber platform between the house and Silver Creek, and Steve found work at the Savage Mine.

But the Savage, too, was laying off miners, and Steve got together a crew of Mexicans and set up a wood camp in Sulphur Canyon, moving over there with his family. One Sunday Jim and his family had gone over to Sulphur to visit, and on their return to the Oasis Orchard they found the tent in front of the house was gone. Fresh wagon tracks led away out into the valley, so Jim and his ten-year-old son, Frank, saddled horses and followed the tracks to the Martyrs' house down near the San Simon Cienega.

There is obviously more to this story than is known today. Whether it was a borrowed tent that was repossessed or it was stolen clumsily, then given up with a shrug, Jim told Bob Martyr that he expected the tent to be returned and restretched by the next day, and it was.

It was mostly the wage-earning men who left the Paradise camp. The serious prospectors continued to comb the slopes of Apache Pass Fault, sinking their picks into seams in the limestone, looking for promising rock. One of these was Duncan R. McDonald, who had several claims in Indian Creek.

McDonald was an experienced miner from Canada who had arrived in Paradise after nearly thirty-five years of hard-rock mining in the Colorado Rockies. For a time he'd been the mayor of a mining camp called Bull Hill, a fact he proudly shared with his fellows, who thereafter referred to him as "Bull Hill" McDonald to differentiate him from Duncan *D.* McDonald, another local miner.

To replenish his funds, Bull Hill had moved over to Paradise from his diggings and worked a couple of years in the Chiricahua Mine. In 1909, with the mine shut down and a new grubstake in his pocket, he went back to his shack in Indian Creek to find that his claims had been jumped. New work had been done, and a broad trail led over the pass into Wood Canyon. McDonald followed the trail to a cabin between Overton Canyon and the mouth of Bitter Creek, where he encountered Byron Clair of the Pawnee Mining Company of Douglas. Clair pointed out that McDonald hadn't done his assessment work and his claims had lapsed.

There were hard words but no hasty action. Both parties were equally firm in the righteousness of their stands. Bull Hill left but let Clair know that he expected him to be out of there when he returned.

Snow had been almost continuous since late November, but Clair continued to work with two employees at getting out ore. On December 31 he started down Wood Canyon with fifty-four sacks of ore on his wagon. A short distance above the Cross J Ranch, he broke the wagon tongue and returned to his cabin, intending to go out to San Simon the next day for a new tongue. Meanwhile he did some more recording work and wrote letters to his partners.

McDonald left his Indian Creek camp early on the morning of January 2, 1910, with a 30/30 and rode through deep snow over the divide into Wood Canyon, arriving at Clair's camp at eight o'clock. Smoke was coming out of the stovepipe, indicating that the Pawnee Mining Company was still in residence.

"Come out here, Clair, you dirty son-of-a-bitch," Bull Hill called out. "I'm going to kill you."

The claim-jumper *did* come out, and Bull Hill did what he said he would do.

The prospector fashioned a makeshift shroud from two ore sacks, lashed the body over the back of one of Clair's draft horses, and led him to Paradise. He pulled up to Chamberlain and Hawkins in the midafternoon and surrendered to Mart Moore.

Judge Jim Hancock presided over the coroner's jury, which found that—in the legalese that Jim was learning to use—"the deceased met his death at the hands of D. R. McDonald . . . contrary to the form of the statutes in such cases made and provided and against the peace and dignity of the Territory of Arizona." In Clair's pockets they found an unmailed letter to his partner, Jim Coombs, saying that Clair intended to confront McDonald and warn him that if he didn't vacate the claims, Clair would go to the sheriff and get an injunction. "May have to fight McDonald but that is my lookout," he wrote prophetically.

At the grand jury in June, witnesses for the prosecution included T. R. Brandt, the San Simon merchant, and Clair's two employees, Octaviano Savela and Felipe Hernández. There was considerable local sympathy for McDonald. John Rock, Dick Brown, Henry Chamberlain, Bill Morrow, Emmett Powers, Jim Reay, and the arresting officer himself, all pitched in to cover his ten-thousand-dollar bond, but he was found guilty of second-degree murder and sentenced to fifteen years in the new penitentiary in Florence.

The same day Bull Hill McDonald plugged Byron Clair, a quieter but more tragic death occurred at the Z Bar T Ranch under Split Rock at the mouth of Whitetail. The two-week-old daughter of Nancy and John Costin died, having survived her mother by only three days. "Nannie" Costin, at seventeen, had been married only a year when her baby was born at the home of her mother, Henrietta Hall. Doctor Richardson was fresh from one of the Paradise saloons when he attended the delivery and wasn't at his best. The young mother died of peritonitis within ten days.

Paradise continued to shrink—and to dry up. Joe Larrieu closed down the Mineral Park saloon and left town. Alejo Bedoya served his last drink in the Monte Cristo and took his family back to Solomonville. John Bendele moved his saloon to San Simon, and his wife, Maggie, homesteaded in Wood Canyon. Mart Moore now owned the license at Boozer's, and it stayed open with Jack Cross tending bar. Pat Walsh's saloon stayed open through most of 1910, but he was his own best customer. Delirium tremens overcame him and he was taken to the asylum for the insane in Phoenix, where he soon died. State law prohibited the sale of intoxicants for credit, but Chamberlain and Hawkins sold bottled whiskey at the store, putting it on the books as "merchandise." Laura Hancock's Arcadia was the only hotel left.

The U.S. Census taken in April 1910 for the first time shows Portal with a larger population than Paradise. There were 125 people counted in Turkey Creek and Whitetail, but 139 between Cave Creek and Sulphur Canyon. The population was still predominantly male, with over twice as many men as women. The latter were fertile enough, however, as 42 percent of the total number were children.

The people thought of themselves as belonging to a single settlement, but there are some interesting comparisons to be made between the populations centering around the two post offices. Paradise was a mining camp. Of the working men, thirty-four of fifty listed their occupation as miner or prospector. Only two called themselves farmer or stockman. And it was a more compact community, with most of the people living within a mile of the short stretch of Market Street. Portal's population was more spread out, reflecting its primarily agricultural orientation. Only seven heads of households were miners; thirty-eight were farmers or stockmen. Spring roundup was underway at the time of the count, and fourteen of those thirty-eight were 7H cowboys.

Paradise's men also averaged older, maybe because it was the younger bucks who were quicker to look elsewhere when the boom was reduced to an echo. There were still at least four old-timers from Galeyville in residence. Though Stephen Reed, at eighty-five the oldest man on the east side of the mountains, was part of the Portal population, Portal men averaged thirty-eight—nearly ten years younger than the Paradise holdouts.

In the larger, combined community there were thirty foreign-born from ten countries. All those with a European origin were naturalized or had taken out first papers. None of the fourteen born in Mexico had become citizens. Among the latter, José Grijalva had stepped through the ethnic barrier and was mining underground for copper.

The census was erratic. Several people known to have been in the area weren't listed, whereas Emma Maloney was counted once at her own home and two weeks later at her mother's house on Turkey Creek. Laurence Mouser was tabbed at the San Simon headquarters and again at his father's house on the Cave Creek Cienega. A growing community of about a hundred drawing mail from the new post office at John Richhart's store at Apache was more oriented toward Rodeo than to Portal.

Itinerants in Cave Creek in the spring of 1910 were Lyman Lindsay, a "showman under canvas," and his wife, Margaret, a "performer," with their three daughters: Vilia, Aria, and Corinne. The census didn't say if they put up a tent, if Lyman in dusty doublet and frayed hose declaimed Hamlet's soliloquy, or if Vilia accompanied Aria's soprano on a battered trumpet while Margaret posed in pink jersey tights.

There was much real estate activity on Cave Creek, reflecting the relative optimism felt about its future. A couple of entrepreneurs from Douglas formed the Portal Horticultural and Improvement Company and bought out Hugh Rowe's homestead, and Bob Herrell bought Rowe's several lots in the town site. Herrell and his wife, Sarah, had farmed in New Mexico before coming to Arizona, where they lost no time digging in. Sarah took over the post office from Ed Epley.

Mart Moore relinquished his interest in the stage line to Coryell and homesteaded 160 acres on Silver Creek at the south end of Limestone Ridge. Hedging his bets, he also had a share in a cattle ranch ten miles north of Stein's Pass. Jim Reay had irrigated a bumper crop of sorghum on fifty acres, taking water from the creek just above the crossing of the lower Paradise-Rodeo road, but he wanted a bigger farm. He and Herrell talked about a cooperative ditch with a takeout farther up the stream where water flowed longer through the year.

Fred Finnicum's brother Walter, a bachelor, joined him at Portal and soon filed for a homestead on Silver Creek between the town site and the Ribern Justice place. He was forty-three, time was short, and eligible women were scarce. He answered an ad in a "lonely hearts" column and apparently made a good case for himself, because before long he drove the spring wagon to Rodeo to pick up a widow with a nearly grown son. If he was taken aback at the formidable appearance of his secondhand rose as she stepped off the train, she was certainly equally distressed to find that Walter's "ranch" was a flimsy board shack and his herd comprised a milk cow and a cat-hammed horse.

Walter didn't enjoy his bride's constant criticism, but he went to work as a fire guard for the Forest Service. When he came down off the mountain one Friday evening, there seemed to be no one at the house, but he put his horse in the wire corral and walked to the door. Something caught his attention and he turned aside just as he pulled the door open, thus escaping the blast from a shotgun that his stepson had wired to a chair just inside the door. Walter was long-suffering but couldn't bring himself to forgive that. He told the lady and her boy they would have to leave. The rest of his life was lonely but peaceful.

Other couples moving into the canyon had more stable marriages. Trustees Fred Finnicum, William Rose (Zachau's office manager), and Hugh Mouser opened the Portal School for the year of 1909–10 and paid Mrs. Ola Martyr seventy-five dollars a month to teach thirty-nine youngsters. Over in Paradise the teacher, Emily Martin, had only seventeen children, including twenty-year-old Clarence May.

The spring of 1910 was Clarence's last at a school desk he'd outgrown. He was only two years younger than the new teacher, the Ericksons' older daughter, Lillian, who was to start the fall term. He'd grown impatient with being penned with children. He was physically grown and wanted to be counted among the men. His contemporaries Fred and Charlie Hall on Whitetail rode horseback everywhere and carried pistols. Just his age, Gould Davis and Lawrence Mouser were punching cows for the H's. George Hall, a year older, was married and had a brand of his own. Much his mother's boy, Clarence mucked in his father's prospect hole, the Humboldt Mine on the north side of Round Valley.

The Mays lived in a small adobe just below the low pass over into Turkey Creek, at a spring that they had developed for domestic water. The few burros they used for packing ore and firewood watered at the open seep. There was no fence around it, so goats owned by others also watered there.

Most often the offending goats belonged to Earl Sands, a young Texan who lived with his wife and baby about a mile south of the Mays in a grove of hackberry trees. Young May resented the trespass of Earl's goats, which fouled the water to the point that the May's burros wouldn't drink. He made it widely know that he wouldn't stand for it. His father advised him to cool down.

On the morning of June 27, the May men took the burros up on the slopes to pack in firewood. After Isabel readied up her kitchen, she walked to the mine, three-quarters of a mile away, to comb the dump for pretty mineral specimens to take to a sick friend in Paradise.

After packing two loads of wood to the house, "Cappy" May sent his son to the mine to do a few chores at the surface until he could join him. He had a letter to write first. Isabel was near the bottom of the dump and was starting for home when she saw Clarence approaching her on his burro.

"What are you doing, Mama?" he asked her.

Before she could answer, three rapid shots were fired. Clarence rose up in the stirrups, pulled a pistol from his hip pocket, and fired three rounds to his right. As she ran toward her son, Isabel saw Earl Sands on foot, running down the arroyo paralleling the road. She reached Clarence's side to catch him as he slid from the saddle. He was bleeding profusely from wounds in his wrist and kneecap and more seriously from his right side. As she held her son in her arms, Sands whirled to fire two more shots in their direction.

Earl and Gertie Sands had been walking to Paradise with three-year-old daughter Jessie that morning. George Shipman, a cowboy from out in the valley, came up behind them from the direction of the

Savage Mine. He offered to take the child behind him on his horse, and Earl walked on ahead as Gertie handed Jessie up and then turned to follow her husband. Jessie didn't feel secure behind the cantle, so George rode slowly to keep her confident and comfortable. The parents were out of George's sight when the shooting started, but Gertie ran back. "Earl has shot Clarence," she cried. "Give me my baby and go get a doctor."

George handed the girl down to her mother and rode ahead to where Isabel May was lying on the ground with her son in her arms. Her clothing was bloody and tears streamed down her face.

"My god, get me some water and go for a doctor," she pleaded in anguish.

As the cowboy rode off toward the closest help, the Savage Mine two miles away, Gertrude Sands came up to the two on the ground.

"My god, is Mr. May killed?" she asked. "Where is Earl?"

"No," Isabel told her, "bring your baby over here and I'll take care of her while you get me some water."

But Gertie Sands was concerned for her husband and didn't know if he, too, might be wounded. She hurried away down the arroyo in the direction he had fled.

When he heard the shots, the elder Clarence dropped his pen and ran toward the mine. From a hundred feet away he saw his wife and son lying together on the ground, covered with blood, and he feared they both were shot.

"Papa, Sands shot me, and I never saw him," his son told him.

The wounded boy was lying between ocotillos on the flinty limestone gravel. By now it was about ten-thirty in the morning, and in the glare of the unfiltered June sun the temperature was close to 100 degrees.

The father caught up the burro and started back to the house. As he urged the beast along, George Shipman overtook him. He'd gotten the word to a couple of men at the mine who were following him on foot. Clarence May asked him to ride to Paradise for Judge Hancock and to ask him to phone for a doctor.

May rode on to his house and returned with a canteen and with a folding cot over the pommel in front of him. He and Isabel got their son onto the cot and, using it as a litter, carried him to the shade of a desert willow in the arroyo, too exhausted to carry him further. The men from the Savage arrived to help take his son home, but when Hancock and the doctor arrived, the boy was dead.

Constable Mart Moore was in Tombstone that morning giving testimony to the grand jury in the case of Duncan McDonald, so Jim Hancock got word to Orvil Hicks, a cattle association range detective living in Portal who, by virtue of his job, had been deputized by the county sheriff. Hicks arrested Earl Sands, who made no resistance and was released pending a hearing, which was postponed for two weeks. There was also an apparent reluctance to bring the killer to account, and many of the potential witnesses were at the McDonald trial.

Finally Hancock brought Sands, his accusers, and witnesses together in an upper room of the Arcadia Hotel, where Sands was formally charged with "shooting said Clarence May with a revolver."

The grand jury exonerated Sands because of young Clarence's own mouth. Several witnesses, including Hugh Mouser, Charles Hall, Laura Hancock, and Gus Chenowth's younger son, Earl, testified to his boastful threats to "get" Earl Sands. Most damning was the testimony of Frank Witt, Gertrude Chamberlain's brother-in-law. During the previous two years Frank had been in Paradise running a livery stable but was now living in Don Luis, near Bisbee. Two weeks before the shooting, he saw Clarence in front of the Pony Saloon on G Avenue in Douglas.

"He came up and shook hands with me and he said, 'Well, Witt, I seen some of your old friends the other day, and I'm going back over there and kill a couple of sons-of-bitches,'" Frank testified.

Witt said, "What's the matter? You don't really mean you're going to kill anybody."

"Yes, I'm going to kill Henry Chamberlain and Earl Sands. They're no good." Clarence pushed back his coat to show the butt of a revolver in his waistband and reached in his pocket to show Frank a handful of cartridges.

"Sands is a goat man," he said, "and no son-of-a-bitching goat man is any good."

Witt tried to remonstrate with him, but Clarence clung to him, repeating that he meant it. "You'll hear of it in a day or two. You'll hear of me killing Sands anyway, and Chamberlain too, if I can get him," he insisted.

Sands was acquitted.

It isn't surprising that Clarence missed Sands with his returning fire. The cartridges that he had shown Witt were .38 caliber. His pistol was a .45.

# Chapter 12

# The Nesters

We got the cream off of the country and we left the skim to the nesters.
**Dilworth Parramore, 1942**

When Clabe Merchant and J. H. Parramore brought their rangy Texas longhorns into the San Simon Valley, there was little competition for that broad spate of country. In 1910, a quarter century later, the 7H's were crowded from all sides. They weren't the only big outfit to feel the pressure. Settlement was heavier in the Sulphur Springs Valley, and the Erie had already folded. The CCC was looking for new territory, the Ryan brothers' range was much constricted, and homesteaders around Bowie and Willcox competed with the Munk brothers for the grass in Railroad Pass.

Mrs. Oscar Roberts, Ernst Ruch's widow, was ready to give up the Triangle Ranch—partly because of homesteaders and partly because with less rainfall than in the upper part of the valley, Triangle range suffered more quickly from abuse. Her second husband of ten years wasn't single-minded in attending to business, and too, she'd been on that bleak place for almost thirty years. She sold out to "General" Eugene McKenzie.

New to the San Simon Valley, McKenzie wasn't new to running cattle. From Midland, Texas, he'd been ranching since 1885 in Lea County, New Mexico. He had the reputation of a rustler, but he didn't suffer for it, even though, after a drive from the Pecos Valley to Dodge

City, he bragged that he got there with more cattle than he'd started with.

Three McKenzie brothers jointly owned the Triangle, but its operation fell to Gene and his two sons, Waller and Jimmy. The cowboys they brought with them were mostly hard cases who understood that the boss didn't frown on harassing homesteaders. One of the latter was lean John Cameron, who lived on the west slope of the Peloncillos north of Doubtful Canyon.

One day John took a wagon into San Simon for supplies. On his way he met several Triangle cowboys, who hooted at him as he passed. To urge him to get a bit more speed out of his team, they fired a few pistol shots in his general direction. They probably intended only to scare him and his horses, but one round went through the back of the wagon seat and wounded him in the genitals. The team *did* move faster and got him to San Simon after a painful ride and some loss of blood.

The event was the subject of conversation in the community for several days. Ross Sloan, one of the Triangle cowboys who hadn't stayed on when the new owners moved in, was in A. B. Hulsey's San Simon store for sundries. Mrs. Hulsey asked him where John was wounded.

Victorian prudery wasn't yet dead, and Ross was stumped for a moment. He looked down at his boot for help and said, "Well, Mrs. Hulsey, if he'd been a woman it would have missed her."

Ross himself had been involved in a shooting before coming to the valley. He'd been in Clifton with a fellow Double Circle cowboy, and after some heavy drinking the two friends let a mild argument get hotter until it ended with Ross shooting and killing his partner. Drunkenness hadn't excused Howard Chenowth, but he had killed three *local* men. In contrast, the Double Circle cowboys were both from out of town, the voters weren't inconvenienced, and both men were drunk. The officers reasoned that Ross was provoked into justifiable homicide, and he wasn't charged.

Ross became one of the cattlemen who edged in on Parramore's country when he got financial backing from a Grant County cattle-man for whom he'd worked in the past and he bought out a man named Toney in Skeleton Canyon.

Ross Sloan got his mail at Apache, a siding twelve miles southwest of Rodeo where bachelor John Richhart had opened a store two years earlier and had become the postmaster for some twenty families in the vicinity. Among them were Julius Lee and Maggie Noland Eaton and their three kids. They had moved from Portal into the valley to settle in the Peloncillo's Skull Canyon near where other members of Maggie's family had recently homesteaded. Eaton, who went by his middle name, often got his mail mixed up with that of James Lee Eaton—no relation—a North Carolinian settler who also went by "Lee."

John and Minnie Marken, on their way from Hampton, Iowa, to California, liked the looks of Apache and stopped with their pretty twins, Nina and Neva. Marken homesteaded and later opened a store in competition with Richhart.

Others whose new homesteads dotted the upper end of the val-ley in 1910 and 1911 included John Lee, his wife, Jane, and their one daughter and seven sons, ranging in age from twenty-one-year-old Ernest down to Dale, a babe in arms. The Lees settled between H headquarters and the mountains with Jane's mother, Eliza Vincent. Lee had farmed in the Texas panhandle but sought to improve his situation, and that always meant moving farther west. He had come alone in 1908 to locate his 160 acres and then went back to bring his family by rail in January 1910, the women and the baby in a coach, John and the boys in the baggage car with all their belongings.

Jesse James Benton in Tex Canyon wasn't quite fifty, but he'd had all the hard work and adventure he needed and was ready for a life of sloth. He sold out to Julius Krentz and moved to Douglas.

Krentz, an Alsatian, had been in Arizona since 1876. He and Ben-ton had been partners on a small ranch in the Tonto Basin for a while, then Krentz opened a butcher shop in Winslow, supplying it with beef from his own ranches and with deer, turkey, and elk brought in by Benton. Krentz was older than Benton and also retired. He turned the Tex Canyon ranch over to his son, Frank.

Henry Hale had been farming near Rising Star, Texas, when an urge to move struck him. He pulled a canvas cover over the wagon bows, hitched a team of mules, loaded his wife, Lulu, and their three small children, and headed due west. Henry's younger brother, Will, came with them. They had an uncomfortable couple of days without water, but they made the seven-hundred-mile trip in forty days and homesteaded about a mile south of H headquarters.

Back in Rising Star, the Hales had been neighbors of Tobias and Emily Roberds, whose oldest daughter, Wardie Edington, had recently been divorced. Henry and Lulu urged Wardie to come out and start anew in the developing country, and they made room for her and her small children, Velma and Ray, when they came out by train. Wardie laid claim to a homestead adjacent to the Hales and lived with them while she was getting a house of her own put up. There was little elbow room in the claim shack that Henry had thrown up with Will's help. It was to become more crowded.

On a cold evening in December, Lulu's time had come and Henry sent Will to Apache with the buggy to fetch Dr. J. R. Phillips. To fortify himself from the weather, Will took along a bottle, which he and the doctor passed back and forth between them on the eight-mile ride. Little nips added up, and when they arrived at the Hales', alcoholic fumes preceded Doc Phillips to the bedside. Lulu wouldn't let him touch her or her baby daughter, Lulu Pearl, who had already arrived with the help of Wardie and a neighbor. The ladies fed the doctor breakfast, and Will took him back. The whiskey was gone, but it was warmer with the sun up.

Like tough Susanna Buckalew, many of these later pioneer women had initiative and independence of spirit. Wardie's younger sister, twenty-two-year-old Lillie Roberds, followed her to Arizona in 1910 and staked her own homestead east of Apache, near 7H Horse Camp. She built a little adobe house and supported herself by opening up a school for the neighbors' kids.

Meanwhile, Susanna herself, now past child-bearing, didn't need Henry any longer. Still exerting her independence, she divorced him.

The steady increase of homesteads in the Arizona part of the valley south and west of Rodeo, New Mexico, put a lot of pressure on the Rodeo school. Between Horse Camp and Portal there were close to a hundred children of school age. Fully half of them lived nearly ten miles from either of those schools, and Rodeo took many of them in. People in this stretch of the San Simon Valley, split down the middle by the state line, often called it Lapland. It was where New Mexico lapped over into Arizona. The people on both sides were all neighbors, but the officers of the states and counties took that line seriously. Grant County wasn't collecting taxes to educate Arizona's children, and Cochise County needed to take care of its own.

Henry Hale, John Lee, and G. A. Threlkeld were appointed to organize a school district, and the one-room Lone Oak School was put up about a mile northeast of 7H headquarters near an isolated live oak tree. Anna, the sister of and housekeeper for the recently deceased Dr. G. B. Richardson of Paradise, was hired to teach forty-eight pupils for seventy-five dollars a month.

Lillie Roberds was teaching school at Horse Camp when she was joined by her parents and her two younger brothers, Birt and Altie. Tobias and Emily Roberds took out a homestead east of her, and eighteen-year-old Birt homesteaded east of them, closer to the Peloncillos. After a year in her Horse Camp school, Lillie replaced Miss Richardson at the Lone Oak School.

Over on Whitetail Henrietta Hall was concerned about the education of her boys. George, twenty-six, and Charlie, twenty-four, could just barely read and write but were too big to sit with the little kids at Miss Erickson's Paradise school. R. D. built a two-room shack behind the house for a classroom and teacherage, and the elder Halls hired Ruth Hodges from El Paso to tutor the boys. She started classes in January 1912, but before summer she and Charlie fell in love and were married. They moved into Bill Shanahan's abandoned Redtop at the edge of the valley.

Charlie and George Hall owned the Ermine Mine, across the can-

yon from the site of Galeyville, but their hearts weren't in it. Cowboying was more to their liking. Charlie had the C + H brand, and
George the Spear O Spear. Together they owned a few cows branded
H +2 on shoulder and hip—a brand that could be made by reworking
7 12, a legitimate brand in New Mexico, though there is no proof that
such adjustment was ever made.

A close neighbor of Charlie and Ruth Hall was Dan Moseley, who
had homesteaded just south of the Redtop after shutting down his
hotel in Paradise. With the 1914 death of his brother in east Texas,
the widow came out with her nine-year-old son, Sam, and after a few
months of cooking in a San Simon café, she claimed a homestead near
Dan's place.

It was a hard time for them. Mora Moseley grew a small garden
and milked a cow, but the only cash income for a while was from selling milk, which Sam took to the Cochise Mine in a jar tied behind the
cantle of his saddle when he rode to the school that the mine's management maintained for its employees' children.

Miller was the commonest name in the valley between Cave Creek
and Jack Wood Canyon—a stretch where the 1910 census counted
185 people on the Arizona side of the state line. Twenty-eight of them
were Millers in five unrelated families. The largest was that of Charles
and Rosalie Miller, originally of New York State.

When the oldest child, Edward, became "consumptive," they
brought the family to Arizona in three stages. High and dry was becoming the popular cure for tuberculosis. Apache, Arizona, was both.
There were seventeen family members in five households when the
outfit filed on several homesteads east of the railroad tracks. Daughter
Jen left her husband's grave in Texas. Adele left a sweetheart there,
and Rollins Pattison, who followed her west a short time later, married her, and joined the clan.

Another member of the family to come to Arizona was Charles's
black servant, now remembered only as L'zann, probably for his
Louisiana birthplace. He was the only black person in the valley.
Adele Miller's daughter, who remembers both L'zann and her grand-

father with respect and affection, says that because of their association some of their neighbors referred to them as the "Nigger" Millers to distinguish them from all the others.

James Redmond Miller was the firstborn of an Arkansas farmer who died fighting for the Confederacy. His mother, Nancy, married Jasper English, and they all moved to Bandera, Texas, where nine more children were born. James married another Nancy and took part in the 1889 opening of the Cherokee outlet. Two of his half-brothers, Frank and August English, came to the Gila, worked on cow ranches, and for a while raised horses. It was to be near them that their now-aging parents came to Clifton with their daughter—a third Nancy. About 1902 Frank and August went to Douglas to find steadier work.

Jasper and Nancy came only as far as Rodeo, where another daughter, Sybil, was living with her husband, Andrew Prather, who was getting established as a merchant and developer. The two Nancys, mother and daughter, opened a boarding house, Grandma's Place, in one of Prather's new buildings.

Meanwhile James Miller had given the farm near Chickasha eleven years. To be near his mother and half-sisters, one of the latter now married to Frank Sanford, he and his wife brought their nine children to a homestead in Post Office Canyon in the Peloncillo Mountains south of Rodeo. James ran goats on the hills behind his place and became "Goat" Miller to his neighbors. By 1910 his two older sons, Chesley and Floyd, had married and filed on homesteads of their own in the valley between Rodeo and Apache, and daughter Maude had married Tim Blevins, the ex-foreman of the 7H outfit, now ranching for himself in Price Canyon.

Another Miller family, with three children, had a place across the valley closer to the Chiricahuas. John and Florence Miller came from Texas and were unrelated to the two larger Miller clans. To help keep him distinguished from them, John was known as "Dutch" Miller.

The two remaining Millers, one a farmer and the other a cowboy, were both single, and neither had a nickname. A few years later an old cowboy, Frank "Shorty" Miller, lived by himself on top of the Peloncillos at the head of Cottonwood Canyon, south of Rodeo, where he ran a few cows. His home was a shack reached only by horseback; his social requirements were few; and he is chiefly remembered for a wound he received.

Before moving to that lonely roost, Shorty had ridden for French's WS, the LC, and other outfits north of the Gila. The question of ownership of some cattle arose, the particulars of which are vague, but one or more of Shorty's suspicious neighbors asked that he leave the country. The suggestion was punctuated one morning when Shorty, while riding over those rolling, grassy hills, was struck by an urge. He dismounted, squatted, and presented a gleaming target for the rifle shot that literally caught him with his pants down. He took the pointed suggestion and left the San Francisco Valley standing in the stirrups.

Carl Washburn came into the upper San Simon Valley from the Gila River. He was seventeen when his parents brought their family from Brownsville, Texas, to settle in a new farming community at the mouth of Red Rock Canyon, up the Gila from old Camp Richmond. This was on the southern fringe of country controlled by the LC Cattle Company, and local boys either worked for them or preyed upon them. By 1906, when Carl came to the Chiricahuas, he was an iron-bottomed, bush-popping cowboy who would skillfully and fearlessly lay his grass rope over anything with horns and slick ears.

In Paradise he ran into old friends from Brownsville: Fitch Wilson, Fitch's sister, Susan Sanders, and their father, W. W. Wilson. Fitch had skills and ambitions to match Carl's, but being three years older, he had more experience riding the rough country. An acquaintance said of him, "Fitch Wilson could move more cattle faster, and over rougher ground in the dark of night, than any cowboy who ever rode these mountains."

The two went into partnership branding 3X Bar. Ed Estes sold them his woodcutters' camp in the north fork of Cave Creek for a base of operations, and they went to mavericking.

The mountains were full of mustang cattle as wild as deer, escapees from the 7H works. Many were unbranded bulls and heifers following branded mothers, but so remote and rough are the canyons that grown, unbranded mother cows had eluded several roundups. Those mavericks became the foundation of many herds. Parramore thought of those cattle as his, but if his cowboys didn't get to them before they were weaned, Carl, Fitch, Jack Maloney, or George Franklin were very likely to do so.

Franklin was born in Kentucky but came west through Texas in easy stages as a child with his parents and did most of his growing up near El Paso. But *his* family also was on the Gila for a while—long enough for George to become acquainted with the Washburns and to marry Carl's sister, Ida. They all made their way south about the same time. The Franklins settled below the mouth of Sulphur Canyon, and George worked roundups for the H's.

Colonel Parramore was aware of the maverickers' enterprise and preferred not to hire any man that had a brand of his own, but he found it increasingly hard to stick with his rule. As the big outfits went out of business or shrunk in size, the ample labor pool of young, single, drifting cowboys diminished. If 7H cattle were to be gathered and the calves branded, Joe Wheeler was often forced to hire the wolves that were nipping at his hocks.

There was a place where a line had to be drawn, however.

The 7H foreman and Carl Washburn started out on a friendly basis, but when Joe came upon Carl standing over a calf to hogtie it while its 7H mother anxiously watched from a hundred feet away, he slapped him over the head with his coiled rope and told him he'd shoot him if he saw him afoot again on San Simon range.

Carl was on a friendlier footing with Kate, Susanna Noland Buckalew's second daughter. Kate was attracted to the good-looking cowboy who was so handy with a catch rope, and he to her—for her looks, naturally, but also because she was a pretty good hand herself. They were married in 1909; Fitch Wilson discretely rolled his bed, and she moved into the rough camp in Cave Creek and proceeded to make it habitable.

As Carl's encounter with Joe Wheeler implies, the fine line between mavericking and rustling was sometimes crossed when a man couldn't wait for a sucking calf to be weaned. One of these impatient fellows separated several 7H calves from their mothers on lower Turkey Creek and hid them in an old abandoned building in Galeyville till their mothers quit bawling for them and drifted away, and the new brands peeled. The venture might have worked if George Franklin hadn't informed on him. A warrant was served on the rustler, and the calves were penned in a small corral on the east side of the creek at the lower end of Paradise, pending a hearing before Judge Hancock.

Several of George's neighbors were upset with him for making trouble for a man who had a family to feed and who, after all, was only doing what many others were doing. George, in turn, was puzzled by the criticism.

"Why, we all agreed to quit," he protested.

It was a situation that called for rectifying action. A fight was staged out in the middle of Market Street in front of Boozer's. A boy was sent for Deputy Mart Moore to break it up, and while all attention was centered on the fracas, Carl and a helper took down the bars of the corral, turned the calves out, and drove them up the creek. Soon all the dogs in town joined in the fun and chased them past Soldier Flat and up the canyon. With the evidence dispersed, it was necessary to drop the charges.

Fitch Wilson didn't always confine his roping to mustang cattle. Lula Walker kept a milk cow, as many did, to help feed her three children. It was her custom to pen the cow at night and turn the calf out so that she could get the morning's milk first and then let the calf strip the cow after she had milked. One morning when she went out to the pen with bucket and lard can, the calf, which was always hungry in the morning and eager to get at its mother, wasn't there. With Georgia's help, Lula searched the neighborhood and the creek bottom but soon gave up to make preparations for her contribution to the afternoon's political rally, of which her husband was a leading organizer.

A potluck picnic was held on the concrete platform at the site of the old concentrator, a short distance down the creek from the end of Market Street. Supplemented by the cole slaw, potato salads, hot rolls, and beans the ladies brought, the main dish was the beef that had been roasting in a pit since the night before.

After the speeches were over and the party was breaking up, someone complemented Fitch for his part in preparing the feed. Laughing, Fitch said in Lula's hearing, "You should thank Mrs. Walker. She contributed the beef."

Lula Walker didn't think it was a bit funny.

Kate and Carl weren't long for Cave Creek. Forest Supervisor Arthur Zachau pointed out to the Washburns that they had no permit to run cattle on national forest land and that they were "squatters" on the old Estes place. It hadn't been occupied before the forest reserve was established, and afterward it was exempt from entry under the Homestead Act. Without any fuss the Washburns went to the homestead that Kate had located down in the valley near Apache when much of the rest of her family had homesteaded there. But the move didn't stop their mavericking, and they left their name on the little fork they had occupied for such a short time. It is still known as Washburn Canyon.

Zachau also confronted Jack Maloney with his lack of a grazing permit and proof of ownership of the ground on which he was planting fruit trees.

"I doubt that you're man enough to put me off," Jack said. "You're wearing a gun. Do you want to use it?"

That's the way Emma told it, and it sounds like her. Another version has it that Zachau, after repeated warnings, told Jack, "If you don't get those cattle off the forest, we'll take action to get them off for you."

Knowing the white-eyed, ring-tailed spookiness of the old snakes in the brushy canyons and on the rocky ridges, Jack agreed right away. "That's just fine, and I'll give you five bucks for every one you can bring to the corral." And that sounds a lot more like Jack.

Jack had a little more legality on his side than Carl. He was living on his father-in-law's place. Joe Sanders hadn't filed either, but his squatter's rights preceded the founding of the forest reserve. Jack stayed.

Range abuse and cattle theft resulted from the homesteader's scramble for an economic foothold. The years 1906–09 had rainfall well above normal, bringing an increase in homesteading. When things returned to normal, anyone who hadn't known better soon found out that you couldn't dry-farm this border country with an average rainfall of ten to fifteen inches a year and an evaporation rate of several times that. Grazing was the only way to survive. Most of the land was public domain, belonging to whoever could get the most use of it. Buying breeding stock was beyond the means of most settlers. Indiscriminate branding wasn't equal in scale to the rustling of the 1880s, when Curly Bill drove off whole herds, but with so many participants it added up.

In 1912 the Cochise County Stock Growers' Association was organized at Willcox for the purpose of taking measures to reduce rustling. Emmett Powers was elected to the board of directors and appointed one of several brand inspectors. He and his son-in-law had a few cows on their homesteads above Portal, as well as on their Hot Well Ranch, and they suspected Maloney of carelessly putting his brand on some of their calves. To set a trap, Emmett made tiny incisions at the butt of the tail of two of their calves, inserted inch-long pieces of baling wire, and turned them loose up the canyon with their mothers.

Jack found the pair as Emmett had intended, and separated them. He penned the slick-eared calves and fed them from a bucket until the mothers finally dried up and abandoned the place. He built a branding fire and went into the pen to catch a calf. When he grabbed its tail, he pricked his hand. Upon examination he found Emmett's implanted wire, and he knew why it was there. He removed the wire, then checked the other calf and found another one. He removed it too and branded both calves.

When the mother cows showed up near Emmett's house without their calves, he called the range deputy and went up to Maloney's ranch with him and accused Jack of stealing his two calves.

"I can prove it," he said. "Mart, you'll find pieces of wire under the skin on the underside of both of their tails." Of course, Mart didn't.

Hopeful prospectors continued to peck around Paradise, but there was no payroll, and the slump showed signs of becoming permanent.

In 1911 Chamberlain and Hawkins gave up and sold the store to George Walker, who still had faith in the camp he'd founded.

Artesian water had been found near San Simon, and farmers were coming in to use it. Henry and Gertrude Chamberlain, following another boomlet, moved down there to open a small hotel. Tom and Eddy Hawkins went with them and raised chickens. Renwick White had been moonlighting with mine promotion and swung the sale of the Black Queen near old Galeyville to the Phelps Dodge Corporation, who never worked it. But the lack of advertisers and readers forced him to put out his last issue of the *Paradise Record*, and he, too, moved to San Simon with his press, where he began to publish the *Artesian Belt*.

Paradise's moribund condition affected the health of its satellite. Lots in Portal weren't selling, but there was growth of another kind on Cave Creek with the expansion of farming through irrigation from the creek.

Jim Reay couldn't water his Oasis Orchard in 1910. Despite some winter moisture, the total rainfall that year was a record low of a little over eight inches—less than half of normal—and the creek dried up. He saved his trees, but there was little fruit, and his sorghum was a complete failure.

Even in that dry summer, water was permanent in the creek bed at the narrows of the canyon a few hundred yards above where Neil Erickson had just completed the new ranger station. To take that water to Reay's fields and to maintain a gentle grade for the drop of 320 feet would require a ditch over three miles long as well as a flume across Silver Creek just above his house. That was a big project for one man, but the route of the canal lay across the land of another man who could benefit from it, and Jim enlisted William Stuart to help him.

Bill Stuart was born in Maine but raised on an Illinois farm. He'd shipped as a sailor for a while before coming to Arizona to work for the Forest Service. At thirty-one, after five years of ranging the mountains for Neil Erickson, he decided to sink roots. From Mart Moore and George Walker, he bought 160 acres that lay between Reay's and the foot of Limestone Mountain and next to Fred Finnicum's place on the creek.

The homestead had belonged to Moore, who had mortgaged a half interest in it to Walker for money to develop it. Their interest in it was speculative at a time when everybody thought Portal was to be the new queen city of the West. They were glad to get three hundred dollars for it—Walker to put into his new investment in the mercantile business, and Moore for the little ranch he'd found north of Steins.

Stuart also filed on 80 acres adjacent to the 160, and he joined Jim Reay in planning a ditch, but he was now out of money. He found a couple of chance takers in Tucson who, as the Portal Horticultural and Development Company, took a mortgage on Stuart's place for the funds for his share of the ditch work.

Another farmer using Cave Creek water was Bob Herrell, who had joined the feeble rush to Portal but had been floundering for a foothold. His family couldn't exist on Sarah's post office pittance, and he couldn't farm his two lots in the undeveloped town site. He and Sarah, who gave up her post office, and Sarah's mother, Mary Shirtz, homesteaded way down Cave Creek just west of the state line. They took water from the creek below Jim Reay's, but Bob hoped tapping the source would improve his flow.

Through much of the year 1911, Stuart, Reay, and Herrell, with picks and shovels, mules and a slip scraper, and the hired help of men like Preciliano Mejía, his son Margarito, and José Grijalva, who had been unemployed since the mines closed, completed the Portal Ditch across Stuart's farm and onto Reay's. Jim and Bob together flumed the water across Silver Creek to Reay's Oasis Orchard. It was Herrell's responsibility to continue the ditch on below to his own place. The nature of the terrain in the valley lent itself to cutting a trench with a "middle-buster" plow.

Meanwhile a more modest ditch was cut to take water from a rock dam about a half mile below the Portal ford to what had been Hugh Mouser's place near Cienega Spring. Dutch Mouser had sold his homestead to Charles and Mahala Bush and moved across the valley to the foot of the Peloncillos to put down new roots at a seep in the mouth of what is now known as Mouser Canyon.

The Bushes had moved from an Oklahoma farm to go into partnership with her brother, Shelton Keeling, intending to add their "Hog Eye" brand to the many small herds on the edges of the San Simon company's range. They had no illusions about making the desert bloom with cotton or fields of grain. Their little ditch was for watering a patch of grass for horse feed.

It was January 1912 and way too early to plant, but Neil and Emma Erickson's son, Ben, was spading the kitchen garden at Faraway Ranch to get the ground ready for spring. He looked up to see Jay Hugh Stafford huffing down the trail from his place up the canyon. The old man's haste was unusual. At seventy-six, he was a little rheumatic, and he customarily strolled deliberately, with his hands clasped behind his back. But this time, as Ben put it later, he was "walking with his hands as fast as his feet."

"Something has got off with your trap and the Hands boys are after it," Stafford panted.

Ben dropped his shovel and ran to catch up with John, Frank, and Percy Hands and another neighbor who had brought a couple of dogs. Percy, Alfred Hands's surviving twin, had recently moved from Scotland. He was working with his brothers near the old Dunn Mine on properties that Frank and John had organized as the Hilltop Silver/Lead Mining Company.

A number-4 wolf trap had been set in the mouth of Rhyolite Canyon just above Stafford's house, and whatever had put its foot in it was dragging the ten-foot logging chain fixed to it. A few good footprints showed the round, clawless sign of a cat, and the men thought they were on the trail of a lion. The chain tore up enough duff to make a broad trail, and tracking was easy until the wire that tied it to the trap broke. The dogs were coursers for running coyotes, had little interest in scent, and proved to be worthless. The men spread out casting for sign until dark.

The next day Frank and Percy climbed back to the mine and Ben returned to his garden, but John returned alone to take up the trail again, believing that as long as the animal was carrying the trap, it couldn't go far or fast. He followed the cold trail up the north side of the canyon to where the creature began to work up the manzanita-clad slope of Sugarloaf Mountain. It's not easy going for man or beast in that country, now part of Chiricahua National Monument, but John Hands had been exploring what he called "the Pinnacles" for twenty years, and he probably knew it better than anybody.

By the end of the third day, he'd followed the tracks to the ridge connecting Sugarloaf to the rocks where Neil Erickson and Louis Prue had found Massai's abandoned meat in 1890. The tracks were fresher, and John knew he was getting close.

On January 12 John returned with his brothers to where he'd left the trail the night before. The three men followed the tracks only a short distance until they disappeared into a crack in one of the rock pillars. Frank worked his way up pill-like scree to get on top of the rock and lay on his belly to peer down into the crack and into a pair of shining eyes twelve feet away. He called to John to bring him the rifle. He fired once, and a jaguar slid out of the crack in the rock at Percy's feet.

In 1912 Neil Erickson supervised the construction of a fire lookout tower on Chiricahua Peak, and Arizona became a state.

After years of lobbying, New Mexico and Arizona were deemed by Congress to be mature enough to govern themselves, providing they could each write an acceptable constitution. Statehood was granted to New Mexico in January, to Arizona a month later.

Of more immediate importance to residents of the Chiricahuas was a long, warm rain on March 10 that fell on a deep snowpack in the high country between Sentinel and Buena Vista Peaks. Rainwater and melted snow flushed a lot of debris out of the stream channels, and Turkey Creek rose out of its banks to wipe out a couple of flimsy shacks in Paradise. Cave Creek threatened Maloney's house, roared down to wash out the dam for the Portal Ditch, and flowed around the juniper piers holding McCord's house off the ground.

The Portal school was on high ground and wasn't threatened. Miss Lillie Roberds, teaching at her third school in three years, could get to school from Jim and Minnie Reay's, where she was living, but many children living on the right bank of the creek couldn't cross it for several days—no doubt to their distress. At the junction of the main creek and its north fork, floodwater lapped at the front and back doors of Stephen Reed's cabin without crossing the thresholds. It was to be the last of a lifetime of hazards to be endured by the old pioneer. Not long after the water receded, Stephen Reed died at eighty-three.

Spring rains kept the water flowing out to San Simon Creek well into the summer, teasing several potential farmers onto homesteads and into irrigation projects. Dr. George Richardson's brother, Robert, planted his family on Turkey Creek's floodplain about a mile west of the Martyrs, on a meadow of tobosa grass. He dug a forty-foot well into the stony alluvium without reaching water, and he plowed a mile of ditch from the lower end of the Reay ranch that was almost as dry. The Chenowth's oldest son, Charles, homesteaded between the Richardsons and the Herrells.

Bill Morrow moved a mile and a half below Paradise, where he built a house and put in a little orchard on the bench above his slaughter house, near the site where Casper and Albert were killed by Indians and buried. He sold his house at the upper end of town for seventy dollars to George Franklin, who moved up from the valley.

The small flood of immigration that started in 1909 tapered off in 1912, but it brought Cliff Darnell into the country. Cliff was born in Kansas. When he was fourteen, his mother took her children to live with her brother, Clarence Tipton, who was cutting ties in Rye, Colorado. Tip left not long after that to work for the WS at Alma, New Mexico, and Cliff was left to be the family's main support. For several years he drove ore wagons at Cripple Creek.

In 1898 Tipton left French's to work for himself. By 1900, with a freight line in operation, he sent for May and her children. Cliff helped his uncle and cousins freight machinery up the narrow switch-backs to the mines of Mogollon with a jerk line of sixteen horses.

In 1910 Cliff began punching cows for the Hatchet Ranch, south of Hachita. He'd been there two years when a horse fell with him and broke his leg. His mother had died by that time, and his sister, Dilly, had married a WS cowboy. He no longer had a home, so while he

healed, he drifted. He'd known Ross Sloan in the country north of
Silver City, so he went to Skeleton Canyon to visit him. Ross told him
of a little place on Deer Creek, a couple of miles north, that could be
acquired. Cliff was thirty-seven and had been sleeping on the wagon
or under it long enough. He rustled up a little earnest money and
contracted to buy the Barker place, its OA Bar brand, and a roof of
his own.

Traffic from Rodeo had dribbled off to the point of unprofitability
to the Moore and Coryell stage, and they quit the business in 1911.
John Lee took over the contract to carry the mail between Rodeo
and Paradise in a trap with a mule. After a year he found it more
convenient to let his homestead lapse unproven and move his family
to Paradise. Jane Lee cooked and cleaned the rooms at the Arcadia
Hotel for Jim Hancock, whose wife, Laura, had given up and moved
to California. Lee helped usher in modern times when he bought a
touring car and started carrying the mail and an occasional passenger
by "motor-stage."

William Stuart still had a government job, and he found it hard to develop his new farm on weekends, but in 1913 he married Eula Lee,
Gus and Mary Chenowth's youngest daughter. With Bill's wages to
live on and Eula's steam to do the farming, the ranch began to amount
to something.

Eula had known Bill Stuart since she was seventeen. She may have
admired him all along, but his possession of 240 acres in Cave Creek
Canyon with a recently completed ditch running across it made him
even more attractive. It is undeniable that Eula Chenowth Stuart was
a go-getter who liked to take charge, and she brought more to the
union than her charm.

Old Gus Chenowth had finally died. His seventy-nine years had
seen the country change from a Mexican wilderness inhabited by a
handful of wandering Apaches to one of the settled United States.
Perhaps some of the treasure he was reputed to have buried was real.
At any rate, upon their marriage Bill Stuart paid off what he still owed
Walker and Moore on his homestead and then quit-claimed it to his

new wife. Eula also bought the adjacent old Rowe homestead. She mortgaged a one-sixth interest in that property, and Bill mortgaged his eighty acres to Stark Brothers in Missouri for 1,647 fruit trees valued at $580.50.

The flood of the previous spring made it clear that there were many places along the length of the Portal Ditch that required reinforcement, and Henry Hale was hired to haul creek-bottom stone for laying up masonry revetments. He kept his team and wagon at the Maloneys' and rode a saddle horse back and forth from his ranch in the valley. He was riding through Rodeo one morning on his return to Portal when he spotted Jack's horse tied in front of Bob McMahon's saloon. He tied his horse to the same rail and went in to see if Jack wanted to ride up to the canyon with him. Jack wasn't quite ready to leave, so to be sociable, Henry took a drink or two with him while he waited. By early afternoon they were both pretty well lubricated when they finally rode up to Maloney's. Emma met them out in front of the house.

"Where in the dickens have you been?" she demanded of Jack as she picked up a big stick.

Jack reined his horse around and spurred away, looking back over his shoulder. While he kept his eye on his irate wife, the horse carried him under a low sycamore limb that swept him out of the saddle. Before he could get up, Emma swarmed over him and, in Henry's words, "liked to beat him to death." Henry backed discretely away toward the barn to hitch his team.

Ed Miller, who had come to Apache for his tuberculosis, found his lungs improved in the crisp, clean air of Arizona. He married John Marken's sister, Laura, and was appointed by the sheriff to serve as the deputy for the Apache district. In that capacity one day in August 1913, he got a complaint about storekeeper John Richhart. Nobody today knows what the complaint was, but it was one of many.

Richhart was a cantankerous, vile-tempered man of sixty-two who was rumored to have left Kansas in a hurry after killing a man (some said it was his wife). At a hint of disapproval or a question about a price, his face would begin to twitch. When those who knew him saw the tic, they were quick to break off the conversation before he blew up. As a consequence he'd lost much of his trade to Marken's Store.

One who still traded with Richhart was James Miller's son, Floyd, who bought a 1913 Model T Ford through the storekeeper. To show his appreciation for the commission he'd earned, Richhart presented Floyd with a new set of tires at no cost. When the family came to the store to buy groceries or settle a bill, Richhart would fill the brass scoop from the scales with penny candy, put it down between the kids on the floor, and let them eat their fill. So the "Goat" Millers, while recognizing that the old man was touchy, thought he was a pretty good fellow.

A man named Turner didn't have such a good opinion of Richhart. He asked Ed Miller to go with him to the store to mediate a disagreement or at least to help keep tempers cool. Turner waited outside while the deputy went in to talk to the storekeeper, who reached the boiling point in short order. Ed, realizing the futility of further discussion, turned and started for the door. He wasn't quick enough. Richhart reached behind the counter for a shotgun and shot him in the back. Knowing that the shotgun had two barrels, Turner was already swinging into the saddle when he heard the storekeeper call out, "Where are *you*, Turner?"

An unofficial posse of neighbors assembled, cautiously circled the store, and talked Richhart into giving himself up.

At the trial Newt Eldridge testified that he had heard Ed Miller threaten the accused "with bodily harm," and Fred Burch told of hearing Ed tell Richhart that he would kill him. That was enough to reduce the charge to second-degree murder. Though Richhart was convicted, Floyd Miller and others spoke up for him. Most telling was the appearance of the victim's mother in court. Rosalie Miller said that sending an old man to prison wouldn't bring her boy back, and Richhart was released on parole.

Stephen Reed's children owned the old ranch in equal shares, but just barely. Stephen had lived on the ranch for twenty-nine years without title and hadn't bothered to file for a homestead before the land was withdrawn from the public domain for the Chiricahua Forest Reserve. In 1908 Supervisor Arthur Zachau had encouraged him to apply for title under special provisions for prior inhabitants and helped him with the details. Final title wasn't awarded until shortly after his death.

None of the children wanted to hang on to the place where four of them had been born and all had been raised. Lula and Claudie had married and left home. The oldest son, Grover, was married to Lyda Justice and working in Paradise. Walter, then twenty-two, was working for the Hands in their Hilltop Mine. Both Frank and John Hands had been close to Stephen Reed since coming into the country in the 1880s, but John—"Uncle John" to the Reed kids—had been a member of the family. The Hilltop Mine had been producing well, and he had a little cash plus the hope of more from interested investors. He bought the ranch from Stephen's heirs and allowed Alice and Bill to stay on as long as they liked. For the time being, he himself stayed in Pinery to keep track of his mining interests.

For over twenty-five years the Hands brothers had been burrowing into the igneous pipes and dikes around Jack Dunn's old mine. In 1913 they extended their exploration over the ridge into the head of Whitetail Canyon. Their modest shipments of lead, silver, copper, and zinc ores had been enough to pay the cost of custom smelting and to keep them in beans and dynamite, but significant development and profitable production required capital to invest in machinery and labor. In 1915 they found a man who had the money—or knew how to raise it.

When Frank and John sold the Hilltop group of mines to John O. Fife and his Chicago associates for a reputed $120,000, they made more money from a California District mine than anyone else before or since. Frank promptly got married and retired to his Pinery Canyon ranch. John used a piece of his share to pay off the Reed children, and he moved over to Cave Creek.

Toward the end of the summer of 1914, the limbs of the apple trees that Reed had planted long ago were so heavy with fruit they were pulled to the ground. John suspected a bear was getting his fruit, and he set a trap under a tree for it. After Stephen's death and before John took possession, Jack Maloney had assumed proprietorship of the orchard and came up one evening to fill a few more boxes. John's trap might have fooled a bear, but it didn't escape Jack's eye. He sprung the trap and took it home—with a box of apples.

The winter of 1914–15 was wet. Between the first of December and the last of April, almost eleven inches of precipitation were measured at the Portal Ranger Station. That helped Warren "Ike" Faust to get his wagon stuck up to the hubs in mud one day in early April when he was returning from Sulphur Canyon with a load of wood. He unhitched his horses, tied them to wagon wheels, and walked in the rain to Henry Hale's house with his four-year-old son in his arms. The boy was soaked through and cold, and Lulu Hale put him to bed with two of her youngest.

Henry, with his own team, went back with Ike to the stalled wagon, and the four horses pulled the wagon to dry ground. On the way back to Hale's, Ike told Henry of his troubles. His roof had been leaking through the long winter rains, and he needed money to reroof the house. He had a job with the railroad and a homestead halfway between Rodeo and Apache, but the bank refused a loan. He asked Henry to put in a word for him.

Like most homesteaders, Henry was struggling to hold his own head above water and wasn't in a position to endorse another man's note, but he wrote the bank to say he knew Ike to be honest and thought he was good for enough to buy some roofing material.

Eventually Henry got a reply from the bank saying that they couldn't make the loan. Having an errand in Rodeo, though it was a little out of his way, Henry drove his buggy to Faust's place to deliver the message. His father-in-law, John Dill, went along for the ride. At the gate, about twenty feet from the house, Henry tied the reins to the whip stock and went to the door. Mr. Dill stayed with the buggy.

Ike met Henry at the door and they both sat down on the step, Henry pulling out his pocketknife to whittle at a stick. John Dill, dozing in the warm spring sunshine, paid no attention to the conversation until voices were raised. He looked up to see Henry walking toward him with blood streaming from the side of his neck and soaking his shirt and coat.

"Harry, what happened?" Dill asked.

"I don't know," Hale answered, still walking toward him.

At a scream from the house, he turned around. Rose Faust was struggling with her husband, trying to take a rifle from him. Ike jerked it out of her grasp and shot Hale in the chest, killing him instantly.

Lulu Hale believed that Faust had accused her husband of not trying hard enough to get him the loan he wanted. When Hale remonstrated with him, Ike, known for an unpredictable temper, lost it and apparently lashed out, causing Hale to stab himself with his own knife. At the Tombstone trial Ike said he thought Henry was going to the buggy for a gun.

Rose Faust took her children to relatives in the Silver City area while Ike served time in the Florence penitentiary. They never returned to the San Simon Valley.

If the winter of 1914–15 had more precipitation than usual, it was dry in another sense. To the disgust of a large minority, the state of Arizona imposed prohibition of the sale of alcoholic beverages, anticipating the national Volstead Act by six years. The drought affected the thirsty population in the interior of the state more than on the fringes. New Mexico stayed "wet" for three more years, so residents of the San Simon Valley were hardly inconvenienced. In fact, some were able to find an economic advantage in the prohibition by transporting booze from New Mexico to the west side of the Chiricahuas. A pass across the ridge between Pine Canyon and Rock Creek became "Bootlegger Saddle" for the frequent passage of mule trains carrying Rodeo whiskey through Barfoot Park into West Turkey Creek.

Rodeo experienced a small boom. Saloons proliferated and hotel business picked up. The eastbound passenger train, once nicknamed the "Drummers' Special" for the cigar and hardware salesmen who used it, became the "Drunkards' Special" for the rounders from Phoenix and Tucson who flocked to Rodeo on weekends for a two- or three-day toot.

In 1915 an old man in Paradise was careless in burning trash and allowed some coals to roll down the slope to smolder against the back of the Arcadia Hotel. By the time the fire was discovered, the building was ablaze and it burned to the ground. Jim Hancock and the Lee boys made several trips into the burning building to bring out furniture, clothes, and papers. Hancock kept going back in after it became dangerous and until Ernest Lee picked him up bodily, carried him out, and restrained him.

The judge had lost not only his home but also his office, which was a small room attached to the north side of the hotel. After the burned rubble was scraped away, Hancock took down an abandoned house and reassembled it on the site, where it served as his living quarters as well as his office as postmaster, justice of the peace, U.S. commissioner, county registrar, and observer for the Weather Bureau. His new office wasn't yet in place when he was called upon in his capacity as a peace officer.

George Coryell, realizing that the road down Turkey Creek ran across his property, discussed the fact with the man who operated the county's horse-drawn grader.

"Yes, I guess you *do* own the road," the fellow agreed.

Ironfoot Coryell saw an opportunity to augment the income from his goat herd, and he fenced off the road, installed a gate, and prepared to collect a toll. Owen Davis and Rube Haddon brought charges against him for obstructing a public road.

Judge Hancock wasn't set up for new business yet, but he joined in the complaint and took it to Herman Precht, the justice of the peace in Apache. Precht told Coryell that he'd been misinformed by the grader operator, whom he should have known had no authority. He found him guilty and fined him five dollars but remitted the fine providing the defendant agreed to take down the barrier. George Coryell was hard-headed and righteous in his cause. He appealed the judgment and demanded the case be heard in the superior court. He should have let well enough alone. The higher court also found him guilty and fined him two hundred dollars and costs.

A happier event that year was the marriage of Cliff Darnell and his neighbor Lillie Roberds. Lillie had frugally saved her salary and bought one of the first cars in the valley. She drove Cliff to Tombstone in her new Model T Ford for a wedding and honeymoon at the county seat.

The six-year-old Mexican Revolution reached the border in 1915 when the armies of Pancho Villa and Venustiano Carranza fought each other in Agua Prieta. Residents of Douglas watched the contest from rooftops with binoculars.

Villa blamed his defeat on the United States, which he believed had reneged on promises of support. He took petulant revenge when he stopped a train in Chihuahua and had fifteen American miners taken off and shot. When illustrated news of the incident reached the border, a mob in El Paso rampaged in the Mexican neighborhood and had to be restrained by troops from Fort Bliss. More than one lonely *mojado* caught on the north side of the Rio Grande in west Texas was shot or dragged to death.

On their ranch east of the Animas Mountains, Bill and Alice Parker were killed by their Mexican cowboy, who fled into Chihuahua well mounted on a Parker horse. The Parkers' two sons, "Dink" and "Ope," with a large posse of neighbors and Diamond A cowboys, took up the trail after the killer but didn't find him.

An American cowboy who was south of the border bringing drifted Diamond A stock back to home range was killed by Mexicans and hung with barbed wire from a windmill tower.

News traveled to rural areas sporadically and arrived third or fourth hand, garbled and exaggerated. People on isolated ranches thought invasion was imminent, and some families around Apache, thinking their houses would be targets for plunderers, went out to sleep in the arroyos at night. For a few nights, at Joe Wheeler's invitation, some men brought their women and children to 7H headquarters for protection and returned to stand guard at their respective homes.

Lulu Hale, now a widow with three children, refused to huddle with the other women and, against the advice of her brother-in-law, stayed on the place. She had the boys bring in wood for the stove and water for the night. She nailed the windows shut, locked the door, and propped the shotgun by it. Her daughter remembers her sitting at the table as the kids played on the floor. If she heard a noise, she blew out the lamp.

One of Villa's soldiers who remained loyal after the retreat from Agua Prieta was Manuel Domínguez, a vaquero from south of Casas Grandes who many years later would raise a large family in Portal and Rodeo. Manuel grew up on one of the huge ranches of Chihuahua and made his first cattle drive to El Paso as a child of seven, riding on the bed wagon and helping the cook rustle wood and water. When he was thirteen, he was in the saddle making a hand, and while still in his teens, he was swept up by the revolution. By the time of the battle at Agua Prieta, he was a veteran with his own *soldadera* following him.

On March 8, 1916, Villa and what remained of his army, some four hundred men, assembled on the Río Casas Grandes. They marched through a moonless night toward the northwest and crossed the border just west of Palomas. A half mile out of Columbus, the column divided to surround the town. Men on foot, Manuel Domínguez among them, crept up behind the buildings and to the stables of the American Thirteenth Cavalry to await the pistol shot that would signal the attack. The surprise was complete. The Lemmon and Romney Store and the Commercial Hotel were burned, some private homes were plundered, and the army kitchen was raided for food, but after a melee that lasted several hours, Villa withdrew. A score of Americans were killed, but he left more of his own men dead in the streets—estimates run from fifty to two hundred.

It is hard to know what Villa intended to accomplish. He may have come unraveled without a clear idea himself, but he was at the end of his rope, and he retired when his army disintegrated. With the disbanding of Villa's Dorados, Manuel Domínguez was out of work. He had no political interest in the revolution and had no conflict of conscience in switching sides. He was soon carrying a rifle for another of the several armies. In a skirmish near Nacozari, Sonora, he killed an officer of the opposing force in a hand-to-hand fight. Manuel's colonel, who saw the action, rewarded him by leaning over to take the dead man's badge of rank and pinning it on Manuel's shirt.

"You are now a major," he told him.

The new Major Domínguez's old sergeant was piqued at being out-ranked by one of his privates, and Manuel wasn't accustomed to han-dling that much authority. It was a difficult situation and not surpris-ing that it turned into a brawl that ended when Manuel shot and killed the noncom.

Mexican military justice was swift. Manuel was sentenced to die before a firing squad and locked in the corner room of a small house in the village. During the night some of his old companions, to whom he was still Manuelito, not Major Domínguez, chiseled a hole through the adobes and got him out to where they had a horse saddled and waiting for him. They gave him a pistol and ten dollars in American money, and he rode north as dawn broke. He rode through that day and much of the next night.

Before daylight on the second morning, he crossed the border two miles east of Douglas. At the foot of a small volcanic mound now known as "D" Hill, he slid off and curled up to sleep next to a ba-saltic boulder. When the sun was high, he cached the saddle and bridle under a mesquite, slapped the horse on the rump to send it back across the border, and walked into town. A bearded Mexican in huaraches riding a horse into town would have been too conspicuous.

By 1916 J. O. Fife had his Hilltop Metals Mining Company well under-way. He started a new tunnel on the west side of the mountain, hoping to intersect the richest ore bodies, and named it the Dad Fife in honor of his father. Walter Reed, who had been working for the Hands brothers, stayed with the mine when it was sold, and his brothers, Grover and Bill, also started work at the Hilltop. Grover had just lost his wife, Lyda, who left him with a three-month-old daughter, Maurine. Unable to care for her himself, Grover left the baby with his sister Lula Walker.

Fife also hired a number of Paradise men who had been working on claims of their own after the Chiricahua and Cochise Mines shut down. Among the movers was Bill Morrow. He and Eva had been on Turkey Creek for fourteen years, had had four children born there, and had seen Paradise grow from a tent camp to a boom town and then wither away. Morrow had been living on the earnings of his butcher shop and a few head of cattle and had been prospecting and speculating in mining property whenever he had time and a little money from his other endeavors. He moved his family into Whitetail Canyon and worked for the Hilltop Mine until the camp grew big enough to support a butcher shop that could feed his family and finance his prospecting.

Up in Cave Creek Canyon one morning, Jack Maloney was just leaving the corral on horseback when Emma called to him from the door.

"Jack, get me a couple of buckets of water before you leave."

Jack sighed, reined back to the corral, unsaddled, turned the horse out, and went back to the house with a shovel and a bar.

For their nine years on the place, they had been dipping water out of the creek and hauling it a hundred feet to the house. But no more. Jack tore up the kitchen floor and dug a ten-foot well next to the stove.

On the west side of the mountain, Neil Erickson reported a band of lobo wolves between Bonita and Picket Post Canyons.

Europeans had been at war with each other for two-and-a-half years when the United States joined them in April 1917. Americans went wild with a patriotism not equaled in their next big war. In a climate of intolerance that renamed German fried potatoes "home fries" and changed hamburger steak to "Salisbury steak," folks with German-sounding names had to suffer questioning looks, if not outright hostility. Ranger Erickson commented in his journal about his respected boss and the ranger in the Dragoons, "Both Zachau and Schoenberg are rather pro-German."

Young men from Paradise who went to war included John and Jane Lee's son, Bill, the oldest Morrow boy, Carson, and Will Sanders, who left his job at the Hilltop Mine. From across the mountain ex-ranger Ed Riggs went into the Signal Corps.

One of the results of nationwide support of the war was increased agitation by the Anti-Saloon League, the Women's Christian Temperance Union, and the Prohibition Party to abolish booze. Drinking was unpatriotic; drunkenness hampered production of the coal, copper, and cotton needed for the war. In their opposition to "Demon Rum," the dry forces got support from some unlikely sources. New Mexico's governor, who later died of cirrhosis of the liver, was an enthusiastic campaigner for a state prohibition act, and a big lobbyist for the bill was later involved in illegal liquor sales.

It was a well-founded fear that 1917 would be the last year of legal and plentiful whiskey in New Mexico. Such an outcome, of course, would also affect Rodeo's Arizona customers. The last months of that year saw an expansion of what was already a boom in recreational drinking in Rodeo and in exportation from New Mexico's liquor establishments across and around the Chiricahuas into thirsty Arizona. Ed Epley quickly paid for his first automobile by running booze to Willcox and Benson.

One of those to join the last desperate celebration in Rodeo was Jack Maloney. It is said that inebriation is never an excuse for meanness because alcohol only uncovers the true man behind the mask. In Jack's case there was no mask. He was jovial, drunk or sober. And he was an agreeable and friendly drunk when he ran out of money in one of Rodeo's saloons one evening, but he was a nuisance as he pestered the bartender for credit and cadged still-solvent patrons. Rodeo had no jail, but finally the constable manacled him to the rear wheel of a wagon out in the street until he sobered up.

Left alone in the dark, Jack got his back under the tailgate and lifted it enough to get the wheel off the ground, and with his fingers he unscrewed the hub nut and removed the wheel. He carried it through the paired swinging doors of the saloon.

"Here, Bob," he said, setting the wheel up on the bar, "this ought to be good for drinks for the house."

In a 1917 reorganization of the Forest Service, the Chiricahua National Forest was merged to become a district of the Coronado

Forest, along with the Santa Rita Mountains, the Catalinas, and the Dragoons. After ten years of good management of the Chiricahuas, Arthur Zachau was transferred to Oracle and Otto Schoenberg was moved from the Dragoons into the Portal station as district ranger.

Neil Erickson had been scaling timber, fighting fires, building trails, and making horse tracks for the Forest Service for fourteen years when he was promoted to take Schoenberg's place as ranger in the Dragoons. He was pleased with the raise in pay, but his journal entries suggest that he missed the Chiricahuas. And at fifty-eight he was slowing down. He didn't bounce back from hard blows as quickly as he had in his youth. His horse kicked him in the left leg. "Black Roxy knocked the taste of coffee out of me," he wrote. And at the end of a long day scrambling through the brush to the top of Mount Glen, he entered in his log, "I don't intend to climb these hills afoot anymore."

California's cornucopia emptied into eastern and midwestern cities, and the rural Southwest had to make do with dried or tinned fruit. But now Cave Creek's orchards were producing well, and Jim Reay's peaches and the apples grown by Stuart, Maloney, and John Hands at the Reed place found a ready market.

Emmett Powers and Fitch McCord were holding the bag of the moribund Portal Land and Improvement Company. Emmett was still involved with the Hot Well Ranch and had bought a machine to shred yucca and sotol, which he claimed to be better cattle feed than alfalfa, but Fitch made Portal his year-round home. He built a house from an abandoned saloon in Paradise, brought it to his homestead in six wagonloads, and put it together again. Then he planted apples in the platted town site and irrigated them with an extension of the ditch he'd dug to water his small hay meadow. It was just as well he had a water right and a ditch of his own because the jointly owned Portal Ditch was in trouble.

Cave Creek's flow wasn't enough to adequately irrigate all the ground that the three owners had broken. Although Eula Stuart wasn't on the scene when the ditch was dug, she energetically protected her interest in it. In her view, her location closer to the head gate constituted a primary right, and since the ditch ran the breadth of the Stuart ranch, she was in a position to see to it that Stuart trees and truck crops were well soaked before any water was allowed to go on past to Jim Reay's place.

The Stuarts had become overextended financially. They sold a one-third interest in their place to Bill's brother, Edward, in Oklahoma. A piece of Bill's eighty-acre homestead was still mortgaged, and they had pledged most of the ranch to the Stark Brothers for the nursery stock. Without reference to any of that paper, Bill and Eula then put up the entire place to the Bank of Bisbee for five hundred dollars.

Bill Stuart was only thirty-eight and in rugged good health when he was stricken with a sudden illness. His wife took him to El Paso, where he died. The court appointed Ernest Lee and Eula's brothers, Earl and Robert Chenowth, to make an appraisal of his estate. There was little to show for his enterprise—"one second-hand automobile truck," $585.45 cash, and a half interest in forty acres. He'd already deeded everything else to his wife.

Charles Miller's widowed daughter, Jen Burns, had married Joe Wheeler and was living at 7H headquarters when she got the word that her son, Kenneth, was killed in action in France. But the great influenza pandemic that swept the world in 1918 claimed more of Cochise County's boys than enemy action. Among the victims were Grover Reed, who died only four months after his second marriage. Two 7H cowboys, Bud Sanders and his brother-in-law, Frank Poteet, were taken on the same day. Bill and Eva Morrow lost their eight-year-old daughter, Kitty May, and Thetus Ball, a settler near Apache, succumbed to the flu, leaving a wife and three children. Ball's destitute widow accepted an offer of marriage from the irascible merchant John Richhart.

The surge of immigration had slowed, but some new faces showed up. On Armistice Day 1918, Bert and Hattie Richards got off the train in Rodeo with four small children. Bert, from Bosque County, Texas, had come to the high desert with the same tuberculosis that had taken his father. He wasn't a stranger to the West. When he was eighteen, he and his brother, Clarence, had taken out adjoining homesteads near Toyah on the northwest Texas plains. They supported themselves for two years by freighting, then sold out to a big cattle outfit and returned to Bosque County, where Bert married and leased a farm until his health failed. Clarence had preceded Bert and Hattie to the San Simon Valley and took them in at his homestead south of Rodeo until they could get established.

A pair of Iowans, David and Irene Banta, who had farmed for years in Louisiana, settled with their three nearly grown children on the New Mexico side of the state line just east of the Herrells. Banta cut a ditch to one of the splayed channels of Cave Creek, where water ran only after long rainy periods, when it was less needed. Claud McDowell claimed a homestead a mile south of the Herrell place, and Milo Gilbert and his brother-in-law James Riley Page moved in between them and built the "Gilbert-Page Ditch" as an extension of Herrell's end of the Portal Ditch.

The Pages had four children, and so that the kids could attend Portal's school, Jim and Minnie Reay invited Mrs. Page and the children to spend the school year of 1917–18 in a small shack they had built near the house while her husband stayed on the farm. The Pages had arrived with little money and too few possessions to equip two households. Ola Martyr, now teaching at Lone Oak, learned of their hardship while passing their place on her way to school. She lent them a small cook stove and a table. Rains were scant that year, and Cave Creek's flow was so reduced that valley farmers relying on it got no water. The Pages pulled up stakes and left the country without returning the things that Ola Martyr had lent them—possibly considering them a gift. Riley had told his neighbor, Claud McDowell, that if there was anything around the place he could use, to come over and get it. That is what Claud did, with a tragic result.

The sparse runoff had heightened competition for what water there was in the Portal Ditch, with Eula Stuart set against all the users downstream from her. More than once when it was his turn to irrigate, Jim Reay found his furrows dry. He walked the main ditch looking for a break, only to find that Eula had turned the water into her own ditches. He would have to remove the canvas dam to let the water pass on down.

To thwart Jim's interference, Eula took to patrolling the ditch with a rifle. Even if she had played fair, there was no chance that there would be enough water that dry year to reach down to Herrell or the Gilbert-Page ditches. But if water couldn't get past the Stuart ranch, it was certain they would get nothing, so those down below sided with Jim Reay. Eula Stuart was pitted against them all.

The Chenowths were a tightly knit family, demonstrated by the support they all had given Howard. Ola Martyr, still rankling over the episode of the tent her husband had had to return to the Reays, quite naturally sided with her sister. She asked her brother Hale to go over to McDowell's to pick up the things she'd lent to Riley Page. Hale was married to Carl Washburn's sister, Emma, but they were living with his mother on the home place on the cienega, a mile from Ola's.

On the morning of January 27, 1919, Claud and Edna McDowell were preparing to go out to cut yucca stalks to build a chicken pen and to shoot a few jackrabbits for baiting coyote traps. Claud was sitting at the grindstone sharpening an ax, with his eleven-year-old son, Basil, turning the wheel, when Hale Chenowth drove up. Chenowth got down from the wagon and walked over to Claud, who got up to greet him and shake hands.

"I've come up to see about the things you took from the Page place," Hale said without any preliminaries.

"Now, wait a minute, Hale," Claud said, "don't be too fast."

Hale, known for a hair-triggered temper, wasn't to be slowed down. He knocked Claud to the ground and started kicking him. Edna McDowell ran over and tried to pull him off, but Hale pushed her away with such force she fell to the ground. He pulled a Mauser pistol from his belt and shot Claud twice. Claud, who was armed for rabbit shooting, struggled to his knees and got off two rounds before collapsing. One shot went wild, but one hit Hale in the abdomen. Hale staggered but fired two more times into Claud's prostrate body, killing him. He lurched over to his wagon, pulled himself into the seat, and took up the reins.

Though badly hurt and slumped over his wounded belly, he managed to drive three-quarters of a mile to David Banta's house, just twenty feet into New Mexico. David and his wife, Irene, helped him out of the wagon, into the house, and onto a bed, and sent their son, Ross, to Rodeo for a doctor. At an inquest the next day, Judge Hancock took statements from Edna and Basil McDowell and charged Hale with deliberate and premeditated murder.

Without waiting for extradition from New Mexico, as soon as he was physically able, Hale went to Tombstone and surrendered to the sheriff. At a May trial the jury couldn't reach a verdict, but at a second trial in November, he was found guilty of the reduced charge of manslaughter and was sentenced to eighteen months to ten years.

The Chenowth family got busy with petitions for a pardon, buttonholing neighbors and calling in old debts. Sheriff J. F. McDonald wrote the governor and the parole board, emphasizing that Hale had voluntarily given himself up and had been a model prisoner. He went on to write, "I feel kindly toward Chenowith [*sic*], and from my experience with him believe he will be law-abiding if released." The sheriff also wrote Charlie Chenowth that he was in contact with the warden and believed that "it will be made as light as possible for your brother while in prison."

There are a couple of ironies connected with the McDowell murder. The hard feelings between the Chenowths and their neighbors on Cave Creek started over water, and the person least involved in the dispute was Claud McDowell. And the rainfall measured at the Portal Ranger Station in 1919 was 27.94 inches, the most ever recorded. The creek ran down to the cienega almost all year long with plenty of water for everyone.

In April, six months after the death of her first husband, Eula Chenowth Stuart married his brother, Edward, thus settling her debt to him. She sold him the forty acres she'd inherited from Bill; they mortgaged the whole place to the Bank of Commerce for fifteen hundred dollars to satisfy earlier debts; and Eula got a new start.

Gus Chenowth had brought the knowledge of whiskey making with him from Tennessee and was renowned for the product he always had on hand to offer to friends. He was pious and god-fearing, but he wasn't government-fearing, and any law he didn't like he flouted. Before New Mexico declared whiskey sales illegal, the state imposed a license fee that Gus always ignored. From time to time an officer was sent down to the cienega to reluctantly investigate a busybody's report.

A deputy from Lordsburg drove a hack up to the Chenowth door one midday with a search warrant. He was reluctant, but someone had made a complaint. Gus invited him in, and after a cup of coffee and a slice of Mary's pie, the officer, accompanied by Gus, searched the outbuildings and the grounds around them without making any discovery. When he went back to climb into his buggy, there was a gallon bottle of pale amber corn whiskey under the seat. No remarks were made about it, and the deputy drove off to start the long ride back to town.

Gus Chenowth's boys had learned the trade from him and inherited his attitudes about government. No doubt they all had turned a hand to production to some extent, but now Howard was in Brazil raising cattle and a family, and Hale was rusting in the penitentiary. It is Charles, the first-born, and Robert, the youngest, who are best remembered for their whiskey.

The last of the Doughboys returned to civilian life in 1920. Bill Lee and Bill Sanders were home from a year of guarding railroads in Siberia. Sanders went back to the Hilltop Mine, and Lee bought a few cows and W. K. Morrow's place on Turkey Creek.

The year also brought prohibition to the entire nation, and the demand for Chenowth whiskey exceeded production. The shortage of beer and whiskey stimulated a market for the distillate of baked mescal or sotol from Chihuahua and Sonora. Charlie made arrangements with Amador Flores of Casas Grandes, Chihuahua, to deliver mescal to him at the border fence near the Culbertson ranch, west of Antelope Wells, at twenty dollars a case.

Since his abrupt departure from army service, Manuel Domínguez had been working on ranches along the border, some of the time riding for Don Juan Slaughter. He was quick to take advantage of the scarcity of liquor in Cochise County, and with a couple of *com-*

*pañeros* he acquired some pack animals and built up a smuggling business. From a still just below the border near the San Bernardino Ranch, they loaded panniers of carefully padded jugs onto burros and led them up the valley through the cinder cones to the Bernardino siding, where they made delivery to a red-haired deputy sheriff they knew only as "Colorado."

It was a profitable business, and after a few trips they were able to buy mules to replace the burros and thus pack a bigger load. It was only about a twelve-mile run from the border, and after unpacking the panniers, they would take off the halters and turn the mules loose to trot back home. After one delivery that netted them eight hundred dollars, they went into Douglas for a celebration, leaving their horses at a livery stable. Walking along the tracks, they noted on a siding a new Ford automobile on a flatcar. They found the dealer it was consigned to and bought it for cash. None of them could drive, but they found a friend who could. They caroused until they were out of money and had wrecked the car. They left it where it died and rode back to their camp.

One day after a delivery to Bernardino siding, Manuel turned his pack string loose and headed south when he saw horsemen coming at him from two directions. He guessed they were revenuers and knew he couldn't outrun them. Near the foot of a cinder hill, he tied his horse at the mouth of a small cave, then climbed the hill and lay flat. The officers thought he'd gone into the cave and, suspecting that he was armed, built a brush fire at the cave mouth, hoping to smoke him out. At dusk they gave up, took his horse, and rode away. He had a six-mile walk back to San Bernardino.

People from the surrounding communities had long used the Chiricahuas as a refuge from summer heat. Early in the 1900s the baseball team from Paradise had fought it out with Rodeo near the tracks south of the shipping pens. Then the mountain community got a diamond of its own when, with the blessings of the Forest Service, a broad piece of canyon bottom at the junction of Cave Creek with its South Fork was cleared of trees and brush. Called Sunny Flats, the clearing became the scene of a community picnic, barbecue, political rally, or ball game nearly every weekend in good weather. Scratch teams from Bowie, San Simon, and the Hilltop Mine joined the informal league after automobiles made it easy to travel thirty or forty miles to a ball game.

Yet tourist travel to the Southwest was relatively new and was largely confined to popular spots near railroads, like the Grand Canyon and Santa Fe. The few hardy pilgrims who somehow found their way to the Chiricahuas had trouble finding accommodations. Among the early travelers were two ornithologists, Maj. Allan Brooks and J. Eugene Law, who spent a couple of weeks in the valley and in Cave Creek in 1913—possibly the first "birders" to do so. John Hands put them up, after a fashion, at the Reed place and also across the mountain in Pinery Canyon. It may have been their visit that put John into the dude ranch business, following Lillian Erickson's example.

In the summer of 1917, Neil and Emma's younger daughter, Hildegarde, started taking guests at Faraway Ranch. The following year her sister, Lillian, left teaching school to join her in the venture, and the two bought J. Hugh Stafford's adjoining property to expand the operation. What they offered their visitors was a taste of ranch life, with horseback rides and picnics in the Pinnacles of Rhyolite and Bonito Canyons.

Certainly by 1919, possibly earlier, with uncharacteristic coyness John Hands had named the old Reed place Bide-a-Wee Ranch and built four furnished shanties, giving them such names as Lucy's Cottage and Stagger Inn, and he hired a Mrs. Houck to care for them.

Gene Law, by then the business manager of the *Condor*, a magazine devoted to western ornithology, returned with his wife to the Chiricahuas and rented John's homestead in Pinery for an extended stay in midsummer. There they were upstream neighbors of Frank and Grace Hands, with whom they became friendly. Law was impressed with Frank's and John's "horseback knowledge" of natural history and with their curiosity about a wide range of subjects. Laura Law, also an ornithologist and a bird bander, was fond of Frank and Grace Hands but didn't share her husband's regard for John, writ-

ing to a friend: "He was a very different individual from Frank. Took
credit for anything that was done right, whether he did it or not, and
disliked any opposition. The longer John stayed over in Cave Creek
the better pleased was everyone in Pinery."

Frank and Grace took the Laws on a pack trip up Pine Canyon to
Barfoot Park, where they camped in the empty ranger cabin for four
days, making side trips to Rustler's Park and Monument Peak. Then
they rode down the east side to spend a couple of days at Bide-a-
Wee. They explored Crystal Cave, the Mules Ears, and Bat Cave, and
one day John took Laura and Grace in the spring wagon down to the
schoolhouse to hear the home demonstration agent talk to the local
ladies about home canning methods. Laura was a bit nervous about
appearing in public wearing trousers—unusual garb for women, even
out in the country—but it turned out that the Portal women were tol-
erant and understanding.

In another outpouring of grievance, Laura's journal complained of
her host:

> He is so surly and dictatorial . . . as for our meals, even simple doesn't
> express what they are. Declare to goodness I don't believe I want to
> see a bean for months and months and months. J. H. however sees that
> he himself has quantities of what is on the table. Thank the Lord, Gene
> hasn't such a pig appetite. Anyone could eat half the amount J. H. puts
> away, and still have plenty. The way he smacked the *old* butter down in
> front of me, while he ate the fresh. Gosh!

Laura wrote that Grace Hands had a similar opinion of her brother-
in-law.

John Hands had no real competition in dispensing even his brand
of hospitality on the east side of the mountains, though Jack Maloney
sometimes guided hunters and Emma fed them and allowed them
to pitch a tent near the house. For the past few years Jack had been
cooking for the 7H roundups and had built up a wide reputation for
his skill with Dutch ovens. He turned his talents to advantage by hosting weekend parties from time to time, when he would pit-barbecue
a deer or a hog fattened on cull apples. Those occasions became more

popular when he poured a concrete slab under the sycamores by the road for Saturday *bailes* with music provided by a guitar and fiddle.

Jack made a more sociable host than John, but his patrons were seldom from farther away than Lordsburg or Douglas. His conviviality wasn't confined to business enterprises. Early in the 1920s Jack got a pickup truck and used it to peddle his apples in Douglas. One day he made a run to town with a load and sold it so quickly there was time for a quick drink before heading home. In Agua Prieta next door, drinks were legal and plentiful. Once started, it was hard to stop, and Jack didn't get home for three days. During that time he'd treated himself to a new 3X Stetson, and when he got back to the house, he took the precaution of tossing his new bonnet in the door to test the wind. Emma promptly scooped it up and stuffed it in the stove.

Col. James H. Parramore died in 1917, and for the next three years his son Dock Dilworth Parramore, or "D.D.," took care of his interests on the San Simon. The ranch was becoming increasingly unprofitable because of deteriorated range and the difficulty of managing a ranch cut up by so many small places—to say nothing of supplying beef to many of the neighbors. In 1920 D.D. started moving out.

The last branding at spring roundup was followed by another work in July, when all the cattle that could be gathered were loaded on cars at the Rodeo shipping pens. The fifteen men on the H payroll and the men who rode along to keep an eye out for their own brands all knew this was the last one. It wasn't a simple job to gather a herd that grew as it moved and ease it around and past the many fenced areas of the scattered homesteads. And midsummer is a brutally hot and dusty time to work cattle in the pens and get them prodded into the cars.

So soon after the spring roundup, the work lacked the usual excitement of the semiannual break in routine—topping off broncs that hadn't been ridden all winter and renewing old acquaintances. Instead there was a sense of nostalgia, and the older men realized that an era was ending. The wagon boss, Joe Wheeler, was seventy and had seen scores of roundups; his brother-in-law, Sam Miller, had been on a few; and Bert Click had ridden for the Parramore outfit for ten years. Frank Eaton, Beuford Martin, and Ross Sloan's nephew, Bob McGinty, were all in their early twenties, but they were conscious of being a part of a big thing—an event they would never forget.

After the cattle were shipped, for fifteen hundred dollars Joe Wheeler bought the remnant—the old skates that hid out in the brush at the heads of the rocky canyons and the occasional cow that was running with another herd. This, of course, was a calculated gamble. Both parties had to guess what was still out there, but Joe was in the better position to make an estimate.

D.D. had shipped most of his cattle, but he still had real estate to dispose of. It takes time to go out of business in an orderly fashion and he was at it for a couple of years. The company still owned 1,240 acres on both sides of the state line in the cienega and several forty-acre parcels around seeps, windmills, and tanks that were claimed under a special act designed for grazers. These plots included the headquarters west of Rodeo and the windmill at Horse Camp. The cienega land reverted to public domain, and Parramore sold the headquarters to Bill Click.

Little remained to be done but to sell the fencing tools, the chuck wagon, the dump rakes and mowing machines, the work teams that had pulled them, and what was left of the remuda. Then the San Simon Cattle Company, after almost forty years of riding high from the craters to the Southern Pacific tracks, and from the Chiricahuas across the valley into the Peloncillos, was out of business.

## Chapter 13

# More Modern Times

I have seen many changes since I first landed here and I can't feel we are as well off now with all our modern conveniences as we were in the olden days before civilization overtook us. . . . Sometimes I feel like taking the red man by the hand and saying, "Brother, the white man's civilization is sure hell on us poor devils."

**James C. Hancock, Paradise, 1933**

After the bountiful flow of Cave Creek in 1919, winter snowfall in the mountains was light, and precipitation in 1920 was below normal. Conditions on the Portal Ditch returned to normal—short of water but long on squabble.

Eula Stuart turned to bizarre tactics. One evening after dark the Reays were sitting around the kitchen table when they heard a racket outside. Jim went out on the porch to see a figure draped in a sheet drifting around in the peach trees south of the house, beating on a wash pan.

"Go home, Eula," Jim called to her. "We know it's you, and you don't scare us."

It was apparent that the problems of sharing the Portal Ditch weren't going to be solved without outside help, and all concerned signed a petition to the state water commissioner for "a determination of relative rights to Cave Creek water."

In July 1920 an official from Phoenix spent two days at the schoolhouse taking testimony from almost everyone who used creek water for irrigation and some who didn't. Although they had no stake in the issue, Earl and Robert Chenowth were there, probably to support Eula's claim. Three new faces were present: young schoolteachers from Bisbee—Helen Brown and Elsie and Myriam Toles. They had just bought Fred Finnicum's place, and they attended to defend their right to the water in the ditch Fred had built below Portal.

In September the water commissioner's representative returned to present his findings at a meeting at the Powers house. It was determined that the first right was Jim Reay's. After Jim had enough to irrigate fifty acres, the U.S. Forest Service, represented at the meeting by Ranger Schoenberg, could water its three-acre hayfield. The Stuarts and their various mortgage holders and co-owners could have 25 percent of what was left, and the Herrells the rest.

The decision defined the rights to the Portal Ditch but didn't address other rights to the creek's water. How much could Hands and Maloney take out of the creek above the head gate? Were the owners of the ditch required to let water go downstream from the takeout for the use of Fitch McCord, the Toles, and the Bush-Keeling ranch? When the water was low, the entire creek could be diverted into the Portal Ditch, leaving McCord's fields to make out with the lesser flow from the creek-bottom spring above his house. In normal years there was barely enough water in the entire system for even Reay's fifty acres. Another thing that mediation couldn't change was that the Stuarts, upstream from the Reay's Oasis Orchard, were in position to take want they wanted.

While others were involved in the water issue, John Hands was negotiating the sale of the Bide-a-Wee Ranch, a process that was cinched when he got his down payment a week before the final water meeting at Powers. John had been quick to seize on the recreation potential of the Reed place at the forks of the creek, in a basin surrounded by soaring red cliffs on two sides and the timbered scarp of the range's crest on the third. He'd been slower to admit that he lacked the disposition of a genial host and didn't enjoy that line of work. The buyers were H. G. Gosman and Frank Officer, promoters from Douglas and

Bisbee, who sold shares in a company to run a resort with plans for several cottages, a picnic ground, and a swimming pool.

John made a profit to add to the sockful remaining from the sale of the Hilltop Mine, and he moved back across the mountain to his homestead in Pinery Canyon.

In March 1921, on the heels of John Hands's departure, Lincoln and Elizabeth Gurnett came to Portal from California to buy out Fitch McCord and Daddy Powers. They were rare birds in the mountains. Most of the recent settlers had been farmers from the southern states, working folks trying to make a living. But the Gurnetts were monied, urbane people of New England stock. Mrs. Gurnett's father, Mexican War veteran and Forty-niner Col. Charles L. Wilson, had become wealthy in northern California by building and promoting railroads. Her husband was involved in the pulp industry and paper mills.

They were preceded in the Southwest by Mrs. Gurnett's brother, Archibald Wilson, who had been dealing in ranch properties and other real estate in Willcox. It was Arch who introduced them to the country and found a ranch for his sister. By the time of the sale, Powers and McCord were the sole owners of the Portal Land and Improvement Company, which they sold to the Gurnetts for three thousand dollars. For another thousand they sold the various lots they owned individually.

This gave the Gurnetts all of the town site except for three blocks at its east end and a few scattered lots, most of which they were able to buy up within the next few years for a total of five hundred dollars. Powers sold his homestead to them for another three thousand dollars. Intending to stay in Portal, Emmett kept about thirty-five acres around his house in the creek bottom. McCord sold his homestead to the Gurnetts for three thousand dollars, having already moved to Douglas the year before to run an auto agency.

The four separate sales gave the Gurnetts a block of roughly four hundred acres of the broad basin at mouth of the canyon. They named their place Sierra Linda Ranch.

The enterprise was more Elizabeth's idea than her husband's. Lincoln was on hand for the negotiations and remained interested in the legal and fiscal aspects of ownership, but when he was satisfied that his wife and their twelve-year-old son, Larry, were well established, he turned his attention to business interests in California and Maine. Another brother of Elizabeth's, Lloyd Wilson, came from the coast to help his sister with the ranch, and all of them moved into the McCord house.

In the first year the small orchard was expanded to cover eighteen acres, and a crew made thousands of adobe bricks for the construction of a more substantial house on high ground at the south end of the ranch, next to the forest boundary, and for a barn near the McCord hay field.

Elizabeth found a good man in Féliz Carrillo from the Cochise Mine, who recruited others to help make and lay adobes. She let him build a small *barraca* of adobe and creek-worn stones across the creek from the north end of the town site. He put a fireplace at one end, used mescal stalks for rafters, and roofed it with sacahuiste thatching. He dug a shallow well for times when the creek didn't run that far down the canyon, and moved in with his wife, Silveria, and their three small children. She put in a vegetable garden, watering it with a short ditch from the creek in front of the house when she could and with buckets from the well when the creek was dry.

The eastern block of lots of the old Portal town site had been purchased at its inception by A. D. Boswell, the saloon owner who had so much trouble with his customers. Only a few months after the Gurnetts bought out Powers and McCord, that block was bought by Raymond Roush and his wife, Anna, who moved to Portal after selling their homestead in Horseshoe Canyon to Cliff Darnell and his brother-in-law, Birt Roberds. The two cattlemen formed a partnership in the TL Slash brand.

Ray Roush, a locomotive engineer from Ohio, was railroading in Texas when he met Anna. Anna Pence was born in Kentucky but raised in Texas, where her father had taken his tuberculosis. She and Roush married in 1907 and in 1913 moved to Douglas, where Ray drove a hog for the EP&SW. In 1914 they bought a forty-acre water claim in Horseshoe Canyon, where Anna stayed. Roush had quarters in rooming houses in El Paso and Douglas, at each end of his run, and came out to the ranch only on occasion. Known as "Ducky," Anna wasn't quite five feet tall but had a lot of grit. She caught a lobo in a trap and shot it with a .22. She couldn't lift it, but she got its forelegs over her shoulders and, grabbing its paws, dragged it home to skin it.

The move to Portal didn't interfere with Roush's job, and as before, it was Anna's enterprise, with the help of her brother, John Pence, that got an adobe house built on high ground. Portal had been without a store for the ten years since the closing of Powers and McCord Mercantile. Anna thought the community could generate enough trade, and she built a small adobe store building in the creek bottom below the house, a few feet north of Ed Epley's old "whiskey tree." A year after leaving Horseshoe, she was selling work gloves and canned milk and kerosene.

When O. C. Davis and his partners closed down the Cochise Mine, they left a watchman, Charlie Welch, who had come from Texas only a year before with his wife, Mary, and year-old daughter, Ruth. By 1920 he'd been twelve years at the Cochise, with its magnificent view across the valley and the Peloncillos to the Burro Mountains on the northeast horizon. He appreciated the scenery, but he couldn't eat it and his job was tenuous.

From time to time the owners scratched up some capital and stirred up the rocks a little, giving Charlie work as manager. But then the money ran out and his salary dropped back to a watchman's pay. And sometimes the partners were in such pinched straits that paychecks were delayed. Welch had a mining man's optimism and enough faith in the future of the Cochise to accept shares in lieu of wages. The past year or two the partners had been trying to divest themselves of the property, but there were liens against it and lawsuits pending. Davis and Alexander had gone on to other interests, but the mine stuck to their fingers and they couldn't shake it loose.

Finally, in the winter of 1919–20, the legal niceties were resolved, and the newly formed King Copper Company took it over. Charles E. Welch was vice president, mine superintendent, chief enthusiast, and principal stock salesman. The plan was to issue one hundred thousand shares at ten cents and to get back into production.

Charlie's ebullient manner and bonhomie sold a little stock locally. Jack Cross, the last owner of the defunct Boozer's Place, couldn't resist picking up a little, but people in Cochise County had seen mines open and close, and they were cautious. Charlie made a trip to New York and took a room at the Commodore Hotel. There, with his knack of making friends easily, he gained the confidence of some eastern capitalists. Contrary to tradition, it's easier to sell an Arizona mine to a New York banker than to sell the Brooklyn Bridge to a country rube.

Soon Welch had men at work deepening the shaft of the King Mine, as the Cochise was now called. Among them were Sam Moseley and Ed Epley's son, Floyd, who ran the hoist.

The Welches and the Zachaus had come into the country at the same time, and Charlie and Mary Welch had been close to Arthur and Julita Zachau before the forester was transferred to the Catalina Mountains. Charlie wrote Zachau to offer him, as one of his good friends, a chance to get in on the ground floor.

"I can see nothing but success ahead of us and that the stock of the King Copper company will be selling for several dollars per share in eighteen months instead of a few cents a share," he wrote; "if there is any one on earth I would like to see make some easy money it is you, old man."

Zachau had left the Forest Service and moved to California, where he got a position with the Kern County Land and Cattle Company, which sent him back to Cochise County to be general manager of their ranch near Fairbank. They had bought the old Mexican grant of San Juan de las Boquillas y Nogales, which branded the map symbol for a spring—a *boquilla*—but cowboys called it the Wagon Rods. Zachau's own capital was scant, and having been on the scene when the Paradise bubble burst, he wasn't quite as sanguine as Welch about the prospects, but he scratched up enough for a $250 personal loan to his old friend.

Edward Stuart, the second husband of his brother's widow, was forty and in the prime of his active life when he came down with an undiagnosed disease in the summer of 1922. He didn't suffer long but died peacefully in bed and was buried on the ranch next to his brother. Eula wasn't inconsolable. She was a self-reliant woman yet needed a male shoulder to lean on. She found that comfort in David Benshimol, the Douglas lawyer who helped her through the tangle of second mortgages and the probate on Edward's will, as he had earlier with William's. Eula observed the proprieties by grieving for a year before she and Benshimol were married.

The promoters who bought the old Reed place from John Hands had difficulty getting their guest ranch into operation. They started to build a central lodge and dug a hole for a swimming pool, but they lacked two necessities—money and a good manager.

Meanwhile hospitality on Cave Creek was offered in the summertime by Elsie and Myriam Toles. Helen Brown had married Shelton Keeling's brother and sold her interest in their place to the Toles sisters, who renamed it El Portal Ranch, and during their summer vacations they took guests.

The tourist business was off to a better start across the mountain, where Lillian Erickson didn't have much money but had a flair for management. Shortly after the Erickson girls started taking guests at Faraway (they avoided the term *dudes*), sister Hildegarde got married and left for California. In 1923 Lillian married Ed Riggs.

The two were a good team. Lillian was a good bookkeeper and knew the difference between profit and loss, but she could be somewhat imperious. Edward Murray Riggs, grandson of Brannick K. Riggs and nephew of Gus and Mary Chenowth, wasn't fascinated by figures but was a relaxed and congenial host with an intimate knowledge of Rhyolite and Bonita Canyons. Ed built trails up to join those that John Hands had hacked out years earlier from the north fork of Pinery. He called the area the Wonderland of Rocks, a name Hands called idiotic, preferring the old name, the Pinnacles. Ed's promotion of the area was so successful that in 1924 seventeen square miles were carved out of Coronado National Forest to create Chiricahua National Monument, with its only access the road that passed Faraway Ranch's front door.

Elizabeth Gurnett had her hands full at Sierra Linda Ranch. The house and barn were finished, and the orchard was planted to eight hundred trees of Stark's Red Delicious, Winter Banana, Winesap, and Arkansas Black apples. A vineyard of Concord grapes was planted in the bottom below the orchard, and near the ditch's head gate, about halfway between the house and the barn, an adobe poultry house was built to house chickens and turkeys. It was intended that Elizabeth's brother, Lloyd Wilson, would do the farming. He was a strapping fellow well over six feet tall, but he didn't like chickens, had little interest in pomology or viticulture, and was even less inclined to ride a sulky plow behind a team of mules. He *did* love the country and spent much time roaming the mountains. Elizabeth leased the ranch to Neil Carr.

Carr was a charming and energetic upper-class Britisher whose brother was the personal physician to the Prince of Wales. Neil was on a summer's tour of the Continent in August 1914 when World War I erupted, catching him in Germany, where he was interned until the Armistice. After the war he came to California to visit an uncle, then to Arizona, where he met the Gurnetts.

Carr converted the adobe chicken house into a two-bedroom cottage, and on open ground between it and the old McCord house, he built a small frame duplex. He was ready to take in guests.

Manuel Domínguez had a wife and a son in Sonora, but he left them there to come north and go to work in a limestone quarry at Steins. One of his fellow workmen at the quarry was Jesús Fimbres from Oputo, Sonora, who introduced him to his sister Josefa. Josefa was housekeeper at the little hotel at Steins.

Manuel and Josefa fell in love and were married. Manuel blew his wages on train tickets to Tucson and a night in the Santa Rita Hotel. They didn't return to Steins. Manuel and Jesús both got work cowboying on a ranch near Willcox.

In 1924 most of the activity and nearly all of the cash payroll in the Chiricahuas was centered around Hilltop, which was reaching its peak of production. Charlie Welch kept up the front necessary for a promoter, dressed well, drove a big touring car, and put a pair of matched bays to a shiny landau for family picnics, but the King Copper Mine itself wasn't prospering.

Arthur Zachau put friendly but insistent pressure on him for repayment of his loan of a few years back. Arthur had used an account of his deceased father's to make the loan, and other members of the family felt that it wasn't his to lend. The rosy optimism of Charlie's replies began to fade. The mine shut down, "deals" were falling through, he had property for sale in San Simon with no takers, and he was looking for a job.

"Just as soon as I do get hold of the money I will shoot it to you, old man," he wrote. King Copper was dissolved in 1925.

By this time the Hilltop had a payroll of forty men and had developed nearly five miles of workings in four major tunnels named for important stockholders. The tunnels were from three to four hundred vertical feet apart—one above the other. The topmost, the Caspar, was an extension of the tunnel the Hands brothers had driven in from the Pinery side of the range. It was now six-tenths of a mile long and went entirely through the apex of the mountain. The other tunnels were driven in below it from the east, or Whitetail Canyon, side of the mountain and were connected by winzes, vertical shafts through which ore could be dropped to a lower tunnel and brought out to the surface in mule-drawn cars without the need to hoist it.

With the shutdown of the King Copper, Sam Moseley and his mother moved up to Hilltop, he to drive a mule in the mine, she to cook in the mine's boarding house. One day Sam had his empty car at the chute for another load. The broken rock came roaring down but hung up about fifty feet above the tunnel. Johnny Underwood, the foreman, said, "Sam, take a bar and climb up there and punch it out."

There was an arrangement of timbers at the side of the chute to provide access for just that contingency, but it was badly rotted and a makeshift ladder of two-by-fours had been rigged. Sam was reluctant.

"John, I'm getting married Saturday to Violet Kuykendall," Sam said, "and I'm not about to go up there."

"If I was getting married I guess I wouldn't either," the boss said. So Underwood climbed up the ladder with a pry bar and began to pick at the ore. The ladder slipped and he fell just as the jam broke loose, and he came down the winze with several tons of churning rock.

Underwood had come from Houston to run the concentrator in Paradise before the Hilltop opened. He and his wife, Belle Rapier, had just bought the Rock House Ranch in the mouth of Whitetail from the Halls. He also left two small boys.

Frank Officer, the dude ranch developer of the Reed place, wasn't doing well with it, only occasionally renting a starkly furnished cabin for forty dollars a month. He saw better prospects in mining and became a director of the newly organized Ainsworth Copper Company, which acquired the old properties of the defunct King Copper. He got a contract to haul the Hilltop ore to the railroad at Rodeo, bought six heavy-duty trucks, and did a little roadwork.

Officer and Hilltop's owners could see a possible need for a spur line to Rodeo and went through the preliminaries of organizing the Arizona Copper Range Rail Road. Fortunately, no tracks were laid, for after shipping almost seven thousand tons of ore by truck, the Hilltop Metals Mining Company ceased operation in 1927.

In the late summer of 1924, it had been thirty-eight years since Geronimo gave up in Skeleton Canyon, bringing to an end the scratchy coexistence of Apaches and whites in the country. An occasional stray Indian passed through the valley, like the unfortunate old man that Al Farr disposed of near Granite Gap. In 1904 the trail of a Mexico-bound party from San Carlos was picked up leading down the crest of the Chiricahuas, though no one saw them. But the memory of the years of conflict was alive in men and women who had lived in fear and had lost family or livestock, and in many more who had heard the stories from the older ones. So in August, when a handful of Chiricahua Apaches wandered up from the Sierra Madre, they caused wild excitement.

It's unlikely that many of that small band had ever been in the Peloncillo Mountains or the Animas Valley, unless it was as small children. But they had secondhand memories of parents and grandparents to guide them.

A Diamond A cowboy blundered into their camp in the south end of the Animas Mountains. A woman saw him at the same time he saw her, and as she fled, shouting to warn the others, the cowboy reined around to make fast tracks for the Gray headquarters. Another cowboy, Frank Fisher, wasn't so lucky. When he came upon them unexpectedly, he was killed.

One night at Tom Noland's ranch, below the mouth of Skull Canyon, his dogs began barking and kept it up all night. Beulah Noland suspected something wasn't right and paced from the bed to the window all night. Tom was away. He and his brother, Charles, who had a place back in the canyon, had gone to the San Simon Cienega with Birt Roberds, Floyd Miller, and others to run wild horses. They returned the next morning through Rodeo, where they heard exaggerated stories of Apaches on the warpath, and hurried home to their families. Tom turned his hounds loose and followed them to find a trail of moccasin tracks about a mile west of the house—heading south toward Skeleton Canyon.

Jim McCauley, working for the XT, was looking for stray horses in Skeleton. In midmorning near the top of the divide, he saw several Apaches in the trail ahead of him and tried to turn back, but his horse was shot from under him as he turned broadside to the Indians.

McCauley managed to step off and pull his Winchester from its boot as the horse fell. He ran back down the trail two hundred yards to a point where could get up the bank into some rocks that offered protection. Though he wasn't followed, he didn't know the Indians weren't waiting for him to show himself, and he lay out in the sun all day without water.

After dark he slipped away to hoof it to the Gray ranch, reaching it at midday, sun blistered and footsore. He returned to the dead horse with three Diamond A men to get his saddle and found from the sign that the Indians had pulled out at the first shots and that he'd spent needless hours in the sun.

Apparently the Indians had crossed the border near San Luis Pass, at the south end of the Animas Mountains, then gone north down the Animas Valley and crossed the Peloncillos at least as far north as Black Mountain and Post Office Canyon. In the San Simon Valley they headed south again, recrossing the mountains via Skeleton Canyon, where they picked up two of Ross Sloan's mules. The tracks went back into Mexico near White Gate, in the middle of the Animas Valley.

From these brief encounters grew a number of tales, the most romantic of which tells of Indians being led by a red-bearded white man who could be none other than the missing Charlie McComas. If the boy had survived, he'd have been forty-seven.

In 1926 the speculators who had bought the Reed ranch from John Hands gave up on it and sold it to Harry A. Clark, another mining man from northern Michigan's copper country, now working for the Calumet and Arizona. He was superintendent at the smelter when he bought the ranch for a summer home for his family and for a hunting lodge where he could entertain important bigwigs. John Schad, a mason, mechanic, miner, carpenter, and all-around ingenious handyman, was hired as caretaker. Schad moved into Stephen Reed's old cabin, and with the help of Cristóbal Rendón, an ex-Dorado of Pancho Villa's, finished the swimming pool started by Officer and added to the frame lodge building.

Clark hit it off immediately with his nearest neighbor, Jack Maloney, and when he brought friends and business associates out to Cave Creek to enjoy the mountain air, he invariably used Jack as a hunting guide and cook—and to provide local color. One evening after Jack had fed the party a satisfying meal of beans and venison, they all sat in front of the big stone fireplace for whiskey and conversation. One of the guests was a prominent brain surgeon from Chicago who gave a detailed and graphic account of an intricate operation he'd performed recently. After he finished, there was a moment of appreciative silence. Then Jack spoke up.

"Harry," he said, "tell 'em about the time you and me give an enema to that old sow of mine."

Charlie Welch was still in Paradise exuding confidence and good cheer. He had letterhead printed up saying "Charles Edward Welch, Practical Mining Engineer and Geologist." At the bottom of the page was "Coming Largest Lead-Silver Producing District in the South-west." For other occasions he used the title "Vice-president of Keystone Lead-Silver Co.," but deep inside he had gnawing doubts.

"I am really ashamed of this whole affair," he wrote Arthur Zachau. "All my deals have stood still."

Zachau wasn't the only one dunning him. In the spring of 1926 Welch moved to Los Angeles to look for work—and to evade creditors in Arizona. Zachau never got his money back. He was killed the following year when he failed to make the curve in the company's Essex. Charlie Welch didn't find a job, and his tangled finances landed him in jail for a short time.

However, there was work for local men throughout 1926. Although the Hilltop Mine was beginning to slow down and a few men were laid off, some of them got work with the Forest Service putting a road over Onion Saddle. Up to then the traffic over the mountain labored up the steep logging road of Pine Canyon into Barfoot Park, then down an equally steep pitch through Turkey Park and Turkey Creek to Paradise.

The new road started at Locust Camp in Pinery Canyon, at the foot of Downing Pass, where the old logging road crossed over into Pine Canyon, then it climbed by switchbacks up Pinery through Oak Park to Onion Saddle, then down Onion Creek and around a point into Turkey Creek, where it intersected the old road. The new road continued from there to climb out of Turkey Creek into the head of Cave Creek Basin and down to join the road Stephen Reed had built up the canyon forty-seven years before. A spur from Onion Saddle went to Rustlers Park.

John Richhart, Apache's short-fused storekeeper, was hard on the three stepchildren he'd acquired when he married Thetis Ball's widow, and they were scared of him, so his wife took them with her when she went to Benson to teach school. They would come back home for holidays and vacations and be off again with the new school year at Benson or to another county school. As soon as they were able, the two boys left home. Their older sister, Laliah, married Sumpter

Logan, and they both taught in the Apache school. There was no longer any need for Mrs. Richhart to get her children away from her husband, but she continued to teach over Richhart's objections.

Early in September she said her farewells to the Logans—she was to leave by train the next morning for her new school term. For the next two or three days, people who went to Richhart's store found it closed. That wasn't unusual. The man had become increasingly independent and opened if and when he felt like it. Potential customers shrugged and went to the old Marken store that C. S. Graves now owned.

One morning at breakfast Laliah said that she thought it was odd that they had seen nothing of her stepfather in several days. So before running up the flag at school, Sumpter went to the door of the apartment at the rear of the Richhart store. Something was obstructing the door, and he had push to get it open. He found his mother-in-law on the floor with her head blown off. She was dressed for travel, and her packed bag and a shotgun were beside her. John Richhart was on the foot of the bed in the next room. He'd shot himself with the .45 that he always carried with him in a small black satchel.

The Reays' Oasis Orchard was a hard row to hoe and becoming harder. They had made molasses of several good crops of sorghum, and peaches and other fruits had done well in the past. Jim was a good farmer with almost inexhaustible energy, but molasses could quickly flood the local market, and selling it at distant points wasn't easy. Sometimes a good harvest of fruit that was shipped to El Paso or Tucson would spoil before a broker took it at a discount.

Jim and his brother, Steve, had augmented farm income for a time by operating a wood camp in Sulphur Canyon with a crew of thirty Mexicans, but to keep going, Jim had to borrow from John Hands, who took a mortgage on the ranch. May Reay was big enough to help her mother, and the two boys, Frank and Jimmy, were grown now and did much of the heavy farm work, but there were five to feed and clothe.

It would soon be six—and then seven—when Frank married Ethel, the daughter of Will Brabbin, who had a little place on Horseshoe Draw a mile west of the old 7H headquarters. With the help of Miguel Duran, a miner laid off from the King Mine, Frank made adobes and built a little house down the creek a quarter mile east of his parents.

Conflict over water continued. One day Frank walked up the ditch to find that the Reays were cut off again. He confronted David Benshimol, and after a heated argument Frank laid a pistol barrel alongside the other's head, knocking him down. Given the vital importance of water and the fact that so many men wore arms, it's remarkable that there was never a killing over the Portal Ditch.

In 1927, having given it twenty-five years, Jim Reay had to give up. He turned the ranch over to John Hands in satisfaction of the mortgage and went to California. At that, he'd lasted longer than most. Between 1925 and 1930 many homesteaders came to realize that even the 640-acre "grazing homesteads" weren't enough to keep a family. People were moving out.

Hands moved into the adobe house that Jim Reay had built, and he began to acquire adjacent property. Charles and Mahala Bush, who lived a mile south of him at the Cienega Spring, sold out to him and left the country. Bush's brother-in-law and partner, Shelton Keeling, sold him his homestead on Cave Creek below the Reay Place. Robert Richardson's brother gave up his "starve-out" in the valley between Cave Creek and Turkey Creek, and Bob Herrell also sold his farm on the dry end of the Portal Ditch on the state line. Charlie Chenowth was working on the Slaughter ranch and was glad to find a taker for his unproductive homestead between Richardson's and Herrell's.

When John Hands bought Ola and Bob Martyr's place near the cienega, nine miles east of his headquarters, he controlled the public land between. John had been a miner for a long time, and by virtue of the sale of the Hilltop, one would have to say he was a successful one. But he'd never had a hand in the cattle business, nor did he have any particular interest in it when he found himself, at sixty-one, with about thirty square miles of range. He put his E J H on the shoulders, ribs, and thighs of his cows, turned them out, and more or less forgot about them. Not all of his neighbors did, however, and some of them with elastic consciences took advantage of him. He had letterhead printed calling his place "Desperation Ranch." The intent was humor.

Hands didn't scrap with Eula Benshimol about water. He didn't care much about farming either, and most of the fruit trees died of thirst.

Bert and Hattie Richards had bought the Pattison place on the Arizona side of the state line, a mile west of Rodeo. But it was tough going. Bert's tuberculosis wasn't as improved by the climate as he'd hoped, and he didn't have the strength to work for wages. Hattie taught at the Lone Oak school one year, but taking care of her husband, growing a kitchen garden, and having and caring for children took too much of her time for outside work. The family of four children they had brought from Texas grew to seven—all big kids—and it took a lot to feed them.

In the crisp autumn of 1927, there was a remembrance of the old days of the San Simon Cattle Company when Joe Wheeler moved the remnant of the H herd to his new range at the upper end of the valley. Several old cowboys who had worked for Joe when he was Parramore's wagon boss, along with some younger men who had not, helped him gather the cienega. The first day's drive took them as far as the Richards place, where Joe had arranged with Bert to use a fenced trap west of the house to hold the cattle overnight.

Hoofs and horns in a cloud of dust and eight to ten cowboys funneling bawling cattle through the gate was pretty heady stuff to nine-year-old Finley Richards. Fin was up at first light to go out where the cowboys were rolling their beds at the wagon and the cook had the coffee boiled. He was handed a tin plate and invited to have breakfast. The biscuits were no better than he was used to, but what he really tucked away was the bacon—the first he'd ever tasted. It had always been salt pork at the Richards table.

Eula Chenowth Stuart Stuart Benshimol became a widow for the third time in ten years when David Benshimol went the way of his predecessors in the early winter of 1928. They were in El Paso when he died suddenly, and the body was promptly cremated. Eula stayed at the orchard but leased it to her brother, Robert, the youngest of Mary Chenowth's twelve children.

When Bob Chenowth was twelve years old, he'd gone out to shoot some quail in the tall sacaton of the San Simon Cienega. While he was crawling between the top two wires of a fence, something snagged the trigger of his shotgun, and he wounded himself so badly that his lower arm had to be amputated. Yet people didn't think of Bob as handicapped. He was strong and did more work with one arm and a stump than many men did with two good arms. Some fellow watching him lift several flats of peaches with his one hand to put on the bed of the truck expressed his admiration.

"What would you be like with *two* arms?!" he exclaimed.

"If I had two arms, I probably wouldn't try so hard," Bob answered, "and I'd be as worthless as you are."

Bob's work in the orchard didn't take so much time that he had to give up making whiskey. He located a source of good water a mile west of the ranger station in a little well-secluded spring in the oaks on the slopes of Silver Peak. There he set up a still that he could tend in his spare time.

Mary Chenowth, at seventy-seven, through inability to pay off a note, had lost the old place that she and Gus had settled fifty years before and was living with Eula. She longed to see her boy Howard before she died. The reckless young cowboy who had rampaged in Silver City was now a responsible, middle-aged estate manager in Brazil and a family man. Mary played upon the sympathy of New Mexico's political leaders for an old pioneer woman. Gov. R. C. "Dick" Dillon, a sheepman from Estancia, pardoned Howard. It was said that family and friends, in gratitude, raised a large campaign contribution for the governor.

Howard's Brazilian wife had died, leaving him with seven children. He brought them to Arizona to a place just south of the cienega near his brother Hale, who had been released from the penitentiary at Florence five years earlier. Hale had married Carl Washburn's sister, Emma, and had a place on the arid and stony slope between Granite Gap and the valley bottom.

For a time Howard helped Hale with his cattle, but while riding one day, Howard came upon Hale and Carl driving eight head of cattle they didn't own. Howard didn't believe that they were in the process of returning strays to their owner. He'd just been pardoned and wanted no more trouble with the law. His protest put Hale in an awkward position with his wife. It seemed best to split, so Howard moved to Portal. There was no room at the orchard, but he rented a house near the school and put up a tent in the rear for the older boys.

The exodus of miners and homesteaders in the late 1920s called for a reorganization of county schools. When Miss Helene Kinsella closed the door of the Paradise school after Christmas in 1929, it never opened again. For the spring semester of 1930, there were Nolands, Underwoods, Morrows, and Walkers from Turkey Creek and Whitetail going to school in Portal. Lone Oak school was also closed, and that district was divided between Apache and Portal. Portal picked up several Richards kids from the closure.

In anticipation of the consolidation, the county had built a new and larger adobe schoolhouse in Portal next to the frame structure just south of Rouse's store. Miss Myriam Toles taught the first five grades in the new building, while Mrs. Dora Patterson had the older children in the old school building.

Six of Howard's seven were of school age, and with Bob's two girls, nearly a third of the Portal school roster in the fall semester of 1929 were Chenowths—and another was coming. Eula's brother, Earl, had died in 1923, and his widow, Zula, became seriously ill and was afraid that she wouldn't make it. Childless Eula agreed to take Earl's son, Jimmy, as her own.

Myriam Toles had her hands full. Except for a few words, Howard's Brazilians spoke only Portuguese. The language was close enough to Spanish for them to communicate with Pancho Carrillo from the Gurnett ranch and with a couple of Arviso children, and Myriam spoke some Spanish. Bob Chenowth took his sister's place on the school board.

The people in the mountains were not always sympathetic with Forest Service policy, but rangers and their families lived in the community and were neighbors. An example of the regard in which some were held is found in a story told by Pegleg Coryell's son, Jim, who packed mules for the Forest Service. One day Jimmy and the ranger, Gilbert Sykes, were riding from the Old Headquarters near Snow- shed Peak down South Fork below Sentinel Peak. It was a hard coun- try for cattle to get into and hadn't been grazed in some time. There was a lot of water and the grass was tall.

"A dozen steers could get fat in here, Jim," Sykes said. "Why don't you put some in here?"

Jim did just that—without the bother of paperwork or fees.

In 1930 Carl Scholefield had been Paradise District ranger for nine years when he was transferred to Globe. His children were in school in Portal, and the family had many friends in the neighborhood and left Portal with reluctance. Not long after he left the ranger station to Sam Sowell and was settled on the Pinal District, he got a letter from Sam.

"You'll never guess what I found in the upper end of the pasture behind the station," Sam wrote. "There's a still up there, hidden in the brush."

"I know that still," Carl wrote back, "and it makes mighty good whiskey, too."

Bob Chenowth traded his lease on Eula's orchard to an older sister, Mary Frances, and her husband, Jesse Simmons. Eula, who had been unmarried for almost four years, married the lawyer who had been helping her juggle loans and leases, Donald A. Rothrock of Washing- ton, D.C., five years her junior. After moving west, he'd been assistant Cochise County attorney. At the time of his marriage, he was in pri- vate practice in Douglas and was candidate for the office of justice of the peace.

Rothrock wasn't successful in his candidacy, but he wasn't cut out to be an apple knocker either. He intended to hang out his shingle in Phoenix, and he didn't want to take Jimmy Chenowth Benshimol with him, so Eula found a buyer for the ranch. Her sister, Frances Simmons, known as "Lady" to her family, adopted the boy and took him to California.

The new owner of the ranch was a Douglas surgeon, Dr. Edward W. Adamson, who took possession in August 1932. In 1910, right out of his residency, Dr. Adamson had come out of Michigan's Upper Peninsula, like so many of Arizona's copper men. He bought the Portal ranch as a wedding present for his second wife, Anna. The Adamsons refurbished and enlarged the house Bill Stuart had built and put up three smaller frame houses for hired help. He put in an apple-washing and packing shed, developed an irrigation well to supplement the ditch, and hired Cristóbal Rendón to build a large stone barn with stalls and hay loft for Anna's horses. Adamson didn't give up his Douglas practice and could seldom find time to visit the place. It was really Anna's ranch and home. She called it the AVA, her initials and brand.

One of the new employees AVA brought to Portal was Manuel Domínguez. After a succession of ranch jobs, this was to be his last. His and Josefa's children, Pedro and Petra, filled a couple of the school seats vacated by all those Chenowths, and as they grew old enough, more Domínguezes were to follow them to school.

In 1941 Elizabeth Gurnett left her Sierra Linda Ranch and moved to Tucson. Her son's heart wasn't in farming, and her lessee, Neil Carr, had left to operate a dude ranch south of Tucson, where he met his end. He'd always been intolerant of Mexicans and abusively pushed one too far and was beaten to death with a two-by-four. Elizabeth sold out to Arthur Greenamyer, a retired steel company executive from Buffalo, New York.

Greenamyer had wanted to be a farmer ever since his boyhood in rural Ohio, and now he could afford to be one. He asked his daughter, Gretchen, and her husband to come and help him run it.

This is where I come in—I was that lucky husband—and this is where I leave it. It's not that the years since 1941 haven't been interesting. They have been so gripping and full of wonder that it's hard to realize that fifty-six years could zip by so fast, or that I have known the Chiricahuas longer than Jack Maloney or Joe Sanders and I know its canyons better than John Ringo ever did. I said in the preface that when I moved to Cave Creek, I wanted to learn all about the country and to know what it was like. By the time I found out, it wasn't like that anymore. But I don't want to include the time I've lived through in a "history." I started out in—and went back to—archaeology and have therefore always been more interested in piecing together scraps of data and fragments of things—and to make sense of them—than in observing current events.

So if you have plowed through these pages this far, hoping to read about Arthur Lee's accidental death at the hands of a dude he was guiding on a lion hunt, or Jerome Clark's drilling of the first irrigation well in the valley and his subsequent death by lightning, or Anna Roush's romance with Sparks Faucett and her later marriage to Lieutenant Pugsley of the CCC camp (and the school kids seeing her brassiere hanging on her clothesline and mistaking it for the gall bladder she'd just had surgically removed), or Herman Kollmar's fantastic career in international finance, shuttling between London and Berlin via Portugal during World War II, which enabled him to buy the Z Bar T Ranch and retire at forty-five—you will be disappointed and I apologize, but I have to quit somewhere.

I *will* bring you up-to-date on some of the characters and places mentioned in the preceding chapters.

Those Chiricahua Apaches who were taken as prisoners of war to Florida, after many years of captivity, were allowed to return partway west when they were moved to Fort Sill, Oklahoma. Then in 1913 those who wanted to—most of them—were allowed to move onto the Mescalero Apache reservation in south-central New Mexico. Many of the descendants of Cochise, Mangas Coloradas, Chihuahua, Victorio, and Massai came to Fort Bowie in 1986 to a commemoration of Geronimo's surrender. Two years later thirty-six of them made a pilgrimage to Embudos Canyon in Sonora and to a stronghold in the Sierra Madre, where the Mountain Spirits came down to dance for them, possibly the first time they had done so in Mexico in 102 years. In the spring of 1995 a great-granddaughter of Martine brought relatives to Cave Creek to cut mescal.

Oscar Olney, the grandnephew of Joe Hill, the cowboy who rustled Mexican cattle with Bill Brocius, helped me more legitimately gather the Z Bar T cattle out of Indian Creek and Jhus Canyon in 1956.

Glennis Hayes, a great-granddaughter of Ike Clanton's friend Billy Byers, who escaped the massacre in Guadalupe Canyon, lives in Portal and teaches school in Animas. Judge James Hancock's daughter, Irene Kennedy, lives in Safford. There is a large tribe of the descendants of Brannick Riggs living in the Sulphur Springs Valley, along with some of Bill Starks's lineage. Several generations of the Chenowth line are scattered from the Rio Grande to California—several within a morning's ride of the cienega. Nolands still run cattle where Mrs. Buckalew settled; Bill Morrow's grandson lives within sight of Galeyville; there are still Reeds in Arizona and Walkers in Colorado; and Sgt. Neil Erickson's granddaughter lives in Hawaii.

The old mountain man Joe Sanders, still trapping in his eighties, tried to step into the saddle with a freshly trapped skunk when his horse went to bucking, pitched him off, and dragged him. He was never so spry again, but he lived to die at ninety-three in 1937. His descendants still own the ranch he left to his daughter, Emma Maloney.

Former Forest Supervisor Charles McGlone, having served his time for misfeasance, returned to Cave Creek in 1935 to explore again and to unsuccessfully promote Crystal Cave as a tourist mecca. After a half century of searching for rock-bound treasure from Jhus Canyon to Cave Creek, Ed Epley was offered $250,000 by a New York company for a mine in Turkey Creek with a good showing of tungsten. That would have been a record for a California District mine, but Ed held out for a half million, his buyer backed off, and Ed lived out his final years on a Social Security check.

After Harry Clark died, his widow sold Stephen Reed's homestead to a dilettante couple, who sold it to another. In 1955 it was bought by the American Museum of Natural History to use as a research facility. Because of the many scientists who have visited the station and made the unique Madrean biota of the Chiricahua Mountains widely known, in the last forty years more biologists and bird-watchers have visited the area than miners in the preceding seventy-five. So many have retired here that Portal now has more Ph.D.'s per square head than any other place in Arizona.

Some of Elizabeth Gurnett's grandchildren come by from time to time to see the place where she lived. Henry and Gertie Chamberlain's daughter lives in Tempe. One of James "Goat" Miller's grandsons lives in Post Office Canyon, and another rides almost every day on his ranch between Rodeo and Portal. Two of Charles Miller's granddaughters live in Douglas and Bisbee. A daughter of Cliff and Lillie Darnell married a son of Bert and Hattie Richards. They live in Cave Creek—my close neighbors and close friends.

Soon those later years I have touched on so lightly will be far enough behind to qualify as historical, but someone else will have to sort it out, sift the seeds of significance from the chaff of data, and examine the various versions of an event to make a stab at determining which, if any, is probable.

The separation of fact from fiction requires strict self-discipline. We all love a good story, and few of us can resist making an epic out of a mundane account—particularly if it involves Grandpa. I don't pretend to be immune, but I've tried to put the brakes on and to be as objective as I could be.

The problem is that before the dust settled and the blood dried, the winning of the West became mythology. While the future cornfields of Nebraska were still teeming with bison, the dime novelist Ned Buntline, with the enthusiastic cooperation of his subject, created a legend when he turned William F. Cody into Buffalo Bill. Before the Civil War, James Hickock became "Wild Bill" as the result of a story in *Harper's*, and the desperados of the 1880s avidly devoured exaggerated accounts of his exploits. Jesse James never reached the Chiricahuas, but someone who admired the bank robber put his name on a side canyon leading into Pinery. Toward the end of the nineteenth century, the Christians and the Ketchums were victims of the myth, playing the role that they felt was expected of them.

Grandchildren consciously, unconsciously, or wishfully sometimes create lives for their grandparents. The life of Gus Chenowth was full enough not to need embellishment, but it has been made into a legend larger than life. I think it is likely that George Coryell really *was* present when Billy the Kid helped his pa fight off the Apaches, but the story is told of others also. Some stories have made Stephen

Reed a friend of Cochise, but the Chokonen chief died before Reed moved from California. If the number of people who are said to have fed Geronimo had really done so, he would never have had to steal horses.

I overheard Emma Maloney, never backward when it came to stringing a tenderfoot along, say that when she was a child in Solomonville, she walked to school one day after an Indian raid to find the schoolhouse door bristling with arrows. She was three years younger than my father, who was born five days before the last Chiricahua Apache boarded the train at Bowie. They had been using firearms almost exclusively for fifteen years by that time.

One warm spring day when a vermilion flycatcher was darting erratically above the walnut tree, Jack Maloney came down to my barn and we went out into the field to judge whether the winter oats were at the cutting stage for horse feed. When we sat down on the ditch bank to fellowship a little, Jack sat on a goat-head burr. He rose quickly and felt at the seat of his denim pants. Though he'd been in the canyon for forty years, he said with surprise in his voice, "I declare, I believe every darn thing in Arizona's got a sticker on it."

Now, that turned out not to be a myth.

# Bibliographic Essay

I'm a bit reluctant to launch into an essay on sources. As I stated in the preface, my intention was to tell a story, and I make no pretense of scholarship. I went through a lot of books, papers, files, and newspapers. I talked to many people, made miles of footprints and horse tracks, and took pages of notes. But since I wasn't going to present this as a thesis or dissertation, I neglected the meticulous niceties of ascription. But in the interests of an academic appearance of some kind—here goes!

## *The Setting*

Adolf Bandelier, pioneer anthropologist and archaeologist, whose 1883 description of the Sierra Chiricagui begins this section, had just finished a long solo horseback trip through northeastern Sonora and northwestern Chihuahua and was returning to Tucson by train. The details of his perilous and somewhat absentminded peregrination are found in *The Southwestern Journals of Adolph F. Bandelier: 1883–1884*, edited by Charles H. Lange and Carrol L. Riley (Albuquerque: University of New Mexico Press, 1970).

The descriptive material in this piece—i.e., the remarks on the lay of the land, the vegetation, on whether or not it is likely to rain—is made up of my own observations. Figures on rainfall were worked up from fragmentary U.S. Weather Bureau records for Portal, Paradise, and San Simon and my own twenty-year record for the mouth of Cave Creek Canyon. For elaboration, corroboration, and maybe correction of the words on the geomorphology of the Chiricahuas, one should see Harold Drewes, "Geological Map and Sections of the Cochise Head Quadrangle and Adjacent Areas, Southeastern Arizona" (*USGS Miscellaneous Investigation Series*, 1982); also Philip T.

Hayes, "Cretaceous Paleogeography of Southeastern Arizona and Adjacent Areas" (*Geological Survey Professional Paper* 658-B, 1970).

### Chapter 1. The Indian Pioneers

Most of what I learned about North American archaeology as a college boy in 1935 has long ago been disproved. Much of what was substituted by 1965 is also in doubt, and the dates for the peopling of the Americas that I gave when writing this chapter are now being hotly contested by people I admire and respect, including my good friend Julian Hayden, who knows more about it than I do. Whether or not men and women inhabited this hemisphere as early as 20,000 or more years ago, there is no doubt there were people in these valleys by the twelfth century B.C. My sources for "early man" include Emil W. Haury, Ernst Antevs, and John F. Lane's "Artifacts with Mammoth Remains: Naco Arizona" (*American Antiquity* 9/1, 1953), and "The Lehner Mammoth Site: Southeastern Arizona" by Haury, Ted Sayles, and Bill Wasley (*American Antiquity* 25/1, 1959). Marie Wormington's *Ancient Man in North America* (Denver Museum of Natural History, 1957), though now almost as old as its subject, is still a good introduction for someone who wants to know a little but doesn't care about the latest theories.

The ecologist Paul S. Martin's proposal that it was man that killed off the mammoths and giant bison stimulated considerable discussion among archaeologists. The idea has many supporters, but skepticism is the soul of science, and the theory has its doubters. The question is discussed in detail in *Quaternary Extinctions: A Prehistoric Revolution*, edited by Martin himself and Richard Klein (Tucson: University of Arizona Press, 1984), and in Larry D. Agenbroad's "The Clovis People: The Human Factor in Pleistocene Megafauna Extinction" (Pittsburgh: *Ethnology Monographs* 12, University of Pittsburgh, 1988).

Sources of information about the foragers and semisedentary horticultural settlers who succeeded the big-game settlers include two by E. B. Sayles: "The San Simon Branch: Excavations in Cave Creek and in the San Simon Valley" (Globe, Ariz.: *Medallion Papers* 34, Gila Pueblo, 1945) and "The Cochise Cultural Sequence in Southeastern Arizona" (Tucson: *Anthropological Papers* 42, University of Arizona, 1983). For an overview of the Mogollon culture for a casual reader, I recommend a book by *another* Paul S. Martin, the archaeologist: *Digging into History: A Brief Account of Fifteen*

*Years of Archaeological Work in New Mexico* (Chicago: Chicago Natural History Museum Popular Series, *Anthropology* 38, 1959).

The pueblos of the 1200s and 1300s are described in A. V. Kidder, H. S. and C. D. Cosgrove's *Pendleton Ruin, Hidalgo County, New Mexico* (Albuquerque: University of New Mexico Press, 1949) and in Eugene B. McCluney's "Box Canyon and Clanton Draw: An Interim Report on Two Prehistoric Sites in Hidalgo County, New Mexico" (Santa Fe: *School of American Research Monograph* 26, 1962). Three publications by Jack P. and Vera M. Mills concern late pueblos in Cochise County: "The Glass Ranch Site" and "The Kuykendall Site" (El Paso: *Special Reports of the El Paso Archaeological Society* 4 and 6, 1966 and 1969) and "The Curtis Site" (privately printed in Douglas, Ariz., n.d.). The last reference is to the limited work in the little that remained of Pueblo Viejo.

It is a shame that not more is known about the prehistory of the San Simon Valley, but the fact is that the summers here are too warm for undergraduate archaeology. Most long-range excavations today are undertaken by university field schools, with most of the work done by tuition-paying students, who are more easily attracted to digs in the pines. It is no random accident that the Mogollon Rim has been so thoroughly investigated.

It was apparently Bartlett who was responsible for the oft-repeated error that the name Chiricahua was from the Apache *tsil*, "mountain," and *kawa*, "great." But the name had been used by Spaniards before they knew any Apaches, and it was through Opata guides and allies that the latter first knew the mountains. An important objective of Adolf Bandelier on his 1883 trip was the discovery of Opata people who still had a remnant of their old culture. Although they had by that time been largely absorbed either by Apache intruders from the north or by Spaniards from the south, a few old men were able to give him a fragmentary vocabulary of Opata, a Piman language. He recorded that *chiri* was "hummingbird" and that *cahui* meant "mountain" (*Southwestern Journals*, p. 283). However, long before Opata had become almost extinct as a spoken language, Juan Nentvig, missionary to the Opatas, in his *Rudo Ensayo: A Description of Sonora and Arizona in 1764*, translated and annotated by A. F. Pradeau and R. R. Rasmussen (Tucson: University of Arizona Press, 1980), after years of preaching to the Opatas in their own language, confirmed that *cahui* was "mountain" but that, rather than the smallest bird, *chiri* was "turkey," the largest.

My principal sources for Chiricahua Apache culture were Morris Edward Opler, *An Apache Life-way: The Economic, Social, and Religious Institutions of the Chiricahua Indians* (Chicago: University of Chicago Press, 1941), and the same author's "Myths and Tales of the Chiricahua Apache Indians" (New York: *Memoirs of the American Folklore Society* 5/37, 1942). Also helpful were Harry A. Basehart's "Mescalero Apache Subsistence Patterns and Socio-Political Organization" (Albuquerque: *University of New Mexico Land-Claims Research Project*, 1960) and Keith Basso's *Western Apache Raiding and Warfare: From the Notes of Grenville Goodwin* (Tucson: University of Arizona Press, 1971). A few notes on language were derived from the *Mescalero Apache Dictionary* by Evelyn Breuninger, Elbys Hugar, and Ellyn Lathan (Mescalero, N.M.: Published by the Mescalero Apache Tribe, 1982).

### Chapter 2. Spanish Exploration

The route Coronado used to get to northern New Mexico after he left the Río Yaqui has been interpreted in various ways. Early historians, who didn't know the country well, had him improbably pushing his sheep and cattle across the Gila and Salt in the vicinity of Globe and up through rugged canyon country and across the White Mountains. Herbert E. Bolton, in *Coronado: Knight of Pueblos and Plains* (Albuquerque: University of New Mexico Press, 1941), proposed a more feasible trail down the San Pedro, leaving the river at Tres Alamos Wash to go through Nugent's Pass into the upper Aravaipa Valley and across Eagle Pass to the Gila, Chichilticale, and the upper San Francisco River. A main objection to Bolton's improvement is that the chronicles make no mention of going through the considerable settlement of Quíburi on the San Pedro.

At a particularly dry time in the 1950s, in order to buy cattle feed, I hired out to the National Park Service to build two privies in Montezuma Pass at Coronado National Memorial, which was established on the presumption that from a high point there in the Huachucas one could probably see the place where Coronado entered what is now the United States. I had the occasion to think about that a good deal while I was there, and I didn't agree. While one might not allow that erecting outhouses gave me sufficient authority to hold an opinion, I brought more than hammer and nails to the job. I had a minor in Hispanic studies, and I knew the topography involved. The *conquistadores* were not blundering blindly but had Indian guides all the way—guides who knew Cíbola from trading expeditions. They would have taken the easiest and best-watered route: from the San Bernardino River down the San Simon to Chichilticale, to the Upper Gila, and on to the Zuni towns by their Salt Lake. The only mountain they would have had to cross was a relatively easy pass in the Gallo Mountains.

When I was promoted from digging waste pits to digging in Indian ruins, I frequently voiced that opinion and was delighted to find that Charlie Di Peso shared my unorthodoxy and said so in his *Casas Grandes: A Fallen Trading Center of the Gran Chichimeca* (Flagstaff: Northland Press, 1974). Later discussions of the question are found in Carrol L. Riley's "The Location of Chichilticale" and Madeleine Turnel Rodack's "Cíbola Revisited" (both published in Santa Fe: *Papers of the Archaeological Society of New Mexico* 10, 1985) and in Riley's "Coronado in the Southwest" (Albuquerque: *Papers of the Archaeological Society of New Mexico* 17, 1992).

For an account of the Vargas military sortie to the upper Gila, see John L. Kessel's *Remote Beyond Compare* (Albuquerque: University of New Mexico Press, 1989) and *The Journals of Don Diego de Vargas: New Mexico, 1691–1693*, edited by Kessel and Rick Hendricks (Albuquerque: University of New Mexico Press, 1992).

I cribbed the fascinating account of Jironza's 1695 campaign into and around the Chiricahuas from Thomas H. Naylor and Charles W. Polzer's *The Presidio and Militia on the Northern Frontier of New Spain: 1570–1700* (Tucson: University of Arizona Press, 1986), though in some cases my interpretation of what places they visited differs somewhat from theirs. Subsequent expeditions to or near the Chiricahuas are described in Kessel's "Campaigning on the Upper Gila, 1756" (Albuquerque: *New Mexico Historical Review* 46/2, 1971) and Donald C. Cutter's *Defenses of New Spain: Hugo O'Conor's Report to Teodoro de Croix, July 22, 1777* (Dallas: Southern Methodist University Press, 1994).

Military and administrative contact of Spaniards with Jocomes, Janos, and Chiricahua Apaches is elucidated by William B. Griffen in "Indian Assimilation in the Franciscan Area of Nueva Viscaya" (Tucson: *Anthropological Papers of the University of Arizona* 33, 1979) and by Max L. Moorhead in *The Apache Frontier: Jacobo Ugarte and Spanish-Indian Relations in Northern New Spain, 1769–1791* (Norman: University of Oklahoma Press, 1968). The continuing "Indian problem" into and through the Mexican period is discussed by Griffen in *Apaches in War and Peace: the Janos Presidio, 1750–1858* (Albuquerque: University of New Mexico Press, 1988) and "Apache

Indians and the Northern Mexican Peace Establishments" (Santa Fe: *Papers of the Archaeological Society of New Mexico* 10, 1985).

### Chapter 3. The First Gringos

The English adventurer George Ruxton's unflattering description of the Americans he met in 1846 is taken from Clyde and Mae Reed Porter and LeRoy R. Hafen, eds., *Ruxton of the Rockies* (Norman: University of Oklahoma Press, 1950).

Two of several sources about American trappers in northern Mexico are Forbes Parkhill, *The Blazed Trail of Antoine Leroux* (Los Angeles: Westernlore Press, 1965), and William C. McGaw, *Savage Scene: The Life and Times of Mountain Man Jim Kirker* (San Lorenzo, N.M.: High Lonesome Press, 1972). The massacre of Compá and his people is told by Rex Strickland in "The Birth and Death of a Legend: The Johnson Massacre of 1837" (Tucson: *Arizona and the West* 8/3, 1976).

Lt. W. H. Emory's report of his 1846 trip to the Gila is reprinted in *Notes of a Military Reconnoisance [sic]* (Albuquerque: University of New Mexico Press, 1951). The story of Colonel Cooke's Mormon Battalion is found in "Exploring Southwestern Trails," edited by Ralph P. Bieber (Glendale, Calif.: *Southwestern Historical Series* 7, Arthur H. Clark Co., 1938), and the trials of Major Graham in traversing some of the same country are told of by one of his soldiers in *Hepah! California: The Journal of Cave Johnson Couts from Monterey, Nuevo Leon, Mexico to Los Angeles, California During the Years 1848–1849*, edited by Henry F. Dobyns (Tucson: Arizona Pioneers Historical Society, 1961). For the encounter of the Duval party with Mangas Coloradas, see Benjamin B. Harris, *The Gila Trail: The Texas Argonauts and the California Gold Rush* (Norman: University of Oklahoma Press, 1960).

Though long-winded, an account that reads like a novel—better than most —is the reprinted 1854 edition of John Russell Bartlett's *Personal Narrative of Explorations and Incidents in Texas, New Mexico, California, Sonora and Chihuahua* (Chicago: Rio Grande Press, 1965).

### Chapter 4. Arizona Territory

Even more exciting than Bartlett's pompous narrative is the life of Andrew Belcher Gray, told in *A. B. Gray's Survey of a Route on the 32nd Parallel for the Texas Western Railroad*, edited by L. R. Bailey (Los Angeles: Westernlore Press, 1963). Unable to get at the primary sources for information about Lieutenant Parke's railroad survey, I borrowed from John P. Wilson's *Islands in the Desert: A History of the Uplands of Southeastern Arizona* (Albuquerque: University of New Mexico Press, 1995).

Stagecoach travel has so captured the interest of western history buffs that there is a wealth of material on the subject. Most useful are Roscoe P. and Margaret B. Conklings' *The Butterfield Overland Mail: 1857–1869* (Glendale, Calif.: Arthur H. Clarke Co., 1947) and Gerald T Ahnert's *Retracing the Butterfield Overland Trail Through Arizona* (Los Angeles: Westernlore Press, 1973). Raphael Pumpelly's vivid account of travel is found in "Pumpelly's Arizona," an excerpt from his *Across Asia and America*, comprising those chapters that concern the Southwest, edited by Andrew Wallace (Tucson: Palo Verde Press, 1965).

The description of the building of the Apache Pass stage station is that of James H. Tevis in *Arizona in the '50's* (Albuquerque: University of New Mexico Press, 1954). Tevis also tells of Agent Michael Steck's meeting with Cochise at the pass—a story told again with more detail and accuracy by Edwin R. Sweeney in *Cochise: Chiricahua Apache Chief* (Norman: University of Oklahoma Press, 1991). Sources for the confrontation of Lieutenant Bascom with Cochise at Apache Pass include Sweeney (*Cochise*) and "The Bascom Affair" by Charles K. Mills (Douglas, Ariz.: *Cochise Quarterly* 22/2, 1993).

For the Civil War in Arizona, the passage of the California Column, and the battle of Apache Pass, I relied heavily on Boyd Finch's "Sherod Hunter and the Confederates in Arizona" (Tucson: *Journal of Arizona History* 10/3, 1969), Darlis L. Miller's *The California Column in New Mexico* (Albuquerque: University of New Mexico Press, 1982), *Life Among the Apaches* by John C. Cremony (Lincoln: University of Nebraska Press, 1983 [reprint of the 1868 edition]), and Sweeney again (*Cochise*).

### Chapter 5. Cochise

Since 1991 it has been impossible to mention the name without reference to Ed Sweeney's monumental tour de force, *Cochise*, and much of this chapter is owed to it.

Captain Tidball's journal kept during his futile campaign into and through the Chiricahuas was printed in the *Santa Fe Weekly Gazette* on October 5, 1864. Jack Wilson alerted me to it and to his reprinting of it as an appendix to the study he made under contract with the Coronado National Forest,

*Islands in the Desert: A History of the Uplands of Southeast Arizona* (Las Cruces, N.M.: 1987). It was not included in the University of New Mexico Press 1995 edition. The account of the campaign given here is an abridgment of my paper "An 1864 Scout Through the Chiricahuas" (*Cochise Quarterly* 21/4, 1992). The adventuresome life of Tidball's guide is told in Ed Sweeney's *Merejildo Grijalva: Apache Captive, Army Scout* (El Paso: Texas Western Press, University of Texas at El Paso, 1992).

For background on Tom Jeffords, I used "Tom Jeffords: Indian Agent" by Harry G. Cramer III (Tucson: *Journal of Arizona History* 17/3, 1976) and C. L. Sonnichsen's "Who Was Tom Jeffords?" (*JAH* 23/4, 1982).

Cochise's attack on the stage and a herd of cattle near the Dragoons and the subsequent running fight and battle in Rucker Canyon is described in L. L. Dorr's "The Fight at Chiricahua Pass in 1869" (Tucson: *Arizona and the West* 13/4, 1971). For some details I am indebted to William B. Gillespie, who with Mary M. Farrell prepared the nomination of old Camp Rucker for status as a National Historic Site. These archaeologists for the Forest Service identified the actual site of the battle.

The events in Horseshoe Canyon and Round Valley are only two of the six in the Chiricahuas between February 1871 and October 1873 that are listed in *Chronological List of Actions with Indians from January 1, 1866 to January 1891* (Washington, D.C.: Office Memorandum, Adjutant General's Office). They are described in "Frederick Phelps: A Soldier's Memoir," edited by Frank D. Reeve (Albuquerque: *New Mexico Historical Review* 25/1–4, 1950); *Pioneering in Territorial Silver City and the Southwest*, edited by Helen Lundwall (Silver City, N.M.: n.p., n.d.); and, of course, in Sweeney (*Cochise*).

Dan L. Thrapp's *Conquest of Apacheria* (Norman: University of Oklahoma Press, 1967) describes in detail the massacre of Aravaipa Apaches at Camp Grant, as well as the subsequent posting of Gen. George Crook to Arizona. Crook's first tour of duty in command of the Department of Arizona is told in much detail in John G. Bourke's classic, *On the Border with Crook*. The original 1891 Charles Scribner's Sons edition is reprinted by the University of Nebraska Press (Lincoln, 1971).

Gen. O. O. Howard's search for Cochise and his eventual meeting with him in the Dragoons is taken from Capt. J. A. Sladen's *Making Peace with Cochise, Chief of the Chiricahua Apaches, 1872*. Sladen's son had his father's penciled notes copied and typewritten. They are on file at the Arizona Historical Society in Tucson. I read a copy at the Cochise County Library. Edwin R. Sweeney has since edited an annotated version, *Making Peace with Cochise, the 1872 Journal of Captain Joseph Alton Sladen* (Norman: University of Oklahoma Press, 1997).

In 1984 the ruins of a building near Apache Springs were excavated and identified by Mardith K. Schuetz, whose "Archaeology of Tom Jeffords Chiricahua Agency" describes the building (Las Cruces, N.M.: *COAS Monograph* 6, 1986).

### Chapter 6. Galeyville

The story of Henry Antrim at Bonito appears in Jerry Weddle's "Apprenticeship of an Outlaw: Billy the Kid in Arizona" (Tucson: *Journal of Arizona History* 31/3, 1990) and in *Billy the Kid: A Short and Violent Life* by Robert M. Utley (Lincoln: University of Nebraska Press, 1989). His encounter with three families of immigrants appears in Miguel Antonio Otero's *The Real Billy the Kid* (New York: Rufus Rockwell Wilson, Inc., 1936). Their identification as the Coryell brothers and their families was told to me by James W. Coryell of Paradise.

"The Autobiography of William Carroll Riggs" (Willcox, Ariz.: *Arizona Range News*, November 8, 1941) is a source for the Riggs brothers' early history. The material on Stephen Reed in this and subsequent chapters is taken from articles by his son, Walter, in the *Douglas Dispatch* for May 22, 1955, and May 29, 1955; from interviews with his granddaughter, Maurine Reed Hicks; and from numerous letters and miscellaneous papers collected by Lillian Slover Reed, made available to me by her daughter, Mildred Reed Clapp. Dan L. Thrapp, in *Conquest of Apacheria* and *Victorio and the Mimbres Apaches* (Norman: University of Oklahoma Press, 1974), describes the Indian scare that put the Riggses and the Reeds into Emigrant Canyon.

Information about Nick Hughes came to me in a roundabout way in a letter to Mamie Franklin from Judd Robertson, Hughes's great-great-grandson, who enclosed copies of two articles by Emma Marble Muir. The first, "The Oldest Ranch in the San Simon Valley," apparently appeared in the *Lordsburg Liberal* (November 14, 1947). The second, entitled "A Pioneer Ranch," was in an undated periodical, *Around Here*, which probably was printed in El Paso.

There is a wealth of material about Galeyville in the Arizona Historical Society's files of James C. Hancock (MS 325). That file and others at the

AHS also contain bits and squibs about Louis Prue, Major Downing, Tex Whaley, Al George, Shanahan, the Keating brothers, William Brocius, and many other local characters, and more was culled from issues of the *Arizona Star, Arizona Weekly Citizen, Phoenix Herald*, and *Tombstone Epitaph* for the years 1880 and 1881. Most of the Galeyville anecdotes in this chapter are taken from Hancock.

A manuscript by Annie Faust Cox at the AHS (MS 189) contains biographical data on Jack Dunn. Whitehead's life is covered by Ellen Cline in "Tom Whitehead: 19th Century Cochise County Rancher and Restauranteur" (Douglas, Ariz.: *Cochise County Historical Journal* 27/1, 1997). Additional material on Al George is found in an article I can no longer find, by his niece, Grace McCool. There is some information about Alex Arnett in "Officer With a Record" by William R. Ridgeway (*Arizona Republic*, June 2, 1963).

John Galey's career is covered in *The Greatest Gamblers* by Ruth Knowles (New York: McGraw-Hill, 1959), with further details in a letter from his son, Thomas Galey, reprinted in the *Chiricahua Bullsheet* for October 13, 1958.

Gus Chenowth's experiences in the 1860s and 1870s are detailed in his biographical file at the AHS. The Indian-killing episode at La Paz is described by Constance Wynn Altchuler in *Chains of Command: Arizona and the Army, 1856–1875* (Tucson: Arizona Historical Society, 1981).

Information on Galeyville's business establishments is found in William C. Disturnell's *Business Directory and Gazetteer of Arizona* (San Francisco: Bacon and Co., 1881), and summaries on the district's mines are found in "A History of Mining in Arizona," edited by J. Michael Canty and Michael N. Greeley (Tucson: Mining Club of the Southwest Foundation, 1987); in "Mineral Resources of the Chiricahua Wilderness Area, Cochise County, Arizona" by Harold Drewes and Frank E. Williams (Washington, D.C.: *Geological Survey Bulletin* 1385-A, 1973); and in a long article by Renwick White in the *Paradise Record*, reprinted in the *Arizona Daily Star* (Tucson: February 21, 1911).

The records of George Ellingwood's court of justice for the period of May into September are on file at the Arizona Historical Society.

### Chapter 7. Cowboys and Indians

Reverend Hall's unflattering view of his neighbors is quoted in Robert H. Keller's "Shrewd, Able, and Dangerous Men: Presbyterian and Dutch Reformed Missionaries in the Southwest, 1870–1882" (Tucson: *Journal of Arizona History* 26/3, 1985).

There are good accounts of Arizona's first commercial cattle herds in *History of the Cattle Industry in Southern Arizona, 1540–1940* by J. J. Wagoner (Tucson: University of Arizona Press, 1952) and in Bert Haskett's "Early History of the Cattle Industry in Arizona" (Tucson: *Arizona Historical Review* 6/3, 1935).

The best account of the activities of the rustlers on both sides of the border is in "When All Roads Led to Tombstone," an unpublished manuscript by John Plesant Gray, in the files of the Arizona Historical Society (MS 312).

The short, violent stay of the Earps in and out of Tombstone has fascinated historians, readers of pulp fiction, and horse opera fans ever since Walter Noble Burns wrote *Tombstone* (New York: Grossett and Dunlap, 1929). Stuart Lake's *Wyatt Earp: Frontier Marshal* (New York: Houghton Mifflin, 1931) was more accurate as to events but was marred by wide-eyed hero worship. William M. Breakenridge, in *Helldorado* (New York: Houghton Mifflin, 1928), was perhaps biased in the other direction, but he had the advantage of having been a contemporary and on the scene. Frank Waters, in *The Earp Brothers of Tombstone* (Lincoln: University of Nebraska Press, 1960), didn't have a high opinion of the Earps. Glenn G. Boyer, in *I Married Wyatt Earp: The Recollections of Josephine Sarah Marcus Earp* (Tucson: University of Arizona Press, 1976), and Donald Chaput, in *Virgil Earp: Western Peace Officer* (Norman: University of Oklahoma Press, 1994), are more objective, but neither has much to say about events outside of town.

An account of the shooting in Eureka is told by an observer in the *Arizona Weekly Star* for June 23, 1881. Almost as celebrated as the "battle of OK Corral" is the legendary Skeleton Canyon hijacking. By far the most believable account is found in the Hancock file (AHS MS 325). The rugged survivor in later years repeated stories of the old Galeyville days to several interviewers and wrote them up himself for newspapers—always adhering fairly consistently to the same version. Hancock didn't take part in the affair, but he knew all the participants and heard their accounts of it within a day or two of the event.

The mass killing in Guadalupe Canyon is recounted by Billy Byers, one of the two survivors, in the *Arizona Weekly Star* for June 23, 1881, and by John Gray, who helped pick up the bodies the next day.

Nana's raid out of Mexico is recorded by Steven H. Lekson in "Nana's

Raid: Apache Warfare in Southern New Mexico, 1881" (El Paso: *Southwestern Study Series* 81, Texas Western Press, 1987).

There are many accounts of Loco's breakout in April 1882, but it would be hard to beat Dan Thrapp's *Conquest of Apacheria*. For details of the chase, accounts by four of those who took part in it are found in George A. Forsyth's *Thrilling Days in Army Life* (New York: Harper and Brothers, 1900); C.A.P. Hatfield's *Expedition Against the Chiricahua Apaches, 1882–1883*, an unpublished manuscript dated 1925 in the Gatewood File at the Arizona Historical Society; the scout Al Sieber's letter to the *Prescott Weekly Courier* for May 27, 1882; and the notes of Neil Erickson in the Faraway Ranch Collection, Western Archeological and Conservation Center, National Park Service, in Tucson.

Loco's activities around Galeyville are mentioned in the Hancock papers and in "When the Cowboys Deserted Galeyville" by Dora Wessells Strumquist (Stillwater, Okla.: *Frontier Times*, September 1966).

The story of Gus Chenowth's hosting of his neighbors in the adobe corral is part of the local legend and was first told to me in 1941 by Emmett Powers, who wasn't here himself until about 1900 but knew most of those who had been involved.

### Chapter 8. Geronimo's Time

Sam Kenoi's opinion of Geronimo, recorded by Morris Opler, is quoted in "A Chiricahua Apache's Account of the Geronimo Campaign" in *Geronimo and the End of the Apache Wars*, edited by C. L. Sonnichsen (Lincoln: University of Nebraska Press, 1986).

The bits about Stephen Reed are from interviews with his granddaughter, Maurine Reed Hicks. The valley ranches of Hancock and Whitehead are described in the Hancock file (MS 325) at the Arizona Historical Society.

There is an abundance of literature about the activities of Geronimo and his followers and the army's efforts to contain them in the four-and-a-half years between April 1882 and September 1886. I gleaned something from much of it, but to list it all would take a small volume. Most useful were Dan Thrapp's *Conquest of Apacheria*, which I have already referred to; Thrapp's *General Crook and the Sierra Madre Adventure* (Norman: University of Oklahoma Press, 1972), which deals specifically with these final years; Angie Debo's *Geronimo: The Man, His Time, His Place* (Norman: University of Oklahoma Press, 1976); *Apache Days and After* by Thomas Cruse (Lincoln:

University of Nebraska Press, 1941); *The Truth about Geronimo* by Britton Davis (New Haven, Conn.: Yale University Press, 1929); and *Chasing Geronimo: The Journal of Leonard Wood, May–September 1886*, edited by Jack C. Lane (Albuquerque: University of New Mexico Press, 1970).

All of the above are from the viewpoint of the White Eyes except for Kenoi. Other Apache versions are *I Fought with Geronimo* by Jason Betzinez with Wilbur Sturtevant Nye (Lincoln: University of Nebraska Press, 1987) and *Indeh: An Apache Odyssey* by Eve Ball (Norman: University of Oklahoma Press, 1988).

The story of the death of Frenoy and Lobley during Chato's raid comes from an interview with John Fife in the *Tucson Daily Citizen* (November 15, 1937) and from "The Graves of Frenoy and Lobley in the Chiricahuas," an unpublished paper by Fred Wynn, in the Frederick Wynn Collection at the Arizona Historical Society. George Forsyth's *Thrilling Days* and Neil Erickson's papers both make reference to the McComas incident in that same raid. Anton Mazzonovich, in "The Killing of Judge and Mrs. McComas" (Tucson: *Arizona Historical Review* 1/3, 1928), describes it in detail.

Hancock tells of the advent of Hall, Parramore, and Merchant in the valley. For background on James Parramore and Merchant, I am indebted to correspondence with Parramore's great-granddaughter, Eleanor Hoppe, of Abilene, Texas, who furnished me with copies of papers from the Ranching Heritage Center at Hardin-Simmons University.

Joseph Amasa Munk's *Arizona Sketches* (New York: Grafton Press, 1905) tells of the Munk brothers' ranch in Railroad Pass, which was the scene of Stewart Edward White's fictionalized *Arizona Nights* (New York: Hillman Periodicals, 1907). Isabel Shattuck Fatthauer's *A Little Mining, A Little Banking, A Little Beer* (Tucson: Westernlore Press, 1991) and Lynn R. Bailey's *We'll All Wear Silk Hats: The Erie and Chiricahua Cattle Companies in the Sulphur Springs Valley of Arizona, 1883–1909* (Tucson: Westernlore Press, 1994) tell of the Tumble T and the CCC ranches. "The San Bernardino Ranch" by Reba B. Wells (*Cochise Quarterly* 15/4, 1985) and *The Southwest of John Horton Slaughter* by Allen A. Erwin (Glendale, Calif.: Arthur H. Clarke Co., 1965) tell the history of Don Juan and the Z brand. George Hilliard writes of the early days of the Victorio Land and Cattle Company and the Diamond A in *A Hundred Years of Horsetracks: The Story of the Gray Ranch* (Silver City: High-Lonesome Books, 1996).

James Hancock is the source of the story of the raid in Wood Canyon and

Lieutenant Overton's futile pursuit, and Hatfield (*Expedition*) for the losses the army sustained in Guadalupe Canyon.

A letter to me from Ruey Darrow of Apache, Oklahoma, dated April 25, 1991, tells of the death of Charlie McComas as it was told to her by her father, Sam Hauzous.

Gilbert's standoff with Ulzana's raiders at the cienega hay camp is told by his son in "Apache Ambush" in *The Southwesterner* 2/10 (Columbus, N.M., April 1963). The killing of Albert and Reese in Turkey Creek in the same raid is recounted in Thrapp's *Conquest of Apacheria* and in the Edward John Hands file at the Arizona Historical Society. Gus Chenowth's near encounter was related to me by his granddaughter, Dorothy Chenowth Jessee, who was also the source of the story of Mary Chenowth feeding General Miles and Geronimo. Neil Erickson's papers repeat the latter story, as well as mention of Emma Peterson's handshake. Jim Hancock told of Lieutenant Johnson's pursuit of the escapees in Wood Canyon. Dorothy Jessee, as well as the John A. Chenowth file at the AHS, tell the poignant story of Farr's disposal of the old Apache.

### Chapter 9. The End of the Frontier

John Gray's manuscript (MS 312) at the Arizona Historical Society mentions the 1887 earthquake, as does Neil Erickson in the Faraway Ranch Collection at the Western Archeological and Conservation Center. For as thorough a study possible so long after the event, see "The 1887 Earthquake in San Bernardino Valley, Sonora: Historic Accounts and Intensity Pattern in Arizona" by Susan M. DuBois and Ann W. Smith (Tucson: *State of Arizona Bureau of Geology and Mineral Technology Special Paper* 3, 1980).

Material on John Hands comes from his biographical file at the Arizona Historical Society and Neil Erickson's journal, as well as numerous oral references by Elmore Walker, Maurine Hicks, Bill Sanders, Jack Maloney, and others.

John Hands describes the big valley roundup. Other data on the San Simon Cattle Company in the 1890s is found in the Special Collections of the University of Arizona Library and in *Sixty-five Years in the Cow Business* by Young Bell (Cisco, Tex.: Longhorn Press, 1961). J. P. Gray (AHS MS 312) describes the death of Comanche White.

Massai's visit to Bonito Canyon is described in Neil Erickson's unpublished paper, "Some Facts about Bigfoot Massai," in the Faraway Ranch

Collection at the WACC. Accounts of his death are found in *They Also Served* by Susan E. Lee (New York: Book Craftsmen Association, 1960) and Henry Walter Hearn's "How Apache Kid Met Death" (*Magdalena Mountain Mail*, December 1, 1988). Massai's great-granddaughter, Anita Lester, tells me that family tradition holds that he was killed by soldiers, but the Apache account of his killing and the subsequent journey of his wife and children to Mescalero is otherwise so close to the cowboys' stories that there can be little doubt they refer to the same event. Joe Chisholm, in *Brewery Gulch* (San Antonio: Naylor Company, 1949), is responsible for the hint that John Slaughter had something to do with dispatching Apache Kid.

The disastrous drought of the early 1890s is told of by James Hancock (AHS MS 325); by Amasa Munk (*Arizona Sketches*); and by Henry H. Collins, Jr., in "The Tragedy of the San Simon" (*Nature Magazine*, February 1940). Ben Pague of Hilltop, who was only about ten at the time, told me of remembering vividly the carcasses too numerous to skin.

The escapades of the Christian and Ketchum gangs are related in two books by Jeff Burton, *Black Jack Christian: Outlaw* and *Dynamite and Six-shooter* (Santa Fe: Press of the Territorian, 1967 and 1979). The lawmen's pursuit of them into the Chiricahuas is described in J. Evetts Haley's *Jeff Milton; A Good Man with a Gun* (Norman: University of Oklahoma Press, 1948); Colin Rickard's *Charles Littlepage Ballard: Southwesterner* (El Paso: Texas Western Press, 1966); and *George Scarborough: The Life and Death of a Lawman on the Closing Frontier* by Robert K. DeArment (Norman: University of Oklahoma Press, 1992). Leonard Alvorsen tells his hard-luck story in his own words and provides the quotation at the head of the chapter in the Alvorsen file (MS 14) at the AHS.

Most of the Susanna Noland Buckalew story comes from an interview with her grandson, Albert Frank Noland, Jr., who also quoted his father's remarks about the later days of Curly Bill Brocius. Jim Hancock was quite firm in his belief that Wyatt Earp didn't kill Curly Bill, and apparently he reflected the widely held opinion of his local contemporaries. Among quotations to that effect are interviews with him in the *Arizona Star* for December 31, 1937, and in Frank C. Lockwood's "Fifty Years in Paradise" (Tucson: *Progressive Arizona* 11, December 1931 and January 1932). An unpublished manuscript by Melvin P. Jones in the AHS files describes his meeting Brocius, whom he had known for several years, after the latter's presumed death at the hands of Wyatt Earp.

Butch Cassidy's and Elzy Lay's short stays in Cochise County are mentioned by William French in his *Recollections of a Western Ranchman,
1883–1899* (Silver City, N.M.: reprint of the 1928 edition by High-Lonesome
Press, 1990) and by Joseph Axford in *Around Western Campfires* (Tucson:
University of Arizona Press, 1970). Axford also speaks of their association
with Clay McGonagill.

The name McGonagill has a ring to it, making it easy to remember. In
1939 my brother and I were negotiating the rutted wagon tracks on the
west side of New Mexico's Puerco River, looking for Indian ruins. Crossing a
deep wash under Mesa Chivato, the car quit. We couldn't reasonably expect
anybody to come along in that lonesome country for a week or two, so we
started to walk south toward Laguna Pueblo, about twenty-five miles away.
In three or four miles a little track led to the west and a weathered board
sign pointed to "McGonagill Ranch."

A mile or so away, tucked back into a little sandstone rincon, was a house,
a corral, and a fellow of about thirty working at a little shed. He introduced himself as Clay McGonagill, took us back to the car with his pickup,
towed us to the ranch, and started with relish to tinker with the motor.
While he was at it, his mother, Annie Laurie, fed us beans and biscuits and
showed us album after album of photos of Clay's daddy, the original Clay, in
action. The house was decorated with old ropes, trophies, and photos, and
Mrs. McGonagill seemed surprised we hadn't heard of the World Champion
Cowboy, who had died when I was four years old. Clay junior may not have
been the steer buster that his father was, but he was a fine mechanic, and
before dark we were on our way.

About ten years later I helped Sparks Faucett pull the sucker rod on
his windmill in the little canyon just south of Cave Creek Cienega. During a break he explained to me that Clay McGonagill "and those other old
rustlers" used to hold H cattle in that canyon until they could safely dispose
of them.

In 1957 George Webb, a Pima living near Snaketown, took me down
through the dense mesquite where the Santa Cruz joins the Gila to show me
the ruins of Maricopa Wells. He told me the area was called "the New York
Thicket" because in 1919, when Clay McGonagill made the great gather of
wild horses in there, he hired a number of rodeo hands who were wintering in Phoenix to help him. Many of them were fine athletes but were city
boys who couldn't follow a track, and several were lost in the brush for a day
or two.

The way the name keeps cropping up is one of the reasons I wanted to write this book. It came up again when I was researching this tale and read Eve Ball's "Clay McGonagill: A Colorful Cowboy" (Oklahoma City: *Persimmon Hill*, Winter 1979).

### Chapter 10. Paradise

With this chapter we are getting closer to where old times overlap into my times, so scraps of paper, overheard remarks, and formal interviews assume more importance.

The *Chiricahua Bullsheet*, however, was more than a "scrap of paper." The thirty-eight typed and mimeographed issues, which were published in Portal between May 7, 1957, and May 17, 1959, by Carson Morrow, a retired border patrolman who had been raised in Paradise, were intended to be a "non-partisan, non-sectarian and non- about everything" gossip sheet and a vehicle for Morrow's "thumb nail sketches of people who resided in or near the Chiricahua Mountains during the period 1903 to 10." I borrowed a lot from his column entitled "Digging up Skeletons" for this and the next two chapters, though I altered some of the accounts a little. Carson was a great storyteller and didn't slow down to dot his i's or pick nits, so I've corrected a date—or picked a nit or two—using data from the 1910 census, several years of the Great Register of Cochise County, or six issues of the *Paradise Record* in the Faraway Ranch Collection at the Western Archeological and Conservation Center in Tucson.

Maurine Reed Hicks was my chief informant about her stepfather, George Walker, with some input from his sons, Reed and Elmore. Ulrich Rieder was the mail carrier when I moved to Cave Creek, but my information about him is from his daughter, Ruby Rieder Marr, and from Maryan Stidham's "Teacher at Hilltop" (Douglas: *Cochise Quarterly* 20/2, 1990). For Dad Colvin and the Halls, see Virginia Hershey's "The Robert Davis Hall Family" (Douglas: *Cochise Quarterly* 25/4, 1995). The background on Laura Wood and her marriage to Jim Hancock was told to me by their daughter, Irene Kennedy, and *her* daughter, Rosalie Gilliland.

Roland L. Frazier of Hondo, Texas, a grandson of Zeke Barfoot, supplied me with information about the Barfoots and Gardners. (Clay McGonagill makes another appearance!)

The confrontation between Benton and Henley over water and range in Tex Canyon is told by Jesse James Benton in *Cow by the Tail* (Boston: Houghton Mifflin Co., 1943). The division of the San Simon Company and

Clabe Merchant's move to a new San Simon ranch is told in "The Merchants of San Simon" by T. Dudley Cramer and Joyce Merchant Peters, in *Cowboys Who Rode Proudly*, edited by Evetts Haley, Jr. (Kansas City, Mo.: Lowell Press, 1992).

The means of getting the boiler up the hill to the Chiricahua Mine was told to me by William W. Sanders. The history of the sawmill in Barfoot, the road from it down into Paradise, and the Sweeney's involvement comes from Carson Morrow, Dorothy Chamberlain, Bill Sanders, and Neil Erickson's journals in the Faraway Collection at the Western Archeological and Conservation Center. From the day he went to work for the Forest Service in 1903 until his retirement in 1927, Erickson made almost daily entries in his log, describing where he rode, what he saw, and who he met on the trail. This record was undoubtedly the single most valuable source for writing the last three chapters of this book.

Erickson's journal, of course, provided much detail on the Chiricahua Forest Reserve, as did Edwin A. Tucker's "The Early Days: A Sourcebook of Southwestern Region History" (Albuquerque: *Cultural Resources Management Reports* 7 and 12, Forest Service, Southwestern Region, 1989 and 1992) and "A History of the Forest Service" by Charles R. Ames (*Smoke Signals* 16, Tucson Corral of the Westerners, 1967). Some of Supervisor McGlone's activities are included in those sources.

Caldwell's murder is reconstructed from the Hancock file, the *Bullsheet*, and from microfilmed Records of the Clerk of the Cochise County Superior Court. Jim Gould's prior criminal career is described in the *Silver City Enterprise*, October 1, 1886. Ted Moore's killing by the Haldermans is described in Robert E. Ladd's *Eight Ropes to Eternity* (privately printed by the Tombstone Epitaph, 1965) and in Territorial Inquest 397, Records of the Clerk of Cochise County Superior Court.

Background on Renwick White, the *Record*'s editor, is found in "Cochise County Characters and Capers" by Archie L. Gee (*Cochise Quarterly* 2/4, 1972). Nearly everything about the Chamberlains and Hawkinses and their store comes from unpublished accounts written by Dorothy Chamberlain, copies of other papers she furnished me, and an extensive interview with her at her home in Tempe in 1994.

Some bits of the story of Howard Chenowth's rampage were told me by his niece, Dorothy Chenowth Jessee, and his nephew James Simmons. I am indebted to George Hilliard for some pertinent facts from the Blachley tapes in the Pioneer Oral Histories of the University of New Mexico Library. The event was the front-page feature in the *Silver City Enterprise* for September 2, 1904. His escape was the big story in the same paper for January 6, 1906.

Judd's fall down the shaft at the Chiricahua Mine was told to me by Bill Sanders, and the ignominious end of Alex Wills is recorded in the *Chiricahua Bullsheet*, February 27, 1958.

### Chapter 11. Portal

Although some of the background for the founding of Portal comes from Carson Morrow's *Bullsheet* and the *Paradise Record*, I relied more on talks with Edward Epley and Emmett Powers. The first days of the Paradise school are found in the *Chiricahua Bullsheet* for May 31, 1957, and in the records of the Cochise County schools.

Most of the material about George Coryell is taken from interviews with his son, James W. Coryell. The facts of George's arrest, trial, and acquittal are found in the Records of the Clerk of the Cochise County Superior Court.

James and Minnie Reay's story comes largely from interviews with their grandson, Herbert Reay. I knew Frank and Nancy Sanford but couldn't have straightened out their story without the help of their daughter, Grace Cox, and grandson, Jim Frank Cox.

Jack Maloney's holdup of the EPSW train has been told several times. This version was Emma Maloney's. There are bits about the Duffners from my own memory, and some from the *Bullsheet*, Junior Noland, A. B. "Blackie" Stidham, the *Paradise Record*, a letter from G. E. Haas, and census records.

Ed Epley, the first postmaster, told me himself of the origin of Portal's name. Conversations with him and Emmett Powers were the source of some of the incidents of its earliest days. Again, the *Bullsheet* and the *Record* were helpful, but it was the Sierra Linda Ranch's abstract of title, in my possession, that made it possible to unravel the story of the Portal Development Company.

Boswell's difficulties with his customers are detailed in the records of the Superior Court. Carson Morrow is the source of information about the disposal of his victims' bodies.

McGlone himself in 1941 told me the story of the creek crossing. Other incidents involving McGlone and the Forest Service are from Tucker ("The Early Days") and Neil Erickson's journal, which also tells in detail of the

Horseshoe Fire. Interviews and correspondence with Arthur Zachau provided information about his father, Supervisor Zachau.

The Maloney wedding was described in an article by Dorothy Bliss in the *Douglas Dispatch* for December 27, 1957. For the faded photo and other information about the couple, I am indebted to their grandson, Pat Stoltz.

The tragic death of Will Noland is common knowledge, but like most common knowledge, the facts are frequently garbled. Most useful, and probably most accurate, were accounts by Dorothy Chamberlain, Neil Erickson, and Judge Hancock and the interview with Albert Noland, Jr.

Information about Joe Wheeler comes from the San Simon Cattle Company file in the University of Arizona Library's Special Collections and from the *Bullsheet*, but more fully from interviews with his niece, Mamie Pattison Franklin.

The story of the marble quarry in MacIntosh Canyon comes from "Marble, Arizona," an unpublished account by Jack M. Kaiser in the files of Chiricahua National Monument.

There is information about the McDonald-Clair dispute in the Hancock file, in the *Bullsheet*, and in the Dorothy Chamberlain interview, but more still in the Records of the Clerk of the Superior Court. The May-Sands tragedy in Round Valley, though thirty years old, was still talked of locally when I came to Portal. I heard versions of it from Sam Moseley, Blackie Stidham, Bill Sanders, and Ralph Morrow, all the same in essence but differing wildly in detail. For those details I relied on the testimony presented at Sands's trial, preserved by the Clerk of the Court. Dorothy Chamberlain gave me the bit about the bloody long johns.

### Chapter 12. The Nesters

For this chapter even more than the last, I relied a lot on things I learned through osmosis over several decades. It will be a little harder to document my sources, many of which were word of mouth—and I'm not sure of whose mouth in every case. Therefore much of this was painfully put together by fine-tuning with data from the county assessor's office, the county register, census figures, and other notes and records.

In November 1942, when I was home on leave from the army, Emma Maloney, learning that I was being sent to Camp Barkeley, Texas, near Abilene, told me that Dilworth Parramore lived there and I ought to look him up. Around Christmas time I called him, and he and his wife had me to the house for a Sunday breakfast that lasted all morning. I learned about the final days of the H's from him that day. Other details were found in the San Simon Cattle Company folder at the University of Arizona's Special Collections and came from interviews with James Finley Richards, Mamie Franklin, and Jeff D. Jordan.

The *Chiricahua Bullsheet* for January 11, 1959, tells of Oscar Roberts and the sale of the Triangles to "General" Mackenzie. There are several references to Mackenzie in DeArment's *George Scarborough*. Some about Ross Sloan came from Ross himself in the Silver Dollar Bar in Rodeo in fall of 1941, some of it from Finley Richards and Jim Coryell years later. Sam Moseley told me the story of John Cameron's accident and Sloan's embarrassment at Hulsey's store. When I helped John load a car of seven-year-old steers at the San Simon shipping pens in the late 1940s, he didn't say anything about it.

Mamie Franklin has filled me in on the early days of Apache and the family of her grandfather, Charles Miller; her Uncle Ed's death at the hands of John Richhart; the Markens; and her husband's family, the Franklins. More about Richhart came from the Records of the Clerk of the Superior Court and from William Miller, who gave me the history of the James Redmond Miller family.

Although I knew three of the Lee brothers slightly, it was before I learned to ask questions, so I've relied on little dabs from the people they grew up with; on Robert McCurdy's *The Life of the Greatest Guide* (Phoenix: Blue River Graphics, 1981); and on *Down on the Blue*, edited by Cleo Cosper Coor (Goodyear, Ariz.: Valley West Printing Co., 1987).

Benton's *Cow by the Tail* tells of his sale to Krentz and his prior association with him.

The story of the Henry Hale family and Henry's death at the hands of Ike Faust was told during an interview with Henry's daughter, Lulu Pearl Hale Larman, and some patchwork was done by Sally and Finley Richards. Sally Richards was my source for the lives of her parents, Lillie and Cliff Darnell.

That word *patchwork* is appropriate. Nobody I interviewed—or just talked with—has ever confined himself strictly to his or her own life or that of a forebear, but conversations are apt to be peppered with comments about friends or neighbors. It is one thing to mention Jim Hancock's low opinion of Wyatt Earp in 1881, but another thing to stir up dust among descendants who are still in the neighborhood. Therefore I won't name those who suggested that Carl Washburn was careless with his branding iron. His daughter, Addoline "Addie" Washburn Hill, wasn't shocked to hear that I had heard it said, and she gave me a long interview about her family, along with a couple of cups of good coffee.

Manuel Dominguez is another that I knew years ago but who died before I could talk to him, and most of what I know about him comes from his youngest son, Leo S. Dominguez.

I first heard the story of the Parker brothers and the hanging from a windmill in Chihuahua from an old cowboy at the Culberson ranch on the Diamond A in 1936. I can't remember his name, so that hardly makes an acceptable citation, but George Hilliard's *Story of the Gray Ranch* mentions the Parker boys.

### Chapter 13. More Modern Times

I learned about the scrapping over ditch water from people who were on the scene or close to others who were: Myriam Toles, Dorothy Jessee, Jim Simmons, Herb Reay, George Newman, and Reed Walker. A record of the meetings with the water commissioner and his decision are part of the AVA Ranch abstract of title, which I was able to examine through the courtesy of Theodore Troller, Jr.

Larry R. Gurnett gave me information about his grandparents Elizabeth and Lincoln Gurnett. The rest of the Sierra Linda Ranch story was just absorbed through years of working the place.

Local knowledge of the ups and downs of the Cochise Mine and Charlie Welch was supplemented by copies of correspondence between Welch and Arthur H. Zachau sent to me by the latter's son, Arthur B. Zachau.

Sam Moseley, who was there, told me of John Underwood's accident at Hilltop. The last days of the Chenowths on Eula's farm at Portal were told of by Amos Chenowth, Jim Simmons, and Dorothy Jessee. I learned of Anna and Edward Adamson's purchase of the AVA Ranch from themselves. Doc Adamson delivered both of my sons.

# Illustration Credits

Illustrations not listed here are from the author's collection.

### The Arizona Historical Society
Merejildo Grijalva (neg. no. 22269)
Loco, a Chihenne chief (neg. no. 30382)
Gus and Mary Chenowth's place (neg. no. 5542)
Frank Hands at his place in Pinery Canyon (neg. no. 5006)
Waiting for the stage at the Hayes Hotel (neg. no. 75064)
A Paradise street scene in 1906 (neg. no. 24,866)

### Dorothy Chamberlain
The first year of the Paradise school, 1906
Henry and Gertrude Chamberlain and their children
Hollis "Holly" Chamberlain Sweeney
Patrons of Joe Wheeler's saloon in about 1909

### Amos Chenowth
Gus Chenowth at his cienega ranch
Howard Pinckney Chenowth
Loyola Agnes "Ola" Chenowth

### Coronado National Forest
John Wethered and Neil Erickson
Charles T. McGlone at Crystal Cave

### Leo Domínguez
Manuel Domínguez

### Karen Hayes
Cathedral Rock in the mouth of Cave Creek Canyon.
Looking down Turkey Creek Canyon
Barfoot Park
The San Simon Cienega

### Virginia S. Hershey
The Hall family at their Z Bar T ranch

### Maurine Reed Hicks
Stephen Reed, Alice, Claudie, Walter, and Bill, and John Hands

### Pamela Hulme
Riding one and leading one up Market Street in Paradise
Alejo Bedoya

### Jefferson D. Jordan
The San Simon Cattle Company headquarters

### Irene Hancock Kennedy
Judge James Hancock and a friend.

### National Park Service, Western Archeological and Conservation Center, Tucson, Arizona (Faraway Ranch Collection)
Sgt. Neil Erickson of the Fourth Cavalry
Emma Peterson
Officers and scouts at the Mud Springs vedette
Chamberlain and Hawkins' store in Paradise
Albert Fink at his Silver Creek camp.
Clowning at Faraway Ranch
John Lee and Albert Fink with the "auto-stage"

### Betty M. Nelson
J. L. Coryell and his son George
Susan Wilson Sanders, Emma, Lizzie, Willy, and Myrtle
The Moore and Coryell stage in Graveyard Canyon
George "Ironfoot" Coryell
William Wesley Sanders

### Albert F. Noland Jr.

Katie and Maggie Noland at the ranch on Oak Creek
Will Noland and two prospectors at "Eagle City"
Henry and Susanna Buckalew, Audie Buckalew, and Maude Noland
Frank and Will Noland at the Buckalews' adobe bunkhouse

### Minnette Harris Smith

Rodeo, New Mexico, in about 1920
James H. Parramore and his 7H cowboys at the cienega ranch

### Special Collections, The University of Arizona Library

A Chiricahua Apache family's camp of the 1880s
Jim Hughes with either Milt Hicks or Jack Mackenzie

### George Patrick Stoltz

Samuel F. "Jack" Maloney

## ABOUT THE AUTHOR

After graduating with a bachelor's degree in anthropology from the University of New Mexico, Alden Hayes worked as an archaeological technician in Texas and Tennessee. He then moved to Portal, Arizona, and ranched for sixteen years before returning to a career as a field archaeologist with the National Park Service. He authored six monographs and three dozen shorter papers about his work at such major sites as Mesa Verde, Gran Quivira, Pecos, and Chaco Canyon. Hayes retired to the Chiricahuas in 1976 and wrote a travel memoir, *Down North to the Sea: 2,000 Miles by Canoe to the Arctic Ocean*. His work now consists of cutting wood in spring and fall and throwing it into the fireplace in winter.